Letters

from the
Lost Generation

Letters

FROM THE
LOST GENERATION

Gerald and Sara Murphy and Friends

edited by
Linda Patterson Miller

Rutgers University Press
New Brunswick and London

First printing April 1991
Second printing July 1991

Library of Congress Cataloging-in-Publication Data

Miller, Linda Patterson, 1946–
Letters from the lost generation : Gerald and Sara Murphy and
friends / Linda Patterson Miller.
p.   cm.
Includes bibliographical references and index.
ISBN 0-8135-1642-0
1. Murphy, Gerald, 1888–1964—Correspondence.   2. Murphy, Sara—
Correspondence.   3. Painters—United States—Correspondence.
4. Wives—United States—Correspondence.   5. Expatriate painters—
France—Correspondence.   I. Title.
ND237.M895A3   1991
759.13—dc20
[B]   90-42139
                                                                              CIP
British Cataloging-in-Publication information available

For Randy

Contents

List of Illustrations

All photographs courtesy of Honoria Murphy Donnelly unless otherwise noted.

Acknowledgments

Many have helped to make this book by sharing with me recollections, photographs, correspondence, and source materials I might otherwise have overlooked. Many, as well, have opened up their homes to me with a warmth characteristic of the Murphys themselves. My deepest gratitude goes to Honoria Murphy Donnelly, whose commitment to her parents and their memory has inspired this book and without whose generosity and support this book would not be possible. I thank Mrs. Donnelly for her permission to publish her parents' letters, and also family photographs, and for the endless hours she has spent talking with me and helping me to sort through the vast Murphy collection, now housed in East Hampton, New York. Mrs. Donnelly's late husband, William, contributed his own recollections of the Murphys and their friends, and I remember him and his indomitable humor with fondness.

Others deserve special mention. Fanny Myers Brennan has guided me to sources, verified dates, and challenged my thinking with her own profound understanding of the Murphys and their era. I thank Mrs. Brennan for her great help and also for her permission to publish from the Richard and Alice Lee Myers Papers, now on deposit at Yale University. The late Archibald MacLeish, who described himself as a beleaguered survivor, remained generous with his written responses to my many questions and enthusiastically supported this project, as did Ellen Barry. Along with her husband Philip, Mrs. Barry played a significant role in this era and talks about it with wit and verve. Others who gave of their time in interviews, in person, by phone, or by way of letters, include: Anne Gugler, Alice Munro Haagensen, Marion Lowndes, William H. MacLeish, Gertrude Macy, the late King Vidor, Adelaide Walker, and Roger Wilcox.

These scholars and writers have generously shared information and ideas:

the late Carlos Baker, Miranda Barry, Matthew J. Bruccoli, Virginia Spencer Carr, Scott Donaldson, Townsend Ludington, and Michael Reynolds. In addition, the following libraries were invaluable resources for this project, making available to me their special collections: The Benchley Papers at the Mugar Memorial Library, Boston University; The Dos Passos Papers at the Alderman Library, The University of Virginia; the Fitzgerald Papers at the Firestone Library, Princeton University; the MacLeish Papers at the Library of Congress; the Hemingway Papers at the John F. Kennedy Library, Boston; the Gerald Murphy/Douglas MacAgy Papers at the Smithsonian Institution's Archives of American Art; and the Woollcott Papers at the Houghton Library, Harvard University. A special thanks to Catherine Keen at the Archives of American Art, to the past and present curators of the Hemingway Papers, including Jo August Hills, Joan O'Conner, and Megan Desnoyers, and to Beatrice W. Agnew, Director of the Palisades Free Library. Gloria O'Mahonney was helpful in opening up to me resource materials at the Mark Cross Company.

Penn State University has supported this project through a Research Initiation Grant and several travel grants, partially funded by Penn State, the Ogontz Campus. I thank as well Dinah Geiger and the wonderful staff at Ogontz who have helped with the mechanics of bringing this manuscript to press. Pierre Cintas contributed considerable French expertise as consultant on the French translations.

Richard A. Davison's enthusiasm for the art of the Lost Generation first inspired my work on this subject, and I thank him for his continued support of my work. Elaine Safer has also stimulated my thinking while reading and commenting on my work in progress. Jackson Bryer, who carefully read and commented on several versions of this manuscript, helped to define its scope. I cannot thank him enough for his time and his considerable insights into this work and this era. Leslie Mitchner at Rutgers Press is the supportive editor every writer dreams of; and Stuart Mitchner copyedited this text with sensitivity and care. My most patient listener and best critic—on this project and in all things—has been my husband, Randall. His encouragement and his support mean everything.

In addition to Mrs. Donnelly and Mrs. Brennan, the following individuals have kindly granted permission to publish family correspondence: Ellen Barry for Ellen and Philip Barry, Marjorie Benchley for Robert Benchley, Elizabeth Dos Passos for John Dos Passos and also Katy Dos Passos, and Patrick Hemingway for Pauline Pfeiffer Hemingway.

Jacqueline Rice, Literary Executor for the Dawn Powell Estate, has granted permission to publish Dawn Powell's 26 October 1964 letter to John Dos Passos.

Richard B. McAdoo, Literary Executor for the Estate of Archibald MacLeish, has granted permission to publish the letters of Archibald MacLeish.

These letters are copyright 1991 by the Estate of Archibald MacLeish and reprinted by permission of the Estate; previously published MacLeish letters in *Letters of Archibald MacLeish 1907 to 1982*, R. H. Winnick, ed. (1983) reprinted by permission of Houghton Mifflin Company. "Words to Be Spoken" is from *New and Collected Poems: 1971–1982* by Archibald MacLeish; copyright 1985 by the Estate of Archibald MacLeish; reprinted by permission of Houghton Mifflin Company.

The Ernest Hemingway Foundation (d.b.a. The Hemingway Society) has granted permission to publish the letters of Ernest Hemingway. These letters are copyright 1991 by the Ernest Hemingway Foundation and quoted by permission of the Foundation. The letters from Hemingway to Gerald and Sara Murphy of March 19, 1935, and to Sara Murphy of July 10, 1935, and February 27, 1936, are reprinted with permission of Charles Scribner's Sons, an imprint of Macmillan Publishing Company, from *Ernest Hemingway: Selected Letters 1917–1961*, edited by Carlos Baker; copyright 1981 by The Ernest Hemingway Foundation, Inc.

Permission to publish the F. Scott Fitzgerald letters is as follows:

Letters to Sara Murphy, August 15, 1935 and March 30, 1936; Sara and Gerald Murphy, January 31, 1937; and Gerald Murphy, March 11, 1938, reprinted with permission of Charles Scribner's Sons, an imprint of Macmillan Publishing Company, from *The Letters of F. Scott Fitzgerald*, edited by Andrew Turnbull; copyright 1963 by Frances Scott Fitzgerald Lanahan.

Letters of Summer 1940 (#187) and September 14, 1940 (#189) to Sara and Gerald Murphy were first published in *The Crack-Up*, by F. Scott Fitzgerald; copyright 1945 by New Directions Publishing Corporation, U.S. and Canadian rights. For British refer to Gerald Polinger, Esq., 18 Maddox St., Mayfair, London, W1R OEU, England. Reprinted by permission of New Directions Publishing Corporation.

Letter of December 26, 1935 (#96), September 21, 1939 (#170) and September 1939 (#173) are from *Correspondence of F. Scott Fitzgerald;* copyright 1980 by Frances Scott Fitzgerald Smith; reprinted by permission of Harold Ober Associates Incorporated.

Previously unpublished material on pages 133 (#81), 239 (#172), 256 (#190), and 261 (#196) by F. Scott and Zelda Fitzgerald is copyright 1991 by Eleanor Lanahan Hazard, Matthew J. Bruccoli, R. Andrew Boose, Trustees u/a 7/3/75 by Frances Scott Fitzgerald Smith, c/o Harold Ober Associates Incorporated, 40 East 49th Street, New York, N.Y. 10017.

Grateful acknowledgment is made to the National Association for the Advancement of Colored People for permission to publish the letters of Dorothy Parker.

Some portions of this work appeared, in different format, in two articles in *Studies in American Fiction*: "Gerald Murphy and Ernest Hemingway: Part

I," 12, no. 2 (August 1984), 129–144; and "Gerald Murphy and Ernest Hemingway: Part II," 13, no. 1 (Spring 1985), 1–13. Grateful acknowledgment to reprint this material is made to Editor James Nagel and Northeastern University.

Further portions appeared, in modified form, in "'As a Friend You Have Never Failed Me': The Fitzgerald-Murphy Correspondence," *Journal of Modern Literature*, 5, no. 3 (September 1976). Grateful acknowledgment to Editor Maurice Beebe and Temple University for permission to reprint this material, copyright 1976 by Temple University.

Introduction

What [a man] knows at fifty that he did not know at twenty is little more than this: that the things he was told were true at twenty and the things he said were true at twenty are for the most part, *really* true—but true with a brutal and inescapable truthfulness and consequence and meaning which would have shocked him had he guessed at it thirty years before. This knowledge is of all forms of knowledge the least communicable because it is a knowledge not of formulas or forms of words but of people, places, actions—a knowledge never gained by words but by touch, sight, delays, victories, sleeplessness, shame, love—briefly by experience of this earth and of oneself and other men.

—ARCHIBALD MACLEISH, *A Time to Act*

Gerald Murphy . . . was intelligent, perceptive, gracious, and one of the most attractive men I have ever known. His wife Sara was the perfect complement to these virtues. If this sounds like a child's tale beginning "Once upon a time there was a prince and a princess . . . ", that's exactly how a description of the Murphys should begin. They were both rich; he was handsome, she was beautiful; they had three golden children. They loved each other, they enjoyed their own company, and they had the gift of making life enchantingly pleasurable for those who were fortunate enough to be their friends.

—DONALD OGDEN STEWART, *By a Stroke of Luck*

This book tells the story of a group of people who were friends and then very close friends. Much has been written about them, and much talk has worked itself into legend. They were the bright ones, and they went to France during the 1920s. All the action was there, on the French Riviera and with the Murphys who, as the legend has it, knew how to throw a good party. The truth of the story goes much deeper than the talk, of course. Legends tend to distort and diffuse, especially when they involve so many flashy characters. But this is not an account of the individuals alone. Most of those truths and sometimes half-truths have been given in biographies and autobiographies. This is an account of the individuals together, interacting, nourishing one another intellectually, artistically, humanly. This story is about an era that had its own special flair, along with its later tragedies. At the center of the story as related in this epistolary "novel" stand Gerald and Sara Murphy.

The Murphys had left America for Europe in early 1921, six years after their marriage on 30 December 1915. They had met eleven years earlier in East Hampton, New York, where both the Murphy and Wiborg families summered. The sixteen-year-old Gerald Cleary Murphy was attracted to Sara Sherman Wiborg's delicate Swedish beauty and poise, and he also appreciated her wisdom (she was four years older). Although the relationship was initially platonic (Sara called him "Cousin"), it grew more complex and durable as Gerald determined that they should renounce the studied ease of life associated with their monied and well-connected families. Sara's father, Cincinnati ink baron Frank B. Wiborg, was well-traveled and cosmopolitan, as was Gerald's father Patrick Murphy, known in New York for his clever afterdinner speeches and his elegant leather goods store, the Mark Cross Company. He had purchased the business in Boston and then moved it to New York in the 1890s, where the Mark Cross insignia embossed on the store's products became synonymous with both prestige and style. Despite the store's solid financial gains, Patrick Murphy resisted efforts to expand the business, choosing instead to keep the shop selective. Although Gerald worked for his father between his 1912 graduation from Yale and his training with the U.S. Signal Corps in 1918, he regarded both the business life and New York City as dismal and confining. Gerald summarized his feelings about the privileged people living in and around New York in a 22 January 1931 letter to Archibald MacLeish: "My God, what a race of people! The hopeless circumscription of their lives, the richness, the sureness, the pompous, leaden dullness of it. Desolation! Sacred staleness."[1]

Gerald believed early on in his relationship with Sara that the two of them could defy this circumscribed life in favor of invention. He told her shortly before their marriage that "together, even among others," they would be able to do things in their "*own* way." "I think we shall always enjoy most the things we plan to do of our own accord." Although Gerald and Sara spent the first years of their marriage in New York, they both knew it would be temporary.

Gerald had no intention of remaining with Mark Cross, and his aviation training allowed him to make the break. Upon his return to New York after Armistice Day, he decided to study landscape architecture. He completed Harvard University's two-year landscaping program and then took Sara and their children (Baoth, Patrick, and Honoria) to Europe. Although Gerald planned to survey the formal gardens of England and France and then return to America, he and Sara found the intellectual and artistic fervor of Paris so invigorating that they remained in Europe for over a decade.

During this decade Gerald forgot his plans to become a landscape architect and became, instead, a painter, executing twelve canvases (possibly fourteen—the number is in question). Picasso saw Murphy as one of the few American painters of his time and told him his paintings were "simple, direct, and it seemed to him Amurikin—certainly not European."[2] Fernand Léger also hailed Murphy as "the only modern American painter to-day." As Murphy noted, "there seemed to be no U.S. painters working in the modern manner. . . . Even Waldo Frank, prolific and gifted, was not contemporary in his point of view.[3] Murphy's contemporary point of view, along with his unexpected career change, can be explained by Paris's postwar energy—what MacLeish called a "conflagration" of the arts and what Murphy described as the "fresh creative activity . . . in the air." "In such a city, at such a time," said MacLeish, "working is not enough. There must be work accomplished, work beyond your farthest expectation of yourself."[4] When Gerald saw the modernist paintings displayed in the Paris galleries, he felt "the shock of discovery" and declared: "If that's painting, it's what I want to do."[5]

Murphy described his painting style as a merger between the real and the abstract. He hoped to "digest" real objects, he said, "along with purely abstract forms and re-present them." His admiration for the exactitude of the fifteenth-century painter Piero della Francesca inspired him to render everyday objects in large scale and with meticulous precision.[6] He established studios in Paris and on the French Riviera as he completed one and sometimes two canvases a year. Although some artists and critics dismissed Murphy as a dilettante, others such as art critic Rudi Blesh, recognized the complexity and the brilliance of his work. His semi-abstract canvases were "so complex in design, so meticulous in craft, and (some of them) so heroic in size (one is ten feet wide and over seventeen feet high)," said Blesh, "that their production could not have been without protracted or concentrated labor."[7] As MacLeish said years later, Murphy turned out by the end of the decade "to have painted some of the most innovative canvases of those years." His paintings of watches and engines and razor blades were so stark and grand, and so original in conception, that they caught the viewer off guard. No one looking at Murphy's painting of a wasp would ever take a wasp for granted again, MacLeish said.

Gerald's passion "was not for the abstraction of experience but for experience itself, 'the thing itself'—the 'thing' so like 'itself' that it would *become* its implications."[8]

As Murphy sought to "*re*-present" real objects in his art, he had to discover these objects by stripping them bare, sometimes probing their interiors and placing them in new and unexpected relationships to their surroundings and to themselves. He brought this same process of discovery and enlightenment to his relationships, which explains his magnetic appeal to the other artists of his day. John Dos Passos admired the "mathematical elegance" of Gerald's mind and the "uncommitted freshness" of his vision, and he acknowledged that Murphy helped him to *re*-see ordinary objects and scenes, such that the streets of Paris became transformed as Dos Passos walked them with Gerald (which he did often during the 1920s). Gerald gave to his friends a "freshly invented world," said Dos Passos,[9] a view which his wife Katy confirmed when she told Gerald (20 June 1935): "It is always so much more fun when you are there, and easier to see things—just as if you had turned on better lighting." Archibald MacLeish reiterated this idea years later when he said that Murphy had given them all "the great creative gift of *sight*—what Rodin meant when he told Rilke that he would teach him to *see.*" This was "what you taught us all," MacLeish told Murphy (2 September [1964]). This was "the treasure you gave us so far as we had strength to take it."

F. Scott Fitzgerald too was drawn by Gerald Murphy's inventiveness and charm, although he recognized Gerald's complications as he came to use him for his fiction. As every Fitzgerald scholar knows, Fitzgerald modeled Dick and Nicole Diver in *Tender Is the Night* after Gerald and Sara Murphy. Fitzgerald had begun the novel in 1925 with the Murphys and the French Riviera in mind, and he completed it nine difficult years later. After its publication in 1934, most literary scholars came to agree with Ernest Hemingway's assessment that Dick and Nicole Diver represent a composite characterization of both the Murphys and the Fitzgeralds, and more the latter than the former. Fitzgerald had merged Sara's image with Zelda's to make Nicole Diver a "psychopathic case," Hemingway said, and he had changed Gerald into "a self-portrait of Scott." As Hemingway saw it, Fitzgerald had captured the Murphys' "surface charm without comprehending their psychological complexities." Fitzgerald knew nothing of the Murphys' faults because he had romanticized them.[10]

But however romantically Fitzgerald might have wanted to see the Murphys, particularly Gerald, he could not, finally, do so. By the early 1930s the reality of life had intruded to destroy the romance, causing Fitzgerald to look more deeply into Gerald Murphy's character as he reworked the novel prior to publication. In the end Dick Diver does not become Fitzgerald so much as he takes on some of Gerald Murphy's basic personality, including one flaw which plagued Murphy and influenced his relations with his friends. Both Diver and Murphy suspected an inner weakness of character which they tried to overcome by acting in ways contradictory to their true desires. As their organizational capacities increased, they suffered a disintegration of self. Beneath the surface charm of both Diver and Murphy was a troubled soul.

Dick Diver's appearance and his actions clearly resemble Gerald Murphy's as Fitzgerald knew him in France during the 1920s. Diver's complexion, like Murphy's, was "reddish and weather-burned," his eyes "bright, hard blue," his nose "somewhat pointed"; and "there was never any doubt at whom he was looking or talking," for his gaze was direct, attentive. "His voice, with some faint Irish melody running through it, wooed the world," and people who were with him "felt the layer of hardness in him, of self-control and of self-discipline."[11] Fitzgerald often thought about Murphy in terms of his actions: "Gerald walking Paris," he wrote in his notebook; or "Gerald's Irishness, face moving first" (a line which he subsequently used in the novel); or his "last afternoon with Gerald, for benefit of two women. Portentousness." He studied Murphy's moves even as he mocked them, for he could appreciate the drama inherent in Murphy's style and in his life, and Gerald Murphy fascinated him. "When I like men I want to be like them," Fitzgerald wrote. "I want to lose the outer qualities that give me my individuality and be like them. I don't want the man; I want to absorb into myself all the qualities that make him attractive and leave him out. I cling to my own innards."[12] His biographer Andrew Turnbull understood it well when he said that Fitzgerald "stood in awe of Gerald's unfailing propriety," and "what he admired about Gerald he put into the character of Dick Diver: the elegance, the turns of phrase, the flare for entertainment, above all Murphy's appreciation of others, his power to draw them out and see the best in them."[13] He also put into the character of Dick Diver the overriding self-doubts that helped form Murphy's identity as both a person and an artist.

Dick Diver, like Gerald Murphy, recognized that his greatest troubles would involve self-judgment. He believed he might be the best psychologist who ever lived, but he also suspected that he was only a second-rate doctor and that he might accept life, professionally and personally, on a lower scale. He thought of Franz Gregorovious who embraced competence, perhaps compromise, rather than greatness. " 'God, am I like the rest after all?'—So he used to think starting awake at night—'Am I like the rest?' " Believing that his inner fears would prevent him from fulfilling his human potential, Diver worked hard to perfect an outer image which might dazzle and detract. He assumed a special style, a dandified presence, which dominated any scene and won people over quickly "with an exquisite consideration and a politeness that moved so fast and intuitively that it could be examined only in its effect." If people chose to submit to the "amusing world" which he opened for them, "their happiness was his preoccupation." Yet knowing the effect he could have on people, he tended to work them over rather than genuinely love them. Nicole came to recognize that Dick's contagious excitement was "inevitably followed by his own form of melancholy." He aroused in others a great love, and the deep gloom came when he "realized the waste and extravagance involved." Then he had to work harder to cover his exposed self-consciousness, to forget that he had failed with his own life by betraying, out of fear and vulnerability, his talent. He wanted to be recognized as a professional, but he also wanted to "be good," "to be kind," "to be brave and wise." Even more than that, he wanted to "be loved."[14]

So it was with Gerald Murphy. His lifelong worry that his character was too weak and that he was not loved for himself led to wild fluctuations of behavior between studied charm and impenetrable depression. Like Dick Diver, the Celtic gloom could descend upon him suddenly ("like the closing of a door," said John Dos Passos); and even Sara learned to respect his periods of seclusion.[15] As Murphy confessed to Hemingway on 14 July 1926, his desire to do things well was one of his great "complications." This overriding desire led him to struggle too hard toward elegance and perfection. He assumed the assured manners and conveyed the quick intelligence seen in Dick Diver, and a sense for composition like Diver's influenced his relationships with landscaping, then painting, then people. Like Dick Diver, he was always the organizer, wanting to feel that he was in control of situations, of people, of himself. He took to wearing French sailor's jerseys and white duck pants on the Riviera, and he often sported a cane, wide-brimmed hats, and a slim leather case. Many people saw him as a dandy and appreciated his style while others felt it was affected and accused him of being pretentious. Dorothy Parker for one enjoyed baiting him, once getting Murphy to pretend to have read somebody she had invented.[16]

Murphy recognized his own pretensions, which only intensified his insecurity. Part of this insecurity related to what he described as Sara Murphy's comfortable sense of self, her ability to put people at ease. Her élan was more natural than his, and it sometimes seemed simpler to fall back on Sara's quiet gracefulness. He had to work hard to be in step, to seem at ease with himself and with life. After one visit with John Dos Passos, Murphy regretted that he had been "painfully superorganizational," working "so hard over nonessentials" that his face "took on a look of absent-minded distraction." "What a misfortune it is not to be able to take people casually," he said.[17] Gerald Murphy was aware of what he called Sara's "very deep and very real feelings" which stood in contrast to his own "ersatz" nature. As he told MacLeish on 22 January 1931, he wanted his friends to "be honest" in not confusing what they felt about him "with Sara." He always feared that friends would naturally love Sara more.

And without a doubt they did love Sara Murphy unconditionally. Hemingway would say in later years that while he "never could stand Gerald but . . . did," he "loved Sara," one of the ones broken but made tougher at the broken spots.[18] He was attracted to Sara Murphy's imperturbable loveliness, and he was touched by her vulnerability in the face of life's terrible possibilities. "Good kind beautiful lovely Sara," he would write.

Archibald MacLeish too recognized that loveliness, which he saw as Sara Murphy's emotional power. He would compare her to a "bowl of Renoir flowers," and in later years he would say that she was "all woman."[19] MacLeish's "Sketch for a Portrait of Mm. G———M———" portrays Sara Murphy's self-containment as it describes the Murphys' sitting room at St. Cloud. The room was "not hers by title," or simply "because she lived in it," but because she had touched it to make it her own. And so "you'd say, 'Her room,'" wrote MacLeish

> as though you'd said
> Her voice, Her manner, meaning something else
> Than that she owned it; knowing it was not
> A room to be possessed of, not a room
> To give itself to people, not the kind
> Of room you'd sit in and forget about,
> Or sit in and look out from. It reserved
> Something that in a woman you would call
> Her reticence by which you'd mean her power
> Of feeling what she had not put in words—[20]

Like MacLeish, most of Sara Murphy's friends, including Fitzgerald, sensed and admired, but could not touch, her emotional depths. Fitzgerald revelled in her direct gaze, and he also studied her moves (much as he did Gerald's) so as to use Sara Murphy in his fiction. In the character of Nicole Diver, a beauty "made first on the heroic scale," Fitzgerald captured a strong and accurate sense of Sara Murphy's presence. He told Sara on 15 August 1935 that he had used her "again and again in *Tender*," but primarily to convey the effect she had on people—"the echoes and reverberations—a poor return for what you have given by your living presence, but nevertheless an artist's (what a word!) sincere attempt to preserve a true fragment rather than a 'portrait' by Mr. Sargent." And so, Nicole Diver in *Tender Is the Night* conveys strength, directness, elusiveness, her face "hard, almost stern, save for the soft gleam of piteous doubt that looked from her green eyes." At times "she gave an impression of repose that was at once static and evocative." She seemed to possess an inner strength which sustained her and set her apart, "her lovely face set, controlled, her eyes brave and watchful, looking straight ahead toward nothing." Often she observed her surroundings "with a lovely peace, without a smile," sometimes "still as still." She could be the silent party, "contributing just her share of urbane humor with a precision that approached meagreness," but she could also "seize the topic and rush off with it, feverishly surprised with herself—then bring it back and relinquish it abruptly, almost timidly."[21]

If Sara Murphy had an ability to speak her mind, sometimes brusquely, she usually did so with a chic that tempered any harshness. She never set out to please, but then did so naturally by her very presence. It felt good to be with Sara, Dos Passos said. "You never lacked just the right cushion in your chair," and you always felt Sara Murphy's warmth, her coziness, her humorous concern for people.[22] Sara Murphy's assessments of people were immediate and unqualified, and when she liked them, they became her friends for life. "You don't REALLY think I am snooty do you?" she asked Ernest Hemingway on 20 May 1936. "Please don't. It isn't snooty to choose. Choice, and one's affections, are about all there are. And I am rather savage, like you, about first—best everything: best painting, best music, best friends I'd rather spend a few hours a year with the friends I love than hundreds with indifferents."

Fitzgerald told Sara what many of their friends felt: that Gerald and Sara formed an integral unit. Hadley Hemingway said that they "matched each other." Dos Passos felt that they backed each other up, complemented each other, and that their marriage was unshakeable. If Sara was the quieter of the two, she was also, as another friend said, the wind for Gerald's sails.[23] Together they embodied an elegance and an originality which people in an age of artistic innovation and upheaval found attractive. Sara's natural beauty, her unpretentious charm, drew people to her, just as Gerald's more contrived style, his cool originality, evoked in others fresher perspectives. Life always seemed gay and imaginative when the Murphys chose to make it so. This Fitzgerald captured in *Tender Is the Night*. As Rosemary Hoyt noticed, the Divers and their set seemed fashionable but different. She sensed in them "a purpose, a working over something, a direction, an act of creation different from any she had known." In essence, "they seemed to have a very good time," Rosemary thought, and all with an air of "expensive simplicity." But Rosemary was "unaware of its complexity and its lack of innocence, unaware that it was all a selection of quality rather than quantity from the run of the world's bazaar; and that the simplicity of behavior also, the nursery-like peace and good will, the emphasis on the simpler virtues, was part of a desperate bargain with the gods and had been attained through struggles she could not have guessed at."[24]

This selection of quality rather than quantity is what determined and then sustained the Murphys' relationships with the artists they came to know in France. And it was the Murphys' search for simplicity amidst life's increasing complexities, their "desperate bargain with the gods," which came to characterize them to their friends. Indeed, the prominent theme of this real-life story, not unlike that in Fitzgerald's novel, is that man's greatest fear is life itself. As Gerald Murphy saw it one year after the publication of *Tender,* what Fitzgerald had said in the novel was true. "Only the invented part of our life,—the unreal part—has had any scheme any beauty," he told Fitzgerald on 31 December 1935. "Life itself has stepped in now and blundered, scarred and destroyed. . . . How ugly and blasting it can be,—and how idly ruthless." Gerald Murphy was speaking as Dick Diver would have spoken in the novel's aftermath, for Murphy himself came to recognize that life will never be as one would like despite one's best attempts to manipulate it. The repeated coming together and jarring of these two incompatible views—the romantic and the realistic— lends the novel its creative tension, just as it came to define as well the metaphoric dimensions of the Murphys' lives. As the Murphys' friends saw life's wonderful and terrible possibilities conjoin in the Murphys' lives, they saw forcefully demonstrated that contrast between life as one would like it to be and life as it is which stood at the thematic and aesthetic center of modernist art. To the degree that their lives both engaged and illustrated the romantic dreams and the nightmares representative of the day, the Murphys became larger than life and an artist's dream to depict.

Edmund Wilson once admitted that with "amusing or romantic" characters such as F. Scott Fitzgerald or Gerald or Sara Murphy, "anecdotes grow rapidly into legends."[25] Certainly the anecdotes associated with the Murphys and life at their Villa America on the French Riviera have assumed, in their various renditions, mythic proportions. Such renditions are difficult to sort through and verify. Perspectives and perceptions differ, and time tends to blend and distort details in order to give shape to a certain feel, an aura which remains in memory as the larger truth. And with the Murphys, because of their zest for living and their determination to remain brave in the face of life's capricious cruelties, people were more prone to mythologize. Certainly those who partook of rich summer days at the Villa America in the 1920s would look back at those times as special. "We will never feel quite so intensely about our surroundings any more," wrote Fitzgerald in retrospect.[26] On the beach and on the Murphys' lush garden terrace, the days were filled with games, conversation, drink, good food, and a general relaxation. Invariably, because of the particular people involved, "whatever happened seemed to have something to do with art."[27] Sara Murphy recalled that the gaiety stemmed not so much from parties as from mutually felt affections. "You loved your friends and wanted to see them every day, and usually you did see them every day. It was like a great fair, and everybody was so young."[28]

The extensive correspondence between the Murphys and their friends helps to clarify the legends, reflecting the Riviera glow and the 1920s flamboyance they experienced and, in varying degrees, relished. It also shows the sadder times within and apart from this Riviera whirl which Hemingway saw as a fiesta and which Fitzgerald looked back to as the best time of all, once telling Maxwell Perkins he would have liked to "live and die" on the French Riviera.[29] These letters, which cover the years from 1925 until Gerald Murphy's death in 1964, also reveal the strong role France and the 1920s would continue to play in the correspondents' lives during the ensuing decades. As early as 1933, Archibald MacLeish would find it "distressing" that all of his nostalgia was "for a few years and a foreign city." As he told John Peale Bishop, the Murphys had just returned to America (they were the last of the group to leave France), and they were "restoring a few of the geodetic points of our lost topography. But otherwise the scattering is still complete. Indeed I have given up all hope of time's ever bringing our other world together again. Time bringeth all things except its own patterns."[30]

That some of those patterns can be seen and felt in this book of correspondence makes for its peculiar evocative power. As MacLeish described it to Gerald Murphy (2 September [1964]), Robert Frost's "freedom of the material" was that "freedom to make those unexpected 'connections' . . . which actually create meaning." "God knows where that 'freedom' comes from or how it can be taught—even by you," MacLeish said. Some of that "freedom of the material" inheres in this book of correspondence as it brings together, sequentially and for the first time, the letters between all these artist-friends who had met in 1920s France. As each letter successively clarifies and illuminates those that surround it, the reader encounters those unexpected connections which create meaning and discovers a picture not yet presented so graphically, or with such immediacy, in separate books of letters, memoirs, and biographies of the era. This book's meanings reside in the chronological interweaving of its text, and it is best read whole. What emerges finally is an expressionistic portrait of individuals, of a group, and of an era.

Decades later Gerald Murphy would say that this era was greatly misunderstood by those who tended to overromanticize it. People in post–World War II America, in particular, had developed "a completely false conception of the life of Americans in France in the twenties and early thirties." The Murphys' experience "was not that of the already established Francophile 'American Colony' in the Bois de Boulogne and Avenue Matignon nor was it the life in Montparnasse as described by Malcolm Cowley [in Exile's Return]." Instead, as Gerald Murphy defined it, it narrowed down "to our milieu of young (mostly married) Americans who were interested in the arts. These people were free of the point of view of the generation before them who attended the Beaux Arts and dabbled in Montmartre and copied the French Impressionists. Léger referred to them as 'faux Bohémiens,'—even to their wearing blue smocks and velvet bérets and baggy trousers which narrowed at the ankle."[31]

Those who were truly "interested in the arts" found common ground in Serge Diaghilev's Ballets Russes—the "focal center of the whole modern movement in the arts" as well as a "kind of movement in itself," said Murphy. Anyone expressing interest in the company "became a member automatically. You knew everybody, you knew all the dancers, and everybody asked your opinion on things."[32] Central to the ballet and a powerful influence on fellow artists was Diaghilev himself. Gerald Murphy would recall the day that Diaghilev told Picasso that he must go with him to Rome. "'I am doing a ballet based on the music of Scarlatti which Stravinsky is to arrange and sharpen,'" Diaghilev told Picasso. "'I shall douse you in the Comedia del Arte of which you know nothing, since you never leave Paris. I will arrange what you are to see there.'" As Murphy remembered it, Diaghilev told Picasso during their last three days in Rome "to spend the rest of his time looking at nothing but Roman sculpture and I don't mean Greco-Roman! Something will come of it! Well, it did: those great big girls which he did on the spot in pastel. They with their huge cylindrical fingers, monolithic heads and thick eye-lids, but running like gazelles down beaches on their piano legs."[33]

As both Gerald and Sara painted sets for Diaghilev's stage productions, and as Gerald studied painting under Diaghilev designer Natalia Goncharova, they began to meet other American artists who came to the same exhibits, recitals, plays, and ballets. By 1925 they had met Donald Ogden Stewart, Robert Benchley, Alexander Woollcott, and Philip Barry (New York luminaries variously associated with the *New Yorker* magazine, the Algonquin Round Table, Broadway, and radio). They had also met the major correspondents in this book: John Dos Passos; Archibald and Ada MacLeish; Scott and Zelda Fitzgerald; Ernest and Hadley Hemingway, and Pauline Pfeiffer, who became Hemingway's second wife in 1927. By 1926 they had met Dorothy Parker, and in 1929 they had met as well Katy Smith Dos Passos, Hemingway's childhood friend who had married Dos Passos that same year. For the most part, these friendships were lifelong and interrelated, although Hemingway later turned on the Murphys in his posthumously published *A Moveable Feast* (1964) and blamed them for the unhappiness which he traced back to his 1926 break with Hadley.

The Murphys had not chosen an easy friend in Hemingway—or for that matter, in Fitzgerald; but their friendship with Fitzgerald matured over the years, until Fitzgerald came to rely on them as two of the few people who knew and loved him for himself. Although Fitzgerald seemed the most dependent recipient in this relationship, it was still mutually remunerative, especially for Gerald Murphy, who told Fitzgerald on 31 December 1935: "You are the only person to whom I can ever tell the bleak truth of what I feel. . . . When you come North let me talk to you." Even though the Murphys did not always "like" Fitzgerald with his selfish and careless insensitivities toward others, they felt free to tell him so; and their repeated candor helped to fortify the relationship.

If the Murphys' relationships with both Fitzgerald and Hemingway were sometimes troubled, this was not the case with John Dos Passos, who was the first of this group of artists to meet the Murphys in France. His friends saw him, accordingly, as a pathfinder. With his "nearsighted, far, far-seeing eyes," noted Archibald MacLeish, Dos Passos "had caught the first glimpse of the whole adventure, the vast experience—a view as wide as Whitman's but a century further on." And after he "had caught the vision of a vision," he "came to Paris year by year to find there what he'd lost."[34] When he found the Murphys in 1923, he was "eternally grateful." He particularly liked the Murphys when they were with their children and his happy memories of those first Riviera days were directly linked with them when Gerald was "Dow-dow."[35] (Gerald liked this nickname which his children gave him and which his friends then adopted, and he sometimes took to signing his letters with what he called the French spelling: Daou-daou; or sometimes just Daou.)

Archibald MacLeish met the Murphys in France shortly after Dos Passos and likewise came to regard his relationship with them as one of the richest of his life. It was, as MacLeish said, "a relation between artists" and on a deeply human plane which "included Sara and my wife, a brilliant singer, in the usual way of such things." As attractive as he found the Murphys and the house at St. Cloud and the villa on the Cap d'Antibes, what MacLeish was most impressed by was Gerald's dedication to his art and the creative vision which inspired it—what MacLeish called his "unerring sense of the *scene.*"[36] MacLeish believed that when the Murphys returned to America in 1932, they carried with them there that same "sense of the *scene.*"

Back in America during the 1930s, the Murphys and their friends wrote to each other often, sometimes giving vent to personal fears. As Fitzgerald worried about money, about Zelda, about his health, about his writing, MacLeish tried to overcome his fear that working as a journalist (an editor for *Fortune* magazine) had destroyed his artistic credibility. Hemingway fought his own inner battles as he grew increasingly moody and alienated even his best friends. Political differences worked to sever the Dos Passos-Hemingway relationship by the late 1930s, just as personal differences finally led to Hemingway's break with the initial group. Gerald Murphy wondered how Hemingway could get away with saying such outrageous things about people and decided finally that he must be voicing his feelings only to Gerald and Sara. This, however, was not always the case, to the dismay of Hemingway's friends. Although Gerald and Sara tried to act as arbitrators during the late 1930s, they could not always patch strained relationships, especially those between Hemingway and the others. They did help to put life into perspective for their friends however, and they did turn to them when they needed them.

Sara in particular would rely on her friends during the 1930s, difficult years wherein Gerald seemed unable to give her adequate emotional support. He recognized that she relied on people more than he did and encouraged her to find sustenance in others beside himself. MacLeish was concerned that Sara's inner turmoil could not be reached, and he told Hemingway that her unhappiness was "about the headaches she has so much of the time and about a lot of other things she won't talk about."[37] Sara apparently did talk about some of these things with Hemingway between 1935 to 1940, years when she saw him often and found in him a special rapport and comfort.

One of the ironies reflected in these letters is that despite the Murphys' incredible gift for friendship, they were not always able to meet each other's needs. When Sara called Gerald to task for this in 1936, it only intensified his sense of deep regret and personal helplessness in the face of what he called his emotional "deficiency." Gerald would apologize repeatedly to Sara, and to their friends, for his inability to convey, sometimes to feel, the appropriate emotion. Rather than confront an emotional crisis in a relationship, Gerald would, at a crucial moment, turn away. When Murphy tried to explain to MacLeish how he had "learned to dread (and avoid) the responsibilities of friendship" because he believed he was "incapable of a full one," he was admitting to his own sense of inadequacy. They had talked about this once while sitting on the Villa America terrace in 1925. John Peale Bishop's ideas on tragedy had stimulated their discussion about terror—which was "the horror of evil, of unexpected, sharply contrasted depravity, of helplessness before one's own nature—*not death, but life and its terrible possibilities.*" Murphy and MacLeish had agreed with this idea: "So completely obvious!—like all profound observations," MacLeish said. "We are afraid of our own lives— and beside that fear, death, which is at least a fact, is a small matter."[38]

Although Murphy knew that he could not meet all Sara's emotional needs, their marriage was nonetheless solid and enduring, and inspired. Perhaps this had most to do with their different orientations toward life and people. Sara was more of the heart. She had told Fitzgerald, after all, that "what one thinks of things" matters far less than "what one feels about them." Gerald, on the other hand, was more of the mind, telling Fitzgerald that "it's not what we do but what we do with our minds that counts." He gradually arrived at "a kind of distant region" within himself where he found his "mind freed." He understood too well Tennessee Williams's dictum that everyone is sentenced to solitary confinement within his own skin, and he also knew, and stated it often, that "grief cannot be shared." Nonetheless, both he and Sara recognized their strong need for each other. As they each acted upon their own perspectives, they indeed complemented and enhanced and, in an inexplicable way, completed each other. Sara would say to Gerald on 7 August 1963: "You *must know* that without you—nothing makes any sense—I am only half a person,—and you are the other half—It is *so*, however I may try."

When Gerald and Sara Murphy and their "three small children" had "set off for Europe . . . for an indefinite period," neither of their families could understand or accept this. But "there were those outside of our families," said Gerald Murphy, "30 years ago—who understood why we had gone. Ernest, Scott, Archie, Dos and others did when we met them there."[39] Perhaps because of this unspoken mutual understanding, the rapport between the Murphys and these friends was immediate and electric—and lifelong. Ellen Barry would never forget her surprise and wonder at discovering the Murphys in Paris. Donald Stewart had personally led Ellen and her husband Philip to the Murphys' apartment, where Sara leaned out the second floor window to greet them on the street below. Her "very adorable, pert, pretty face and her hair done up in a high French twist" was framed suddenly within the window and in fresh contrast to the rough-hewn brick. From the first glimpse of both these "very original people," remarked Ellen Barry, you knew they were "extraordinary."[40]

Throughout their years in Europe and in America, the Murphys and their friends tried to see one another often, and when they could not, they missed one another and said so in their correspondence. In times of need, they provided verbal and financial encouragement and a physical and spiritual presence—acts of love which helped to temper life's inequities. Their good-humored acceptance of petty annoyances and human foibles and their talk about visits, travel, boats, water, houses, food, music, theater, film, children, and mutual friends reflect their desire for day-to-day continuity besides providing a means for assuaging the larger pains they did not always want to name. That these artists talk less in their letters about art than they do about life should come as no surprise given "the unfinished nature of real life," what Patricia Frazer Lamb has called "its artless messiness." As Lamb notes in a discussion about women and their letters, artists might feel a stronger need than most to "re-structure their past histories into a semblance of sanity and order." This they do in their art (if it is any good). Their letters, in contrast, "convey wonderfully the chaos, the changes of mind, the growth of self."[41] As Fitzgerald told Sara Murphy on 30 March 1936, "Willy-nilly we are still in the midst of life and all true correspondence is necessarily sporadic but a letter from you or Gerald always pulls at something awfully deep in me."

Although most of these correspondents wrote eloquently and with a distinctive style, Gerald Murphy's letters in particular are masterpieces of conception—small paintings on paper. His exact and elegant print neatly fills the spaces of a postcard, lining up around the sides to form a frame. Katy Dos

Passos would comment that Gerald was the only one to create a "Post Card Style." "I am planning a monograph on this with examples," she told Sara Murphy on 8 April 1945. "It will be known as the Murphy Telescope Style or something of that kind—probably just known as 'The Murphy Style.'" Archibald MacLeish thought that if Gerald were not a painter, he could have been a writer, and that he wrote like a poet. Overall, Gerald Murphy's letters are grammatically sound and rich in literary allusion, and they reflect his intellectual bent, his tendency, sometimes to a fault, to organize. Although Murphy's letters bespeak a certain candor, they sometimes seem veiled because either too controlled or too hyperbolic.

Sara's letters, on the other hand, reveal her open, spontaneous personality. They move rapidly from thought to thought with little regard for punctuation and with sporadic use of ampersands, contractions, and underlined words (sometimes double-underlined for emphasis). Sara could be particularly emphatic when writing to Fitzgerald, and her letters overall—similar to Hemingway's in their free-flowing character—could be disarmingly candid and pointed. She invariably signed them with "love."

The women correspondents probably wrote about ongoing daily life more often than the men, and Katy Dos Passos's letters are particularly witty and zestful as she informs Sara about trips and housekeeping troubles and the need to see friends. Gerald would say to Sara (2 March 1951) that there was no one as funny as Katy in that "quaint quiet way." Pauline Hemingway's letters from the thirties are not unlike Katy's in their wit and charm. As she writes from Florida or Wyoming to detail Hemingway's latest fishing or hunting feats or to plan for Sara's regular spring visits to Key West, she provides a counterpoint to the letters from Ernest to Sara, which grow increasingly somber as the decade nears its close. Indeed, more than the other writers, Hemingway's letters (and especially those to Sara) are spirited and self-revealing. MacLeish's letters, on the other hand, are not unlike Gerald's—artfully modulated with an undertone of restraint which gives them emotional resonance. John Dos Passos, of all these friends, wrote the sketchiest letters. He was always on the go, and he preferred being with his friends rather than writing to them. Dos, as his friends called him (pronouncing it with a short "o"), was known to show up unexpectedly, and he was always welcome.

Alexander Woollcott's correspondence, primarily with Gerald Murphy during the 1930s and early 1940s, reflects his and Gerald's shared love for drama and the dramatic. Woollcott, like Murphy, took to completing an outfit with some unusual flourish—often a sweeping cape or a jaunty cap—and to becoming his own self-caricature. What perhaps most drew them together was their underlying insecurity and sensitivity—sometimes disguised by the outward show. When Woollcott died of a heart attack in early 1943, Murphy told Archibald MacLeish that "Alec—behind all that nonsense—had something very human. He had become more tractable and was dining *alone* quietly with us each week. His gift was to make the people he loved feel valuable. Few have it."

Along with the letters between the primary correspondents, there are some which speak directly about the Murphys and their friends. One of the most remarkable of these letters is from Dorothy Parker to Robert Benchley in the fall of 1929. A 1964 letter from novelist Dawn Powell to John Dos Passos on the death of Gerald Murphy helps to round out the book.

Letters from the Lost Generation comprises a nearly complete collection of extant correspondence, with the exception of some more perfunctory letters and cards, particularly during the 1940s and 1950s. The 1920s correspondence is limited because the Murphys and their friends were together often during those years, and also because many of the letters to the Murphys from that period were lost, probably left behind at Villa America. The surviving letters from the 1920s are primarily those of the Murphys to Scott Fitzgerald and Ernest Hemingway, with the bulk of the correspondence centering on the 1930s, years which appear more tragic in contrast to the gayer surroundings of 1920s France. By late 1940, Fitzgerald had died, and Zelda Fitzgerald's letter to the Murphys about Fitzgerald, and about all of them together in France and in America, completes the middle section of the book. Most of the final section (letters between 1941 and 1964) consists of correspondence between the Dos Passoses, the MacLeishes, and the Murphys. Personal letters exchanged between Gerald and Sara and their families have generally been excluded along with roughly one-fourth of the letters from Katy Dos Passos, who wrote often, sometimes several days in succession when she and Dos Passos were traveling. Of the letters published here, most have not appeared previously, and never in this form—a group portrait wherein the participants are allowed to tell their own story.

Although so many correspondents, each with individual quirks and foibles, test the editor trying to maintain an editorial policy that does not at some point betray the distinctive style of each writer, the general rule has been to transcribe the letters exactly as they were written, with the following minor exceptions. Obvious errors of typing (misalignments, jammed words, omitted letters) and unintended slips of the pen, including sometimes sloppy punctuation and Gerald's tendency to misplace apostrophes in contractions, have been silently emended. Grammatical and spelling errors are atypical, of course, except that Fitzgerald was a notoriously poor speller and Hemingway, when going with the flow of the letter (especially when he typed it), could be idiosyncratic. Since Gerald sometimes used ellipses to indicate pauses in thought, the reader should note that these ellipses do not reflect editorial omissions. Indeed, all these letters are printed in their entirety, save for two in which some lines were deleted at the request of family.

Each letter provides in its major heading the name of the writer and the recipient, the place of origin, and the date. Datelines have been regularized to follow Gerald's format: the day preceding the month and year. Gerald invariably dated his letters carefully, whereas Sara seldom did, occasionally giving the day and the month but not the year. Most of the undated or partially dated letters in this book can be dated with a good degree of accuracy, either by an accompanying postmark or internal evidence. Dates so ascertained are bracketed.

Scholarly apparatus has been kept to a minimum. Introductions to each section provide background information and analysis as needed, and occasional commentary between letters serves both to clarify references and to place the letters in context. For the most part, the letters themselves—when read as a continuous whole—provide their own continuities and clarifications. References to people or events are identified only when deemed necessary to understanding a particular letter, and footnoting overall is spare so as to allow the writer's voice to keep the pace. Whenever it is possible to do so without disrupting the letter, necessary clarifications are made in brackets, and translations of foreign phrases, unless common knowledge, are also provided within brackets. The frequent use of French words and phrases offers evidence of the time the correspondents spent in France and the degree to which French life became a part of them.

The numerous name and place references generally become clear in context. It is helpful to know some of the basic references associated with the Murphys' lives. Some of their household staff over the years included Celestine, a cook; Clement, a chauffeur; Ernestine Leray, a housekeeper who was with the Murphys in France and also in America; and Mrs. Wessberg, a household worker in America until after Gerald Murphy's death. Joseph Revello was head gardener at Villa America, and he and his wife Baptistine named their only child after Gerald Murphy. The Revello family stayed on at the Villa as caretakers after the Murphys left for America in 1932, and after the Murphys sold Villa America in 1950, they remained there in what had been Gerald's studio. The Murphys had renovated several of the outbuildings associated with the Villa. Gerald used one of these as his studio; the "Bastide" was the cottage where Dos Passos, among others, stayed; and the "Ferme des Orangers" was a former donkey stable in the orange grove directly across the road from the Villa which Gerald and Sara had made into a fully-equipped housekeeping cottage. After Robert Benchley stayed here, he rechristened it "La Ferme Dérangée." Hale Walker and Harold Heller were New York decorators who helped the Murphys with the interiors of their various residences, including the Villa America, their East Hampton homes (in particular Hook Pond and Swan Cove), their various New York apartments, and Cheer Hall, at Snedens Landing, New York. From the beginning of their years in France, the

Murphys employed Vladimir Orloff ("Vova") to oversee the sailing and maintenance of their boats. A cousin of Diaghilev's, he became a close, lifelong friend of the Murphys.

The originals of the Murphys' letters to their friends are located as follows: The Hemingway Papers, John Fitzgerald Kennedy Library, Boston (JFK); The MacLeish Papers, The Library of Congress, Washington, D.C. (LC); The Fitzgerald Papers, Princeton University Library (PUL); The Dos Passos Papers, University of Virginia Library, Charlottesville (UVA); The Woollcott Papers, Houghton-Mifflin Library, Boston (HL). Dorothy Parker's letter to Robert Benchley is with the Benchley Papers at the Mugar Library, Boston University (BU). The letters to the Murphys (except for Katy Dos Passos's letters, which are part of the John Dos Passos Papers) are in the Donnelly Collection, as are miscellaneous copies of Murphy letters to others. The abbreviated reference at the close of each letter keys the reader to the letter's location.

PART ONE
1925–1932

The Riviera
in the Summer

Now I am working in a red plush room at the Murphy's place at Antibes where I'm being "entertained" as the New York Herald would say with great elegance and a great deal of gin fizz. Wonderfully good bathing. The Riviera in summer is a strange and rather exciting place.
—JOHN DOS PASSOS, *The Fourteenth Chronicle*

When John Dos Passos met Gerald and Sara in early 1923, he caught their enthusiasm for Diaghilev's ballet and helped to paint sets for Stravinsky's *Les Noces*. He and Gerald spent days—and sometimes nights as the June 17 deadline neared—painting sets in the hot theater lofts, and they worried that nothing would be finished on time. After rolling paint on huge canvas sheets, they sometimes took breaks at a local brasserie which served beer "in glasses the size of goldfish bowls." On opening night ("we were all mad for it," said Dos Passos), they marvelled that everything fell miraculously into place.[1]

Around the time of the premiere, Archibald and Ada MacLeish and their two children had also arrived in Paris. "Where else would you go but Paris," MacLeish's friends said, "if you were crazy enough to turn down a partnership in the best law firm in Boston to write—what?—*poems*?"[2] The MacLeishes rented an apartment on the Boulevard St. Michel and met the Murphys shortly thereafter. Soon they too were enjoying life with the Murphys in Paris and on the French Riviera, where the Murphys had decided to buy a villa. During the extensive renovation of Villa America prior to 1925, the Murphys stayed at the Hotel du Cap in Antibes, where they held "open house for a bunch of Americans,"[3] including Dos Passos, the MacLeishes, and

Gerald's younger sister Esther. When Esther Murphy and Dos Passos returned to New York in late 1923, they regaled their Long Island friends (John Peale Bishop and Scott and Zelda Fitzgerald among them) with tales of the Murphys and the good life in France. The Fitzgeralds decided shortly thereafter that they should move abroad, and they looked up the Murphys in the spring of 1924. From June through October they rented a villa in St. Raphael to be near the Murphys at Antibes. As Edmund Wilson assessed it later, the Murphys, and by 1925 Ernest Hemingway, "came to constitute Europe for Scott."[4]

Fitzgerald's intimacy with the Murphys may have led to Hemingway's finally joining the group, despite his resistance at meeting those Donald Stewart called the "right people."[5] The two authors met shortly after the spring 1925 publication of *The Great Gatsby* and prior to the fall 1925 publication of Hemingway's *In Our Time*; and Fitzgerald had begun thereafter to talk of Gerald and Ernest in the same sequence, writing Gilbert Seldes, for example, that he had seen Ernest "a great deal" and also Gerald—"both of them . . . thoroughly charming."[6] When Hemingway met Gerald Murphy in late 1925, he succumbed to his charms and wondered that he had waited so long. Hemingway found both Gerald and Sara "grand people" and took them sufficiently into his confidence to read to them—straight through—*The Torrents of Spring*. Sara "slept through most of it, sitting bolt-upright on the sofa," and Gerald, along with Dos Passos and Hadley Hemingway, "found the book in questionable taste."[7] Its bitter satire of Sherwood Anderson's *Dark Laughter* caused Liveright (publisher of *In Our Time*) to reject the manuscript, and Hemingway went to New York in February 1926 to negotiate with Scribners, who published the book and became his publisher thereafter.

When Hemingway returned to Schruns, Austria, Gerald and Sara and Dos Passos joined the Hemingways there for a week of skiing which Dos Passos likened to "living in an oldfashioned Christmas card." They stayed some of the time at the Taube inn, and they spent their time eating and skiing, hiking up the mountain trails until the deeper snow required them to use their skis, with sealskins attached to the bottoms, as snowshoes. The wonderful food and wine at the Taube made "every meal time . . . a great event," said Hemingway; and as Dos Passos remembered it, they usually relived the day's activities during the evening meal and "could hardly eat for laughing." At the end of this week (during which Hemingway read them the revised *The Sun Also Rises*), the troupe parted company as "brothers and sisters."[8]

By the 1926 summer, most of these friends had spent time at the Murphys' Villa America, where life had already established its special charm and beauty. Dos Passos's description of a typical day there conveys the ambience which Fitzgerald attributed to Gerald's ordering of the day's events, "spaced like the day of the older civilizations to yield the utmost from the materials at hand, and to give all the transitions their full value."⁹

It was marvelously quiet under a sky of burning blue. The air smelt of eucalyptus and tomatoes and heliotrope from the garden. I would get up early to work, and about noon walk out to a sandfringed cove named la Garoupe. There I would find the household sunbathing. Gerald would be sweeping the seaweed off the sand under his beachumbrellas. We would swim out through the calm crystalblue water, saltier than salt, to the mouth of the cove and back. Then Gerald would produce cold sherry and Sara would marshal recondite hors d'oeuvres for blotters. Saturated with salt and sun, some in cars and some walking, the company would troop back to the terrace, overlooking the flowers and vegetables back of the villa, for lunch.

One of Sara's favorite dishes was poached eggs with Golden Bantam corn cut off the cob and sprinkled with paprika; homegrown tomatoes cooked in olive oil and garlic on the side. Sometimes to this day when I'm eating corn on the cob I recapture the flavor, and the blue flare of the Mediterranean noon, and the taste of vin de Cassis in the briney Mediterranean breeze.¹⁰

Although Dos Passos would return to America and remain throughout 1926, the others, including the MacLeishes, the Fitzgeralds, and the Hemingways, would be in Antibes for a good part of the 1926 summer. Hadley Hemingway came ahead with Bumby in May and was soon established in the villa which the Fitzgeralds had loaned them. Ernest Hemingway was pleased to learn, upon his return from Spain in early June, that Hadley "had the villa running beautifully" and that it promised to be "like the good old days." They "would swim and be healthy and brown and have one apéritif before lunch and one before dinner." "Scott was not drinking, and starting to work and he wanted us to come," said Hemingway. "No one drank anything stronger than champagne and it was very gay and obviously a splendid place to write. There was going to be everything that a man needed to write except to be alone."¹¹

One of the difficulties for Hemingway was that Pauline Pfeiffer was also at Villa America that summer. The Hemingways had met Pauline and her sister Virginia the previous spring in Paris, where Pauline worked as an editor for *Vogue* magazine, and they all became good friends. But once Pauline had come into the Hemingways' lives, nothing was ever "the same again." Hemingway described how "an unmarried young woman becomes the temporary best friend of another young woman who is married, goes to live with the husband and wife and then unknowingly, innocently and unrelentingly sets out to marry the husband." When Hemingway had finished his work, he had two girls waiting. "One is new and strange and if he has bad luck he gets to love them both."[12] Not surprisingly, Hadley Hemingway felt a sense of impending disaster as the month of June "dragged on for an eternity."[13]

As the Hemingways pretended that all was well, the Fitzgeralds were doing their own posturing, acting out the charades which had begun to strain their relationship and their friendships. Gerald said that they worked together that summer like a "pair of conspirators." "They would begin together in the evening; you would see some look come over them . . . as though they were waiting for something to happen; they didn't want entertainment, or exotic food; they seemed to be looking forward to something fantastic. . . . It was that they were in search of, and they went for it alone." When the Murphys threw a champagne-and-caviar party to welcome Hemingway's return from Spain, Scott Fitzgerald arrived "intent on social sabotage." According to Gerald, he thought the caviar-and-champagne idea the "height of affectation" and made derogatory remarks accordingly. He also stared rudely at a girl at the next table, began tossing ashtrays, and throughout it all, laughed "with sophomoric glee." Gerald left the party in disgust and Sara later wrote Fitzgerald a letter scoring his behavior. Ada MacLeish spoke for everyone when she said they all "learned to avoid like the plague" these "Fitzgerald Evenings."[14]

When Donald Stewart came to the Villa America in June with his bride Beatrice Ames, he sensed a change in both Antibes and his friends. The Villa America had become a "celebrity circus," and the writers there felt that "something was constraining them, interfering with their thoughts." Malcolm Cowley found that "as the colony grew, there were jealousies, boredom, gossip, intrigues," and artists complained that "these interruptions" inhibited their work. Dorothy Parker, who had met the Murphys that spring and then remained with them throughout the summer, confided to Stewart upon his arrival that the rich made her nervous and that her work had suffered.[15]

Partly to escape the crowds of monied tourists, the Murphys, along with the Hemingways and Pauline, left for Spain in July. During this trip Gerald recognized that Hemingway had a strong influence over him—something to do with Gerald's desire to be liked and Hemingway's idea of toughness. "The preoccupation with masculinity never let up with him," Gerald remembered. "He was obsessed with courage, and with toughness. 'You'd like him, he's tough,' he'd say of someone he admired." During their stay in Pamplona, Gerald chose to wear "a darkish cap" pulled down over one eye. Hemingway told him that the cap was "just right. Just the thing to wear. You look tough." On this same trip. Hemingway encouraged him to enter the bullring at one of the morning amateurs. "Ernest had a very strong sense of what you could take in the way of physical punishment," Gerald said later. "And when you were with Ernest, you didn't say, 'I think I'll stay here.'" When Murphy found himself being charged by one of the bulls, he moved his raincoat to the left, narrowly escaping injury by performing a quick and unwitting veronica. "I've never been so terrified in my life," Murphy admitted later.[16]

At the end of the July fiesta, the Hemingways remained in Spain while the Murphys and Pauline took the train to France. Gerald wrote the Hemingways from Villa America to say: "You're so right: because you're close to what's elemental. Your values are hitched up to the universe." Shortly after this letter, the Murphys and all the Hemingways' friends were surprised to learn that Ernest and Hadley planned to separate. "When you get fond of a couple," Dos Passos said, "you like them to stay hitched."[17] The Hemingways stopped in Antibes before heading for Paris, where Ernest would stay in Gerald's studio at 69 rue Froidevaux—a sculptor's studio in "a single ground floor building with a ceiling 30 feet high" which allowed for Gerald's "very large canvases."[18] As Gerald and Sara talked with Hemingway throughout August and September, they encouraged him to persist in his separation from Hadley. Hadley's belief that certain people, and particularly Sara Murphy, had ganged up against her in favor of the more stylish and aggressive second woman seems justified in light of the Murphys' letters to Hemingway that fall, letters which confirm that they would not be sorry to see Hemingway's relationship with Hadley end.

After counseling Hemingway that fall, the Murphys left for America to visit family. The Fitzgeralds saw them off, as Scott reported it to Ernest back in Paris. "Got stewed with them (at their party)—that is we got stewed—and I believe there was some sort of mawkish reconciliation," Scott wrote. "However they've grown dim to me and I don't like them much any more."[19] These feelings were shortlived, however, more a reflection of Fitzgerald's own sense of failure than his regard for Gerald and Sara. As Fitzgerald's biographer Andrew Turnbull emphasizes, with Europe and the Murphys "Fitzgerald came as close as he ever would to finding perfection in the real world, and in a way the rest of his life was a retreat from this summit."[20] Zelda captured the summer's aftermath and the Fitzgeralds' sense that time was running out when she wrote Maxwell Perkins that "all the gay decorative people have left, taking with them the sense of carnival & impending disaster that colored this summer."[21] To Scott, "it might all have happened at Roslyn, Long Island," for it was a "futile" as well as a "petty" summer. He had hoped to complete the novel begun in 1925, but its lack of direction reflected his own disorientation. When the Fitzgeralds left for America in December 1926, Scott saw behind him the "huge Garoupe standing desolate."[22]

Back in Paris prior to the Fitzgeralds' leavetaking, and on through the winter, Hemingway saw the MacLeishes, staying with them for periods of time, and also kept in touch with the Murphys. Although he was anxious for them to return, when he saw Gerald, after marrying Pauline in May, the reunion was constrained and troubled. That Hemingway associated Gerald with the broken marriage about which he still felt remorse, had something to do with this, as did Gerald's own growing preoccupation. He had entered one of his most productive artistic periods as his work became increasingly complex, moving beyond precisionism to cubism and finally to sophisticated surrealism, fantasy as "an unintentional by-product of the quest for 'reality.'"[23] But if Murphy was producing some of his best work during 1927, he was also questioning his identity as a man and an artist and retreating from his relationships in the process.

"And what are you up to?" Archie MacLeish asked Hemingway that June. "Down at Antibes are you? And listening to the Murphys tell how they broke with the MacLeishes because they really couldn't let anyone act as though anyone could ever have responsibilities toward anyone? Or how?"[24] The MacLeishes were in New England for the 1927 summer, and they had last seen the Murphys that spring, after the Murphys had returned from America to meet up with the MacLeishes for a "dash through Central Europe." Apparently Archie had suffered his own quarrels with Gerald during this troubled period; yet he was pleased (but with reservations) to hear by August that Ernest and Gerald had had a rapprochement.[25]

Although Gerald and Ernest patched their quarrel that summer and then continued to see each other sporadically thereafter, their relationship never reassumed its former intensity and candor. In fact, Gerald would come to believe later that Hemingway put him and the relationship to the final test during the spring of 1928 in Paris. Murphy remembered that Hemingway "was talking about homosexuals, kidding, as people did then when there weren't so many, or at least they weren't so in evidence."

> He was extremely sensitive to the question of who was one and who wasn't. He said, casually, 'I don't mind a fairy like X—, do you?—and for some reason I said 'No,' although I had never met the man. I have no idea why I said it, except that Ernest had the quality of making it easier to agree with him than not; he was such an enveloping personality, so physically huge and forceful, and he overstated everything and talked so rapidly and so graphically and so well that you just found yourself agreeing with him. Anyway, instead of saying I had never met the man I agreed with him, and he gave me a funny look. Afterward I almost wondered whether it had been a trap he laid for me. In any case, after that I always felt he had a reservation about me, and I was never nearly so close to him as Sara.[26]

When Gerald and Ernest had this encounter, Hemingway was wearing a bandage around his head due to one of his stranger accidents (he was peculiarly accident-prone throughout his life). He and Pauline had returned from dinner with the MacLeishes (back in France after their summer reprieve in

America) when Hemingway unwittingly pulled the bathroom skylight on his head, severely cutting his forehead. Pauline resummoned Archie to help get Ernest to the hospital, and the incident seemed to hasten both the Hemingways' and the MacLeishes' departure for America. The Hemingways would stay in America while Pauline had her baby (a boy, Patrick) and the MacLeishes would return for another summer stay in New England, where they also had their third child, Peter, who became the Murphys' godchild.

Nearly crossing paths at sea with the MacLeishes and the Hemingways that spring were the Fitzgeralds, on their way to France after a difficult year in America. Scott Fitzgerald had decided early in 1927 that he hated screenwriting, and he and Zelda left Hollywood for Wilmington, Delaware, where they moved into Ellerslie Mansion. Although Fitzgerald hoped to complete his novel, his work still faltered as the Fitzgeralds became known, once again, for their drinking and their parties. By the beginning of 1928, the Fitzgeralds believed that they might find new solutions in France. "They hadn't much faith in travel nor a great belief in a change of scene as a panacea for spiritual ills," Zelda would write later in her autobiographical novel *Save Me the Waltz* (1933), but "they were simply glad to be going."[27] From the start of their sojourn in America, they had been homesick for France. Zelda wrote Scottie from Hollywood that the weather made her think of Paris in the spring. "And I am *very* homesick for the pink lights and the trees and the gay streets. So is Daddy, also for the wine and the little cafés on the sidewalk."[28] When they finally arrived in Paris after more than a year away, they took an apartment across from the Luxembourg Gardens and stayed until September. Fitzgerald was soon boasting to Hemingway, still back in America, that they were friends with the Murphys again. "Talked about you a great deal," Fitzgerald added, "& while we *tried* to say only kind things we managed to get in a few good cracks that would amuse you—about anybody else—which is what you get for being so far away."[29]

Still far away also was MacLeish, who had decided during the summer of 1928 that he and his family would have to live in America. It was becoming less cheap to live in Paris by the end of the decade, and MacLeish accepted a position as a writer/editor for *Fortune* magazine, a position he retained for a decade in order to support his family. Later he would envy Hemingway for being able to live off his writing. "There is no way to write except to live as you do doing something with your body and letting the line float off somewhere," MacLeish said to Hemingway, but "how in Christ's name do you arrange it? I am getting soft and losing my wind and my mind runs on an overhead trolley that meets all the trains and I haven't let her slide for a year now. There doesn't seem to be any way out."[30]

In September 1928, MacLeish wrote a letter/poem to Gerald which reflected his sense of feeling emotionally torn between commitment to two countries, France and America. He associated France directly with Gerald—

the "humming pines and the surf and the sound / At the ferme Blanche," and "Port Cros in the dusk and the harbor / Floating the motionless ship and the sea-drowned star." He kept thinking of "the dolphin at Capo di Mele" and seeing in his mind "the taut sail / And the hill over St.-Tropez and [Gerald's] hand on the tiller." He associated America with an overwhelming loneliness— "to be born of no race and no people" and to live in open spaces where "here it is one man and the wind in the boughs."

When Gerald received MacLeish's "American Letter," he and Sara were planning their own visit to America, to Hollywood. Fitzgerald had introduced Gerald to film director King Vidor that summer, and Gerald had agreed to assist in the production of *Hallelujah!*, an all-Negro film. Gerald's extensive collection of Negro folk songs and spirituals, some of which he had discovered in the Boston Public Library, intrigued Vidor, who recalled later that Gerald assisted him, through consultation, with the music and also with the photography. "I thought that the type of painting that he did would fit very well into the type of photography that I was going to use for the Black approach . . . a sort of dynamic approach to the Black people's environment . . . rather than . . . a classic country down south type of thing." Vidor further recalled that Gerald "was terribly interested in the project, not because it was Black, but because of the new idea in films. He felt that being an artist he could contribute an artistic viewpoint. He wanted to see it done in the manner that he expressed in his paintings—very mechanistic."[31] In the end, Gerald found the film a disappointment primarily because Vidor tried to make the black aspects of the film palatable to a white audience. Gerald also found California, with its own ersatz milieu, equally disappointing and compromising. He told Dos Passos that the whole thing was "a dull sham . . . without one single one of the virtues of its ten thousand defects," defects which Gerald colorfully enumerates to Dos Passos in a letter from January 1929.

When the Murphys arrived back in France early in the new year, the Fitzgeralds were also there, as were the Hemingways, who had warned Maxwell Perkins not to give Fitzgerald their address. Hemingway feared that Fitzgerald would disrupt his domestic calm with unannounced and disorderly intrusions. He would see Scott in public places but not in his apartment.[32] Fitzgerald felt the snub but still saw Hemingway often—largely under Hemingway's conditions. When the Hemingways left for Spain in early July, the Fitzgeralds returned to the Riviera for the rest of the summer and fall. During this time, Gerald helped to arrange ballet lessons for Zelda with Madame Egorova, head of the Diaghilev ballet school and teacher both to Catherine Littlefield (Zelda's teacher in Philadelphia) and the Murphys' daughter. Although Gerald questioned the wisdom of Zelda's new ambitions, he felt that unless he saw to Zelda's introduction, "something awful would happen."

When he and Sara watched Zelda dance at rehearsal, they knew "she had taken up the dance too late." There was "something dreadfully grotesque in her intensity" as she danced, the Murphys felt, for the muscles of her legs worked against each other, pulling and stretching, and her body appeared too tall and gawky.[33]

During the summer and fall, as the Fitzgeralds saw the Murphys regularly, Scott Fitzgerald kept Hemingway informed of their doings through his letters sent to Spain. Increasingly, he conveyed to Hemingway his growing depression and sense of isolation which his drinking and his unfinished novel only intensified. He wrote in September: "I stay alone working or trying to work or brooding or reading detective stories—and realizing that anyone in my state of mind, who has in addition never been able to hold his tongue, is pretty poor company. But when drunk I make them all pay and pay and pay."[34] The Murphys felt that they had begun to pay when Fitzgerald scrutinized them for his fiction, being then in the process of modeling Dick and Nicole Diver after them. Fitzgerald confessed to Hemingway in August that he and Zelda were "desperately unpopular and not invited anywhere." They continued to see Gerald and Sara "once a week or so" nonetheless—Gerald "older, less gay, more social, but not so changed as many people in five years."[35]

Despite the Fitzgeralds' "poor company" that summer, the Murphys had good visits with Donald Stewart, Robert Benchley, and Dorothy Parker who, according to Fitzgerald, was having "the time of her life" with the Murphys.[36] Parker stayed in the Bastide guesthouse, where she "was content to live quietly," taking breaks from her writing to swim in the surf (a passion which Gerald shared) and to play with the Murphy children in the garden. Sometimes her underlying loneliness and depression revealed itself, as when the Murphy children's tutor noticed Parker in the villa garden "looking a little lost."[37] She had not yet recovered from an unresolved love affair with New York investment banker John Garrett.

As the summer lingered into a late fall and then into winter, the Murphys anticipated seeing John Dos Passos and his bride Katy Smith. Katy and her brother Bill had been childhood friends of Hemingway's in Michigan, and Katy had come in later years to treat him affectionately, like a younger brother. Dos Passos had met her while visiting with Hemingway in Key West in 1928; and after they married in 1929 he planned a "triumphal tour" of Europe so that he could introduce Katy to "old haunts" and "old friends."[38] His joy at the prospect was dimmed, however, by news of his friends' misfortunes. October had brought its warnings. The stock market bottomed out in America, and in France, Scott and Zelda left Antibes to winter in Paris, but not before Zelda began to slip into the schizophrenia from which she never recovered, and not before the Murphys' youngest child, Patrick, age nine, developed tuberculosis. The Murphys realized later that Patrick had contracted the disease from a tubercular chauffeur in Hollywood, which only confirmed Gerald's view that California was like "too bad Green fruit softening in the sun off the tree but no ripeness yet."

With Scott drinking and Zelda "far from being in her right mind," Dos Passos found it "heartbreaking" to be with the Fitzgeralds in Paris that December. It was somewhat easier to be with the Murphys, however, for they were "handling their disaster in high style." They had closed down the Villa America to take Patrick to a sanitarium in the Swiss Alps, where they remained for roughly the next eighteen months. The Hemingways, the Fitzgeralds, and the Dos Passoses, along with Dorothy Parker, gathered at Montana-Vermala to make Christmas as cheerful as possible for the Murphys and for Patrick. "For a while it worked," said Dos Passos. "The Murphys were determined nobody should feel sorry for them," and they all enjoyed each other's company, skiing during the day and then laughing together during cozy "white wine evenings" before the fire.[39] But the laughter could not entirely cover the Murphys' pain. As Donald Stewart later described it, "a night with the gay Murphys of Paris and Antibes in that rarefied cold silence and atmosphere of death" was "terrifying." Together, these friends saw the year and the decade to its crashing close.[40]

Gerald put aside his art and never, as it turned out, picked it up again. One of his last paintings, *Portrait*—a starkly segmented collage—captured his sense of personal fragmentation, which would intensify throughout 1930, a difficult year for everyone involved in the struggle for Patrick's life. After most of their friends had returned to America, the Murphys stayed on, clinging to a kind of life-in-death in the Alps. Parker had helped to close down the villa and oversee the transfer of goods and dogs and servants; and "nothing is more horrible," she said, "than a dismantled house where people have once been gay." The Murphy entourage, including Parker, who would stay throughout most of 1930, took over a string of rooms at the Palace Hotel (really a sanitarium) where Gerald and Sara and Dorothy gathered in the evenings next door to Patrick's room. In heavy woolens against the cold sanitarium air, and talking in whispers, they drank wine from hospital cups and toasted their friends in America, including Robert Benchley. Parker's November 1929 letter to Benchley graphically recounts the Murphys' early determination to remain gay and keep to an even keel.

By May 1930, Patrick had improved sufficiently for the family to move to a chalet near the Palace, and Gerald and Sara also transformed an old house into a working bar and restaurant. Harry's Bar became a gathering spot for their friends as the Murphys continued to keep up a brave face during their ordeal. Midway through the year, however, the strain had begun to show on Gerald, who from the beginning had assumed Patrick's direct care. Parker recognized early on "that morbid, turned-in thing" in Gerald "that began with his giving up his painting and refusing to have it mentioned." By the time Gerald traveled to America in late summer 1930, he had grown so preoccupied that he avoided his friends, including MacLeish, who told Fitzgerald in September that Gerald was there but that no one had seen him: "Skulks like a shadow. Why I can't think. He likes us all. But he has deflated the world so flat he can't breathe in it. I'd love to see him."[41]

Gerald's long and analytic apology written to MacLeish upon his return to Montana-Vermala in early 1931 helped him break free of his emotional paralysis, as did the fact that Patrick seemed to be mending, or at least holding his own. He was able to join the family that summer in the Austrian lake country, where they rented Ramgut, a house large enough for guests, including the Fitzgeralds. Scott had placed Zelda in a hospital near Paris in April 1930, when she had her first breakdown, and she remained there for ten days. In May, she had a second breakdown, and Fitzgerald took her to the Valmont Clinic in Switzerland and then to Prangins, near Geneva. Zelda remained virtually "lost" during all of 1930 and into 1931, difficult days during which Scott drifted "from town to town in Switzerland" looking for the stability which only his brief stopover visits with the Murphys seemed to provide.[42] When Zelda seemed to be improving in early 1931, she requested that her first outside visitor be Gerald, who felt "terrified" by the responsibility of his mission. He recalled the interminable walk across the hospital courtyard where Zelda waited for him and how she seemed so "altered" and "distrait." Later in the summer, when she and Scott visited the Murphys at Ramgut, Zelda seemed much improved.[43]

By the following spring, Patrick seemed much improved also, and the Murphys now talked about reopening Villa America. Early in 1932 Sara and Honoria took the overnight train from Switzerland to Antibes, which was, they reported back to Gerald, "a paradise" with "mandarines, lemons, oranges, camelias, anemones, mimosa, & lunch on the terrasse." Gerald wrote MacLeish immediately about all this and confirmed, with an upbeat note, that someday they would indeed "all be together again"—all of them, all as they liked to remember it during the better days. In the meantime, Gerald waited with Patrick back at Montana-Vermala where the days were "cloudless" and "windless . . . sun melting,—above ice,—gleaming ice." Gerald used these days of transition to go up the mountains, "*without* skis, climbing." By February 11 he had joined Sara and Honoria at Antibes, and Baoth arrived from his German boarding school two weeks later. As Honoria remembered it, they "had reopened the Villa America for a final stay before returning to America." Patrick's doctor, as it turned out, advised against his returning to Mediterranean air, and the Murphys saw him off to America, with his nurse, in May. The family followed a few weeks later, and Dorothy Parker and Archie MacLeish were in New York to meet them.[44]

Although there would be summer visits to Villa America thereafter, the Murphys were in America to stay. With the Mark Cross company floundering following Mr. Murphy's death in late 1931, Gerald took over the business. He settled the family in New York, where they oversaw Patrick's continued care, and he dubbed himself the Merchant Prince as he worked to reverse the company's downward trend. In August, the Murphys left Patrick with his nurse and took a trip west, staying for three weeks at the Nordquist ranch at the invitation of the Hemingways.

Gerald's letter to MacLeish from the Nordquist ranch (8 September 1932) underscores his recognition that his personal relationship with Hemingway was over—he had been excluded from the inner "Sanctum." The letter also contains some observations on America, a country which he had perhaps taken for granted. He suspected that too vast a territory dulls the senses and that America, "overpowering in scale and awe-inspiring in formation," fails to inspire us "with the awe . . . that it did the native Indians. Its scale is felt in distances and its fantastic variety as freakishness." His talk about America and how one discovers it through exaggeration and from afar concurs with what John Peale Bishop said later in explaining the expatriate movement of the 1920s. They had gone to France during the 1920s because they were seeking a break with the past which would reveal themselves to themselves: as individuals, as artists, and as Americans. They intuitively knew that "the way to discover one's own country was to leave it; that the way to find America was to find it in one's own heart, one's memory and one's spirit, and in a foreign land."[45]

By 1930, most of the group had returned to America. Dos Passos still longed to travel, but he had always claimed America as his home, and he would spend more of his time there than in Europe from 1926 on. Fitzgerald would pine for the Riviera, yet he was an American writer who had captured for his countrymen an America "coming of age," and he would never return to Europe after 1931. By 1928 Hemingway had begun to switch his allegiances from the Paris cafes and the Spanish bullrings to the open spaces of America's West and the Gulf Stream waters of Key West. MacLeish had returned, in most respects ahead of the rest, and he would later declare that none of them comprised an expatriate group, nor were they—as Gertrude Stein and everyone else thereafter dubbed them—a lost generation. "It was not the Lost Generation which was lost" after World War I, MacLeish said, but "the world out of which that generation came. And it was not a generation of expatriates who found themselves in Paris in those years but a generation whose *patria*, wherever it may once have been, was now no longer waiting for them."[46] When Gerald Murphy returned to his patria in 1932, he was the last of the group to do so, and he did so under duress.

12

Scott and Zelda Fitzgerald spent most of August 1925 in Antibes with the Murphys. Scott Fitzgerald was working on—or at least talking about—his new book (not to become Tender Is the Night *until 1934), and he was still aglow over the spring 1925 publication of* The Great Gatsby. *The Fitzgeralds boarded the train for Paris in early September, leaving behind the Renault which they had purchased the previous year. The Murphys' mechanic, Albert, saw to its overhaul prior to the Murphys' rejoining the Fitzgeralds in Paris later in September. Around this same time, the Murphys would meet Ernest and Hadley Hemingway.*

1. GERALD MURPHY to SCOTT and ZELDA FITZGERALD
Villa America, 19 September 1925

Dear Scott and Zelda:—

There *really* was a great sound of tearing heard in the land as your train pulled out that day. Sara and I rode back together saying things about you both to each other which only partly expressed what we felt separately. Ultimately, I suppose, one must judge the degree of one's love for a person by the hush and the emptiness that descends upon the day,—after the departure. We heard the tearing because it was there,—and because we weren't able to talk much about how much we do love you two. We agreed that it made us very sad, and sort of hurt a little—for a "summer holiday."

Most people are dull, without distinction and without value, even *humanly,*—I believe (even in the depths of my expansive Irish heart). For Sara most people are guilty of the above until they are proved innocent. All this one can believe without presumption or personal vanity,—and the proof that it's true is found for me in the fact that you two belong so irrevocably to that rare race of people who are *valuable*. As yet in this world we have found four. One only *really* loves what is rare and valuable to one, in spite of the fact that one loves first.

We four communicate by our presence rather than any means: so that where we meet and when will never count. Currents race between us regardless: Scott will uncover for me values in Sara, just as Sara has known them in Zelda through her affection for Scott.

Suffice it to say that whenever we knew that we were to see you that evening or that you were coming to dinner in the garden we were happy, and showed it to each other. We were happy whenever we were with you. My God** How *rare* it is. How rare.

The matter of the bath-house, umbrella, etc. is fixed and I owe you 50 francs. Albert is very leisurely putting the Renault in order. You can stop the engine now without running up the steps of the Hotel de Ville to stall it. The painting comes next, replacing of mudguards, etc., and then I think we'll be able to enter it in the Flower Parade at Pasadena,—as its stands.

We are coming to Paris toward the end of the month for a week of hilarity at the Exposition [of Industrial and Decorative Arts]. We'll wire you in advance. My heart leaps up, etc. at the idea of seeing you both.

One thing I regret: that we didn't all go out on a short cruise on the "pica-flor." But if you come to Nice there'll be plenty of chances: she'll be in commission all the time and we'll seize a good spell and make for the open seas. We might all four take that Campagnie Generale trip to Tunisia. Just three weeks, very cheap. High-powered cars with Arab chauffeurs meet you at the boat and you course thro' the country staying as long as you want in each town. More like being a guest than a tourist, they say. Wonderful hotels even in the desert. [Count Étienne de] Beaumont told us about it.

Honoria's ballet teacher is Madame Egórova (Princess Troubetzkey), top floor over the Olympia Music Hall on the Boulevard. The stage entrance is on the side street, 8 or 10 Rue Caumartin. You walk up thro' the wings while the performance is going on, and her studio!! A big, bare room just for learning to dance in.

Sara's yelling that she misses you. Good-bye until the end of the month. It gives me an awful thrill to think of the imminence of the novel. For me such things are the most important in the world. I suppose for the same reason that you two are important. Take care of yourselves, please.

Thank God for you both,
Devotedly,

dow dow

14

What lovely letters you both wrote. It did our hearts good. The Children
are *still* at the hotel. Fevers running. It was the grippe they had.
PUL

*During one of the Murphys' several trips to Paris that fall, they met Er-
nest and Hadley Hemingway. Ernest Hemingway talked with Gerald
Murphy as he was preparing* Razor *and* Watch *for exhibition in the December show "L'Art d'Aujourd'hui," and the Hemingways and Mur-
phys began to plan for a late winter ski trip. The trip was to include Dos
Passos, who had been traveling in Morocco following the fall publication of* Manhattan Transfer, *which had already gone into several print-
ings by the time Hemingway ("Transatlantic Charlie") left for New
York to negotiate a change of publishers from Liveright to Scribners.
When Hemingway had returned to Paris en route to rejoining Hadley in
Schruns, Austria, he saw the Fitzgeralds back from their winter in the
Pyrenées. Fitzgerald was pleased to hear from Hemingway that the stage
version of* The Great Gatsby *was doing well, and he urged Hemingway
to accept the Murphys' invitation to Villa America, where they could all
spend more time together. The Great Gatsby, scripted by Owen Davis
and directed by George Cukor, had opened at the Ambassador Theater
on 2 February 1926.*

2. GERALD MURPHY to HADLEY HEMINGWAY
Villa America, 3 March [1926]

My dear Girl:—

Try and get out of your visit to Antibes! It's *our whole point* in getting family out of the way before April. Come when you want in latter March or April.
If we go to Moscow it'll be late in May. We feel like skunks about Munich, but
you see, as I thought, Dos cabled from Tangiers "Broke Coming to call,"—
and if we'd been away he'd have gone home as he's been threatening. We want
him to be here when you come. Scott & Zelda fresh from triumphs in the
Basses Pyrenées arrive at Nice to-morrow.

Gosh what news of Transatlantic Charlie! It certainly broke prettily for
him. That's the important thing after all: not trips to Munich, I suppose. My
God this world of success! Scott's "Gatsby" is to run all season; Dos' debts to
be defrayed by M.T. [*Manhattan Transfer*],—and Don [Stewart] sends us an
Intimate Portrait Study of himself by a Culver City Lady Photographer of
note. Did you get one? We had it passe-partouted loyally and sat it on axis

with our beds (on the mantel)—but he peered at us so we had to muffle it. We got to feeling guilty, somehow.

Lots of love and welcomes to the guy who brought the news from G. to A. & congratulations! What he settled is going to make "glorious summer" etc. It is a great title "The Sun Also Rises." Some day he'll write "Yet the sea is not full"—or its equivalent. We read it the other day & were blown out of water afresh.

Gerald.

Bumbie would be no trouble Sara says!
JFK

Following their week together in Schruns, Austria, in late March, the Murphys returned to Villa America while Dos Passos returned to New York. Hemingway finished his rewrite of The Sun Also Rises *as he and Hadley planned for a trip to Spain. When Bumby took ill, Hadley remained behind, bringing him to recuperate at Villa America. After the Murphys' English doctor determined that he had the whooping cough and should be quarantined, the Fitzgeralds offered Hadley their villa for the remainder of its lease as they had rented the larger Villa St. Louis nearby. Marie Cocotte, the Hemingways' housekeeper, joined Hadley on the Riviera to help nurse Bumby, while Gerald Murphy wrote Hemingway in Spain to explain the situation.*

3. GERALD MURPHY TO ERNEST HEMINGWAY
Villa America, 22 May 1926

Dear Ernest:—

There is only one outcome which could have proven more inconvenient,— and that is that Bumby might have been left last Thursday in Paris with M. C. [Marie Cocotte] where the cocluche [whooping cough] would have developed and been prolonged (absence sun, air, etc.) with Hadley off in Spain.

Bumby has got it. Mildly but *it*. Sara's drastic measures were based on *the one* thing we've learned: that well children (especially 3) are no encumbrance to life and one's time,—but that sick children (especially 3) are hell to be with:—and that any precaution vauts la peine in the end. It leaves you free. We've never yet had to pass anything up on account of sickness!! Thanks to old Lord Lister, Pasteur, J*no* Hopkins, the Rockefeller Inst. etc.

Hadley seemed so tired when she arrived that we just drove thro' the situation so that she'd at least be spared the haunt of soon hearing the 6 Murphy-MacLeish-Fitzgerald tribe of children barking *their* heads off. She's in great form now and resting finely. There's no doubt that Bumby's better off. We have the best doctor we've ever known: an Englishman. Hadley likes him. It's one of those crazy train of incidents which seems to lead to a situation somehow good.

Don't worry—you. Incidentally Hadley is benefiting,—and Bumby is not coughing in Paris with a nurse who was none too used to a sick child. He'll doubtless be through it very soon,—and he's getting fresh vegetables du jour from the garden. These months are important (the dr. says) as it's the bone-building period and you've got to offset his coughing up his lunch. He looks fine and is gay.

Write me if there's anything special I can do.

Hadley is much less worried in seeing him thro' than she would be to leave him too soon. All this you know, but I somehow wanted to write you. At a distance, things look so funny. If H. stays I'll send the bike with P. Pfeiffer. Lots of love from us all. Don't worry.

Gerald.

JFK

When Hemingway returned from Spain in early June, the Murphys greeted his arrival with a champagne-and-caviar party which Fitzgerald chose to sabotage. Although the following letter is undated, Sara most probably wrote it after this party, which included the Fitzgeralds, the Hemingways, and the MacLeishes. Scott Fitzgerald's note of apology, which apparently followed this letter, has not survived.

4. SARA MURPHY to F. SCOTT FITZGERALD
Villa America [c. summer 1926]

Dear Scott,—I've generally said to you what I've thought. And it seems another of those moments.

We consider ourselves your friends—(of course if you don't want us as such but as objects for observation or something—you have only to say so,—& if I were you I shouldn't even bother to read this—)

However we do.—But you can't expect anyone to like or stand a *Continual* feeling of analysis & subanalysis, & criticism—on the whole unfriendly—Such as we have felt for quite awhile. It is definitely in the air,—& quite unpleasant.—It certainly detracts from any gathering,—& Gerald, for one, simply curls up at the edges & becomes someone else in that sort of atmo-sphere. And last night you even said "that you had never seen Gerald so silly & rude"—It's hardly likely that I should explain Gerald,—or Gerald me—to you. If you don't know what people are like it's *your* loss—and if Gerald was "rude" in getting up & leaving a party that had gotten *quite bad*,—then he was rude to the Hemingways & MacLeishes too. No, it is hardly likely that you would stick at a thing like *manners*—it is more probably some theory you have,—(it *may* be something to do with the book),—But *you ought to know at your age* that you *Can't have Theories about friends*,—If you can't take friends largely, & without suspicion—then they are not friends at all—We *cannot*—Gerald & I—at our age—& stage in life—*be bothered* with soph-omoric situations—like last night—We are very simple people—(unless we feel ourselves in a collegiate quagmire)—and we are *literally* & *actually* fond of you both—(There is no reason for saying this that I know of—unless we meant it.)

And so—*for god's sake* take it or leave it,—as it is meant,—a straight ges-ture, *without* subtitles—

Yr old & rather irritated friend

Sara

PUL

5. Sara Murphy to F. Scott Fitzgerald
Villa America [c. summer 1926]

Dear Scott,

Thanks for your note Don't you think of it again—I haven't.

Why are we *all* so riled-up lately?? Probably the World's Climate is chang-ing, or its electrical voltage or something & we are all 'Sustaining Contusions'——And anyway there's always the Revolution Coming——

So nothing surprises one.

———————

Love to both—& a bientot—

Sara.

So glad to hear you're working—
PUL

The Murphys, the Hemingways, and Pauline Pfeiffer left for Spain in early July. Following their week together, the Hemingways remained in Spain while the Murphys and Pauline took the train to Bayonne. From there the Murphys went on to Villa America, where they were expecting Donald Stewart with his bride Beatrice Ames to arrive for the month of August. The letters from Gerald and Sara that follow were enclosed in the same envelope.

6. GERALD MURPHY to ERNEST and HADLEY HEMINGWAY
Villa America [14 July 1926]

Dear Hadern:—

There's not even a seismograph that could record our feelings of what we owe you two. So as Villalta says: "I won't try to thank you for the flowers."

We clicked up that superb Gascony valley—alone—where men were straining up-stream hooking fish,—with a sense always of Spain over those Pyrenees. Sadie said: "Isn't it a relief *not* to know why we feel as we do about Pamplona and those men." But it didn't prevent our talking far beyond Toulouse of what we thought we felt. It kept unearthing and ever-topping the best we've known together since we've known each other—22 years. It's the finest thing we've ever experienced,—certainly humanly and emotionally the most important.

Those men, living, as it seems to me in a region all their own—and alone each, somewhere between art and life,—and eclipsing at times each of them,—make you feel that you are as you find most other people—half-alive. They are a religion for which I could have been trained. This knocked at my heart all the time at Pamplona. It cut into my desire to "run" and go into the ring;—but when I got into the ring I saw that I was wrong. I had not wanted to feel or look a fool in the face of the thing I respected. Sadie said: "I'm sorry you didn't run. It would have been a great feeling afterwards." So am I. Next year I will, and I'll do it well, Papa. To want to do a thing well even at first is still one of my complications. I was wrong.

As for you two children: you grace the earth. You're so right: because you're close to what's elemental. Your values are hitched up to the universe. We're proud to know you. Yours are the things that count. They're a gift to those who see them too.

We are very lonely. Antibes looks like the back of the scenery for Romeo and Juliet. We left an awful hunk of something on the other side of the Pyrenees,—too heavy and too valuable to carry back into France. Some day we'll go back and shape it into something.

A long, very funny and affectionate letter from Don [Stewart] helped the home-coming. Photo enclosed: the girl looks great,—and very gay. He's

19

superbly happy. They sail July 31st to come directly here. He seems to count on it so. You see, we'll yank something out of it yet, tho' after Pamplona,—one doesn't deserve much.

The frontier reminded me of the peseta we forgot here it is and here's my heart damn it in thanks,

> Your spent, dwarfed, but *elated*
> friend—
>
> dow dow.

Lunch alone—more Pamplona viz. the Spanish are the only ones who deserve a religion (because they don't *depend* solely upon it. The wops have made it theatrical, the frogs intellectual, the Americans political. Why should an Irish servant girl pray 1/2 hr. for the salvation of her soul when she's only going to cross 42nd St. There's not a soul but you people to say this to so that's why. 25 extra pesetas for chauffeurs keep not put on my bill.
for Godsake send us the Bandillero music,—it's become our leitmotif. Just a transcription of those thirds the horn-pipes do.   G.
over on acc't of Sara
JFK

7. Sara Murphy to Hadley and Ernest Hemingway
Villa America [14 July 1926]

Dear Hadley & Gros Patron,—

Gerald as usual has said everything—so there is nothing else for me to say except that I enjoyed myself,—being a Mistress of under-statement. We left Pauline regretfully at Bayonne—slept the rest of the way in & out of Couchettes—found everything fine in the Home—Baoth *delighted* with his guitar—& the others with their various gifties—((I wont give up the Drum))—and my father arrives tomorrow—Don & bride early Aug., & you must plan to be here same time so that we can meet the train with a *number* of musical instruments—(see how useful the drum is going to be?) *You were so good to arrange everything*—and I shall *never* (nor g. either, as you may have noticed) forget it—and no one has anything on me about liking bullfights—, even if I don't like seeing bowels—But *that* is just a woman's whimsey and does not count. Tomorrow we go to see Bumby & will wire—I enclose panicky letter from Tiddy will you answer it? The poor little thing—so worried. We are now very sorry we didn't buy a donkey I could have carried *one* I saw under the left arm & He would have been so useful for cutting flowers. This is getting a long letter to send so far. & how far away it seems! (Spain is a grand place.)

Much love to you both,—& *thank you* for being so *nice* to 2 amateur matadors.

O that Banderillo Blues!!

and Ernest, do not pick that scab. and don't make me speak of this again. Affectionately yr. old Spanish Compatriot—

Agna Callient Sal.

JFK

By early August, upon their return from Spain, the Hemingways had stopped off at Antibes, announced their planned separation, and then left for Paris, where they established separate residences (Ernest in Gerald's studio). Hadley had made a divorce contingent upon Ernest and Pauline's one-hundred-day separation, and Pauline spent much of that time back in America.

8. GERALD MURPHY to ERNEST HEMINGWAY
Villa America [6 September 1926]

Dear Ernest:—

We found we couldn't leave Paris without acting on the hunch that when life gets bumpy you get through to the truth sooner if you are not hand-tied by the lack of a little money. I preferred not to ask you: so Sara said just deposit and talk about it after. I wanted to speak of it that night we left but couldn't in front of Hadley, and didn't want to call you back from her.

I think we're right, Ernest,—often an arbitrary mechanical gesture on the part of someone that you ultimately trust, clears the air. I wanted to put it to yr. $a/c to do with as you wished. You didn't have one, so I changed $400.00 and put it to yr. fr. a/c.

What follows will be read by only you and me: There is one phase of your situation which disquiets me,—and that is the danger that you may temporize: first because Hadley's tempo is a slower and less initiative one than yours and that you may accept it out of deference to her,—secondly because of a difficulty in settling the practical phases of it all: Hadley's comfort, Bumby's.

21

Should either of these things deter you from acting cleanly and sharply I would consider it a dangerous betrayal of your nature. I admire like hell the way that you've both slowed down the situation and let the facts march by in review,—but I fear in both your natures the tendency to a probational period together and the awaiting of a solution.

The facts in the case are so clean and clear that they deserve to be allowed to act.

Hadley and you, I feel, are out after two different kinds of truth in life. All this is outside of the fact that you care for each other. After we question the validity of the relation of two people as man and wife, there remains to question the one as man and woman. I suppose what we all are is

Man	Woman
$\left\{\begin{array}{c}\text{Breadwinner}\\\&\\\text{Husband}\end{array}\right.$	$\left\{\begin{array}{c}\text{Wife}\\\&\\\text{Mother}\end{array}\right.$
$\left\{\begin{array}{c}\text{Artist}\\\text{or}\\\text{Worker}\end{array}\right.$	**?**

Hadley (and I say this as one who likes her personally and has his own relation with her) happens to have been deterred from facing the fact of being your wife (in the sense of material service rendered, this accentuated by your placing yourself in the breach),—also of being a mother (in the sense of material service rendered). I do not think Hadley's nature will change: I think that yours will become more like itself. Hadley is saving herself for some personal truth,—you are destined to enrich and remain where you are—in the stream of life. Hadley is miscast, now,—I feel.

(As you read this for Christ's sake don't think of me as some impertinent pup,—but I'll go down (in your estimation if necessary) fighting just to state my belief and godalmighty valuation of that thing in you which life might trick you into deserting)

There's a side of you too sensitive not to be yangled by the hunk that life has thrown in your lap and will continue to throw.

You and Hadley should go away from each other. There's a sane probation for you! What situations need is space and distance as well as time. But above all things you should act.

For years conditions have allowed of Hadley's drawing upon your personal energy to face the efforts of the day. It's true that 3/4 of the race lives upon the energy of the other 1/4,—but when a man finds himself replacing a woman in her own departments of life,—then it's a kind of death.

I have not spoken of you as much as of Hadley because of the fact that your remorse and self-reproach (natural but not related to the truth of a solution) have already tended to blur the facts.

I trust you to believe that I have thought in values and with no sense of personal criticism of anyone concerned (God knows I haven't the right) it can't be necessary to remind you that I hold in very sacred respect the thing which Hadley and you have enjoyed between you.

If you will allow me I'd like to speak further with you when I come to Paris. I write because of my fears for you both.

Believe me
your affectionate friend,

Gerald.

We sail the 22nd returning just before or after Christmas. Early in January I am going to Bâle or Germany or somewhere to work. Sara was almost hurt to learn that I had been wanting to and had not suggested it to her. I believe in it for many reasons. Husbands and wives should take steps to keep each other fresh for each other, thus making a bum of marriage, who knows?
Your heart will never be at peace to live, work and enjoy unless you clean up and cut through. GM
JFK

The Murphys probably hand-delivered the following notes when they stopped in Paris prior to sailing for America on 22 September. The notes were no doubt enclosed in the same envelope which bears the address— 69 rue Froidevaux—in Sara's writing. There is no postmark or stamp.

9. GERALD and SARA MURPHY to ERNEST HEMINGWAY
Paris [c. fall 1926]

My dear boy:—

We said to each other last night and we say to you now that: we love you, we believe in you in all your parts, we believe in what you're doing, in the way you're doing it.

Anything we've got is yours: somehow we are your father and mother, by what we feel for you—

Gerald.

Dear gros Patron

We *certainly* believe in you as Gerald says—Thank you for talking to us— and don't think you were the only one helped by it! In the end you will probably save us all,—by refusing (among other things) to accept any second-rate things places ideas or human natures—Bless you & don't ever budge—Much much love—

from   Sara

[scribbled on back of envelope] both sent off a note to Hadley   S.
JFK

Shortly after the Murphys arrived in America, Hemingway's The Sun Also Rises *was published by Scribners in New York. It was doing well both critically and financially, and the Murphys forwarded to Hemingway a recent review, probably from an American journal or newspaper. Hemingway wrote the following letter on the back of a copy of his* Today is Friday, *a Stable publication of 1926. This story was reprinted in his 1927 collection* Men Without Women. *Hemingway inscribed the pamphlet to the Murphys on the cover page, above the Jean Cocteau line drawing of a human figure.*

10. ERNEST HEMINGWAY to SARA and GERALD MURPHY
Paris [c. late fall 1926]

Dear gents—

Thanks for the review. Archie read me a grand letter from Sara to Ada. I will write you a fine letter soon—but today it is raining.

I am very comfortable at 69 (rue Froedevaux he hastens to add) and about as happy as the average empty tomato can.

Archie and I went to Zaragoza and had a fine trip. He took away from me—with a couple of books and his fine legal mind—the Popes, Caesar and Shakespeare (all Fairies) and the Holy Grail (just a goddam lie or legend) and gave me in exchange A Great Yale Football Team (they'd just beaten Dartmouth).

Well we got home and the next Sunday I read the paper and Holy Cross or some place like that had beaten Yale 33-6. So I wrote Archie a poem and said I was sending back the great Yale Team including their great new quarterback and would he return me by return post all the Popes, Caesar, Shakespeare and The Holy Grail.

But so far I haven't got them back.

However I love you both very much and like to think about you and will be shall we say *pleased* to see you—

It is swell that Gerald is working so well and I will be pretty excited to see the stuff—

When do you come back? My love to Patrick Baoth and Honoria. Bumby and I lived together for 10 days while Hadley was on a trip and one day when I brought him an harmonica and a glace and he was holding the one and eating the other at the café he said, "La Vie est beau avec Papa."

Ernest

[Inscribed on front] For Gerald and Sara with more than all of Papa's love— and don't mind the Cocteau Drawing—They bought that first
HMD

The Murphys had just arrived back in France after several months in America, where they saw both John Dos Passos and Pauline. In late December, Dos Passos left for Mexico and Pauline returned to France. She and Ernest would not marry until May, and Hemingway continued to use Murphy's studio as home base until then.

11. GERALD MURPHY to ERNEST HEMINGWAY
Villa America, 13 February 1927

Dear E.

What news of you? Are you well? Did you receive a wind-breaker from us near Xmas? I forgot to write love and kisses on the card enclosed. We plan to go to Moscow early in March. We're swollen with USA drink but r. well. Everyone in America is discontented, unhappy or complaining. We hid all day then went forth alone at night until 4–5 AM.

G.M.

Dos is in Mexico with his revolution!!
JFK

The Murphys came to Paris in early March and probably saw Pauline, but not Ernest, who had left on an Italian trip with Guy Hickok. Instead of going to Moscow, the Murphys went with the MacLeishes to Germany before the MacLeishes left for America. Gerald's new interest in experimental photography and film had been quickened during his stay in New York. Although he and Fernand Léger talked about collaborating on a film, nothing seems to have come of it.

12. GERALD MURPHY to ERNEST HEMINGWAY
en route from Berlin, 19 March [1927]

en route
Dear E:—

Just before I left Paris saw Leger who wants to begin our film (secret!). This means that 69 [rue Froidevaux] must be empty as possible for 1st week May on. Vladimir is coming soon to Paris to get some of my stuff. I won't be able to let you leave anything there unfortunately as the place going to be torn to pieces for "installation." Berlin was fine. I like it. Saw a splendid new film "Metropolis," laid underground a big city. Also a new opera (half revue half film—ballet—& moving abstract scenery, stern light etc.) by a guy 27 yrs. They [the Germans] certainly are *the* big technical experimentors. And thank gawd for it. Hope bella Italia seemed all right. Hope we cross in Paris later anyway. Best to P. the Pifer. She looks finely. Is a good chicken. And I'd like to see her get along.

Yrs.

Gerald

JFK

Ernest and Pauline had a small, quiet wedding in Paris on 10 May 1927, and they were probably still honeymooning on the Grau du Roi when this letter—written the day after Charles Lindbergh's solo flight— would have reached Paris.

13. GERALD MURPHY to ERNEST HEMINGWAY
Villa America, 22 May 1927

Dear Ernest:—

Sara and I are getting to Paris Wednesday am. If you are about and this reaches you and the sun doesn't get in your eyes, come around to the quai. We shall be very much alone and wearing red-moustaches in the side streets. We've forgotten how to talk to people without barking.

Bob Benchley cables that Don [Stewart] has been "very ill" and that they are to come over together soon. Don has been in NYC about his play [*Los Angeles*]. Word from Dos says that he is "hopelessly involved in the theatre here." (Can't you see him having, with difficulty, two little theatre movements a day?)

Thank God that somebody like Lindbergh does something like what he's just done some of the time. It tightens the main-spring. We've been swimming since April 15th. Quite far.

Old Mamma Austerity and I send you much love. Our love to Pauline. I hope we'll get to see you. We'll be there a week in all.

Gerald.

JFK

14. GERALD MURPHY to ERNEST HEMINGWAY
Villa America, 18 June 1927

Dear Oiniss:—

It was good to have news of you both.

It would be nice to have a chance to talk about almost everything with you both. Often it gives you a sense of covering ground, when you can have a good talk. I often think that life gets a little denser chemically during talks,—not conversations. Not that there's anything to be settled, God knows,—but as Sadie says: "I don't want to see those people, they tire me because I can't say *any*thing that I think in front of them." It's true: Almost Everyone carries with him some constraint,—ultimately you like people who leave you free to say what you think.

You're right. The ballet's as dead as the theatre. The world needs to know what it's looking at and listening to for a while. La Chatte was at least clean visually, though a little diaphanous,—and the only proof you need that such dance is decadent is when the boys get to doing Roman riding to get off a stage.[1] L'art has just discovered les sports, and if you chase a butterfly across the stage with a Wright and Ditson racket: you got a ballet. Next year Diaghileff will be keeping a 350 Supersport Terrot a culbuteurs sans soupapes

---

1. Diaghalev's *La Chatte* had premiered in Monte Carlo on 30 April before coming to Paris 27 May.

and casting him for the juvenile lead, with an augmented orchestra of 60 spare parts.

I've bought a 4cv Terrot motocyclette,—and my God: it and she does 90 kilos without losing a spangle. You are directly responsible, because you described some races to me once, and now I think I'm a racer. It weighs a ton and has a *new* kind of power about it. You feel as if you'd been taken by the seat of the pants from in front and yanked along. It's about as close to having Pegasus around as you know. I wish you were here to try it. You must know it's a very beautiful experience: a little like skiing except that the motive power comes from the opposite pole and you flatter yourself that you control it more. But there's a mystery in the equilibrium that gets me.

You do both know that we'd love to have you come to us if ever you just suddenly feel like it. You could have our room. That's what we do now when we have people,—and go to the bastide ourselves. The Cap isn't at all bad, because we don't know anyone well except Phil and Ellen Barry who are at Cannes and they're grand. There are a few floosies, but they're the superior kind which lets us out. The swimming is superb and the Picaflor more faultily faultless, icily regular, splendidly null than ever. She doesn't bother me now on account of the other hot boat [*Honoria*] coming along: you do get a good ride out of her. She's like a machine or an instrument.

I'm working all the time and feel that I've knocked one or two things on the nose. Before I die I'm going to do one picture which will be hitched up to the universe at some point. I feel it now and can work quietly.

No news of Don [Stewart] except that he's pretty well knocked out physically and financially. We wrote the other day. Bob [Benchley] won't make it I suppose. His last rescue work failed pretty badly evidently, because of the fact that the frail, blonde piece of flotsam whom he found at the Dizzy Bar and followed to a gambling hall where she was the virtual prisoner and slave of a fine dark fellow in evening dress,—proved to be about one of the best and famousest players of the badger game on the Sixth Avenue beat and Bob just had enough sense not to follow her into the last house that she'd led him to. He stepped out the other door of the taxi and did the 220 low hurdles up 8th Avenue while she with the help of a few male attendants called from indoors for the purpose took the taxi apart and didn't put it together again. The chauffeur got a stocking filled with sand at the base of the brain.

Well, here I am, writing a newsy amusing letter. I must stop.

We'll have to have a four cornered yell together some day,

lotsoflovetoyouboth

daou-daou.

JFK

28

Following Gerald's letter to Ernest, John Dos Passos arrived on the Riviera after being away for over a year. It would be a quiet summer without either the MacLeishes there or the Fitzgeralds, who had left for Hollywood in late December 1926. Two months later, the Fitzgeralds moved to Ellerslie Mansion near Wilmington, Delaware.

15. SARA MURPHY to ZELDA FITZGERALD
Villa America, 28 June [1927]

Dearest Zelda—

At last I have your address—from Esther [Murphy],—(and what an address!)—to send you back that money—how worried you must have been! I *could* have sent it care publishers, but I have always distrusted publishers—Anyway we are terribly sorry to be so late as you were *too lovely* about running our entire place while we were away—& taking so much trouble that you must think of us as borrowing nuisances—and I apologize *very much,*—and do borrow $25 from us and never give it back at *all* just as a revenge—We wonder very often how you both are—not forgetting Scotty—and affection wells up in our hearts believe it or not as you may, Scott especially—who considers us a lot of old scrap granite or something—and I was *delighted* to get your letter fr Los Angeles and carried it around quite a lot reading aloud to complete strangers therefrom—I'm sure you can't have been sorry to leave Los A.—(now that I have near-read one of Mr. [Carl] Van Vechten's articles on it)—(I do wish he would come here & write about Antibes too & clear the place out a bit)—But why Wilmington? Don't answer if you don't want to, but I just wondered. Perhaps its very lovely? and your house—(according to Esther)—is palatial & then some—You keep, it appears, only fourteen of the 27 bedrooms open & only 3 drawing rooms—and you and Scott have a system of calls & echoes to locate each other—readily—Do you ever have a hankering for Villa St. Louis?—& the sedan chair cabinet & the neighbor who turned off your water (or was it on) at night? We've had a grand quiet spring here, Gerald working & me blowing up the gardener to our hearts content—following a hectic 5 mos in U.S. counting crossings—& a dash through central Europe with the MacLeishes—But we never went to Russia as planned as by the time we got visas the theatres had closed & the snow started to melt not to mention opening of the season for Executions—

People have now started to crowd onto our beach,—discouragingly undeterred by our natural wish to have it alone—However, by means of teaching the children to throw wet sand a good deal, & by bringing several disagreeable barking dogs & staking them around—we manage to keep space open for sunbaths—It will go on no doubt, until Sept—when we leave ourselves—

The Old guard of last year has changed, giving place to a new lot of American Writers & Mothers—The [Charles] Bracketts are back, also Wymans—the Barrys in Cannes,—& Walker Ellis who has bought an awfully nice boat—upon which we (with les Barrys), went on a trip to St Tropez the other day & had a lovely time. Ben Finney & Dos are back at the hotel, but no R. [Ruth] Goldbeck & I think no Miss [Grace] Moore—*Dozens* of others as well

We miss you & MacLeishes dreadfully—Every now & again I think I see your old rat Renault whipping around a corner—

Is Scott working? And how's the book coming on? We haven't had any fights but then the season is barely opened—give us time—We saw Ernest on a flying trip to Paris—& he was *fine*—I think he is on his way to Pamplona by now—

Well do let us know how you're getting on, & plans, if any—as Lord knows *when* we'll get back to U.S.,—our late expedition having taken our last Sou—We had an idea you had *all* gone into the movies, and that some night at the "Select" or the "Grand" we should suddenly see you appear.

Why don't we *all* go into them? (Regardless of course of whether we are wanted or no) advertising as: 2 Flying Riviera Families—or nifty nine or something—plots & costumes by F. Scott Fitzgerald

Gerald sends his best love & so do the children (they are getting *so* tall & violent!) & how is cute old Scotty? Don't forget us, because we don't you—& won't ever,—I am afraid) In fact we think about you both much more than you know & certainly a lot more than you would believe—so there's no use going on any more about it—With *much* love to you—& the "Laughing Dancing Devil of J-les-Pins"—from myself too—

Your old but Enthusiastic friend

Sara—

Really we *should* so like to see you both!!
PUL

16. GERALD MURPHY to ERNEST HEMINGWAY
Villa America, 16 October 1927

My Dear Boy:—

Vladimir (who appreciated your message of bon jour: his face lit up) and I have been down the coast to a presqu'ile [peninsula] this side of Toulon with a beach on each side of the neck, which itself is only about 100 feet wide. It's 15 kilos from a RR and ten from a house, a deserted douane [customs] house (there used to be contraband landed there up until last year, now they go into port with it). We brought lines. Slept on the beach under stunted stone pines. Had Heinz Beans in Tomato Sauce with and without Pork. Have you ever tasted Libby's *canned* Sweet Potato and Corn on the cob? My god. Vladimir kept saying: "C'est mortelle! C'est mortelle!" We left the Garoupe here at one AM with the land-breeze, and sung down the coast with a three quarter moon up on the left. Not a sound nor a ship. At four the sun came up out of the sea, rose; above and on the right the moon made all the coast and cliffs cold gray, for about ten minutes you were on two different planets at the same time. It was all linked up with

Those Goddamn stories of yours [*Men Without Women*, 1927] that kept me rooted and goggle-eyed all the way into Germany the other day. I never even *saw* France. I had never *even* read "the Undefeated." You should have kind of told me, on account of that weak bladder of mine. It's like a tower in a field. "A Canary for One" is made of incorruptible stuff if you will. My God, but you've kept your promise with yourself. "A Simple Enquiry" settles it for all time: bitten out of copper with acids, if ever I saw it. "Now I Lay Me" is eternal. They're superb, and varied, and simple and free of any bunk that you can mention. And the sensibility of them all. The first 25 words of the "Enquiry" are all that dowdow demands of words, poetry, and carry a beauty to me that is pretty goddamn moving. Every time I read them something builds up before me piece by piece. I don't know what, but it's all I want.

I forgot to say that toward day-light a Spanish Tramp oozed out of the mist, crossing us. She saluted and the stokers came up and peered at us as if we were a phantom, a slim black racer in full sail before the wind. When she'd gone by she belonged to us.

Sara is rustling among the galleys [of *Men Without Women*] now. Then I'll send them back. It was good to see you and Pauline the other night. Thanks for coming 'round. You both look splendid, and seem so free. What else do you want. Your minds were all muscled, I felt. Take care of yourselves is the wish of

daow-daow—
(french spelling)

JFK

17. GERALD MURPHY TO ERNEST HEMINGWAY
PARIS, 5 JANUARY 1928

Dear Oiness:

There are a pair of heavy shoes here [at 69 rue Froidevaux] that must be yours. Do you want them? Do you happen to know where my skis were put? I hope your throat is better and that you have snow all around you [in Gstaad, Switzerland]. My love to the Sister Act [Virginia Pfeiffer and Pauline]. Paris si (to be read "is") a joke burg, which allays the pain, what with a smoke screen of work, it goes. Have you read in the Sous-Marin [Submarine] where *eight* of them were on the floor of the sea talking to each other 58 metres down? With destroyers circling above

best,

Gerald

JFK

The Fitzgeralds arrived in Paris in April to spend the summer. Fitzgerald had met King Vidor in Hollywood in early 1927, and his introduction of Vidor to Gerald Murphy led to Murphy's later stay in Hollywood. The reference to "Ingraham" means Rex Ingram, who directed Mare Nostrom, *a 1926 film based on the novel by Vicente Blasco Ibañez.*

18. GERALD MURPHY to F. SCOTT FITZGERALD
Villa America, 15 May 1928

Dear Scott:—

On the contrary, thanks very much for giving a letter to King Vidor. I've always admired his work and have heard a lot recently about "The Crowd" [1928].

I only hope we're here when he passes through. We come to Paris tomorrow for a week, I think.

It's too bad he isn't in Paris to meet Léger. It would interest him enormously as L. has just been looking into the cinema business in Germany.

We'll be at 14 Rue Guynemer (on the Luxembourg). It will be great to see you both again, because we are very fond of you both. The fact that we don't get on always has nothing to do with it, Americans are apt only to feel fond of the people of whom they see the most or with whom they run. To be able to talk to people after almost two years is the important thing.

Affectionately,

Gerald.

Had I found Ingraham as "hard and bright" as I found him "neat," I should have been pleased. That moving mass of mush "Mare Nostrum" bespeaks

his demi-soldier-of-fortune-Spanish-American-War-correspondent-Richard-Harding-Davis mentality with a dash of Professional Irishman thrown in. He's a fake, and that American Field Clerk uniform indicates it.
PUL

While John Dos Passos traveled throughout Russia, the Murphys oversaw his mail and kept him up on the news. Gerald Murphy had encouraged Dos Passos to contact Alexander Tairoff, director of Moscow's Kamerny Theatre, a group the Murphys had supported in Paris.

19. GERALD MURPHY to JOHN DOS PASSOS
Villa America, 5 August 1928

Dear Dos:—

Many thanks from all of us for the cards en route. It was most reassuring to receive them, as it's hard to believe that anyone IS on the way to Russia. Your letter from Leningrad has come, and we are amazed to hear that it functions so well. Armandine and others prefer to believe that it doesn't. For years, I suppose, it will be pictured to us as the great example of confusion. Is there much poverty and suffering? Not much more than New York, I guess. They've always felt their winters, and want to, Vladimir says. I have to-day sent off an envelope containing 12 letters and one post-card, and a package of magazines and newspapers. As you will see, I have the Brandt and Brandt check. Should it be easier for you to have money sent you by me through my Russian bank in rubles (more advantageous), just let me know. Tell me how many dollars you want, for instance, and the Guaranty Trust draws on our dollar account and changes them into rubles IN PARIS and sends them as such. You may have difficulty cashing a US check there, or it may take too long. We shall be here until October when it looks as if we'd have to go to NYC and stand in a row in front of the TWO FAMILIES for a week or two.

Ada MacLeish writes that Pauline has a 8 3/4 pound "Patrick." Ireland is doomed if THAT name is going to take on literary and poetic values and go the way of Michael, Shane, Moira, etc. I thought it was fool-proof.

The cruise was great fun. I've never been exposed to an incessant excitement day AND night for 21 days before. We left Marseille, a strange crew, Orizio 70 at the tiller, Vladimir, Henry and myself. The gréement [rigging] of the top-sails and spinnaker had been changed and never tried. In fact Orizio had never had the boat under sail. People came to the stern and kept suggesting that the boat was fast, and we'd reply that we didn't know. They took this as canny American racing tactics, and we were soon known by the other crews as "le cochon noir américain" [the dirty American beast]. 23 yachts left Marseille. Being a cotre franc [free cutter] our handicap from the larger schooners was somewhat diminished, and we gave to several boats of our own size who were marconi-rigged or of other types. It was all very fair, however. A wind from the West so Orizio made for the open sea, the others hugged the coast. When far out we tacked up toward Toulon, the wind dropped, but the Honoria decided to keep going and going. We cut an aisle through the rest of the boats under no visible means, and arrived at Toulon at 4 am, 44 minutes after the "Eblis" the largest and fastest of the cruise who owed us one hour and a half handicap for that etape [section]. We arrived 44 minutes before the 3rd boat, the "Barbara" to whom we owed 30 minutes handicap for that run. We left Toulon with a stiff breeze, went out to sea, and sailed up toward Cannes where we hit 2 hours calm and got in an hour and twenty five minutes after the Eblis who owed us two hours, and one minute after the Barbara who owed us still seven or eight minutes. And so at Cannes we were first place in las Course Croisiere de la Méditerranée. We left Cannes in a stiff breeze, sixth across the line at the port and second by the time that we passed the islands to go to sea. Wind SW. We cut, against the wind, 22 degrees E. of S. directly for Ajaccio, 130 miles away. The Eblis and the Hobo a very fast pilot sloop (American) held the same course. The rest went before the wind E to Cap Corse. M. le Baron de la Grange of the Barbara having horreur of being out of sight of land left us. On we plugged with a fresh wind until 3 o'clock the next morning, when a calm fell which LASTED THIRTY HOURS. We travelled 6 miles in those 30 stricken hours (Sara had come on board at Cannes otherwise we would have died of thirst, heat and hunger), but she whipped the boat into a kind of temporary-hospital, and we came through the affair cool, well-nourished with beer on the ice until Ajaccio. The hardest part was to see all those other boats one or two kilometres away creeping up the coast toward Ajaccio from bay to bay, cats-paw to cats-paw at three six nineoclock in the morning while we shared our nourishment with baby cachalots, marsouins and tortoises. It was very beautiful, but the anguish of keeping twenty three boats in their place all day and those cross-eyed red and green lights (screened by some to fool you) was about as accablant [oppressive] a chase as you'd want. Toward ten we picked up a breeze and made a Princeton finish by cutting behind some islands through a pass about two metres and a half deep and ten wide. It was Orizio's big moment. We were then seventh in position (the others had come up out of the night with the shore winds), we finished third at Ajaccio, but the cautious Baron to whom we owed 40 minutes was in an hour before us with his shore winds, and the superb Eblis had reached Ajaccio at mid-night before, she had been brought to the entrance of the port by the wind which failed us at three. The Honoria is a superb boat, but needs a fresh wind, for which she was constructed. All the coast is admiration for Vladimir. The de la Granges have very sportingly arranged a race between us for the 15 août as the result of the race they consider was much faussé [distorted] by the paralysing calm. Next year it's to be Monaco, Barcelona, Balearique Isles and return. She really is a great success, and a most original version of speed and sturdiness.

We think of you so much. Léger has been here for three weeks with us. It's always great to back up once a year and take on a load of him. He's very exciting on the subject of the Surrealiste direction. He feels that it's the end of something and not the beginning, but that with all revolutions in art that it has dragged some real values onto the stage, and that one should encaisser [collect]: I am. My last things are a moving mass of looseness and liberation (for me).

Lots of love to you from all of us. The children ask always of your whereabouts and then talk about it to Mlle. Rouselle during geography,

Gerald

Tairoff writes me from Paris. He's there for a month.
UVA

While Dos Passos was traveling in Russia, the MacLeishes were back in America, where they had decided to live permanently. MacLeish worked through his sense of regret and ambivalence about the move in his letter to Murphy, which became "American Letter: for Gerald Murphy"—published with minor changes in New Found Land *(1930).*

20. ARCHIBALD MACLEISH to GERALD MURPHY
Conway, 1 September 1928

Dear G:

The wind is east but the hot weather continues,
Blue & no clouds, the sound of the leaves thin,
Dry like the rustling of paper, scored across
With the slate-shrill screech of the locusts. The tossing of
Pines is the low sound. In the wind's running
The wild carrots smell of the burning sun.
Why should I think of the dolphins at Capo di Mele?
Why should I see in my mind the taut sail

And the hill over St. Tropez & your hand on the tiller?
Why should my heart be troubled with palms still?
I am neither a sold boy nor a Chinese official
Sent to sicken in Pa for some Lo-Yang dish.
This is my own land, my sky, my mountain:
This—not the humming pines & the surf & the sand
At the Ferme Blanche, nor Port Cros in the dusk & the harbor
Floating the motionless ship & the sea-drowned star.
I am neither Po Chü-i nor another after
Far from town, in a strange land, daft
For the talk of his own sort & the taste of his lettuces.
This land is my native land. And yet
I am sick for home for the red roofs & the olives,
And the foreign words & the white of the sea fall.
How can a wise man have two countries?
How can a man behold the sun & want
A land far off, alien, smelling of palm trees,
And the yellow gorse at noon in the long calms?

It is a strange thing—to be an American.
Neither an old house it is with the air
Tasting of hung herbs & the sun returning
Year after year to the same door & the churn
Making the same sound in the cool of the kitchen
Mother to son's wife, & the place to sit
In the dusk marked by the worn stone at the well head—
That—nor the eyes like each other's eyes & the skull
Shaped to the same front, & the hands' sameness.
Neither a place it is nor a blood name.
America is a cliff & the wind blowing.
America is a grey sea & the snow.
A tree, a white bird, the rain falling,
A drifted log on the beach & the gulls' call.
America is neither a land nor a people.
A colt's eye, it is, a hawk's sleep.
America is alone—never together;
Never the hand's touch, the mouth's breath
Of many having the same fathers among them.
Never so, but alone and the dumb tongue.
America is alone & the gulls calling.

It is a strange thing to be an American.
It is strange to live on the high world in the stare

Of the naked sun & the stars as our bones live.
Men in the old lands dwelt by their rivers.
They built their roofs in the vales in the earth's shelter.
We just inhabit the world. We dwell
On the half earth, on the open curve of a continent.
Sea is divided from sea by the darkness. The dawn
Rides the low east with us many hours.
First are the capes, then are the shorelands, now
The blue Appalachians faint at the day rise:
The willows shudder with light on the long Ohio:
The lakes scatter the low sun: the prairies
Slide out of dark: in the eddy of clean air
The smoke goes up from the high plains of Wyoming.
The steep Sierras arise. The struck foam
Flames at the wind's heel on the far Pacific.
Already the noon leans to the eastern cliff:
The elms darken the door & the dust-heavy lilacs.

It is strange to sleep in the bare stars & to die
On an open land where few have perished before us.
(From the new earth the dead return no more)
It is strange to be born of no race & no people.
In the old lands they are many together. They keep
The wise past & the words spoken in common.
They remember the dead with their hands & their mouths dumb.
They answer each other with two words in their meeting.
They have life together in small things. They eat
The same dish, their drink is the same & their proverbs.
Their fears are alike. They are like in their ways of love.
They are many men. There are always others beside them.
Here it is one man & another & wide
On the darkening hills the faint smoke of the houses.
Here it is one man & the wind in the boughs.

Therefore our hearts are sick for the south water.
The smell of the gorse comes back to our night thought.
We are sick at heart for the red roofs & the olives.
We are sick at heart for the voice & the foot's fall.
Nevertheless we are born to this wood's silence,
These unknown mouths, these unfamiliar eyes.
Nevertheless this is our land & our people,—
This that is neither a land nor a race. We must reap
The wind here in the grass for our soul's harvest.

37

Here we must eat our salt or our bones starve.
Here we must live or live only as shadows.
This is our race, we who have known, who have had
Neither the old walls nor the voices around us—
This is our land, this is our ancient ground—
The raw earth, the mixed bloods & the strangers,
The different eyes, the wind, & the heart's change.
It is this we cannot leave though the old call us.

The sun is over the pines. The wind falls.
There are only the bees now & the bronze cicadas.

I think of the surf at Cette & the sweet rain.

Arch.

HMD

Shortly after Gerald received MacLeish's "American Letter," the Murphys themselves left for America to see their families and to travel to California, where they stayed with King Vidor in Hollywood. As Gerald assisted with Hallelujah!, *he also saw John Howard Lawson and Laurence Stallings, who were earning large salaries writing film scripts. Dos Passos had just arrived back in New York, where the New Playwrights Theatre would produce his* Airways Inc. *in February. Dos Passos had seen Alexander Tairoff in Russia and had tried to convince him that he owed the Murphys no money. Dos Passos had not yet heard about the elaborate treasure hunt which the Murphys and Vladimir Orloff had staged for the Murphy children that summer, a hunt complete with map, clues, and, finally, buried treasure in a cove beyond St. Tropez. Portions of Gerald's letter along its fold lines are worn through and illegible.*

21. GERALD MURPHY to JOHN DOS PASSOS
Beverly Hills [19 January 1929]

How does a man like Lawson STAND it? Life's so short. Laurence Stallings says we'd like it if we knew some of the "real drunks." But nobody can stand more than two drinks here, we find.

Dear Dos:—

You're back. You big bum. Gosh we envy you Russia, especially since we've been out here. Thanks for burdening your brain with all that high finance of Tairoff's. I wish he wouldn't think about it so much. He *made* us *lend* it to him, and he's never been able to forget it. He wrote me so many letters that he wanted to pay it that I finally wrote forchristsake pay it, and forget it. I'm afraid he didn't "quite" understand. I'll write him. I'm so glad you saw him.

We can't wait to hear of every inch of your travels. Isn't Alice Coonen very beautiful? Pretty damn troublante. We'll go to Moscow to spend our rubles. The dollar begins to have a tarnished look to me.

And My God what a place this is, while you're up: what goes on in this free country? Anyway. The whole works has gone quaint, since we were here. The kitchen utensils have enamelled handles in *pastel* shades. Bootblacks and barbers wear indigo and jade-green smocks at their toil. The milk-man has a blue and white striped livery (cut dairy-wise) with the name of the firm embroidered in red across his back, cap to match. Waitresses are costumed as Watteau Shepherdesses, Matadors, Holland Maidens (with wooden shoes), Sailors, (the effect somewhat marred because of the prevalence of make-up and plucked eye-brows. God, the work that is being put in on those once at least pretty faces!) And just as the vanishing race of waitresses so goes the restaurant. One cannot bear to eat unless it be in "Mammy's Shack," "The Dutch Mill," "The Monkey Farm," "The Lighthouse" or Ye Bull Penn Inn, a Cafe Unique. Each one of these is built in loving imitation of the spot chosen. And don't think they're fantastic or gay or even crowded, they're not. There is a monstrous brown derby where you "eat in the Hat," and very badly I suppose. The electric lights inside are brown. There is a monster ice-cream freezer (all over town) with a giant handle which turns ceaselessly, where one enters and, of all things, eats ice-cream, in order to keep from crying. There are also gargantuan ice-cream cones. Don't think it's spectacular. It isn't. One eats in them. Ice cream cones. If there were only some gayety with it all. It's so solemn.

Oh God, the *need* to be quaint, with it all. You eat at the Sip and Bite, or the Goodie Fountain, well here goes a list——

The Snack Shop
The Hippedy-Hop Cake Shop
The Optimistic Doughnut
The Oakwood Storknest Hospital (maternity)
The Caress Courtesy Service Station (gasoline)
The Goodie Fountain (soda, in my day)
The Naughty Waffle Sandwich
The Piggly Wiggly Stores (grocers chain-stores)
Mitey Nice Bread
Holsum Wonder Bread
The Kit Kat Malted Milk Shoppe
Buddy Squirrel's Nut Shop (nuts)
The Miracle Cafeteria

Or like the race of romantic materialists that we are, we've dressed up life cap-a-pie such as

The Lovers' Delight Sandwich
The Green Orchid Ice Cream Salon
The Youth Is Wonderful Tie Shop
The Spartan Grocers
Ead's Castle for Eats (crenallated roof)
The Miracle Mile of Wiltshire Boulevard
The Angel City Cheese Company

Or in case that commerce appear a lowly pursuit

Rite Spot, the Home of the Aristocratic Hamburger
Ritzy Rolls
Facial Aesthetics (beauty specialist)
The Home of Harmonic Framing
The Funeral Home
Correct Feminine Apparel
Exclusive Remembrances (gifts)
Distinctive Interiors
The Bedspring Luxurious
Ethele Francis, Face Rejuvenator (Beauty specialist)
Milady's Salon, Where an Atmosphere of Quiet Prevails.
Manndel's Fascinating Slippers
Stoner's Beautiful Shoes
The Swelldom Department Store
The Face Exchange (beauty parlor)

Or the importance of well-being:——

The Health Temple
Magnetic Inn Sandwiches
Health Again Water
Health Restorium
Marys'es Candy Studeio
Crescent Milk, Protected in 27 Different ways.

The eye grows horny for signs like

Bud and Mabel's Good Eats
Charlies Noodle Cafe
Prompt Delivery, If it breaks our backs.
Sea Food Grotto

Tebb's Steak House, Private Tables for Ladies.
                    Booths for Ladies.
The You'll Come Back Cleanateria.

But in the parks the grass is protected by signs reading:

PLEASE GIVE ME A CHANCE TO GROW

My God, the country's gone nonce. These are verbatim signs out of Los Angeles, NOT Hollywood.
On the way to town there's a sign:

"Helping a Great City to Grow Artistically
Lawn Forest Memorial Park (a cemetery)
Historic Objects
Foreign Statuary
Moses, by Michael Angelo."

Now don't sit down and defend all this. It would be all right if they weren't so smug. That combined with their ignorance. Their ignorance combined with their "prosperity." The wealth of it all takes the heart out of you. Vladimir only lasted six weeks in all. Lost weight, tormented by night-mares, got the miseries,—and we didn't have the heart to ask him to stay. He crossed the continent all alone, and sailed away. He got to Paris in time to arrange my paintings for my exhibition at Bernheim Jeunes. January 15th. He kept saying while here: "Mais avec toute cette richesse il n y a pas d'espoir. C'est terrible. Ils sont perdus. etc." [But with all this opulence, there is no hope. This is terrible. They are lost.] As for the movies, and how they're done. Well I guess we won't go into it: but to see what I have seen, hear what I have heard. Zowie.
    There is no vestige of a visual aspect of the goddam art-industry. All "trick angles" have been exhausted by the Germans according to them. They don't know what a "picture" of any kind is. And they're all so rich.
    I've been officiating for six weeks at a picture: should have been sure-fire stuff: 80 negroes combed from out the southern states: (the only white people here, I'll tell you), but in two weeks they had it so full of scenes around the cabin door, with talk of chittlin's and corn-pone and banjoes a-strummin, that it was about as negro as Lew Dockstader's Minstrels. When they got LIONEL BARRYMORE to coach these negroes in the use of dialect, I resigned. My God! But it is considered most daring, original, planet-displacing on King Vidor's part to not have one single white person in the cast. Just think!
    And poor devils stand in line at 11 a.m. to go into dark, warm, scented cinemas, with a blur of red lights and quivering organ-music to see this other race of people ducking about in spangles and dress [illegible] and

high-powered cars. They've set a profile boy up as ideal male and a monstrous little girl with organdy ruffles from her ears down, curls like [illegible] shavings, a huge shaggy head, who lisps and minces and plays the [illegible] whether she be 20 or 35 years of [illegible] woman over [illegible] Europe a woman is apt to be considered a bore until she's 30. Here the women wear pinafores, I assure you,—and dancing pumps with instep straps. Their eyebrows are plucked however.

One of the directors here told Dorothy Parker that he had "a $150.000 liberry with a first edition of *Edith* St. Vincent Millay."

Well, well. What I keep thinking of is when could you come over and go on a cruise to the Balearic Islands or Corsica. There are great places to go on either one of them.

At the grocer's the other day Sara asked the Jap who was waiting on her so nicely what his name was and he said "Kenneth." That was all right. But later to the head-man she said she wanted a box of saltines. "You mean Cupid Chips, lady?" "Why no. I don't think so. In my time they were called saltines." "Well, same thing, I guess." "Not at all. A big man like you calling things Cupid Chips!" He didn't like it.

The children want the rights to telling you about the pirate cruise. It was such a success that sometimes I feel it didn't ever happen. Nature and chance were on our side to such an extent that we were all hurled back into the 18th century, willy-nilly. They still refuse to mention the treasure which they found before people for fear that the French Government will take it up. They buried the loot in the garden before they left France.

We speak of you so often, and think of you for luck, with our fingers crossed for fear that we won't have you with us somewhere someplace soon. The rest of the time we spend in the Mexican quarter, from which we send you under separate cover our most Mexican wishes. It saves our lives, that place. It cuts the grease of Marion Davies and Mary Pickford. What a dull sham the whole thing is, without one single one of the virtues of its ten thousand defects.

I don't demand good art of a country, but when they can't cook a decent meal or sell a vegetable with any taste to it, then something's up. There is nothing to eat, except when Sara cooks it. What do people live on. I hope they really want the money they earn. It's all too bad Green fruit softening in the sun off the tree but no ripeness yet. Excuse this blast.

Love from all

Gerald.

UVA

42

The Murphys arrived back in France early in the new year, and the Fitzgeralds were soon there to greet them. Their lease on Ellerslie Mansion had expired, and they now talked about a more permanent stay in France. They spent March on the Riviera with the Murphys, and they spent most of the spring in Paris, where the Hemingways had also arrived in late April. When Gerald wrote Ernest to see if he could join him on a two-week sailing race, Pauline was sick with a septic sore throat which persisted and then spread to baby Patrick.

22. GERALD MURPHY to ERNEST HEMINGWAY
Paris [c. spring 1929]
10 A.M.

Dear Ernest:—

I am *thinking* of signing up for the Course-Croisiere, June 15th

Cannes—Marseille 105 *miles*
Marseille—Palma (Majorca) 240ᵐ
Palma—Barcelone .160ᵐ
Through about June 28th.
Vladimir, myself, Henri and Guillaume (two Breton sailors).

Would you consider joining?
Sara and I are dining alone to-night. Would you all three be free? We leave Monday.
In case you can come telephone Littré: 38:37. Otherwise don't bother.
If Pauline isn't up to it, would you come and talk about the cruise. Prize of 4500 pesatas to be divided,—also prix d' equipage,—etc.
In any case think it over,

Yrs.

Gerald.

In these cities people are not thinking *at the same speed* at which they are living. This would kill any animal. A biologist said so. Maybe we're still part animal & are being killed.
Sara & Pauline could join us at Barcelona.
JFK

Although Hemingway was tempted to join Gerald, he finally declined because he was finishing the proofs for A Farewell to Arms. *As it turned*

out, Gerald never completed the cruise. After leaving for it on 15 June, he eventually turned back because Sara had implored him not to go and he began to feel guilty. Sara's main concern was Patrick, who had begun to show signs of illness in early 1929. Although the doctors initially diagnosed stomach trouble and prescribed a non-fat diet, they modified the diagnosis in late summer after discovering a spot on Patrick's lung. When Patrick had not improved by October, Gerald took him to Dr. Armand De Lille in Paris, who confirmed that Patrick's lung infection was tuberculosis. Both Jinny Pfeiffer and Dorothy Parker were with the Murphys when the disease was identified. Hemingway's A Farewell to Arms had been in print for two weeks when he received Gerald's letter.

23. GERALD MURPHY to ERNEST and PAULINE HEMINGWAY
Paris, 12 October 1929

Dear Ernest—Pauline:—

Thanks for what yr. petit mot brought with it. We both backed up and took on a much needed load.

He's taking the injections of gas like that brick. He gets 300 cub. centimetres of it each time through a thick needle under his arm between the ribs. It surrounds and collapses the lung, immobilizes it, stops the spread. He's living on the good lung. They hope to keep it good. Altitude and sun-treatment will help. Injections—one every 15 days to keep up the gas pressure,—for two years.

His case indicates that he has no tendency,—very strong lungs,—but was *impregnated* by *contact with some one* over a considerable period of time. The fever of 3 wks. last May (diagnosed as intestinal infection, with heart-pains) <u>was</u> the beginning!

Something must be said about Jinny. What a very remarkable and very beautiful (interior) person she is. Most disturbing and moving to Sara and me. We wonder what she's doing all the time. She's very haunting. We feel there's something imminent about her. Something she must have. (I don't mean to talk as if I meant a "problem,"—I don't) She'll always be the same. Will always want that thing,—and never be sure she's going to have it,—in fact not sure enough. Sara says she's so simple that most people must find her complicated. A *real* innocence she has,—and presents it as a flat surface to the world. I imagine most people aren't good enough for her (I mean in *my* opinion.) We're crazy about her: always have been. Very rare distillation of something. It's been a privilege to be with her. Don't ask to take her back for a couple of months. We worry about her—for *no* good reason.

Sara leaves for Antibes to-morrow night. Patrick takes his 4th injection Tues.—maybe a 5th Wed. He and I leave for Montana-Vermala, Verlaise, Suisse (Palace Sanatorium) on Thu. night. Will find a house for the rest of the family. The map looks like very good ski-trips,—it's at 1500 metres with lots of cabanes in the mts. above and no villages beyond us. If you don't go USA maybe you'd come. The most sun in Suisse,—8 hrs. of it on Dec. 22.

Have my own copy of F. to Arms. Thanks for the one sent. Sara's boiling up and down over it. Of course it's good. So was Big 2 Hearted [River, a story included in *In Our Time*, 1925]. Our love to you both, (and Patrick H.)

Gerald.

[Enclosed in Gerald's letter was a picture of Patrick with a note attached:] Taken in bed Oct. 11th (to shift him from Sara's to my pass-port)—Please keep it and hunch. For luck.

JFK

24. SARA MURPHY to PAULINE HEMINGWAY
Paris [12 October 1929]

Sat—eve—

Dearest Pauline—after having the children xrayed at Antibes the dr. wires us Honoria bronchials show speckly—so in the light of all that has been happening—& as naturally the other 2 children have been exposed to this germ unwittingly all along,—I've wired to have her come *here*,—leaving Antibes tomorrow, & Jinny is bringing her. We feel dreadfully about Jinny's visit having fallen on such a gloomy time—& only *hope* the slight change of air she's had has done some *slight* good—She really is so sweet, & we all like her so much! They are supposed to leave Train Bleu about 5 tomorrow p.m. & they arrive quarter to 10, Mon. a.m. My own idea now is to get H[onoria] straight to the best specialist—& have no more delays & fiddling by any optimistic fools—I'll go to the gare [train station]— & meet them—Just wanted to let you know—Jinny was coming back—She has *got* to come & stay with us in Suisse this winter—Because I counted on her visit—we were so looking forward to it—Any more news of whether you're going, to U.S.A.—soon? *Crazy* about Ernest's book (as you can well imagine)—and to Hell with Isabel Patterson, & her kind (if such there be).[1] What can we do to Isabel Patterson?

1. Isabel Paterson was a columnist for the *New York Herald Tribune* who published Morley Callaghan's claim—and the retraction of the story—to have knocked out Hemingway in a June boxing match. Sara was using Paterson's name as representative of the larger group of literary critics who might choose to find fault with Hemingway's writing.

We are here all day—if you'd feel like coming up in the p.m. Much love to both—

Sara

Room 68 [George V, 6 rue Piccini]
JFK

By late October, the Murphys, along with Dorothy Parker, were in Montana-Vermala at the Palace Hotel. Parker had helped to close down Villa America, which saddened her; and she continued to be depressed over her ill-fated novel and her relationship with John Garrett. Parker understood the Murphy's growing isolation from their two families in America, and she sided with them in their feelings for Sara's sister, Hoytie Wiborg. Many of the Murphys' friends resented Hoytie, especially after she broke with Sara because of serious disagreement over the Wiborg family estate. Gerald kept both families posted during Patrick's illness. Both Parker and Benchley had been with the Murphys at Antibes during the summer.

25. DOROTHY PARKER TO ROBERT BENCHLEY
Montana-Vermala [7 November 1929]

So last night, Fred, I was standing out on my balcony at midnight looking at the Alps in the moonlight, when I was startled to hear a sudden loud, tearing noise in the still air. And I found, much to my surprise, that it was me, standing all alone in the night, making that sound with my mouth at them.

Now you can see for yourself how this typewriter is working. And then they want a person to write novels. (((The lines had become jammed together.))) Write novels, write novels, write novels—that's all they can say. Oh, I do get so sick and tired, sometimes.

Well, Fred, if you had told me last year that this November I should be in a sanatorium for the tuburcual in Switzerland, I should have said—well, I should have said (collapse of story) "That's great!", because last November I was in Hollywood, and any change would have been for the better. And NEXT November, Fred, I do hope that you are going to be able to find time to come visit me up at the Death House in Sing-Sing.

Because Palace Hotel my eye, Fred,—they are all called hotels, and all Palaces, Splendids, Royales, Grands, Magnifiques, and Collosales, at that. But they are all sanatoriums for the tubercular, and jolly no end, no end whatever. The halls are full of doctors dressed in butchers' coats and nurses who come as Edith Cavell, and it is forbidden to make a sound, much less click a typewriter between two and five in the afternoon and after eight at night, and everyone walks on tiptoe and speaks in whispers, and Baby is going right out of her mind. And though it may be pointed out—though never by you, Fred— "What an ideal place to work," it isn't at all, because it has sent me into that state of slow, even heebs where I can't write or even read—I just sit looking ahead of me. But not at the Alps, Fred. I wouldn't do that on you. I get my chair all turned around before I begin my looking, and then I do it at a clean white towel they have thumbtacked up over the washstand. It's a good thing to look at. You can go all around the edges very slowly, and then you can do a lot of counting the squares made by the ironed-out creases.

I know, Fred. This is the kind of thing of which, when you get tired of it, you say, "Oh, WHY did I ever leave the sanatorium? It WAS so peaceful there. I really think those were the happiest days of my life." And while it is going on, you are running a really corking chance of going nuts, in the desperation of your melancholy.

So anyway, Fred, here I am on top of this God damn Alp, and I really do not see how I am ever going to get off it, because nothing could coax me back into that funiculaire that brought me up here, the coward. As long as it takes to get to Stamford, going absolutely vertical, with nothing between you and your Maker but a length of frayed cable! No. I'll stay here among the bacilli. I'm no fool.

Well, you big shit, I cabled you before I came and asked your advice because I have one of those dandy superstitions about it, and either you were away at one of those places beginning with W, or else you never answered, or both. So I came anyhow. But I think you'd have said to. Because a prize horse's a-- I would be, walking out on the Murphys now.

And sometime you must try that trip up from the Midi with three dogs, two of them in high heat, and the baggage the Murphys left behind, which consisted of eleven trunks and seventeen handpieces. Well, it was the God's own mercy we had to change trains only three times. And laugh, trying to get the dogs through the customs at Geneva! They told me at good old Thomas Cook's, in Nice, that the Swiss are wild to get dogs into their country—were, in fact, making a drive to entice them here—and it would be no trouble at all. So what you have to do is pay several kings' ransoms, and let the Swiss Guards, one after another, have their way with you.

And I will draw that veil over the last days of shutting up the place in Antibes. Because what is more horrible than a dismantled house where people have once been gay?

Well, Fred, I have always thought of Switzerland as the home of horseshit, and I see no reason to change my opinion now. For what does anybody want with a country that has no history except William Tell, and I don't know to this day whether he was a legend or not? Also, I have had a hard time all my life getting the Swiss and the Swedish mixed up, and it is too late for me to change now.

I have put off talking about the Murphys until now, because truly, Mr. Benchley, it would break your heart. Ah, why in hell did this have to happen to them, of all people? Patrick's treatment will take two years, they say. Gerald has absolutely isolated himself with him—does every single thing for him, and takes his meals with him. I didn't see anything at all of him the first few days I was here; and then I caught a glimpse of him, hurrying along the balcony, with a pot-de-chambre in one hand and a thermometer in the other, and he was dressed in Swiss peasant costume, with a green baize apron with a chain across the back, and it was the most touching thing I have ever seen. They are so damn brave, and they are trying so hard to get a little gaiety into this, and it just kills you, Fred. And now the doctors have found that Honoria—well, there are no positive germs, but she has a constant fever and her lungs are spotted, so they are giving her a three months rest cure, and then they are going to see. It's too much, isn't it?

The doctors have traced the incubation of Patrick's illness back to last February—when they were in Hollywood. Sara thinks it was probably that nice Negro chauffeur they had—they recall now, as people always do, that he had a frightful cough.

Sara and Baoth and I dine in their little salon—the rooms are regular hospital rooms, but Sara, of course, has made it all different, and Gerald, of course, has insisted that it be made regular ham Swiss decorations. I remember having some idea that I would always wear little chiffon pretties for dinner on account of morale—the Englishman-in-the-jungle school of thing. Yes. So what you wear for dinner is a tweed suit, a coat over it, a woolen muffler tied tight around your neck, a knitted cap, and galoshes. When you go outdoors, you take off either the coat or the muffler. But it is much colder inside, with no sun. They have to have it that way on account of the sicks. Outside, you find that that is all true about your not feeling the cold at all. You really don't. And I never knew there could be such glorious air. And you can have it on your birthday.

There is no real drinking—I believe stiff liquor is supposed to kick the tripe out of you at this altitude, although I am getting rather willing to try it—but every night we have a solemn glass of gluhwein (I think that is the way you spell it) before we go to bed at nine. Poor Gerald (and those lights are out in the Hippodrome, Mr. Benchley, when you think of Gerald Murphy as "poor Gerald") has tried to recapture the old spirit and he has fixed up a table as a little bar—it has on it just a bottle of wine and a bag of cinnamon and some lemons and a spirit lamp. He is also making the room into a gluhwein parlor, with mangy white fur rugs on the floor, and all the horrid Swiss decorations he can get. I gave him a cuckoo clock and a parrot—an awful beast. Gerald is scared to hell of her, and carries her on his shoulder, with his neck bent forward at a hitherto undiscovered joint, saying in a quavering voice, "Ah, de sweetheart. Ah, de goose-girl," and then the goose-girl bites a wedge out of his ear. I got her because she was just the right smell for a gluhwein parlor.

So we sit there, Fred, for about twenty minutes after Patrick is settled for the night, in that freezing room, all done up in mufflers, and talking in whispers, of course, because Patrick is on one side and some one strange and older and sicker on the other, and poor Gerald importantly makes gluhwein, and we talk about you. "Ah, old Boogles Benchley. Ah, old imaginary good lucks. Let's cable the old fool to come over." Because they have just the same feeling about you that I have—if you were here, everything would be all right.

Ah, gee, Fred, last night we were sitting there and Gerald suddenly got up and raised his heavy hospital tumbler, and said—of course in a whisper—"To Tiggy Martin, the Wickedest Woman in London," and this is the kind of thing you couldn't stand, Mr. Benchley. I can keep from crying much longer if people aren't brave.

To-day was Sara's birthday, and we had a little party. Everybody gave everybody presents—not just Sara. Even the dogs—the complete five are here— and the canaries and the parrot had things. We had a cake, and Honoria was carried into Patrick's room for the event, and a very nice nurse and the housekeeper and one of the doctors came (all the doctors have it; they are great specialists who had to drop their careers in their own cities and come here for the climate). And we had champagne, and when Sara's health was drunk, Gerald kissed her, and they twined their arms around—you know—and drank that way. Jesus, Fred, I can't stop crying. Christ, think of all the shits in the world, and then this happens to the Murphys!

There aren't any people, Mr. Benchley, except you and the Murphys. I know that now. Ernest is pretty damn good, but he isn't it. There are only you and Gerald and Sara. Nobody else. Sara is a great woman. I didn't know women could be like that. And Gerald is a great man. And you are a great man. Please lend me your handkerchief—Timothy (((her dog))) took mine. He eats them. Now that his name has come up, he loves it here. "Now this," he says, "is what I mean by climate. You and your Riviera! The cesspool of Europe, that's what it is."

The Murphys have six rooms along in a row on a balcony, and Clement and Ernestine (((the typewriter ribbon switched from black to red))) have rooms somewhere, and I have one on the floor above. They can't use the car, so Clement is employed in beguiling Baoth, and I don't know exactly what Ernestine does, but it involves a terrific amount of bustling.

49

I honestly don't (how did this red happen? I must have hit something.) I don't know how long Gerald can stand it, Fred. I don't know what goes on in his head. I don't in the least minimize his devotion to Patrick, truly I don't, but there is something else in this absolute immolation, for after all, a nurse could do as well and better all the routine things that must be done. I think there is something of his denial of illness in it—something of "say it will take two years, do they? Why I'll show them this child is not sick—I'll have him up and about in a couple of months." And there is something else—that morbid, turned-in thing that began with his giving up his painting and refusing to have it mentioned, and went on through his turning back from that cruise before— and thank God it WAS before—we came to Antibes. It wasn't a broken mast, Fred; Vladimir told me. Every time they touched a port there would be tele- grams and special deliveries from Sara telling him it was his duty to come back and be with his children. And I think there is a little of "Very well; since all I'm good for is to be a nurse, then I'll BE a nurse" in his position now. Damn it, these things always sound so much more than you mean when you say them, but you know what I mean. He looks like hell; all the points of his face have gone sharp and turned up, like Esther's. He works every minute—all the en- ergy that used to go into compounding drinks and devising costumes and sweeping out the bath-houses and sifting the sand on the plage has been put into inventing and running complicated Heath-Robinson sick-room ap- pliances, and he is simply pouring his vitality into Patrick, in the endeavor to make him not sick. He is already cracking; he goes into real tantrums of irrita- tion when the child's fever doesn't go down or he doesn't gain weight, al- though the doctors have told him these things aren't expected for a long time. But he was so sure he could lick them, it drives him crazy that he can't.

Their families, of course, have been of enormous assistance. Mrs. Murphy writes that all they have to do is to act and to think as if Patrick were twice as ill as he really is, and then everything will be all right with God's help. (Gerald got that letter just as he was about to stagger out of the room with four laden trays piled one on another. "With God's help," he kept saying, when he re- sumed his burden. "With God's help. Oh, my GOD! with God's help.") Mr. Wiborg points out that this doubtless would never have occurred if the chil- dren had not been brought up like little Frenchmen. And Hoytie, good old Hoytie, cabled: "Dont be forlorn I will be over after Christmas". When he heard that one, Dow-Dow's face lit up just like the Mammoth Cave.

Fred, I frankly don't know quite what to do about me. I do think they want me—I don't mean on account of its being me, but I think a friend around gives them a little touch with something outside this death-house. But I see them, all told, perhaps an hour and a quarter a day. Later on, when they are sys- tematized so that only one of them need be on duty at a time, perhaps, and the other will want to play, I may be of more use. But that will be some time later on, Fred, and it is pretty expensive here. And And I am not, really, very happy here. It isn't that I am tormented by thoughts of here is Life slipping by and me not living—that is so much velvet to me. But it IS pretty lonesome and gloomy, right now.

On that old other hand, I have no place to go but New York, and I am scared to hell of it. It may be Murphy influence, it may be that sinking feeling when I think of what used to crawl out of the drains into my brandy-and-soda of an afternoon, and it may be (and this is my guess) repercussions of the Garrett Blues. Please make a lap, Fred,—I want to dump a lot of shit in it. I honestly don't know where John leaves off and I begin. I mean, I don't know how much I have built up for myself of his boyishness and gaiety and sweetness—even of his good looks. I honestly can't remember what it was like to be alone with him; I couldn't possibly recall any of our conversations. I have a foggy impression that he used to talk a lot about the war, and about that time he flouted Gargoyle, up at Williams. But there *Must* have been more than that. I honestly can't remember. You see, Fred, all through that two-year idyll, we were both pretty fairly tight.

I might be able to go back and see him and talk to him, and think only, "Well, for God's sake, is THIS what it was all about." I might even be able to go back and have him never see me or telephone me—which is what I am so sickeningly afraid of now—and not even miss it. I am immeasurably better and stronger—well, why wouldn't I be, after all this time with the Murphys?—and I might be able to go back and be all right. But that "which is what I am so sickeningly afraid of now" shows the way to bet. You see, Fred, except for the little spots I am with Sara and Gerald each day, I don't see a soul, and there doesn't seem to be anything else to think about.

I guess the best thing to do is stay on for a while anyway. It can't do me any harm, as the housemaid said when she swallowed the egg-cup full of laudanum. Because pretty soon, one of three things must happen—I'll get up and go, my money will give out, or I'll get used to it here. So there really isn't any use in worrying, is there, and Mr. World is a pretty good old feller after all.

You know, I'd love to come back to New York for a little while—as you do, with the idea of returning to Europe. I'd give an eye to see you. I should love to see Seward.[1] You know your sweetest little girl in the world—ah, she's such a dear little girl? Well, he's the sweetest little boy in the world—ah, he's such a dear little boy. But I think maybe I'd better stay a little while longer—I sort of think of it as if I were taking the cure, like the kids, only I am not sure if this is

---

1. Seward Collins contributed articles to *Vanity Fair* and *The New Republic* during the 1920s, and he also pursued Parker during 1925–1926. Although they traveled together in Europe the spring that Parker met the Murphys (1926), Parker found him an uninteresting lover and continued to see him thereafter as a friend.

the right one. But don't you think this is best to do? Why don't you SAY something? Really, Robert, for a bright boy—

Fred, your letter was simply meat and drink to the Murphys and me. It is all worn out from reading. It is the loveliest letter I ever saw, and you are the loveliest and funniest and gamest person. I thanked you for it in that cable—oh, and in case you didn't get it, Fred, I said in it what Sara told me to tell you—to shut up about money. She has enough troubles, she says, without your money.

Look, if you have any friends who usually send their old magazines to the Salvation Army or the men in lighthouses, will you ask them to save out a few for the Swiss Family Murphy? We haven't seen a magazine in weeks. It's no good having any truck with Brentano's in Paris—they just don't send things. And is there any news? I understand there has been some little trouble in Wall Street—that hits us hard, doesn't it, Fred? What about Alec's play?[2] I heard Ring Lardner's was swell.[3] Where and how are the [Donald] Stewarts? Any one we know wiped out in Wall Street? What ever became of Merton Powell, the big stiff? Whom do you see? Is Jock back?[4] Muriel[5] wrote me that Eleanor Chase and her Swiss squirt went though Paris without leaving any spoor at all, save that they gave a dinner at which the bride got stewed and took the ladies into the toilet to tell them she felt just as she always had about Jock Whitney, but unfortunately he wasn't the marrying kind. She is not in love with her husband, so everything stacks up just dandy for the boys back home. Have you seen Marise? How is Marc [Connelly]? What do you do? Has everybody forgotten me, or has it appeared in Walter Winchell's column yet that I have tuberculosis and am in a sanatorium in the Catskills? Seward cabled me that my O. Henry prize was five hundred dollars, but no one else has mentioned it to me and my fingers are still unsullied by the touch of money, so I guess it was just some devil's mockery of his.[6] I enclose this letter of Ernest's to show you how sweet in the mouth are the fruits of success. He is just finding out what you knew ten years ago—what's the sense of being considered a good writer,

---

2. Alexander Woollcott had collaborated with George S. Kaufman on *The Channel Road*, a comedy which lasted only fifty performances on Broadway.

3. Ring Lardner collaborated with Kaufman on *June Moon*, a spoof of the songwriting business which experienced a successful Broadway run.

4. Parker had recently met Benchley's and Donald Stewart's high-society New York friends, including John Hay "Jock" Whitney. She wonders how the bankers, such as Merton Powell, have fared following the October 1929 stock market crash.

5. Journalist Muriel Draper lived next door to Edmund Wilson for a short time, and she joined with many of the American writers who supported left-wing causes during the 1930s.

6. Parker's "Big Blonde" had won the O. Henry Prize for the best short story published during 1929.

when look at the people who consider you that? The Hemingways are going back to Key West next month. I had to write a piece about him for the New Yorker—that was a pretty job. All I couldn't say was anything about his father or his divorce or anything he ever did or said.[7]

Oh, Fred, Sara told me Mrs. Benchley sent me some photographs of Timmy [Parker's dog]. Damn it, I never got them—I moved from the Napoleon to the Saalburgs', and all my mail was lost. Would you thank her and tell her how disappointed I am? Sara says they are swell. Would she by any chance have kept the films? That makes me sick, losing a respectable person's mail that way.

Please give my love to Betty and how is her little Tony, and did you ever get Max the Dog?

I'm awfully sorry about the eye-strain of this letter, but what can I do? You'd think typewriter ribbons grew on trees, the way this is acting.

There's no more paper, but oh, my God, there's so much love from us all!

Dorothy

BU

---

7. Parker acknowledged Hemingway as the "first American artist" and talked about the Hemingway hero's "grace under pressure" in her profile "The Artist's Reward," which appeared in the 30 November 1929 *New Yorker*.

The Hemingways and the Dos Passoses, along with Dorothy Parker, were with the Murphys for Christmas, and by May 1930, Patrick had improved sufficiently for the family to move to a chalet near the Palace Hotel. Despite Patrick's improvement, Gerald began to grow increasingly preoccupied and reclusive. When he traveled alone to America late that summer, he refused to contact the MacLeishes and then wrote Archie the following letter upon his return to Montana-Vermala.

26. GERALD MURPHY to ARCHIBALD MACLEISH
Montana-Vermala, 22 January 1931

Dear Archie:—

When I see you again, I hope that I shall be able to talk to you. (Possibly it will not be necessary!) It is difficult for me to write clearly of what I should tell you. I shall, of necessity, be tiresomely ego-centric. I know, however, that I owe it to you and Ada. What has happened concerns-implicates-only me. Please believe me in this.

After all these years,—and in one sudden year,—I find myself, pried away from life *it*self by the very things that went to make up *my* life. (This is not "Mid-channel." I am *not* tired, bored or sick. I do *not* feel old or forty odd.) I awaken to find that I have apparently never had one real relationship or one full experience. It would seem that all my time has been spent in bargaining with life or attempting to buy it off. And this *although* it has occurred to me from the beginning that I must surely be paying some other price for all that I was enjoying without earning. But it is never quite possible to believe that *all* that one does is unreal, or that one is *never* oneself for a moment,—and that the residue of this must needs be a sense of unreality, all pervading. I don't think that I hoped to beat *life*. Possibly I thought that mine was one way of living it, among many thousand ways.

My terms with life have been simple: I have refused to meet it on the grounds of my own defects, for the reason that I have bitterly resented those defects since I was fifteen years of age. (I once tried to tell you that I didn't believe in taking life at its *own* tragical value if it could be avoided. It was this I apparently meant.) You of course cannot have known that not for one waking hour of my life since I was fifteen have I been entirely free of the feeling of these defects. In the vaults of the Morgan Museum on Madison Avenue I was shown once when I was twenty the manuscript of Samson Agonistes, and while I was listening to a recital of its cost, I read "O, worst imprisonment! To be the dungeon of thyself." I knew what it meant, then. Eight years of school and college, after my too willing distortion of myself into the likeness of popularity and success, I was left with little confidence in the shell that I had inhabited as another person.

And so I have never felt there was a place in life as it is lived for what I have to give of myself. I have doubtless ended by trying, instead, to give of my life as I have lived it.

My subsequent life has been a process of concealment of the personal realities,—at which I have been all too adept. They were not the most important things necessarily, but they were the things which nourish human relationships. What I have contributed to this was "ersatz",—and I have begun to pay for it. The effect on my heart has been evident. It is now a faulty "instrument de précision" working with accuracy in the direction of error. It makes a poor companion, I assure you.

Thus I have learned to dread (and avoid) the responsibilities of friendship (as being one of the realities of life), believing, as I do, that I was incapable of a full one. I have *become* unworthy of one.

I have never been able to feel *sure* that *any*one was fond of me, because it would seem to be too much claim, knowing what I did about myself. I have been demoralized by coming under the banner of what Sara gives people and what she demands of them in the way of affection. This seems to have deceived even you and Ada. It is she who has floated our friendships on the flood of her very deep and very real feelings. You *know* that you have always known that Sara has given you what she was and is. You have never known that I have given you what I was not,—am not. You have *felt* it. That I know.

(I hope that this doesn't sound like a lot of crap. If it were, I think it would probably be easier to say. Maybe we'd better just say that I am rather an ornamentally footling person, whose life has been inconsequential,—and sterilized even of the virtues of its defects.)

In refuting this self-recrimination (as one is always tempted to do by instinct) do be honest in not confusing me and what you feel about me with Sara. But rather recall that she is incorruptibly modest, and has never accepted (much less taken) even to herself, for what she does, what we give out, and what she is. This rare alchemy of nature has distilled a deceptive elixir, for which I have always received and taken too much credit. The process has left me impoverished,—spiritually,—as it should.

One thing more. Don't worry about anything that I have said. Things are perfectly all right. They were not in September. I am long since (thank God!) bored by the very *nature* of what was my unhappiness. There seems to me to be such a lot of second-rate suffering going on about. Americans have gone in for it. My problem has no proportions,—or rather I have preferred that it shouldn't have.

Have I made myself clear enough to have you see why I could come to America and dread the possibility of seeing you and Ada, and risk disfiguring one of the few phantom realities of my life, my friendship with you both? I preferred to skulk it and take the consequences. I have become desperately jealous of such things. You will say that this is a strange way to preserve them. It was rude, unkind and selfish of me. Please pardon it, if you can.

Before I left for America, Sara said that I should cable you I was coming. Over an hours argument I said that I didn't want to, didn't *feel* I had a right to, in fact couldn't, because I *knew* I couldn't follow it up. I tried in vain to state my reasons. Sara could not, naturally, understand them. At last she said: "I think that you are *afraid* to have people like you." And I knew that what she said was true, and that I couldn't see you or anyone whom I like,—or *know,* or who likes or knows me. Dorothy Parker had cabled Bob Benchley I was coming. He met me at the pier unfortunately. It made my heart sink with guilt, somehow. I like him. I do not know him well,—nor he me. I saw no one else except rather fantastic strangers,—all by accident. I was at Southampton [New York] most of the time—and most certainly saw no one there. My God, what a race of people! The hopeless circumscription of their lives, the richness, the sureness, the pompous, leaden dullness of it. Desolation! Sacred staleness.

* * * * *

May I say such things now? Namely: that we are so disappointed that we're not going to see you. We've been talking a lot about you in connection with a dreamlike plan. All this in spite of the fact that we should be as worried about matters financial as you, poor dears,—but somehow our remoteness from the seat of the epidemic divorces us from it. We know that we should be worried, the families, all of them, have done their best to effect that, but we've had enough of another kind for over a year and we have no heads for figures. In any case what in God's name can we do about the goddamn situation and keep our balance on this Alp at the same time?

In spite of thunder we are going to build a very simple, very broad, very comfortable and spacious goélette [schooner]. Not very long, 27 metres on deck. The Honoria was 16. Nice and deep, with head-room below. We're taking as model those little schooners that come from the Balearic Islands and ride in the rade Juan les Pins, loaded with oranges. But of course we'll have a regular big New England deck-house, and big awnings. She will be a composite of all that Sara found the Honoria not to be. She will be under-sailed: jibs that come over automatically, a fixed stay-sail on the front mast, and on the main-mast both marconi *and* regular rigging, according as one is cruising or coasting. She'll be a regular sea-going schooner, very steady and domestic, and very comfortable.

When you cabled that you were not coming I wired Vladimir to put the Honoria on sale (Sara had been out in her all October, every day). In a week she was sold, and very well, fortunately, too, as the ports are full of boats for sale. A young Englishman bought her. He will remove her bowsprit, lower her mast one third, change her to marconi rigging, paint her white and use her for fishing! How strange! It was the inventory that enticed him. The powder-blue plates in enamel that I got from the Girl-Scout headquarters on Third Avenue! Strange!

The Villa is being tended by Joseph [Revello] and his wife who have a little baby. The house is blind, the garden still. People have rented the Ferme. We shall try to sell the Villa America, the Guynemer apartment is gone. Patrick will not be able to stay at sea level on the coast, but it seems a voyage at sea is good from time to time. We shall use the goélette by way of educating the children, taking them along the coast of Spain, Africa, Italy, Greece, etc. When all this is to be, we are not sure, but we are building the goélette, by God!

You and Ada and the children have got to come. Think of it,—no rent and no restaurant expenses for any of us. Sara's cuisine is to be a beaut so she says, she's having a frigidaire and glacière [freezer]. We'll have a 30,000 HP Diesel that goes on butter (true you know!) with electric lighting. She's going to be built at a chantier [shipyard] where they build commercial boats. She will not be a yacht. No mahogany or blue velour upholstery.

It is this that we plan, thinking of you all as we do it. You're the only people who would really like to do it with us. Think of bringing the children up the Adriatic to Venice, or to the Balearic Islands! It can be done.

* * * * *

I gave "New Found Land" to the little British Library here, and I wish that you could hear some of the things Miss Spencer, the librarian, hears said of it. There's an extremely nice crowd of simple, intelligent, liberal-minded English here// It's beautiful. Sometimes Sara and I read it aloud at break-fast. We have a long room that looks down the valley of the Rhone to the Mont Blanc massif which is the first to receive the sun at eight o'clock. Then Hell breaks loose in the way of light. Every morning it seems the first time.// The other day a fellow passed us in the village on skis, pushing on his batons in rhythm to "He— walks—with—Ernest—in the—streets—of Sar—agossa." This is fame, if you will.[1]

* * * * *

Poor Sal, I think, is feeling better as her horrors slide back into last year. She got some awful wallops, one after the other. Turned them under the soil and paid later. She has a kitchen all her own with Honoria, where she evolves desserts which are down-right conspiracies. Patrick is progressing with Miss Stewart (who helped us, at the last moment, bring all three into the world), he sleds every day and will ski next month. His nature has opened up most beautifully. For Christmas he asked for oils,—and you'd be amazed at his facility. If ever I saw someone who was *meant* to paint. Honoria is tall and gracious, with great sweetness of disposition, (where she got it *I* don't know, nor Sara either) she's being very pretty too. We have an excellent teacher for them both: an Englishwoman. Boath is eating up his school. After six weeks of study he had really got German in hand and a composition of his on "Lions" was published in the monthly school paper for its excellence. It's an ideal life for him

---

1. *New Found Land* came out in 1930 and contained MacLeish's poem for Gerald, "American Letter," along with "Cinema of a Man," an autobiographical poem based on MacLeish's years in Europe. The line Murphy quotes here is from the stanza which reads:

He walks with Ernest in the streets in Saragossa
They are drunk their mouths are hard they say que cosa
They say the cruel words they hurt each other
Their elbows touch their shoulders touch their feet go on and on together

and he prefers it so much to what we have had to offer him here. The orderliness, organization and simplicity of the life is just what he needs. It's odd that he should like it, too.

* * * * *

From this welter, I hope you'll believe me when I say that I'm very fond of you and Ada and the children, and that I couldn't imagine the future without seeing you and being with you. Please *accept* my feelings as poor stuff as they are, for I have had to learn to

Gerald.

My human relationships have been effected always by the existence of a fact,—a defect, over which I have had only enough control to skotch it from time to time. It has not been always bearable. I hope this letter does not offend your taste,—or whatever that thing is that gets offended—and you can never feel the same about the person afterwards. I *know* that I could have *told* you this without offending you.

LC

Patrick continued to improve and joined the family that summer in Austria. Although Zelda Fitzgerald's health remained precarious, she was well enough by August to see the Murphys at Ramgut.

27. GERALD MURPHY TO F. SCOTT FITZGERALD
Bad Aussee, Austria [c. summer 1931]

Dear Scott:—

How great that everything seems to be going so well and that you can all really come here. We had begun to worry a little and expect an ugly letter from you. You've doubtless got my telegram saying that the fourth August will be fine. We return from Salzburg on the afternoon of the third after Patrick's next injection which takes place that morning. We stay at the Grand Hotel de l'Europe when there. It's not a bad idea that we see each other there that day, unless you're coming by another way (Zurich—Munich) to Bad Aussee.

Bring bathing suits.

The name of the property is RAMGUT, Bad Aussee, Steyrmark, Austria. Telephone number 1. We are about 85 kilometres or two hours and one half easy going from Salzburg. I should suggest that you come by Zurich, Buchs, Innsbruck, Salzburg,—or if you want to go to Germany from the Swiss border and then South to Salzburg, go by Munich,—but by Innsbruck and the Austrian Tyrol is lovely.

Our schedule may be too tight a one to allow of our going to Vienna with you, as it will be just the moment that we are without a trained nurse for Patrick, the present one leaves August 3rd and Miss Stewart does not land until the 10th. But you and Zelda must go, Scottie can stay with us so easily until you come back to get her. It will give you and Zelda kind of a fling alone;—and we are on your way back.

The termination of your letter with its patter of baby feet had what you would consider the desired effect upon Sara: sharp local pains followed by excessive retching.

Our love to you all. We *are* looking forward to seeing you,

Gerald.

Bring Express or A.B.A. checks for Austria & Germany,—otherwise it's difficult,—and if possible put USA somewhere on your car,—otherwise you're apt to be eaten for a Frog. With USA they strew roses.
[Written at the top of letter]: Vienna is 5 hrs. (at most) due East of us by motor. We are on the direct road between Salzburg & Wien.
PUL

The Fitzgeralds' stay at Ramgut was relaxed for the most part, although Honoria Donnelly recalls that the visit ended "suddenly" and "sadly" one morning when the Fitzgeralds left Scottie behind with a nurse, who had come with them. Most probably the Fitzgeralds had departed for the side trip to Vienna Gerald had suggested they take. Following the Fitzgeralds' visit, Gerald learned of his father's sudden pneumonia, and he sailed to New York. Mr. Murphy died on 23 November 1931, and Gerald was back in Montana-Vermala by Christmas.

28. GERALD MURPHY TO ARCHIBALD MACLEISH
Montana-Vermala, 8 January 1932

Dear Archie:—

There is need of talking to you,—or someone like you,—and there being no such person that I know of, there is need of talking to *you*.

Poor Vladimir: he made the 2000 miles from Fécamp to Gibraltar against head winds (except in the Golfe de Gascogne, where she averaged 13 knots an hour with rotten, borrowed "voiles de route" [sails]). In coming up from

Gibraltar they hit the hurricane that almost got Alain Gerbault in a two-day bout off of Toulon. They were driven into Barcelona, then came out twice and were driven back each time into Las Palamas a little port under the north-easterly Cap of Spain. Finally they got to Marseille. Vladimir says that the "Weather Bird" is indestructible and that he has proof. Of course the "usure" [wear] to the tackle has been considerable and it will take her a month to get into condition. We are going down to Antibes in a week or so to try her out, and are planning a cruise for the Easter vacation. Unfortunately the Doctor will not let poor little Pook go to Antibes. We must keep him here until just before we sail the end of April. This cursed thing is the worst imprisonment for him, as he grows older he chafes more and more under it. The other day he said: "O,—I wish I had another sickness!" Instead of less, unfortunately, he feels *more* and more the things that Baoth & Honoria can do, without thinking or asking. It is cruelly hard for him,—and there remains no choice for us. We have, I am afraid, become identified for him with constant, constant deprivation.

On leaving I had such need of mouthing to myself the old-fashioned wrath that I felt about hard-hearted women, or girls rather, (I intend reserving the word "women" from now on more jealously than heretofore),—that I found myself asking the library steward on the suffocatingly decorated "Bremen" or was it the "Europa,"—if there was aboard a copy of Shakespeare's Tragedies. There was,—all bound in chaste, impersonal khaki canvas. And so I fumed and boiled up and down the deck for five days, unloading at every step such as

> "To shake all cares and business from our age
> Conferring them on younger strengths, while we
> Unburthen'd crawl toward death."
> or
> "He cannot be such a monster—
> To his father who tenderly and entirely loves him."
> and
> "We have seen the best of our time: machinations, hollowness,
> treachery, and all ruinous disorders, follow us disquietly to
> our graves."

> "And the noble and true-hearted Kent banished! His offense
> honesty!"

> "Ingratitude, thou marble-hearted fiend,
> More hideous when thou show'st thee in a child
> Than the sea-monster!"

"Life and Death! I am ashamed
That thou has power to shake my manhood thus,
That these hot tears which break from me perforce
Should make thee worth them."

"This milky gentleness—
I will forget my nature. So kind a father!"

"Monster ingratitude!"

"Maybe he is not well: Infirmity doth still neglect all
office whereto
Our health is bound; we are not ourselves
When nature, being oppressed, commands the mind
To suffer with the body."

"O me, my heart, my rising heart,—but down!"

"—and thou, all-shaking thunder,
Smite flat the thick rotundity o' the world!"

"Is it the fashion, that discarded fathers
Should have thus little mercy on their flesh?
Judicious punishment! T'was this flesh begot
Those pelican daughters."

"THEN LET THEM ANATOMIZE REGAN; SEE WHAT BREEDS
ABOUT HER HEART. IS THERE ANY CAUSE IN NATURE THAT
MAKES
THESE HARD HEARTS?"

A., We think a great deal of our god-child [Peter MacLeish] and are so
proud of him. Blow in his neck for me. It smelt so nice, his neck. Love to my
Mimosa girl [Mary MacLeish] too.

G.

LC

61

*Not long after arriving back in Switzerland following his father's fu-
neral, Gerald Murphy learned that his mother had taken ill and would
probably not recover. She died on 25 April 1932, but Gerald did not
make the return trip home.*

29. GERALD MURPHY TO ARCHIBALD MACLEISH
Montana-Vermala, 4 February 1932

Of a sudden it's ↗ fev. 4, '32
I know of nothing that has happened to us that has shaken us as deeply as your
cable. Sara said: "*Only* Archie could have thought of that." What a rare
occurrence,—an act, one, so personal, so peculiar that it waits a life-time to
come into being,—and stands afterwards like a shining monument and forever. Everything else seems valueless beside such a one:—and suddenly you
see clearly that one of the reasons you lived was to have it happen to you.

Mother's mind failed before I could have got to her,—*had* I been able to
consider going. She has *no* lucid intervals at present. My letters were read to
her. She is not suffering. She may live for weeks, for months. It is sad that she
cannot die. She wanted to. But this life-in-death continues.

From my very grateful heart—thanks,—
and love to you both,

Gerald.

Sara & Honoria have gone to Antibes. The Baroness-instutrice (in the order
mentioned & Paris hotel—life did not work out & was ruinous. She (H.) goes
to Mlle Fontaine's school in Cannes. Baoth in [boarding school in] Germany
until Mch. 18. Patrick & I here. P. preparing for the home-stretch. Very attractive, very intelligent,—but a being apart, I fear,—or do I,—fear? "Weather
Bird" is a thing of great solid beauty says S. Antibes a paradise: mandarines,
lemons, oranges, camelias, anemones, mimosa, & lunch on the terrasse. Some
day we'll all be together again. G.

No ski-ing *at all*. Cloudless, windless, days—sun melting,—above ice,—
gleaming ice. Have been up only twice,—now I go *without* skis, climbing.
LC

*Patrick Murphy left for America with his nurse in May, and the family
followed a few weeks later. In August, they would travel west to spend
three weeks with the Hemingways at the Nordquist ranch.*

30. GERALD MURPHY TO ARCHIBALD MACLEISH
Nordquist Ranch, Wyoming, 8 September 1932

Archie:—

All this is rumination: (possibly maundering!)

I wonder if the habitation of a vast and a rich territory might not tend to blunt rather than sharpen the perceptions, the sensibilities of its inhabitants. I wonder.

For I suspect that just as the vastness of our industry and amassed fortunes in the East seems to have dulled a great portion of our people spiritually,—so here in the West the reaction of the people to their vast and spectacular Natural surroundings and resources is not as fine as one would expect,—not as fine, by far as that of the Indian (represented as it is now by wretched popularized versions of his once pure arts).

What I probably mean is that this country, overpowering in scale and awe-inspiring in formation, does not seem to have inspired us with the awe (even unsuperstitious) that it did the native Indians. Its scale is felt in distances and its fantastic variety as freakishness,—or seems to be,—for this is rumination.

Beef is plentiful—men ride out in the morning and round in the cows from the hills nearby which are slaughtered,—all most conveniently. But the beef is tasteless, without variety,—and indifferently cooked,—and never remarked as being either better or worse beef than the beef before.

The lakes and streams are stiff with trout (weighing up to two pounds and more),—thirty are caught in a day, one drools in anticipation of the evening meal after a long ride,—and one is disappointed. The trout are adequately and not at all badly cooked,—but somehow they have neutralized. They have not been done respectfully,—or as individuals, specimens, cases, examples of trout, cooked as such with feeling and understanding. For trout *should* be regarded as such and not as beef,—which is another very different thing, fortunately. A sense of the "essential" (not even the "quintessential") is lacking.

The horses are numerous, but there is little choice among them although they have been bred and broken here on the ranch. One recognizes that they possess the various elements that should go to make a good horse—or at least some better among others—but not so, they are introduced to you as possessing in *lesser* degree certain bad traits. None of them seems to approach a positive perfection—none of them has been singled out and directed towards this perfection. I ride a gelding that has thoroughbred blood and which has sired four colts here, all excellent material,—one of the colts was broken last year and given by Ernest to Pauline ceremoniously,—but he is only a good horse, and most indifferent to ride. Nothing has been demanded of him.

I do not want to appear to you to be a 45 year old Boy-Exquisite, with the jaded palate of a Lucullus seeking the lost sensations,—but I have known good beef here in this country, I have eaten at Absinthe House in New Orleans, I have breakfasted at Glen Castle outside of Louisville on beaten-biscuit and all that comes after (to the Yale Glee Club), I am still haunted by our shad-roe and cod-fish balls in Boston on Sunday morning as a boy; I remember still the taste of Mallards and Canada Geese which I helped the dogs retrieve on Barnegat Bay years, years back; I know of two women who set the alarm at night and went down from their warm beds to keep devoted vigil during twenty four hours over doughnut batter. Where has all this gone out of our land? Why has not this vast country with its plenitude and its peace brought forth some such thing?

For it is sad to say but I do recall trout that we ate not many years ago au Moulin des Rouats, the ham and bread at Vézelay approached perfection, the cheese (unknown to us) in the open field beside a stream at the foot of the Val de Mercy was a benediction; I ate some plums in Menton which broke the heart of envy, I once heard you exclaim for a running twenty minutes at the sustained taste of four different coddled eggs which you were eating; we have had omelets which we could recall together,—I could eat one now,—or some of the turkey we had at Conway *that* Thanksgiving.

At Christmas Vacation we are going to open your house at Conway and Sara and Ada are going to cook a goose with its accessories and I am bringing the choicest wines and liqueurs of the 1916 Manhattan Club cellar which I have inherited from Father,—and the shot will be heard 'round the world. Our names will be found engraved on the goose's heart. Enough of these herds of cattle. I want a side of beef for myself and my friends, I want to hear Ada ask the sweet potatoes whether they prefer to be cooked with pine-apple or a marshmallow crust, I want to see Sara make a giblet-sauce out of the parts which are condemned out here: The wine it is not fair to speak of.

Ernest is going to Cody to meet a friend [Charles Thompson] from Key West and they are being given the run of a preserve containing five hundred pheasant. If they do not taste good I shall not say so,—but I shall be a very saddened person.

* * * * *

One thing is so sure,—and O how sure it is!:—Ernest's affection for you, Ernest's admiration of you, Ernest's great respect for your work; Ernest's great affection for you both, Ernest and Pauline's great admiration and affection for Ada. They adore you from the ground up,—the pair of you. It's a privilege to hear them speak of you. We love being by,—after the miserable parcelling of feelings that goes on among people in New York.

I think that I have discovered something about Ernest which bears upon your disappointment at one moment at Key West: he is never difficult with the people he does not like, the people he does not take seriously. He has crossed swords with Sara and Ada, with you, with Dorothy (whom he likes), with Dos. But he will never do it with me, there has been no real issue with Don or with Scott whom he no longer respects. For in spite of his love of approval there is the Sanctum to which he has admitted a few. This has grown on him,—he is indifferent to a great many more people than formerly,—to the point of open inattention, which is no longer as hurting as it used to be. I find him more mellowed, amenable and far more charitable and philosophical than before,—more patient also. But the line has been drawn very definitely between the people whom he admits to his life and those he does not. I have never felt for a moment a claim to his affection and do not receive it (and rightly,—we are of opposing worlds). Sara does and receives it unstinted. He is fast taking on the protective qualities which are necessary to a working artist,—and he *is* of the race.

* * * * *

It is superb here,—the country, I mean. Ernest and Pauline have done everything to make it ideal for us. They go Mountain Sheep hunting for two weeks on the 12th, we are motoring through the Park to Cody, Denver and Colo. Springs. on the 16th, a day after school (or so) we shall return East. Come down once again to E.H. [East Hampton] and we'll bathe in the October sea. Much, much love to you both, very dear people,

Gerald

The children adore it here. Baoth is as if just off the Reservation and Honoria is fast becoming a horse,—it's Paradise for them, and Ernest has been an angel about arranging their lives,

G.

LC

PART TWO

1933–1940

The Sunlight
of the Winter Streets

[The 1920s] was an easy, quick, adventurous age, good to be young in;
and yet on coming out of it one felt a sense of relief, as on coming out of a
room too full of talk and people into the sunlight of the winter streets.
—MALCOLM COWLEY, *Exile's Return*

Following their summer visit with the Hemingways in Montana, the Murphys returned to New York. Because of Patrick's health, the children's schooling, and the Mark Cross company, they had declared America their home. This did not prevent them, however, from traveling often, making at least one and sometimes as many a three trips a year to Europe. When they were not sailing the ocean for Europe, they were often cruising the Mediterranean aboard their *Weatherbird*, which they had decided to build while Patrick was ill at Montana-Vermala. The boat would be "a composite of all that Sara found the *Honoria* not to be," Murphy had told MacLeish in January 1931.

Shortly after the *Weatherbird* was completed, by early 1933, the MacLeishes joined the Murphys on board. "It is built like a fishing boat with all the money in the hull where it belongs and in the decks and only light wood painted partitions inside except that Sara has had comfortable beds put in and there is a bathtub but you can't use that because it takes too much water," MacLeish told Hemingway. "The only trouble is that with a crew of five you can't lift a finger and you just sit around and eat. But she sails fine and she is big enough to take anything and Vladimir much to my what do you call it was perfectly willing to go out in a Mistral and we did twice. His only trouble is that he keeps the motor going all the time to charge the battery because the frigidaire takes so much juice. Ada calls it a bateau à frigidaire."[1] Later that summer, as John Dos Passos was recovering from a bout with rheumatic fever, the Dos Passoses came aboard for a trip along the coast of Spain. Patrick was not well enough to join them that summer, but he was able to take short cruises during the next one.

Hemingway had also acquired his *Pilar* in early 1934, and the Murphys (but most often Sara) joined him for spring cruises thereafter off the Florida coast. The Hemingways had purchased and begun to renovate a home in Key West in 1931, and Hemingway increasingly acted on his love for boats and water and fishing. He had told Thorton Wilder as early as 1929 that "when you'd been out day after day . . . in a small boat with people you like and were black from the sun and never wore shoes or underwear and had champagne in the water butt covered over with a chunk of ice and a wet sack . . . when with only so long to live, why . . . come back to cafes and all the little sniveling shit of literary politics."[2]

That the Murphys (and, to varying degrees, their friends) had the means to travel and to maintain costly boats reinforces how right Fitzgerald was when he said that the rich are different. He realized that it had less to do with money than with an inevitable immunity to how most people live. Although John and Katy Dos Passos did not have much money during the 1930s (he made little off his writing), they did maintain, nonetheless, two homes on Cape Cod and they also traveled yearly (sometimes with the Murphys), renting homes and apartments and hotel rooms wherever they happened to stay. As Hemingway's books began to make money, he too traveled and lived well, although he continued to resent what he saw as the corrupting influences of money and of the monied. Fitzgerald made lots of money off his writing, which he spent in the process of moving from place to place and in his continued support of Zelda's care throughout the 1930s. If the Murphys maintained, correctly, that they were not wealthy (in the manner of J. P. Morgan, for example), they did live well, and they were also generous with their money. They gave it to friends but never in great amounts and usually to underwrite trips or rent or a child's education, as was the case with Scottie Fitzgerald. They also gave their friends regular gifts of records and clothes and household goods, especially to the more strapped Dos Passoses. They usually gave these gifts quietly, although it was hard to avoid, in the process, a certain paternalism. The extent to which the giving and accepting of money embarrassed Fitzgerald and angered Hemingway can be seen in Fitzgerald's last letters to Gerald Murphy and in Hemingway's posthumously-published *A Moveable Feast*.

Although Gerald's father had willed the company assets of roughly two million dollars to Gerald and Esther, he had turned over control of Mark Cross to his secretary, Lillian E. Ramsgate, who dissipated capital holdings drastically until she resigned in December 1934. Gerald took over the presidency with reluctance and worked to resolve the growing legal and economic difficulties. One of his first acts as president was to move the business to a new location at Fifty-second and Fifth Avenue.[3] As Gerald worked to reverse the company's decline, the family lived in various apartments in New York City. After John Dos Passos saw Gerald during the 1935 summer, he noted to Hemingway how Gerald "spends all his time on Mark Cross and the Fifth Avenue Association" which "gives him something to use his brains on—he's like he was years ago when he was painting—I certainly hope he sticks to it—there's nothing like economic pressure."[4]

Besides the economic pressures of these years, however, the Murphys experienced emotional pressures much more devastating in their aftereffects. Although the Murphys had money even with the Mark Cross company's economic strains, it could not protect them from the deaths of both their sons—Baoth in 1935 and Patrick in 1937. When Baoth died it seemed too cruel an irony. Everyone had feared the worst for Patrick, not Baoth. It was "fancy. *Fancy,*" Archibald MacLeish said, "There's no other word for it. They could have thought & thought for a million years & they wouldn't have been able to think of one like that."[5]

Baoth had returned to St. George's School in Rhode Island from his 1934 Christmas vacation when he contracted measles and was confined to the infirmary. Sara was in Key West at the time, where she was sharing a rented home near the Hemingways with John and Katy Dos Passos and Ada MacLeish. Gerald had remained in New York because of Mark Cross, and he kept Sara advised by way of letters and telegrams about both Patrick and Baoth. When Baoth's illness took a sudden and grim twist in late February (a double mastoid ear infection had developed into spinal meningitis), Gerald was summoned from New York and Sara was contacted in Key West. In the dead of night, Hemingway sped Sara and Ada on board the *Pilar* along the Keys, landing them on the Florida mainland to get a plane to Boston. For two weeks, the family kept a vigil by Baoth's bed at Massachusetts General Hospital, where on 17 March he died. James G. Vermillion, a master at St. George's School, saw Gerald slip quietly into the corridor outside of Baoth's room, and he remembered that Gerald, in that one tragic moment, remained as "contained and poised and gentle as ever, as if long-since steeled against the inevitable." The Murphys were two of the most "gracious and civilized persons" he had ever known, Vermillion told MacLeish later.[6]

MacLeish had been there too during part of the ordeal, and he recalled how Sara kept Baoth "alive for four hours sitting beside him saying Breathe Baoth! Breathe Baoth." The "poor kid" was "tortured with knives—wracked with agony," MacLeish told the Dos Passoses on 20 March, and he didn't know Sara, "but the will came through & he went on. Sara could not believe he was dead." MacLeish concluded that Sara "fights all her enemies in the gate. Once they break into the house she has no doors to close. She would like to lie in the gate facing them." Whereas Sara was "all of a heap," Gerald had been "superb but . . . really heart-broken."[7] When the Dos Passoses and the Hemingways, still in Florida, were notified of Baoth's death, they each wrote letters which acknowledged that nothing could be done—or said—to ease the Murphy's burden. All of the Murphys' friends tried, nonetheless, to give the Murphys emotional sustenance during the difficult weeks and months that followed.

Fitzgerald, like the Murphys' other friends, recognized the Murphys' irreplaceable loss when he wrote a poem which was only later found among his papers:

For BAOTH 2nd Stanza Poem

There was a flutter from the wings of God
And you lay dead
Your books were in your desk
I guess and some unfinished
Chaos in your head
Was dumped to nothing
By the great janitress
Of destinies.[8]

Fitzgerald went to see the Murphys shortly after Baoth's death, and MacLeish participated in a memorial service at St. George's School two months later. A tree and an octagonal bench around it were dedicated on a "clear open May morning." MacLeish read his poem "Words to Be Spoken," written "for Baoth Wiborg son of Gerald and Sara Murphy who died in New England in his sixteenth year and a tree was planted there."

O shallow ground
That over ledges
Shoulders the gentle year,

Tender O shallow
Ground your grass is
Sisterly touching us:

Your trees are still:
They stand at our side in the
Night lantern.

Sister O shallow
Ground you inherit
Death as we do.

Your year also—
The young face,
The voice—vanishes.

Sister O shallow
Ground
          let the silence of
Green be between us
And the green sound.[9]

Years later MacLeish would still recall his difficulty getting through the reading of the poem. "Ogden Nash, whom I had not met, was there that day—old St. George's boy. I broke down reading the poem. He came over—across the lawn—in complete silence and took my hand."[10]

As friends gathered around the Murphys, they were especially supportive of Patrick as well, writing him letters and sending him gifts, and also visiting him. Hemingway had some of his African animal trophies mounted for Patrick's room, and Alexander Woollcott aired for him a special segment of his "The Town Crier" radio show. This popular family weekly, which had debuted in 1934, incorporated Woollcott's folksy storytelling and literary readings along with music. He liked to play a "serenade" each week dedicated to a special person (often a celebrity and/or friend), and he prefaced the chosen song with a character sketch of the individual. The Hemingways and Dos Passoses huddled around their radio in Key West on the evening of 31 March hoping to catch snippets of the show in between static interference, but Patrick and the Murphys back in New York got a clearer reception. Honoria recalls how she and her parents gathered in Patrick's room, and at the end of the orchestral rendition of "Country Gardens," Woollcott said, "Good night, Patrick. I hope you're feeling better."[11]

The double tragedy of Baoth's death was that it coincided with the period of Patrick's worst relapse. The Murphys thought that they had beaten the disease when Patrick had been well enough to spend the 1934 summer with the family in Europe—at Villa America and cruising on the *Weatherbird*. "He seemed very well all summer," Sara wrote the Hemingways upon their return to America in September, "& we did everything the dr said to,—& now, at a routine (we thought) visit to the dr—he is discovered to have another patch on his other lung." Patrick entered Doctors Hospital where he had a fine view of the boats overlooking the East River. "It was about as cheerful there as any such setting could be," Honoria recalled. "He had his hobbies to work on— wood carving, painting, and stamp collecting. . . . I would visit him on weekends home from school. I was struck by how white and frail he looked. He was engulfed in pillows in a huge hospital bed, which he hardly ever left." The Murphys rented an apartment near Patrick at 439 East Fifty-first Street which also overlooked the river, and they sometimes took the Fall River Line boat which sailed between New York and Newport, Rhode Island, near Baoth's school.[12]

Following Baoth's death, and on into 1936, Patrick's disease steadily worsened, despite periods of slight remission. Sara and Gerald took him to Saranac Lake, New York, where the cool upstate climate and treatments at the Trudeau Institute might stem the disease. They had just settled for the 1935 summer at Steel Camp, a group of cottages which they had rented, when John Dos Passos came to visit. The Murphys were on "a handsome northwoods lake— somewhat trampled by Guggenheims and Untermeyers and speedboats," he wrote Hemingway, "but it has the advantage of being in the State Park so that it has less camps and possibly more bass and Whitefish than most such places." Dos Passos was struck by how "terribly small and thin" Patrick looked and by how "very thin and pretty and in better shape than [he'd] expected" Sara looked.[13] But Sara's outward ebullience belied her inner despair, as friends and Gerald increasingly came to recognize. Between 1935 and 1937, as the Murphys moved to different residences in and around Saranac (both summer "camps" and winter homes), Sara fought the loneliness, the cold, and the mounting strain associated with Patrick's illness and their extended stay at Saranac. After Baoth's death and as she struggled with Patrick during the last months of his life, she refused to believe in any of the sickness, and she willed into being a life which seemed better than it was. "It's a great world," she told Hemingway without a hint of sarcasm, and a day later, on 30 July 1936, Gerald wrote Fitzgerald. "She is gay,—energetic—but is not well," and "there is little one can do for her."

When the Dos Passoses came to visit that Christmas, they found things "pretty horrible." As John Dos Passos told Hemingway on 9 January 1937, "Gerald and Sara both behaving so well in their separate ways that it's heartbreaking."[14] Shortly after he received this letter, Hemingway came to New York to collaborate on the documentary film *Spain in Flames,* and he came to see the Murphys at Saranac. Honoria vividly remembers Hemingway's arrival and how he asked abruptly to see Patrick. She and her mother, with Hemingway, walked into Patrick's room. "It was late in the afternoon and getting dark, but I could see Ernest's face, and I had never seen him look so sad." He began to talk to Patrick, mainly about fishing, "but it was soon obvious that Ernest was having difficulty controlling his emotions." Later, in the hallway, Hemingway wept—openly: " 'He looks so sick,' he said. 'I can't stand seeing that boy look so sick.' "[15]

Hemingway stayed a couple of days before returning to New York, and many of these friends, including the MacLeishes and Alice Lee Myers, came to help out during Patrick's last days. On 29 January 1937 Gerald wrote Alexander Woollcott that "the days are like the tick of a clock." The next afternoon, Gerald and Sara telegrammed Scott Fitzgerald: "PATRICK DIED PEACEFULLY THIS MORNING LOVE SARA GERALD." "Fate can't have any more arrows in its quiver for you that will wound like these," Fitzgerald wrote the next evening. The telegram had made him sad the "whole afternoon" as he thought of Gerald and Sara "and the past and the happy times" they once had. "The golden bowl is broken," Fitzgerald concluded.

In many respects, as Fitzgerald wrote this letter, he was also talking about himself. Hemingway resented it when Fitzgerald tried to draw this parallel, for the Murphys' troubles might be compared to Napoleon's retreat from Moscow, he told Sara, "from which Scott would have deserted during the first week." [16] Nonetheless, the fact remains that Fitzgerald's life continued a downward course throughout the 1930s, after he and Zelda had returned to America. Many of his friends, including Dos Passos, felt that he had changed noticeably by 1933, a decline which continued into the decade. Andrew Turnbull noted how his "light-heartedness" became "replaced by a haunted sense of hope lost and time run out." [17]

Although *Tender Is the Night* finally saw print in 1934, it brought few remunerations, either financial or critical, and Fitzgerald came to believe he could no longer write. When he visited John Dos Passos, who had entered the Johns Hopkins hospital in spring 1933 to receive treatment for his rheumatic fever, Fitzgerald would sit "bleakly fidgeting" as Dos Passos tried to encourage him about his life and his writing. "Actually Scott was meeting adversity with a consistency of purpose that I found admirable," Dos Passos admitted. "He was trying to raise Scottie, to do the best thing possible for Zelda, to handle his drinking and to keep a flow of stories into the magazines to raise the enormous sums Zelda's illness cost. At the same time he was determined to continue writing firstrate novels. With age and experience his literary standards were rising. I never admired a man more." [18]

In order to come to terms with himself and with life, Fitzgerald wrote three personal essays for *Esquire* entitled "The Crack-Up" (February 1936), "Handle with Care" (March 1936), and "Pasting It Together" (April 1936). Although Fitzgerald's contemporaries questioned his professional judgment in publicly baring his soul, the essays are masterpieces of self-analysis as well as provocative reminders, as Fitzgerald saw it, that only the remembered past held beauty and promise. Gerald Murphy shared Fitzgerald's sense of loss about the past, and about life's tarnished promises, just as he also admired Fitzgerald's head-on confrontation with the "dark night of the soul." He agreed that one could overcome emotional bankruptcy only by regarding it dispassionately and intellectually. It was Sara who disagreed completely with what she saw as Fitzgerald's naiveté. "Do you *really* mean to say you honestly thought 'life was something you dominated if you were any good—'?," she wrote on 3 April. "Even if you meant your *own* life it is arrogant enough,—but life!"

As Sara's own emotional resistance wore thin, she felt deepening alliance with Zelda Fitzgerald and defended her against such detractors as Hemingway, who believed that Zelda had ruined Scott. Gerald would recognize and say years later (after Zelda's death in 1948), that Zelda and Sara were very much alike, especially in their retreat inward; and as Gerald felt increasing frustration in the face of Sara's inner turmoil, he would turn to Fitzgerald for help. He confessed on 6 July 1936 that "even her loneliness I cannot reach." He hoped that Fitzgerald might have some answers.

Ironically, Fitzgerald had been the one to ask the questions during the 1920s. In fact, he earned a reputation for his questions which some friends felt were inappropriately personal and curiously lacking in sincerity. Dos Passos had found these persistent questions "silly" and then began to feel hounded by the end of the decade.[19] Some friends believed that Fitzgerald designed his questions to generate his literary material, and Donald Stewart, for one, resented the way Fitzgerald would watch him, "with that green-eyed Mona Lisa smile, as though he were taking notes." "It was that note-taking watchfulness of his," said Stewart, "that kept me from ever feeling that he was really a friend."[20] MacLeish saw the deeper implications of Fitzgerald's questions when he decided these questions were prompted not because Fitzgerald "thought the world was made of answers, but because *that* world, he thought, must *know* the answers—even to the question he could never bring himself to ask."[21] As Fitzgerald toward the end of the decade increasingly came to face that question—when it was three o'clock in the morning and always the dark night of the soul, he reached out to Gerald, who gave both financial and psychological support and proved himself to be Fitzgerald's "friend through every dark time."

The letters between Fitzgerald and Murphy during 1939 and 1940 are unusually sensitive and candid as now Gerald, rather than Sara, admonished Scott for his unthinking disregard for others' feelings. Murphy became particularly irritated when Fitzgerald detailed his physical ailments (especially his fears about tuberculosis), as if he had a corner on illness. After one of Fitzgerald's graphic accounts "about the awful lapses and sudden reverses and apparent cures and thorough poisoning effect of lung trouble," Gerald responded testily (26 August 1940): "Don't think me without heart:—but just as you—so have I—seen much illness around me." Sometimes he tried to make light of Fitzgerald's latest accounts of his physical failings, recognizing perhaps that the most dangerous aspect of any illness is one's own preoccupation with it.

Certainly, as the Murphys experienced most directly, physical illness did play a strong role in the lives of these correspondents. Besides the tragic diseases of Baoth and Patrick, and also Zelda, both Gerald and Sara suffered physical ills which the emotional stress related to their sons' illnesses may have exacerbated. Gerald suffered from persistent throat infections leading to a tonsillectomy in July 1936; and Sara suffered from nerve-related muscle spasms and also stomach troubles which resulted in a gall bladder operation in the spring of 1939. Both the Murphys were concerned, perhaps to excess, with infections. Sara, in particular, took elaborate precautions to avoid her family's exposure to germs. John and Katy Dos Passos also suffered persistent physical problems during the 1930s. John Dos Passos's recurrences of rheumatic fever sometimes curtailed his writing and required that he remain in warm climates. Katy Dos Passos's chronic viral and gynecologic difficulties landed her in hospitals from Baltimore to Boston for tests and treatment. Regarding all of this sickness, which had already begun to take its toll by late 1934, Katy would write to Sara (27 November 1934): "We've been in a very dreary phase, I must admit, but I think we're all coming out of it now."

In a strange way, these correspondents associated some of this physical illness during the 1930s with America, and particularly with California, where Patrick Murphy had been infected with tuberculosis. When John Dos Passos went to Hollywood in the 1934 summer to work on film scripts, he was soon confined to bed with his rheumatic fever. He wrote Hemingway on 27 July to say that, although he had felt sick flying over, "the look of this lousy suburb (Hollywood)" had given him "the sick" even more.[22] In the late 1930s Fitzgerald also went to Hollywood, where he suffered debilitating fevers and where, in 1940, he died. He told Gerald on 14 September 1940 that his "great dreams" about California were "shattered" and that it was "such a slack soft place—even its pleasure lacking the fierceness or excitement of Provence—that withdrawal is practically a condition of safety." The consensus among those in the group traveling between the east coast and Hollywood during the 1930s seemed to be that while California may have offered the shimmering promise which the French Riviera had embodied, it had betrayed them in the end.

In order to deal with all of life's compromises—its sickness both of body and spirit—the Murphys and their friends variously sought some kind of faith. They looked to Catholicism, the Christian Science Church, the power of positive thinking, even to a faith in life itself—what Archibald MacLeish would call a belief in suffering which is redemptive. Pauline Hemingway, a Catholic, saw no need to be refined by suffering, as she told Sara upon the death of Patrick Murphy. Yet Pauline had lit a candle for Patrick and she was praying for him, too. Gerald Murphy had told Hemingway back on 14 July 1926 that the Spanish men who lived "somewhere between art and life" were "a religion for which I could have been trained." By 1936, after his first son's death, he proclaimed himself "an ascetic without belief" and vowed "not to take life at *its own* tragical value." As he told Fitzgerald around August of 1936 he would no longer read magazines and newspapers, the stuff of the real world, preferring to find in books that "distant region" midway between art and life where he could "enjoy living." There "I find my mind freed." When Sara Murphy flirted with the Christian Science Church during this same period, she suggested that Fitzgerald should try it also. He told Sara on 30 March 1936: I "finally decided to try it but the practitioner I hit on wanted to begin with 'absent treatments,' which seemed about as effectual to me as the candles my mother keeps constantly burning to bring me back to Holy Church—so I abandoned it."

Which is what most of the group ultimately did when it came to organized religion. As for Sara, she would go so far as to raise her fist defiantly in the face of a heartless God. Directly following Baoth's funeral service at St. Bartholomew's in New York, she ran from the church and down Park Avenue. When Archie MacLeish "caught up with her, she looked up in the sky and cursed God."23 At Patrick's "bleak, blank memorial service in an empty New York Church" two years later, MacLeish said that "the silences were like the confrontation with the Voice out of the Whirlwind in the Book of Job."24 As for Fitzgerald, the Bishop would not allow his burial in the family Catholic cemetary in Rockville, Maryland, since he had died a "non-believer." Instead he was buried in the Union Cemetary nearby. The funeral was a simple, secular affair in an airless funeral parlor, and about twenty or thirty attended in all, including Gerald and Sara Murphy.25

Directly following Fitzgerald's death, Hemingway told Sara: "No one could ever help Scott but you and Gerald did more than anyone." Fitzgerald, to a great extent, had agreed, and had told Gerald on 11 March 1938, "As a friend, you have never failed me." By the time of his death, he believed that most of his friends had abandoned him, seeing him as a drunken failure, a washed-up artist. When Hemingway and John Peale Bishop made derogatory remarks in print, Fitzgerald was thoroughly angered. Even his literary agent, Harold Ober, felt him a poor credit risk and refused to forward any loans. In a letter to Max Perkins in May 1940, Fitzgerald stated unequivocally that, "You (and one other man, Gerald Murphy) have been a friend through every dark time in these five years. It's funny what a friend is—Ernest's crack in *The Snows*, poor John Bishop's article in the Virginia Quarterly (a nice return for ten years of trying to set him up in a literary way) and Harold's sudden desertion at the wrong time, have made them something less than friends. Once I believed in friendship, believed I *could* (if I didn't always) make people happy and it was more fun than anything. Now even that seems like a vaudevillian's cheap dream of heaven, a vast minstrel show in which one is the perpetual Bones."26

If Fitzgerald believed by the time of his death that Hemingway had criticized and then abandoned him, the other friends from this group also felt estranged from Hemingway by the end of the decade. MacLeish's relationship with him had grown tense as early as 1932, when they had "been together too long out in the Gulf Stream, fishing." MacLeish admitted later that "it was a childish business"—a "simple conflict of overexposure," but "anything we said to each other infuriated us." MacLeish came to realize that such quarrels with Hemingway seemed inevitable, and their "terrific quarrel" in "about '33 or '34" he attributed to a mutual touchiness and the fact that "fame was not sitting well with Ernest." "He was fed up with the world and I was fed up with him." MacLeish would speak for most of the others when he declared later that Hemingway was a "wonderful" but nonetheless "impossible friend."[27]

John Dos Passos felt the same, particularly when he and Hemingway quarreled over the Spanish Civil War. Dos Passos had become angered at what he saw as Hemingway's growing conceit and concomitant insensitivity toward his friends. He and Katy had tried to keep Hemingway "kidded down to size" during their visits together in Key West, but bitter confrontations over Spain during 1937 made these efforts seem futile. When Dos Passos sought to understand why the Communists had executed his friend José Robles, a longtime Loyalist supporter, Hemingway admonished him to accept the Communists' assessment that Robles had been a Fascist spy and supposedly told him that "if he did not clear out, there would be trouble." As a result, Dos Passos felt that Hemingway had betrayed him.[28] Although Hemingway never formally renounced ties with Dos Passos, or any of the others, occasionally communicating with them until his death in 1961, the relationships were never quite the same once Fitzgerald had died and World War II had begun. In late 1940, Hemingway divorced Pauline and married Martha Gellhorn, and they established their residence at Finca Vigía in Havana, Cuba.

These correspondents were concerned about the impending war in Europe during the late 1930s but seldom directly acknowledged it. As Pauline told Sara on 8 July 1937, the war was "always there like a dirty backdrop." In her 8 October 1938 letter to Sara, Katy Dos Passos drew a parallel between the political scene in Europe and the storm which had hit the east coast and demolished the Murphys' East Hampton garden as well as uprooting decades-old trees in the town. "Do you think these convulsions of nature are accompanying political disturbances like they used to in Sartonius," she asked. "It's funny we have a hurricane just while Hitler is starting to march." A few days before the storm devastated it, Gerald had described their home, Swan Cove, as "a Paradise of flowers, trees, places to lunch outside: like some place in a distant land."

Prior to war, and once it seemed inevitable, Fitzgerald had almost defied it even as he acknowledged it, sending his daughter Scottie over in 1938 so that she could see Europe "as it was," before it was too late. Although Fitzgerald had wished to go also, "with the sort of wishing that is remote and academic," he had told Gerald on 11 March 1938 that he knew there was no turning back anymore. "I don't care much where I am any more, nor expect very much from places," he concluded. When Scottie returned from Europe, she sailed with the Murphys; and Zelda was momentarily well enough to meet them at the dock in New York. Seeing Gerald and Sara again after eight years, and hearing Scottie's tales of Europe, saddened Zelda. It was too vivid a reminder of her wasted youth and past happiness, both of which she associated with the Murphys and with France.

"Do you suppose they still cook automobiles at Antibes, and still sip the twilight at Kaux," Zelda asked Scott in a letter to him that fall. "And I wonder if Paris is pink in the late sun and latent with happiness already had." Zelda felt strongly the passage of time—another summer "half gone, and maybe there'll never be anymore sun-burns and high hot moons." She also recognized that somehow the Murphys had been able to survive under personal hardships whereas the Fitzgeralds had not, a phenomenon which Zelda attributed to the Murphys' "remunerative relationship." The fact that they remained "very engaging" and that "age and the ages" had left them "untroubled and, perhaps, as impervious as possible" caused Zelda some resentment, almost as if she blamed the Murphys for introducing her and Scott to an elegant lifestyle without also providing them with the personal resources to sustain it. "If they knew how much of other peoples orientations that they had influenced, they would less resent any challenge to their own," Zelda concluded.[29]

In 1939, Sara and Honoria had returned again to Europe. As they cruised on the *Weatherbird* and revisited all the old haunts in Paris throughout the summer, Gerald Murphy and most of the Murphys' friends were back in New York, marvelling over the New York World's Fair on their many visits there together and swimming off the Atlantic coast as the summer grew oppressively hotter. On the other side of the Atlantic, the world was quickly closing in, effectively shutting off Europe. Gerald waited anxiously back home to hear about the safe return passage of Sara and Honoria and also Richard Myers, who was there with them trying to negotiate a quick exit. "What days!" Myers wrote on 27 August 1939. "We have been living in a state of tension that is a definite test of nerves. Rumors fly thick and fast—planes fly over Paris, soldiers go off to their posts—and every day somebody you know is missing—and you know they have left for their regiment. . . . Last night we spent in a darkened Paris—and it brought back memories of the night Alice Lee and I arrived in Paris on Nov. 10th 1918—only this time it seemed more poignant, for then we were used to war—and now the mere thought of it nauseates most sensible people."

When Gerald had sailed back to America from a visit to Europe in 1937, he wrote on September 9 from on board ship to Sara, who had stayed in Europe longer: "For the first time I feel that I do not know what is ahead of me in America. There's a strange impermanence about it . . . and all thro' the world if one reads the papers. I'd like once to be long enough in a place to see hay around the house taken in, fruit and vegetables grow and pumpkins and apples ripen. Not to speak of flowers." The Murphys and their correspondents seemed to find permanence in America finally, but only after war had been declared and enacted in Europe, putting to rest their unspoken belief that it might still be possible to return to that more idyllic time they had known in France in the 1920s.

Gerald had been plagued with a serious throat ailment when he wrote Dos Passos, who would himself enter the hospital with a recurrence of rheumatic fever shortly after receiving Gerald's letter. Katy had also been suffering a bad throat which led to a tonsillectomy that April. Both the Dos Passoses had spent most of the fall of 1932 and early 1933 in Provincetown, where they had a home at 571 Commercial Street. From there they took some short trips throughout New England, as Dos Passos was also thinking about the publication of Three Plays: The Garbage Man: Airways, Inc.: *and* Fortune Heights. *He and Gerald may have talked about producing one of these works, although nothing seems to have come of the project.*

31. GERALD MURPHY to JOHN DOS PASSOS, Bedford Village, New York, 9 March 1933

Dear Dos:—

I am at home again,—rather rickety and looking too much like the Phantom of Crestwood for Sara's comfort, I think.

Thank you a lot for your very cheerful cards of inquiry. It was good to get them, believe me,—and what superb houses at Wiscasset. One forgets they still stand. They make Radio City look silly— and the trees around them!

Such a nice letter came last night from Katy. How sweet of her to write it! Is *her* throat all right? I suppose it's those wretched tonsils causing such things. Your country sounds beautiful,—from Katy's letter. And how I know that Maine, too: the Saco, Biddeford and Kennebunk of thirty five years ago. There were Indian encampments,—they taught me how and where to find sweet-grass and make baskets. The smell of a sweet-grass basket at the notions-counter to-day hurls the whole thing back at me.

I am deep in the play and terribly excited. Gosh it would be fun to do. I can see it. I'll write you about it.

Should you have occasion to come back to NYC. Stay with us. We'll leave you to your own plans and a Family ticket will bring you both in and out as many times as you want to go. At least make it your head-quarters. We're here until the 4th May,—when we cut for Antibes for 2 months.

There will arrive chez vous soon, I hope, by some devious banking route the sum of three hundred dollars, which is a chip of a little legacy that mother left me and which I'd like you to use for something you shouldn't. I tell you this for the reason that the transaction was started before this holiday-making and interrupted. It may now come to you in the form of wheat or Kleenex (scrip), and I don't want you to be startled.

I am forwarding also a mess of records for which I should prefer not to be held responsible. Should you not like them, just stand on the corner of Commercial and hand one to each passer-by until they are disposed of. I'm relieved that the Phonograph is going.

What a ridiculous and dreary city New York has become! No place to meet your friends. No place to go. No place to eat. It's *all* as silly as Radio City.

Much love to you both and many many thanks from the heart for being so thoughtful when I was low. It meant a lot. I'd never been sick before and now I know. Sara joins me.

Gerald

UVA

The Murphys sailed in May for Antibes, and the Dos Passoses followed "in great style" a few weeks later on tickets the Murphys had purchased for them. The Dos Passoses spent June and July with the Murphys at Villa America and cruising on the Weatherbird, *including a trip down the coast of Spain. By August, the Dos Passoses were in Madrid, as were the Hemingways—on the first leg of an extensive African safari. They would not return to Key West until the following April. En route home, they saw the Murphys in New York and also Fitzgerald, there to celebrate the publication of* Tender Is the Night. *Shortly after the Hemingways arrived back in Key West, Sara Murphy came to visit, along with*

Ada MacLeish. They shared a rented home with the Dos Passoses on Waddell Street, which led to Sara and Ada's nickname thereafter—the "Waddell Girls." The Dos Passoses remained in Florida throughout the spring, and John Dos Passos would return to Provincetown after joining Hemingway in Havana for the May Day celebration and some fishing. Gerald had remained in New York to oversee critical changes at Mark Cross.

32. ERNEST HEMINGWAY to GERALD MURPHY, Key West, 27 April 1934

Dear Gerald:—

I am afraid this is not as much as I owe you so will you please let me know? I lost the ticket envelopes so am going on a basis of $60 tickets—$5.00 (something at the station that I don't remember about but believe it was $5.00) plus $15.00 for the brief-case—I believe it was $5.00 to Alvin you advanced when there was no change for a $20.00 but then there was probably something else so will you let me know—also about the briefcase—It was probably more—

It was lovely having Sara here but we missed you very much. You would like it I think. It is a good ocean—not as old as some and very rich in thoughtless fish everything badly organized and chasing everything else like in the early days—we eating them in the end. You would have a good time on it—we had no decent weather—But tried to get something out of what there was. With good weather its hard to believe how fine it can be.

Scotts book, I'm sorry, is not good—but then I've never read these great books by Scott that he has written—Its necessary to be intelligent to write prose after 30 but then when you get intelligent I suppose a thing has to be damned important before you care about writing about it—There's been too bloody much flashy writing—There is almost no true writing and people do not like to read it—

Poor Scott, though—Poor Scott—

So long Deáu Deáu

Thank you for letting Sara come down—

Good luck,

Ernest

Thanks ever so much for sending Uncle Gus the brief case.
HMD

33. ERNEST HEMINGWAY to SARA MURPHY,
Key West, 27 April 1934

Dearest Sara:

I love you very much, Madam, not like in Scott's Christmas tree ornament novels but the way it is on boats where Scott would be sea-sick. And don't ever let them humiliate you because we are the old indestructible bastards of the world Unite you have nothing to lose but the next grouper.

It was so fine to have you and Ada here and we missed you like the devil. Dont let's go so long without all seeing each other again. It's not worth it. We really do something against the world when around together and the world is always trying to do all these things to us all when we are apart.

Am working fine now—But I would rather have a good life than be a bloody great writer—(who says he's a b.g.w. Nobody) Have written *plenty* and will write *plenty* more. And I will be as good as I know and I'll know better all the time. But every day is a day and its *my* lousy life—not posterities. Oh well. Hell. Anyway goodbye and thank you very much for coming down. We wish you were still here.

Love from Papa—

Ernest

Pauline will be writing. She is housing today.
Am good friends with Dos—Stopped being mean—we are going to Havana
    together next week.
Write if you get time.
Oh yes. Sidney is Sidney Franklin
    1538 East 24th Street
    Brooklyn
    Nightingale 4-1759
HMD

34. PAULINE HEMINGWAY to SARA MURPHY,
Key West [17 May 1934]

Dear Sara—

I have read your letter to friends, acquaintances at the dock, important mercantile gentlemen, and I am afraid perfect and abject strangers. There *are* people who are saying I'm becoming a public nousance like my peacocks.

Those people, however, are not among the better element or fish lovers. Mrs. Murphy, you have writen an aspiring epic.

We miss you and your friend [Ada MacLeish] very much and I have forgotten the name of your tax man which somehow seems to make the break with the time you were here more complete. It's like another age now where nothing very much seems to happen or get done. I look back on buckets of lime juice and dozens of chocolate covered cup cakes and corn bread like Helen of Troy and Hindoooo and you and Ada and Ernest swaying the width of the living room, drunken laughter making the-what-is-it ring. And all those other heroic things. Now I spend the time sewing on buttons and seeing that baracudas are put around the right palms. Needless to say (again) I notice the change.

The presents from the Waddell girls are too lovely. Looks like, Jimmie says, Mrs. Hemingway, they wouldn't a called it beetle ware—he's picked his weight in beetles lately. We took the dishes up to Miami to meet the boat and they fit great and we had a most delicious chowder that Bra made.[1] It seems he can cook like an angel but try to get him to often. I think this was a sort of tribute to the Butler. *And* the super thermos. There's something that represents luxury and high standards. I feel just the way Bra does & Ernest takes it every time he goes out—to keep the fish hooks at an even and attractive temperature I think. Thank you for these beautiful things.

About Hueve.[2] I'm not just unreliable, but I'm pretty sure he's on the Pacific Stops now. He had a Hollywood engagement, and I didn't know just where to write and besides I think it would be better to write to New York when he's there. Why dont you call Vanity Fair and ask about him. I'm pretty sure he'd like to do the children and I remember talking about you to him on the boat and he seemed to have heard a lot about you and if he is in N.Y. and you still want me to write him *leave me know* and I could send him a night letter or something. I have a very vivid recollection of letters addressed to absentees at both Vogue and Vanity Fair getting kicked about and to death with never a word to either owner. Yours to oblige.

Mr. H. is like a wild thing with his boat.[3] I see him at ten minute intervals, hours apart and from notes on doors saying why he cant get home until 3

1. Bra Saunders, a professional fishing guide based in Key West, often accompanied Hemingway on his fishing expeditions in the Gulf.

2. Hueve was probably an illustrator who also did portraits. Nothing seems to have come of the project to "do" the Murphy children.

3. Hemingway had ordered *Pilar* when he arrived in New York that spring. It arrived as promised within roughly a month's time and fit Hemingway's specifications, including bunk space for six to eight people.

instead of 12:30. Wish you were here to fish. Out in the Gulf yesterday they saw a lot of sail fish and got several strikes.

> Much love to you and your unbelievable
> Dow Dow   From Ernest too
> From your old friend in the backwater

> Pauline

Even Patrick [Hemingway] says that was a nice time when Mrs Murphy was here and we got presents everyday, wasn't it mother? You might mention this to Dow Dow. Hope you had a nice Mother's Day

HMD

Zelda Fitzgerald suffered a relapse in early 1934 and had to be taken to Craig House in upstate New York. When she had not improved by May, Fitzgerald brought her back to the Sheppard and Enoch Pratt Hospital outside of Baltimore, where the Fitzgeralds had been renting a row house. Fitzgerald continued to live there during Zelda's roughly two-year stay at Sheppard-Pratt, and from this location he sometimes commuted to New York. He often tried to see Gerald and Sara, although he occasionally wore out his welcome. Internal evidence places this undated letter in the later part of May 1934 when Dos Passos had stopped to see the Fitzgeralds in Baltimore and then the Murphys in New York en route to Provincetown. He had left Key West directly following his May Day trip to Havana with Hemingway, Katy having preceding him north. When Dos Passos stopped to see the Fitzgeralds in Baltimore, Zelda must have just returned from Craig House in New York; and although she seemed "so well" to Dos Passos, her condition was often deceptive to the outside viewer because of periodic moments of relative stability.

35. SARA MURPHY to F. SCOTT FITZGERALD, New York [c. May 1934]

Dear Scott,—

We were sorry not to see you again—but it seemed, under the circumstances better not to—

Please don't think that Zelda's condition is not very near to our hearts,— (& we hope & *pray* it is & will not be as serious as you seemed to think)—and that all your misfortunes are not, in part, ours too—But at times it seems best, for the very sake of our affection for you,—not to let your manners (let us call it)—throw it off its equilibrium—even momentarily—We have no doubt of the loyalty of your affections (& we *hope* you haven't of ours)—but consideration for other people's feelings, opinions or even time is *Completely* left out of your makeup—I have always told you you haven't the faintest idea what anybody else but yourself is like—& have never (yet) seen the slightest reason for changing this opinion, "half-baked" as you consider it! You don't even know what Zelda or Scottie are like—in spite of your love for them. It seemed to us the other night (Gerald too)—that all you thought and felt about them was in terms of *yourself*—The same holds good of your feelings for your friends—in lesser degree;—why,—for instance *should* you trample on other people's feelings continually with things you permit yourself to say & do—owing partly to the self-indulgence of drinking too much—& becoming someone else (uninvited)—instead of the Scott we know, & love & admire,—unless from the greatest egotism, & sureness that you are *righter* than anyone else? I called it "manners" but it is more serious—It is that you are only thinking of yourself.

Be as angry with me as you like, Scott—it may be true that "toute verité n'est pas bonne a dire" [All truth is not good to say] but I feel *obliged* in honesty of a friend to write you: that: The ability to know what another person feels in a given situation will make—or ruin lives.

Please, please let us know Zelda's news—Dos is here & says she seemed *so well* when you all went out together 10 days ago—I think of her all the time— Forgive me if you can,—but you *must* try to learn, for your own good, & your adored family's good—Some distrust for your behaviour to *all* other human beings. Your infuriating but devoted & rather wise old friend—

Sara

PUL

Although the Dos Passoses lived at 571 Commercial Street, Provincetown, the house which had been Katy's and her brother Bill Smith's prior to the Dos Passoses' marriage in 1929, the new house Katy talks about may be the one next door at 565, which the Dos Passoses purchased and then rented to Katy's longtime friend Edith Foley Shay and her husband. The Dos Passoses established a garden between the two homes. They also owned a cottage in nearby Truro, purchased shortly after their marriage.

36. KATY DOS PASSOS to SARA MURPHY,
Provincetown [c. May 1934]

Dearest Sara,

I was just running around the house when you called, stuffing tulips and lilacs into vases in your room, in the hope that you and Gerald might appear. I am afraid I sounded awfully feeble minded talking over the phone, but your voice was only a sweet faint twitter like a mouse in the wall, and I couldn't understand but a few words because of the connection. But I made out that you weren't coming and had been planning to come earlier. Dos and I did not go into the fits of disappointment and frustration that we felt coming on because we were afraid to make a scene over the telephone and thought it might be too hard for you to take the long drive with so little time. But it was awful afterwards when we sat looking at the phone and the tulips and whiskey and native delicacies we had brought from Truro for your pleasure trained senses. It was very hard. The weather was wonderful too and we wanted you to see the new house and advise with us about the sea garden. Oh dear.

But here's a card saying Baoth is to be in the neighborhood, so you will be migratory to this district in the future.[1] But June is coming with a whirring sound and you will be sailing. We feel lonesome in advance. But we are coming to New York Monday or Tuesday, driving up from here. Dos has to see people and do a little work in the library for a few days. So we will see you then. We will call up on arriving. Dos sends his love and I send my love. Next time you come this way we will set a trap in Boston. Lilacs are all out on the Cape now and the air tastes wonderful after Key West, where everything had gotten very overdone, except the gulf stream.

Love, and hasta la vista

Katy

UVA

---

1. Baoth was to be enrolled that fall at the St. George's School in Middletown, Rhode Island, near Newport.

The Murphys sailed for Europe on 9 June and spent the summer at Villa America and cruising on the Weatherbird. *Patrick was well enough to be with them that year.*

37. SARA and GERALD MURPHY to PAULINE and ERNEST HEMINGWAY,
On board *Weatherbird*, Spanish ports, 21 June 1934

Dear P & E.:—

What a country—what a country. Even after "Gib," Algeciras, Tangiers, Tetuan, Cerita, Malaga. To-day 260 kilometres of wheat, sun, mules

threshing,—oxen drawing, hats , Tio Pepe,—well you know.

Love. G.

Oh dear, why aren't you both here?—The boat (& the sea) were never so nice (or so blue) & we wish for friends—next summer? Hope you are having a *lovely* time—much love   Sara
We tried *everywhere* for Ernests hats 7 3/4 no luck—
JFK

38. SARA and GERALD MURPHY to JOHN and KATY DOS PASSOS,
Malaga, Spain, 28 June 1934

If we can *stand* what we're seeing we'll be all right. We turn to you suddenly in market this a.m. Thro' narrow streets with balconies bulging came the dead Archbishop in robes, carried high, his blue face to the sky,—followed by purple, green, black and red figures, bells tolling high—soon, the whole punctured by anti-religious fights at every corner.

G.

We do miss you dreadfully. Mustn't do this again without you. Everything too lovely—& the sea really *too* blue—

Love S.

UVA

The Murphys had an idyllic time at Villa America that summer with the whole family together. Patrick seemed well, although thinner, as the family enjoyed cruising on the Weatherbird, *which they kept anchored off the Garoupe. "We bathe and lunch on board," Gerald wrote Harold Heller (designer and decorator for Villa America and also "Hook Pond" in East Hampton). "We have an entirely Russian crew who speak their own language and it sounds like a Tchekov rehearsal. . . . The portable phonograph works to perfection, and the new French and German music is great." Gerald added in this 22 August 1934 letter (HMD) that Patrick was "very anxious to go to Harvey [School, in New York] so we're going to try it." As it turned out, however, Patrick never entered school. His relapse was diagnosed shortly after the Murphy family docked in New York on 7 September, and Patrick went into Doctors Hospital in New York to undergo further treatment. The Murphys had planned to see the Dos Passoses in Provincetown until they learned that John and Katy were still in California, where Dos Passos had gone in late July to work on the Marlene Dietrich film* The Devil Is a Woman, *directed by Joseph von Sternberg. He suffered another attack of rheumatic fever shortly after his arrival in Hollywood and spent August convalescing there. Katy joined him in late August following her father's death in Columbia, Missouri.*

39. KATY DOS PASSOS to GERALD and SARA MURPHY, Hollywood, 18 September 1934

Dearest Gerald and Sara,

We thought you ought to have this, it shows so beautifully how Hollywood views the world through the Hollywood mirror. I particularly liked the phrase a *Molliere production.* Dos is picking up almost as fast as cold molasses—but he's really a lot better and we think next week will be up. He's up and around his bed right now. Then we may set off for Havana. I hate Havana.

Oh it's so awful not being home when you were coming to visit us. You were really coming and we not there. This is one of the associative catastrophes of the big main catastrophe but it's very hard to bear. It's so funny and awful here we can hardly bear it without you, anyway. When Dos was doing his work for Mr. Von S. he used to throw his hot water bag clear across the room. Von S. was really very nice though and it is wonderful to see him—he is entirely imaginary from head to foot. He thinks he is a Vienese intellectual of the old regime, and his accent almost never fails him. There is a touch too much of the Guardsman about his suits perhaps, but it wouldn't seem noticeable here. I never saw anything like the way the men dress here—it's all blended tones. I see them on the lot and think I'm dreaming. One yesterday had on a henna flannel coat, white pants with a henna stripe, a henna felt hat, a henna tie and shoes and a henna rinse. They go into white and cream like a first communion and you think it's Easter at Elizabeth Ardens. Snow white flannel is the uniform for the lot, and you can't be niftier than when thickly swaddled in cream flannel with cream shoes and face and just a touch of color at the throat in the form of a cowboy scarf in pale blue. Blue is good—if it's *all* blended blue, and I've seen some pinks worn in flannel, of course.

It's wonderful here too. I'm going to write you all about it—please send us a little scratch. How is my dear Mrs. Puss? How are you all? Welcome home and I wish we were home to welcome you.

I saw a lovely sign out at Long Beach the other day, crowded in among the oil wells and decaying Italian villas and all the realtor wreckage of bungalows and Venetian canals and collapsed stucco. It was outside an imitation English manor with the plaster coming off, and it was a large painted sign in the front yard. It said: PUPS 15 CENTS AND UP.

Much Love from

Katy

UVA

40. SARA MURPHY to ERNEST and PAULINE HEMINGWAY, East Hampton, 18 September [1934]

Dearest Hemingways,—

Thank you for the lovely homecoming wire—we needed some cheering I can tell you, as we are in bad luck again about Patrick (god, how I hate to write bad news in letters) He seemed very well all summer, & we did everything the dr said to,—& now, at a routine (we thought) visit to the dr—he is discovered to have another patch on his *other* lung. & we are to be sent out West or god knows where. I just wanted you to know about it, although it is very mean bad luck to write about to anybody—

Patrick as usual has been very brave—braver than any of us by a good deal—although his plans, school, fishing—& shooting have all been broken up, for months to come.

Isn't it *horrid*?—And what a fool's paradise it is to ever think you have won a victory over the White plague!!—Well, he *is* going to be allright ultimately, & all our fighting blood is up again—& perhaps this is that set-back that is so common when children go into puberty—but at times it *does* seem too much,—Especially as he himself is so decent about it all.

All the rest of us are fine, & thank Heaven you all are—& we had a wonderful summer, one of the nicest we have ever had. Which is something—& we are crazier about our boat than ever—we want to see yours sometime, Ernest & how *good* that it's turned out so well! Are you really coming north end of Oct.?

We will let you know our plans as soon as they become definite. Baoth has gone to school (St. George's,—near Newport.) and Honoria goes back to hers—at Greenwich—Oct. 1—so it looks as though we were going to start again to "faire la navette" [run a shuttle-service] between the members of the family! As we did for so many years! May you all cross our feverish path very soon!—We all think of you often & send you much love, and you are a comfort to us.

And in the meantime we are here, with Patrick in bed—& the thermometer going again—But I am sure, not for as long as the last time—

Yr old & affectionate shipmate

Sara

Dow dow sends best love
I wish I knew some more words
JFK

41. ERNEST HEMINGWAY to GERALD and SARA MURPHY, Havana, 30 September [1934]

Dear Sara and Gerald:

It's such a damned shame poor old Patrick should have to go through all that with another lung. We feel awfully about it and send Patrick and you all our love and sympathy. At least, though, you and he have been through it once, know how it is and how it turns out. So there isn't the desperation of something unknown. But it is such a damned brutal thing to have it all to go through again. Fortunately no one in the world is better about it than you two—and no one has more sense, more patience and more acceptance of things than Patrick.

Do you know where you will be going if you do go West? We would like to know because it would be some place to go to. Always want to go out there but never have a good enough reason. Cant you go somewhere where we could put Patrick in ambush and we could all throw foul eggs at Mable Dodge Tony as she rode by?

The shirts are wonderful. These are the first swell looking clothes I have had since the last swell looking clothes you gave me and am creating considerable stir along the water front. Some wonder whether Some Woman has not come into my life that I am such a nifty dresser since day before yesterday. Others think am getting money from Moscow.

Speaking of Moscow how is that old pillar of Radicalism MacLeish the man who trampled on the Constitution and spat on the starry flag? I had a letter from him in July about how bad it was to know November was approaching and wrote him a cherry and drunken answer but no reply. For a while I was afraid November 7th had come and looked for it daily all through August but my Calender and Nautical Almanac show only October 1 so far— give the flag trampler and Constitution spitter my love and also Mrs. Mac-Leish that great beauty, songster, and all around ornament to any home and Cordon Bleu too—what a woman— why did she marry a man who made a mock of all our institutions and joined the Redo just to make his poetry popular and get the Hiram Norton Pulitzer Prize.

Damn it I wish we could see you—I would even like to see that old Radical MacLeish.

We (I) have caught 10 of these fish—420—324—243—228—etc etc— down to 104 lbs. The weather is still good and there are no hurricanes yet— Have gotten through fifteen days of the bad hurricane weather and if we get through next 20 are all right. Are all right anyway—I mean we can fish without having to tie up somewhere up some creek—Hope to get a big fish at 900–1200 lbs. Boat has been lovely—comfortable and a marvellous sea boat—all we hoped for and more—

Our African heads, except a few we have had mounted and sent down, are still at Jonas Bros. I want to give Patrick either a Grants Gazelle or an Impalla—whichever he'd like—They are really no trouble—(housebroken) very clean and light and quite beautiful to look at when you're in bed— Impalla is the most beautiful I think and have a record one he would like— Can you tell me where to have it sent? It will take about 2–3 weeks for them to finish it and they will send it direct. Tell Patrick they are the ones that float in the air when they jump and jump over each others backs. There is a good picture of one in Jock of the Bushback.

We are going to build a swimming pool—45 feet long—with a trophy room around it—The side walls—as soon as I make some money—to run out from my little house and across the back of the yard—shutting out those jig houses. Dont you think that is a good idea, Sara? Then can always have exercise as soon as finish work—

Have been working hard on this long thing [Green Hills of Africa] and now have 50,000 some words done—

We had a fine cool summer—it was cooler in K.W. [Key West] than anywhere in U.S. Very lucky—

This seems all the news. We hope Patrick is going along fine from day to day.

Please let us know your plans as soon as you have any.

Thank you very much for the three beautiful shirts.
With very much love

Ernest (Poor Old Pappa)

The camera you gave me takes <u>Wonderful</u> pictures—Will send you some
as soon as get some prints from the negatives.

Please give my love to Honoria and best to Baoth—

Pappa

HMD

42. JOHN DOS PASSOS to GERALD and SARA MURPHY,
Havana, 30 October [1934]

Dear Gerald—Sara—

We are most anxious to hear how and where you all are. Do drop us a line
when you get a chance. Havana is pleasanter than I have ever known it. We are
in an agreeable Spanish hotel in two agreeable rooms with a view of the port
and the Morro—not a tourist or a Havana blonde in sight. I'm beginning to
pick up again and am now almost back to where I was last summer on the
Weatherbird. I shant go north at all this winter—but shall try to toast myself
in the sun and to take all possible measures to get this infection out of the
system. It's a great pleasure to be on my feet again—

Hem's in wonderful shape, got a lot of dope about the marlin this summer,
and discovered thirty six unlisted varieties of fish but had poor luck in size;
they wouldn't come larger than 300 lbs.

This is certainly not the moment I would have chosen for navigating the
Antilles but we are going to make the most of it. I'm going over to K.W. for a
month while Katy goes north—then we'll get to some very hot island for six
weeks or so, then, in the latter part of the winter, we thought we'd go and look
you up in Tucson or wherever you've decided to nest in the injun country. By
that time I ought to have a good deal of dope about curing the rheumatics—
Are you & Sara going to be in New York before Christmas? Would like to
know address.

Oh I wish you were all down here and everybody was well. We could have
some sessions again with the Camerones and the Marquis of Riscal, that
splendid nobleman. Langostinos, no hay, but shrimp and stone crabs to a
superlative degree. The cookery in Havana is magnificent as always—

People are still horribly poor down here and their main sport is still setting
off small bombs in butchershops and lately in yachts and sailboats—but in the

sun on the roof of the hotel it's very agreeable for us valitudinarians

love to all

Dos

HMD

43. ERNEST HEMINGWAY to GERALD and SARA MURPHY,
Key West, 7 November [1934]

Dear Gerald and Sara:

Christ men its the seventh of November.

Just got your wire (damn this machine)[1] forwarded by Dos who says he answered it. Impertinet fellow. It was fine to see Dos in such good shape really.

We are all fine and Dos is much finer than he thinks too according to a very good doctor (friend of mine) who examined him in Havana when Dos thought maybe he had had a heart attack and told me Dos had the soundest and healthiest heart he had ever listened to. Not a flaw and is marvellous. What he had feared was an heart attack was heart-burn caused by over-eating. Pasos's appetite remains the same and is satisfied accordingly and when you are in bed, of course most people can't eat quite as much but Dos can and will eat more. He is really getting along fine and convalescing very well and it is wonderful luck that the r. fever never has hit his heart. He seemed in grand shape in the head and is due here in a couple of days to occupy the house the Canbys are going to have in December until they arrive. Katey has gone up North to closeup there. We had a fine time together and very funny in Havana.

Dos is very funny on Holywood. So is Kate. All the Comunists make a "minimum of" a thousand dolars a week including Jack Lawson who says that no child has ever been born in one of my books because I am afraid to face the future. (Make out of that what you can and will)

Stewart makes 90,000 a year and has thirty suits of white flannels while believeing Irving Thalberg is the greatest genius of the age. He is a specialist on Smilin Through films and is gretly esteemed because of his contacts with Society.

All Dotty, Stewart etc. talked about whas how I had betrayed Ring Lardner. (Probably because he a the mos beautiful man in the world)

---

1. Hemingway's typewriter was double-typing letters and omitting others, creating more spelling errors than typical for Hemingway, despite his recognizable free-flow letterwriting style. Some of the more obvious and intrusive type-overs and omissions have been emended in transcription.

Who shall I betray next?

We picked a good night to come across as soon as the hurricane warnings were down and before a norther should start and raised sandkey in nine hours forty minutes lead on the shipchannel bouy. Pretty good with a five knot current to figure and it rough as hell in the middle of the gulf with a beam sea. Had been blowing like hell for a week. (But I fear the future)

Am having Jonas Bros send the Impalla to your address. You can take it to the hospital. It is really very light and clean and think Patrick will like. Tell him I killed it with one shot with the 6.5 mm mannlicher at 220 paces. It was the biggest buck in a herd of about fifteen and is big enough to rank in Rowland Ward's Records of Big Game. He was shot near the Serenea river in Tanganyika.

How are you merchants? I had an infected finger then hand for about a month so didn't write. Wrote on my book mornings then kept it in a sling and now is o.k. Was a slow funny infection travel around from place to place. Antiflgistined it until it gaveup and quit.

Give Patrick all our love. If by any chance we can possibly get up will do so but have to wk like hell. Am going very well and am into 60,000 words [*Green Hills of Africa*].

Oh I hope Mr. Thalberg will like it.

If Gerald isn't too godawfully busy and he probably is will he buy me records to the value of enclosed check and send down here? Also will you buy another record of that Victor redseal of Experiment with Snowball on other side. It was a lovely record and it got broke when the phonograph rolled over coming across

Goodbye citizens. Much love.

Ernest

Pauline has been writing you for some time/ It is lovely indian summer weather here now—Place looks beautiful—Have lots of pep for working—Anytime either of you need a rest come on down!

HMD

When Luis Quintanilla was being jailed for conspiring against the Republican government in Spain, Dos Passos and Hemingway tried to raise money for his support through a show of Quintanilla's etchings. The show was well received and did much to advance Quintanilla's cause.

44. ERNEST HEMINGWAY to GERALD and SARA MURPHY
Key West, 16 November [1934]

Dear Sara and Gerald,

    Luis Quintanilla, who is a great pal of ours in Madrid, is having a show of etchings at the Pierre Matisse gallery in the Fuller Blg. starting November twentieth. You will only have to see them to know how damned wonderful they are. I was bringing them over and arranged the show because of how much I believed in them and then Quintanilla, in the last revolution, and now they're trying to give him sixteen years of hard labor so we're trying to make as much fuss about them as possible because it will help him and also he's dead broke. Ordinarily, there wouldn't need to be any fuss made about them because they are good enough to carry it all by themselves as you will see the minute you clap your old Norwegian and Irish, respectively, deadlights on them. If you have any time at all would you go on the opening day as a favor to me and to Dos, let alone Art with a capital P. Dos and I have written introductions for them in the catalogue and I paid for having the prints pulled and am putting up for the show. If you wanted to buy one or a couple it would be swell, but I know with Patrick ill you must have God awful expenses. But do please go and see them anyway and let me know how you liked them.

    I didn't know what it was you were worried about when Dos sent me your cable. He is in swell shape now, by the way, and is on a fine diet and looking and feeling very well. The weather here is perfect now, cool and fresh and swell for working. I finished my long thing, 492 pages, today [*Green Hills of Africa*]. Feel pretty good about it. We're all fine and there's nothing to worry about here. Please let us hear from you when you have time and tell us how Patrick is. Tell him I haven't heard yet from Jonas when the Impalla will be ready. I told them to send it direct to you.

    I do hope Archie can steam up some of his ten dancing dowagers about the Quintanilla show. I wrote him about it. I know he's probably awfully busy, though. Quintanilla is such a good guy it's just as though they had Dos in jail, really just as bad. Thank God they haven't and that the old bastard is getting to look better every day.

    Best love to you all. This is written in somewhat of a hurry and me very pooped after finishing. I think you, Gerald, will like this book. Well, we'll see. Much love again,

Ernest

or

Poor old Papa

HMD

45. GERALD AND SARA MURPHY TO ERNEST HEMINGWAY
New York, 21 November 1934

YOUR RECORDS SHIPPED PARCEL POST YESTERDAY WOULD LOVE TO SEE
YOU LISTENING TO THEM QUINTINILLA SHOW SUPERB SPLENDIDLY
HUNG GOOD GALLERY INTELLIGENT MAN IN CHARGE FINE ATTENDANCE
FOUR SOLD FIRST DAY TRYING TO SCARE UP SOME WRITEUPS SARA SURE
YOU NEED CLIMATIC CHANGE PLEASE COME STAY WITH US JINNY IN
GREAT FORM WHAT A GIRL ALL IN READINESS TO SHOW YOU A TIME
LOVE= MURPHYS.

JFK

*John Dos Passos remained in Key West while Katy went North for medi-
cal tests and treatment. She failed to keep either Dos Passos or the Murphys posted, and everyone was worried about her.*

46. KATY DOS PASSOS to GERALD and SARA MURPHY,
Boston, 27 November 1934

Dearest Gerald and Sara

What a toad I must seem to you, but please don't. I was so dismally sick
when I got to New York I could do nothing but lie in bed, and there was no
phone in the house to call you up. I kept thinking I'd be better in a day or so,
but just seemed to decline and was afraid I'd turn into a case of some kind, so
the first minute I could I went to Boston to see the doctor. I thought I'd better
see the Boston quacks because they had all my records and I had to go to
Provincetown anyway to close up the house—I had tests in Boston and went
on down—When I got to Provincetown about midnight I was told Gerald had
called—a message left at the house—but we had no phone and it was too late
to wake up the neighbors—Next day came your wire—Thank you so much
dear Gerald and Sara—it was awfully warming to hear from you—but I had
had a reluctance to worry you—you've been so troubled lately—It was awful
to learn you'd been worried anyway at long distance. I had no idea Dos was
worried—I had not gotten his wires at all and so hadn't answered them.
    I tried to write you a long fine letter in Provincetown, but was pretty low

there too, and kept thinking I'd improve and would not send you a long-distance whine until I had some idea what was the matter or felt well enough to make a plan. It was all a dimwitted effort not to worry you darlings, or Mr. Parsons [John Dos Passos]. I wish now I had rushed to you with the whole thing and never gone in for the strong silent hermit at all—I would have liked to come mewing to you at once, but was really frightened I might be a terrible care to my dear Sara—you've had such a fearful worry, Mrs Puss darling. I've thought of you both and Patrick, all the time—Cried like mad when Dos sent me your letter saying he was better—I had had a feeling he was better—very queer feeling indeed—I know what it is to live in a trance of fear—was in it all the time in Hollywood, and that was why I wasn't able to write you very well.

Please write me here how Patrick is now. I've been seeing Doctors and they've been taking pictures and I'll have to stay here till Saturday to get a verdict, but whatever it is, it's not serious, as I feared, and I can come back to New York Monday or Tuesday, and I'm feeling all right again—

Darlings could I stay with you a little while in New York really? I would love to—I'm crazy to see you—It's very lonesome-making here—I don't think I will *ever* try for strong silent again—

Oh that lovely Patrick, how I think of him. I'm writing him a letter but don't know where to send it, and I'm not sure of the address—Dos sent it to me, and I lost it coming up here—yours too. I got yours off the telegram.

You're not angry, are you? Oh please don't be put out with this damnable Miserable. Please write me about Patrick. I know he is going to be well—all over from head to foot. It's a promise.

Oh Sara and Gerald I so want to see you—it's really my chief ache now—as the other aches disappear I feel it even worse—It's quite a gnaw—I've a lot to tell and talk about—We've been in a very dreary phase, I must admit, but I think we're all coming out of it now—

I'm in the New England Baptist Hospital where they are giving me all sorts of tests—they think it's a kind of sensitiveness to protein that's been making me so sick, and are trying to find out through food-tests—pictures—and all sorts of gloomy mixtures taken in the most unnatural ways.

But I'm out Saturday. Leaving for good and coming to New York Monday or Tuesday—Do send me a little scratch—Hospital address is 85 Parker Hill Avenue After Saturday, the Brunswick—

Now I've begun to hate to stop—Just a card would be a fine thing to have. Forgive me for being such a dope—Love you inordinately—

Katy

Love to Baoth and Honoria
UVA

47. KATY DOS PASSOS to GERALD and SARA MURPHY,
Boston [2 December 1934]

Dear Sara and Gerald,

Here's your wire in my hand and it feels good—it's very queer I didn't get the telegram you speak of because I called up the Brunswick and asked, but there's a very mean old man there who won't tell you anything and I imagine he does not believe in Western Union or lipstick and won't be a party to telegrams.

I hoped to be out of here [Boston Hospital] today, but had to stay a day longer, but tomorrow they give me five dollars and a hair-cut and let me go—I am so crazy to be gone I am gasping and will rush the red lights all the way to New York—but I won't get there till Thursday or Friday I think, as have some things to do in Boston.

Your wire came from Easthampton and at once I saw you all there in the winey fall, and you all looked lovely and so did the house and the sea. I am very anxious to hear about Patrick, and will snatch up the telegrams at the Brunswick tomorrow. I'm all right now and quite lively again. Did I tell you that Ernest was translated when seen in Havana? You remember how irascible and truculent (can't spell) he was before. Now he's just a big cage of canaries, looking fine, too—and followed around all the time by a crowd of Cuban zombies who think he is Hernan Cortez—He was sweet, but had a tendency to be an Oracle I thought and needs some best pal and severe critic to tear off those long white whiskers which he is wearing—We talked about you a lot and our words flew around like doves.

I'll telephone you when I get to New York—Oh I do long to see you—I would love to come for a few days—Love to my dear Patrick, and to you all,

Affectionately

Katy

UVA

48. ERNEST HEMINGWAY to GERALD and SARA MURPHY,
Key West, 14 December [1934]

Dear Sara and Gerald:

The records were marvellous. There are fine loud ones, like Fats Waller, that are marvellous while trolling and bring the fish up. On the other hand

Lucienne Boyer is very good in the cabin sitting around drinking in the evening with a norther blowing. Youre The Top and Thank You So Much Mrs. Lounsbourugh Whitney are bloody marvellous.

It is grand to hear you are coming down. You will like the boat and fishing is comfortable and wonderful with her. Dos is crazy about her. He is in marvellous shape by the way and it has been swell having him.

I'm glad you like the Impalla. Give Patrick my love and best regards. Also best to Baoth and love to Honoria and you both and Merry Christmas. Very Merry Christmas. I would have loved to come to N.Y. and so would Pauline. You were nice to send the wire. Thanks too about Quintanilla. They sold 30 etchings.

We are driving to Piggott [Arkansas] day after the day after tomorrow. Will start driving back on about New Years.

Merry Christmas again and much love from us all.

Ernest

HMD

Dos Passos may have stayed with the Hemingways while Katy was east taking care of her medical problems. She returned to be with Dos Passos by Christmas, and the two of them would continue to remain in the south because of his heath. Although they would stay primarily in Key West, they also traveled in early January to Jamaica. Around this same time Sara Murphy had begun to plan her second annual spring trip to Key West.

49. PAULINE HEMINGWAY to SARA MURPHY, Key West [c. January 1935]

My Dearest Sara—

We are very pleased and excited to hear that you are coming to Key West if you can get a house. And you *can* get one, because if we cant find one we shall just step out of ours and live in Ernest's little house and you can have ours. So I can hardly see now how you wont be able to come and shall we call the matter settled. Oh yes.

And will Dow-dow come too? I dont think we could *bear* it if Dow-dow didn't come. We play his records all the time and miss him very much. We are sure there is no one on this side of the Atlantic, or in Europe or Africa who can pick out records as well as Dow-dow. We sing them all the time. I hear Patrick (ours) going around singing over and over I'm celophane.

When will you come?

We've had a fine Christmas with the family. Found Jinny in fine shape. Ernest is out after quail today.

We are sending you under the conventional separate cover a zebra skin which Ernest shot. I'm afraid it has a good many holes (not all bullet holes) but it has a nicer pattern than the ones that didn't have holes. Maybe you can have lackeys stand on the holes, with trays of little hot sausages—will never forget your little hot sausages. Hurry up down here, and love to you both and Patrick—Will you write us how Patrick is?

Affectionately

Pauline

Thanks for the fine Christmas telegram.   P.

HMD

After Dorothy Parker had returned to America from her long stay with the Murphys in Switzerland, she met Alan Campbell in New York. Robert Benchley introduced them, and the relationship would prove to be one of Parker's happiest and most durable. Eleven years Parker's junior, Campbell was a strikingly handsome actor and writer, primarily for the New Yorker. *In June 1934 Campbell and Parker drove west together, sending the Murphys a telegram on 8 June as the Murphys were leaving for their summer in Europe.* "THIS IS TO REPORT ARRIVAL IN NEWCASTLE *[Pennsylvania]* OF FIRST BEDLINGTON TERRIERS TO CROSS CONTINENT IN OPEN FORD. MANY NATIVES NOTE RESEMBLANCES TO SHEEP. COULDNT SAY GOOD BYE AND CANT NOW BUT GOOD LUCK DARLING MURPHYS AND PLEASE HURRY BACK   ALL LOVE = DOROTHY." *On 18 June Campbell and Parker married in Raton, New Mexico, and by early September they were in Hollywood. They had signed on with Paramount Pictures as a husband-wife writing team, Parker getting top billing and top salary ($1,000 per week). After they rented a house at 520 North Canon Drive in Beverly Hills, they installed expensive white carpets and settled into Hollywood life.*

50. DOROTHY PARKER to GERALD and SARA MURPHY,
Beverly Hills [c. January 1935]

Dear Sara and Gerald Murphy,

I am a little girl of 56, and this is my first fan letter. I have admired you ever since I first saw you, and you do not know how happy it would make me to have your autographs on a letter.

I live in a big white house with tall columns and magnolia trees, so that I often feel like the Little Colonel, only crosser. I have a friend named Alan Campbell who is also a Sara-and-Gerald-Murphy fan and we often exchange letters. I have two Bedlington terriers and a dachshund, none of which is housebroken, so you can see I am pretty busy—My hobby is the hives, which I have had ever since setting foot on California soil. I scratch a great deal, which has won me the title of Miss Glamour of 1935. It is very pretty here and I like it very much, all except my work at the studio, which stinks.

Well, I must close now, as Fraulein, the dachshund, has just done everything but have puppies on the white carpet which her host and hostess went without eating for a month in order to acquire. She is a very cute little dog, if only she would stop going to the bathroom for five consecutive minutes, and sends love.

I wish I was this letter, so I could go in a plane and be with you *quick*.

Dorothy—

[The back of the envelope bears a Paramount Picture insignia under the following inscription: "If it's a Paramount Picture it's the best show in town!" Parker writes underneath this:] (This is an outrageous lie)
HMD

Stella Campbell (1865–1940) was a London stage actress who had been a friend of Sara's mother, and who also had a long-term relationship with George Bernard Shaw. He wrote Pygmalion *for her at the peak of her career, and they maintained a feisty correspondence until her death. During the early 1930s, the Murphys loaned Mrs. Campbell (the Murphy children called her Aunt Stella) the Ferme des Orangers. Stella Campbell cruised with the Murphy family on the* Weatherbird *when they came for their brief stay before returning to America, and she too came to America shortly thereafter to try to make a new career in film. She landed only bit parts, however, and remained semi-impoverished*

until her death. The Murphys remained concerned about Mrs. Camp-
bell and tried to cover her basic living expenses.

51. STELLA CAMPBELL to SARA MURPHY,
Beverly Hills, 7 January 1935

Darling Sarah—

I love the picture of the beautiful Yacht—oh how happy I was on it! and how lovely you both made life. . . . To think you have been married 19 years—I think you have been wonderfully wise and clever both of you—you have kept ugliness out of your lives—You have done much more than "Pretty well" and that river of love that pours unceasingly from your heart and makes all cool and sweet and lovely around you. Nobody ever realizes their own spiritual gift—that is yours. . . . Your ever loving heart but never tires—Personally I think you are wonderful people, and I dont say that lightly—for I have known and loved some rare folk—Mrs. Percy Wyndham—Margaret Mackail—Bessie Chapman—Mrs. Lyttleton—Darling Mrs. George Sykes a Boston-ian—her father was a doctor—she loved my Beo [her only son, killed in World War I], and he her—but that was a long long time ago and last, but far from least your dear generous loving Mother.

There is something wrong with Dorothy [Parker]—she is sweet and char-ming and gentle as a Dove—but she seems to me always *preoccupied*, and a little lost. Whether she foresees money difficulties which are very serious in this country (you can get no credit, and they just walk away with your car or trunks) or she may be nervous about her husband—I *know* nothing—but she is a little strange. . . . a little story as an example:—I went to call for her to take them both to a cocktail party; the flagstones across the grass in her garden are about 3 inches higher than the turf, so of course I caught my foot against one and came down a real cropper; her husband and my chauffeur helped me up—she offered me whiskey . . . we went to the party and all she said to me as I drove there in agony was "I dont like that house, the last people in it were discovered, and so were the people who lived in it before, I am not going to take any risks." I didn't see that had anything to do with my fall still I said cheerfully "you must tell your landlady to have those flagstones laid level with the turf." She said merrily in reply "I never think of those things." When we arrived at the party I could only get out of the car with help so I had to tell the host I had hurt myself . . . he and Constance Collier got some stuff they put on two places on my leg that were bleeding and wrapped a handkerchief around my leg under my stocking also there was a bad place on my arm that had to be attended to . . . Dorothy never alluded to it or rang me up, and I have never heard from her since. The next day I had to stay in bed for I couldn't move. I had hurt my shoulder. . . . The feeling I had about Dorothy was she was thinking of something else all the time, and hadn't in the least realized what had happened to me. I have given her your address twice, she told me she had—either cabled or telephoned to you, and that Patrick was better—I wrote at once to you and told you I had heard it from her. She doesn't look unhappy but just 'away'.

I see the cheque you have sent me is from Gerald—it is splendid of you both. My landlady is accepting $100 a month instead of $175 so it will pay my rent and that is a great load off my mind, and I am very grateful. I have a little left from the earlier allowances—

I dont think it is very lucky to speak of business before things are signed and sealed but there is quite an important conference going on to-day between author and producer about a leading part for me in a Harwood play—a comedy—it would mean many weeks work. Even if everything is settled in my favour it will take a few weeks before the script is far enough advanced for them to shoot—so if I am very embarrassed I will let you know and return out of my first week's pay. You wouldn't know me I am so so, careful!

You are both angels to me—I wish there was something I could do for you—I dont know what "hunch" is, but if it has anything to do with longing and praying with all my heart and soul that your beloved Patrick will be strong enough to enjoy life and be a blessing to you both for many a long day I am 'hunching' allright!

I didn't expect Gerald to write to me but I would have burst if I hadn't written to him.

I wish I could send Patrick safely my two tiny Finches, they are heavenly birds—I didn't think the nest they had made for themselves in the cage quite comfortable—so I bought one that is always sold for tiny finches and hung it in their cage—They at once got into it—and then both jumped out and brought all the pampas grass bit by bit out of the old nest and put it in the new one and there they are as cozy as can be, and only come out to eat and have their bath. It is the rainy season and a little cold for them. I had no idea such tiny birds were so clever—I will be excited when they have babies.

Alas I have been terribly depressed—I believe it is my liver and I dont know what to take for it. I expect though if this business goes through I will cheer up—and if I could only hear from you that Patrick was eating well and there was nothing more to be alarmed about I would feel quite well. Oh so grateful otherwise

Bless you always darling your loving

Stella

HMD

52. JOHN DOS PASSOS to GERALD MURPHY,
St. Ann, Jamaica, 11 January [1935]

Dear Gerald—

That check I found in my stocking has turned into various things notably a bottle of Madeira that we find remarkably good with roasted breadfruit—at last after all these years we are eating breadfruit and it's remarkably good, tastes like the skin of a baked potato—also into the rent of a car driven by a brownish smoke with an oxford accent—and into a small rowboat in which we are about to navigate the cove in front of this small English boarding house—Jamaica is very beautiful to look at if you can shake off the dreary English air that makes the towns look like grainy bits of London which mysteriously turned black and fringed with coconut palms. Wish you and Sara were here to ride around the island with us and to look at the little fishes in the clear water over the reef across the mouth of the bay—it's in one of these bays that Columbus put in such a horrid winter when his ships went to pieces on him— and to drink the madeira and eat the roast breadfruit—There are the most extraordinarily bright fireflies that come into our room at night some green and some pinkish, and chameleons run up the pipes of the plumbing. It's really quite fine here and at night there are millions of crickets and lisping insects of various kinds and the sound of the waterfalls pouring into the sea and the rustle of the coconut palms—It's really a little too much like the early south sea island movies.

We'll be staying here until we are ready to go back to Key West at the end of the month—as I dont think we can do better and might very well fare worse— Kingston is a singularly dreary dump. We greatly hoping that you'll come down to take a look at the coral reefs and coconut palms either before or after if you couldn't come with the Waddell Avenue girls—it really would be worth taking a peek at, and Havana's rather agreeable this year—and the landscape of Cuba we discovered by going to Matanzas, is not to be sneezed at. And Hem's boat is darned agreeable for his friends, as is the old master himself. And the abandoned tobacco factory is going to be quite agreeable too, in spite of being heavily infected with Salvador Dali and Jean Lurcat as to the outward aspect.

We'll be hoping to find news of Patrick when we get back and of you all. Yrs. truly considerably mended. Love to Sara.

Saludos

Dos

Address Ambos Mundos Hotel Havana and then Key West
HMD

53. KATY DOS PASSOS to SARA MURPHY,
St. Ann, Jamaica, 12 January 1935

Dearest Mrs. Puss,

Every day we've been traveling I've wanted to send you a snow-white dove with a message tied to his pink coral foot, as the plain mails aren't good enough for you—I also thought of embroidering letters on silk, but hadn't the skill, and would have just written anyway, but found everything so confused when I arrived that I never secured the moment to write you suitably. Dos wasn't so well, had found no Key West house for us all, it was cold, and rather crowded and bleak at the [Canby] Chambers bungalow, and the New Dealers had snapped up all the houses in town and were living in them like hermit crabs. The Arch New Dealer of them all told us that if we liked any house we found inhabited by a FERA expert he would make the cowbird move, "Clear him," was the phrase. We did find several such houses, but the owners appeared to be armed and hostile. I'd go back to the Head Man and he'd pound on his desk and shout "I'll clear them!" And I'd explain, "but Mr -X- they won't let me in to look at the house—how can I tell when I can't get in?" And he'd say, "Look in through the windows!" But you can't look in through the windows when the tenants are looking out at you. Some even pulled down the blinds. One family whose house we were considering pulled down all the blinds, locked the doors, took the keys and left town. Se we were pretty desperate till Mrs. Kirk offered us her villa. It's not bad—I do hope you'll like it—it even has a garden full of tropical plants, a vine-covered cistern to have meals out doors on, and the beach is only a short distance—There are four nice bedrooms and a really pretty living room, bath extensive in size, with some fine old marble, private bannes and considerable solitude. The rent seemed excessive ($300) but that takes the house for as long as next November if we want it, and Dos will probably have to have a tropical base well into the summer, so we agreed, but think we should pay part, and dearest Gerald and Mrs. Puss darling, how can I express the gratitude and devotion felt by your constituents. It's wonderful to have the house there so snug and pleasant to go back to. We have it from January 15th, and will be going back in a week or ten days now—

We're in Jamaica, in a very sugary south-sea island paradise right now—it's really an incredible place—set in a grove of coconut palms on a blue-green sea, with two beautiful glass-clear rivers running down in a series of waterfalls and pools into the cove, pink and yellow fish brushing your toes as you wade—I'm going to write Patrick all about it—but the whole thing is too much—all made out of sugar-candy like an Easter-egg. I never imagined a place so much like what I had imagined. Wish you could be here—there's nobody but us, four blacks, and an English spinster lady who keeps the inn, and spends her time talking about "the Royal Honeymooners," and embroidering horrid little mats for "the tea interval."

The natives here are very depressing—they make nothing, do nothing, are nothing, and the English the same. Jamaica is almost solid black, only 2% white, I've heard, and it is a most dismal and rundown civilization—travelers are persecuted all the time by refined English smokes teasing them to buy nasty little trinkets made of celluloid or strings of shells and beads. Dos said the other day that time brings in its revenges, because first the foreign visitors to the island pestered and cheated the natives with beads and trumpery, and now all the natives pester and cheat the visitors with the same trash they brought in—It is funny—But the island of Jamaica is far finer than I ever dreamed—the vegetation magnificent and green, intensely rich and varied, and the climate delicious. Oranges and lemons grow wild—the coast is extremely lovely—we have been eating bread-fruit and yams and little clear—I mean fresh — water lobsters, and the coffee is good. The whole island is very interesting. Oh I do wish you were here.

Oh I had such a lovely time with you all—felt so built up and restored and it was so fine to see you, only now it seems as if I had hardly seen you at all, and Mr. Parsons acts very wild and restless when I tell about you, and wants to head for New York, though he is up to his neck in glamour right now.

I hope you are well—how is your throat please Mr. Murphy sir, as they say in Jamaica. It's too beautiful here to be a human—you need to be a beast or a bird—Please Mr. Murphy we have been very happy with that Christmas money found in envelope signed by you. Oh Mr. and Mrs. Murphy we love you so much. How is Patrick? Give him our love. I'm writing him a letter—Please write to Key West—just Key West, General Delivery—Love to Baoth and Honoria—Con amore

Katy

UVA

54. KATY DOS PASSOS to SARA MURPHY,
Kingston, Jamaica, 24 January 1935

Dear Sara

We're still here bottled up in Kingston like lobsters in a pot, and the only way to get out seems to be backward like a lobster, by going to Panama and then to New York and then to Havana and then to Key West in the form of a cruise costing $150 per man. We were quite desperate for a while but have finally found a german boat that will take us to Cuba disguised as freight. But first we have to sign a paper renouncing all our rights as passengers or voters of any kind, and promising not to complain of anything or annoy the crew. We have signed this and hope to sail to-morrow—under what conditions we don't know.

Oh I hope there is a letter from you at Key West. We're very anxious to hear and want to know about Patrick. We think of him so much. We think of you something terrific here in Jamaica—I've a lot to write about the place. Tell Patrick we're sending him a letter as soon as we get to Havana again—

More pretty quick
With love

Katy

Dos is thriving. He sends Love.
UVA

55. KATY DOS PASSOS to SARA MURPHY,
Havana [c. late January 1935]

Oh my Dear Sara,

Here's your wire and we are so pleased—pleased *double* because you're coming, and that must mean Patrick is improving. We were cast down by your telegram before, but now rising like rockets and hoping for good Patrick news. I'm writing him today, with pictures. Hurray and Yankee Doodle you're coming to town. We are prepared for you with shouting and you shall have music wherever you goes. And speaking of music—we haven't got our phonograft as through some blunder it was left in Provincetown so if you had a small one to bring it would be a great thing. We have a piano for Miz Laetitia the Farmington Nightingale [Ada MacLeish].

Oh hurray the long Arctic winter is over here—sun warm (not too warm) breeze, birds, flowers, fresh shrimps and Hemingway plovers ($10,000 fine for eating them so you see we don't spare expense)

But dollings—don't be surprized when you see the town—There's been changes. The New Dealers are here—they are called New Dealers but what they really are is Old Bohemians, and Key West is now a Greenwich Village Nightmare—They have stirred up all the old art trash and phoney uplifters that sank to the bottom after the war, and they're painting murals on the café walls, and weaving baskets, and cutting down plants and trees, and renting all the houses (with Washington money) and arranging sight-seeing tours, and building apartments for tourists so they can observe the poor Hemingways. They even wrote to Jed Harris[1] sister that she could have an apartment "with a view of Ernest Hemingway," and all the dreary international smart-alecs are turning up as they always do about six years later, "discovering" the place, and horrified to see each other but getting together just the same, and you can't stir out of your house without being run over by a little Jewish woman on a bicycle, or a beach wagon full of new government appointees just coming off the train or plane—The little Jewish women are always either circling around the Hemingway house or else taking their book reviews to the post-office. It's a paradise of incompetents, all floating around in a rich culture of humanitarian graft, a kind of hierarchy of the Dole—There is even a band of fake Cubans with velvet pants and red sashes that meets the train every day and the sky is full of aeroplanes and the speakeasies are jammed with drunk and cynical newspaper men. They are putting in Tea Rooms painted in black and Orange (The Old Village Flag) and those fearful cork candlesticks and fishnets. They are trying to introduce native crafts, but the natives have no crafts (Except bootlegging and cigar-rolling) and the shoppe-keepers are furious because the natives *won't* weave, but just take their $5.00 a day FERA money and sit in the Speakeasies drinking beer and gaping at the paintings. "We can't get them to work," one shoppe-keeper said to me, almost crying, "I could sell dozens of those raffia hats, but they *won't* weave." Well, Sara, I ask you, would you weave yourself?

Now I'm tearing to put this on the plane. We're wild with joy you're really coming. Dos sends his love to the girls. Please let us know about Patrick. How is Gerald? Much love to Gerald from Mr. Parsons and yours

With love

Katy

Excuse blots—
Over-excited
UVA

---

1. Jed Harris was a New York Broadway producer who would become briefly involved with the unsuccessful production of Hemingway's play *The Fifth Column* during the winter of 1938–1939.

56. KATY DOS PASSOS to SARA MURPHY,
Key West [c. February 1935]

My Dearest Mrs. Puss,

We just arrived yesterday and found your letter—a great pleasure and relief—we'd been bottled up so long in Kingston, unable to break out, and had begun to wonder if we'd ever get back before spring. We were anxious too, for news of Patrick—and felt very far away. Oh dear, my *dear* Mrs. Puss, I want that Patrick to be well. I wonder about him every day—is he able to eat any more—how he's feeling—and when I think about the weather I think about the winter in Patrick's room and how he's seeing the river. I wish we could visit him. I found I missed seeing him so much after I left—he was so sweet, and so entertaining, and funny and brave as an Indian Chief. And of course we were very distressed about the temperature flare up—Of course those things do go up and down even if the general course of things is going well, and I'm hoping now he's already begun to pick up again. I know how hard it must be for him to eat, not feeling hungry ever. I should think for that it would be important to keep his morale and he is so good and courageous that he does a lot of it himself, but it can't do any harm to write him and if he likes it we will write him a lot and send small gadgets and widgets. Ernest is delighted that his Impalla had such a success—he and Pauline were in quite a state because your letter came before we did and they saw the envelope and the first thing they said was "Go right home and read Sara's letter—it's been here for days."

I wish we had gotten it sooner, but we were held back from getting here as if by a bogy—I think you'll like the house—we're just settling into it—and it has lots of room. A big bathroom, one large bedroom with twin beds, another middle-sized bedroom opening into the bathroom, a living room dining room, kitchen, a cozy bedroom and study for Dos and self—a small garden and the vine-covered cistern, which we are counting on you to convert into a tropical bower—I haven't done anything about arranging your quarters, my dearest Mrs. Puss, as you will do it so much more brilliantly than I could, but I warn you it will take all your skill to cope with the color-schemes with which the house is really crawling. Mrs. Kirk has heard of colors and that you can do wonders with a can of paint, and she has indeed, aided by the Women's Magazines and Homemaker's Page—One of the rooms is Blue—completely Sky Blue—there's even a solid blue Batick—one is pink and green—one is Lavender. I haven't changed anything because I wanted you to see all the blended tones and act accordingly. Oh we'll be so glad to see you, and Ada.

About things to bring—it's chilly, and I thought you might possibly bring along a rug or blanket—We've enough unless it gets very cold, but it *has* done that. We're short on table cloths—and silver—I brought some—and got some knives and forks and spoons—but the array is meager. If you could bring one of those fascinating things you call a throw, or something to put over your high-bred feet and legs, it might be wise. The weather is really not very hot—it's lovely, but it's not hot. Almost no mosquitoes, and almost no swimming. But it may change any day now. The New Deal here you must see for yourself. Also Ernest's new book [*Green Hills of Africa*]. Dos says it's fine. I haven't read it yet.

Dos and Ernest are very anxious for Gerald to come down—We wish he would. He would like it. Dos and Ernest are crazy to get him here—Ernest is a Dove complete with Coo.

Sara, the hundred dollars is here in our paws, and how to thank you, my dear and generous lavish beloved Mrs. Puss dear except to thank you con amore—But we can't have you paying for the whole thing—not so—and would like to make the third payment a Parsons payment—

Is Ginny [Pfeiffer] coming with you? There's room enough—only let us know, so we can get in a few extras—Oh I'm so crazy to see you. Please tender to Gerald the most profound assurances of our undying regard.

Now I run for the airmail—Am writing Patrick. Dos sends his love—

Hasta la vista

Katy

Address just 1920 Sidenburg Ave (d as in dog)
Key West
UVA

57. KATY DOS PASSOS to SARA MURPHY,
Key West [c. February 1935]

Mrs. Murphy Darling Now it's getting really wonderfully warm and no need at all for blankets—so just maybe you might need a beach rug or something. Our cistern is a delirium of vegetation and the weather is like honey.

Oh I hope Patrick is better—We're all running and barking here because the Waddell girls are coming.

Had a card from Daou Daou who we see will have to be kidnapped from the air. Ernest is now planning to take the girls out every minute on land or sea, and the Hospitality League and Waddell Entertainment Committee meet every day at five with gin and soda.

Much love to you and Gerald. I had a cute letter from Honoria. Would like to have heard Baoth's Sinclair debate. Love to that Patrick and tell him his illustrated news has been delayed but is being sent right away.

I don't seem able to spell today. I know how, but just can't remember, so will close with a brief easily-spelled four letter word meaning

Love

Katy

UVA

Gerald remained in New York, despite pleas from the Hemingways and the Dos Passoses for him to join Sara in Key West. He felt that he could not leave the business during this crucial period of transition, particularly as related to renegotiating a loan from Robert W. Goelet, the owner of the building formerly occupied by Mark Cross. Goelet wanted fifty percent ownership in the company as collateral on the loan Mark Cross had been forced into during the Depression. Gerald was keeping Sara advised about Patrick, who had closely followed the trial of Bruno Hauptmann. On 13 February Hauptmann was found guilty of kidnapping and then murdering the Charles Lindbergh baby. As Gerald wrote this letter, he was waiting to hear from St. George's School about Baoth's measles, and he expected he would be leaving soon to pick up Baoth and bring him home. The Barry family was leaving for California, where Philip Barry would begin writing for the movies.

58. GERALD MURPHY to SARA MURPHY, New York, 15 February 1934 [1935]

Dear Sal:—

I'm glad the trip down was comfortable and the weather good when you got there. I hope it's warm enough.

Patrick has been in fine form with his air-planes and sketching. His appetite has held up well too. Nectarines and pink grape-fruit are the order of the day. His face is very full. It's wonderful what Miss Sonderby gets into him. To-night he complained that his milk was creamy but she talked him out of it— and later admitted to me the amount of cream she had concealed in it.

He got about twenty valentines which seemed to please him. The [Charles] Macgregors sent one, Hale [Walker], Harold [Heller], the nurses, Honoria, the Barrys, etc. The ones he sent surreptitiously also were a great success.

He sketches and airplanes mostly these days. I think it's an actual relief to him that the Hauptmann trial is over. The radio did serve to keep it before him quite a bit, I'm afraid. He now avoids any such programmes.

Honoria was chirping and simply wanted to know about us all. I'm calling her up to-morrow. We have deferred her visit indefinitely until I know about when Baoth is coming.

I've written Merrick to advise me when I can come to get him. I will probably drive up and come down in the boat and then drive Baoth back.

Miss Ramsgate returned yesterday from Atlantic City for 24 hours. Goelet is to be away until the 24th (visiting Wm. Potter of Garritus) and Johnson is to be away from the 19th till the 24th. Miss R. has asked that G's. lawyers put into writing the terms which Goelet wants. Copies are being sent to her and me and then we can decide whether they can be accepted,—or whether they allow of the Mark Cross Co. going on. Nothing can be decided until the 24th. It is such a personal matter between Goelet and Miss R. that I have suggested their meeting and settling for once and all their differences,—then we can talk business. Goelet, oddly enough, is the intriguant. He has used every underground means to bring the advantage around to himself.

Esther [Murphy] telephoned me to-day that she was to be married. When you were in Newport she came for dinner. At the last moment she brought for cocktails a young man called Chester Alan Arthur, III. Thirty four years of age he is. I persuaded him to eat something before going to his meeting of California Utopians. He seemed very nice. A trace of nervous impediment in his speech but gentle and with a nice spiritual quality. Visionary, intelligent but not an intellectual,—at least not uncomfortably so. An idealist. He left. She said nothing. To-day she telephoned that she had decided that night after three weeks reflection to marry him. They've known each other three months. She is 38. He was married eleven years and divorced in 1933 to a Miss Wilson of Santa Barbara. He's grandson of the 21st President. He seems very much of a gentleman, was so taken with the photograph of Patrick and asked if he might be allowed one day to go to see him.

They are apparently very sensible about it and realize that it is not a romantic match. Esther tells me that they have a great many of the same values and principles and values. He is not well off,—but may eventually be, as both his mother and father who are divorced have money in trust for him.

He joined the Irish Republican Army for four years. He apparently has a mania in favor of the Irish.

Apparently they've both had the same kind of a bad time and are most sympathetic. I can't say I'm sorry, because Esther's life is so dreary. She is affectionate and warm and they seem to be drawn together. I do hope she gets some happiness out of it. She might very well. She's asked me to announce their marriage (at City Hall) in about a month. I think they know what they're doing.

Do enjoy every minute of it. Patrick and Honoria are so excited that you've gone. Lots of love from us all to the H's, D.P's [Hemingways and Dos Passoses] and loads to yrself.

dow.

The Barrys leave to-morrow. I got gifts for the boys & am driving them to the train.

d.

HMD

59. GERALD MURPHY to SARA MURPHY,
New York, 18 February 1935

Dear Sal:—

I wrote Olga, saying there was no news from day to day and that that was why she had not heard from us.[1]

Each day I expect orders to proceed and gather up Baoth.

Honoria has all of Friday free: "to run wildly up and down stairs, have any magazine we want and chew gum." But must stay on bounds. If I'm passing that way during the week-end I'll drop in on her.[2]

Everything's fine here. Great scrubbing and cleaning and economizing. Our bills remain big. I find you have expensive house-keeping tastes.

We *are* still behind on our bills, I can't get ahead of that Doctors' Hospital, nurses, doctors, etc. Not that they're not reasonable, but so steady as an expense.

Think a long time before you decide to make a gift (45.00 dollars) of the phono,—as it looks as if the *only* actual thing we *can* cut down for *some* months is gifts to people. Of course if Dos does seem to lack one,—why——

As for the records. I have a lot of recent ones which Ernest already has and that I can send to Dos if the phono remains,—in which case I'd give all the *new* popular ones to Ernest that I sent with you. He has all the ones I'll send Dos,—if I do send them. I've written Ernest that you have some for him. Some new "fats Waller" I'm sending in a day or two.

I've ordered a cake (black chocolate with marshmallow gunk between) for

---

1. Sara's younger sister Olga was married to Sidney Fish, a New York lawyer turned California oilman and rancher.

2. Honoria had entered Rosemary Hall, a boarding school in Greenwich, Connecticut, in the fall of 1933.

Honoria and her friends to eat in honor of the Father of our Country,—such as it is.

The city is a little grim with its elevator strike. Every office building and apartment house is picketed and policed. Our staff is non-union so they're laying for them.

The Mark Cross problem marks time until the 26th. Miss R. [Ramsgate] returns again on Wednesday.

All other news I'm wiring you.

Do please have a good time every minute. You don't know how glad everyone is and delighted that you did decide to go down. Peggy, the Myers, Patrick, Ernestine, Baoth, judy, the Barrys, etc.

Saw them [the Barrys] off for Hollywood, went to the train, transporting Jonathan. They take his convalescence so casually. I think I was the worried one. Gallagher. Ellen and Phil teary,—and so solicitous for Patrick. (I've written Olga about their baby.)[3]

The Brahms was arresting. He was considered sane and astringent in 1860–1880,—but he has a hard time keeping away from the melodies. Some good tortured dissonances would *make* his stuff,—but he gets murky and sardonic instead. My mind is still open. The next concert will tell,—me, at least.

Lots of love, Sal. Get sun, get tanned and get fun. Love to all that quartet. I suppose there's no better one in existence. Ada goes with you,—and you know what that is.

We think of you all the time,

daou.

HMD

---

3. The Barrys' eighteen-month-old daughter had recently died of an undiagnosed infection.

60. GERALD MURPHY to SARA MURPHY,
New York, 20 February 1935

PATRICK CONTINUES SAME WAS DELIGHTED WITH YOUR FISHING NEWS LETTER RECEIVED THIS MORNING ALREADY FORWARDED TO HONORIA SHE IS FINE TELEPHONED DR JACOBY SAYS BAOTH IS MENDING EVERYTHING GOING NICELY HERE PLEASE ALSO GET SOME REST YOURSELF WE ALL SEND YOU VERY MUCH LOVE =

GERALD.

HMD

Shortly after this telegram, Baoth's illness rapidly reversed itself, and Sara was summoned from Florida. Baoth died at Massachusetts General Hospital on 17 March. Gerald Murphy never again acknowledged St. Patrick's Day (a grim reminder of his own dark-sided Irishness). The Hemingways and Dos Passoses, back in Key West, were immediately notified of Baoth's death.

61. KATY DOS PASSOS to GERALD and SARA MURPHY, Key West, 18 March 1935

Beloved Sara and Gerald

How our hearts shrank with dreadful pain when we heard yesterday—Last night we longed to speak with you and there was no way, and no word to say—I think of Baoth—so handsome and sweet—so valuable—as I saw him at Christmas, and it's too cruel—Darlings we cannot help you in this disaster but you are so brave you will master it somehow and go on with your good and beautiful lives, so dear to us all—

Deep love

Katy

UVA

62. JOHN DOS PASSOS to GERALD and SARA MURPHY, Key West [18 March 1935]

You've been so brave through all this horrible time that it seems hard to write that you must go on and be brave. We admire and love you and wish so there were something we could do to make you feel just a little better. Perhaps later we will be able to cheer you up a little—just now we feel its too frightfully hard for anyone to bear—perhaps it can be a slight too slight consolation to feel that you have friends who feel what you feel—even if dimly and far away—and that you play a large part in their thoughts and feelings. And we want you to go on living traveling and looking around at the world in spite of everything—I wish I could have said goodby to Baoth. Trying to think of some kind of cheerful word to end a letter with I cant find any.

Love

Dos

HMD

63. ERNEST HEMINGWAY to GERALD and SARA MURPHY,
Key West [19 March 1935]

Dear Sara and Dear Gerald:

You know there is nothing we can ever say or write. If Bumby died we know how you would feel and there would be nothing you could say. Dos and I came in from the Gulf Sunday and sent a wire. Yesterday I tried to write you and I couldn't.

It is not as bad for Baoth because he had a fine time, always, and he has only done something now that we all must do. He has just gotten it over with. It was terrible that it had to go on for such a long time but if they could keep him from suffering sometimes it is merciful to get very tired before you die when you want to live very much.

About him having to die so young—Remember that he had a very fine time and having it a thousand times makes it no better. And he is spared from learning what sort of a place the world is.

It is *your* loss: more than it is his so it is something that you can, legitimately, be brave about. But I cant be brave about it and in all my heart I am sick for you both.

Absolutely truly and coldly in the head though I know that anyone who dies young after a happy childhood, and no one ever made a happier childhood than you made for your children, has won a great victory. We all have to look forward to death by defeat, our bodies gone, our world destroyed; but it is the same dying we must do; while he has gotten it all over with, his world all intact, and the death only by accident.

You see now we have all come to the part of our lives where we start to lose people of our own age. Baoth was our own age. Very few people ever really are alive and those that are never die; no matter if they are gone. No one you love is ever dead.

We must live it, now, a day at a time and be very careful not to hurt each other. It seems as though we were all on a boat now together, a good boat still, that we have made but that we know now will never reach port. There will be all kinds of weather, good and bad; and especially because we know now that there will be no landfall we must keep the boat up very well and be very good to each other. We are fortunate we have good people on the boat.

With all our love to you both and to the Duke of Taxidermy [Patrick] and to Honoria of the Horses and to old Baoth

Ernest

HMD

118

64. PAULINE HEMINGWAY to GERALD and SARA MURPHY, Key West, 19 March [1935]

Dear Sara and Dowdow—

I can't realize yet that Baoth isn't going to get well. I keep seeing him the way he was out West, so strong and handsome and fitted for life. Of all the boys I can think of, he had the most abundant and radiant health.

I know I can't say anything to comfort you or help you. I can only think of how kind and lovely and dear you are and how much you are suffering.

Your very loving friend

Pauline

HMD

65. GERALD and SARA MURPHY to KATY and JOHN DOS PASSOS and PAULINE and ERNEST HEMINGWAY, New York, 21 March 1935

BAOTHS ASHES STAND ON AN ALTAR IN SAINTBARTHOLOMEWS UNTIL SUNDAY WHEN THEY WILL BE LAID BESIDE HIS GRANDFATHER AT EAST-HAMPTON OH THIS IS ALL SO UNLIKE HIM AND ALL OF US WE TRY TO BE LIKE WHAT YOU WANT US TO BE KEEP THINKING OF US PLEASE WE LOVE YOU=

SARA GERALD.

UVA

66. KATY DOS PASSOS to GERALD and SARA MURPHY, Key West [23 March 1935]

Sara and Gerald Dear

We think so constantly of you that we can't help writing, but alas what can we say—except that we are crushed with sorrow and would give anything to help you. How like you to say in your wire that friends *could* help—oh we love you so truly and share your suffering now and our hearts are desperate to comfort you—We would have come to New York if not afraid for Dos—we want so much to stand beside you and touch your hand.

It is something to think of Baoth's sunny life and how his youth had all the best things of youth—I am glad to have such sweet pictures of him in my mind—days on the boat, and many other things—I remember when I saw him at Christmas I had a feeling of pride and pleasure in him—his beauty and promise—and I thought then what he must mean to you—It is a great disaster, but you are brave, and strong too, and so many people love and count upon you—Dos says to tell you he is going to write you himself—He is broken-hearted—

When you can, do send us a few words—we think of you always—

Your loving

Katy

UVA

Some family members, including Sara's sister Olga, later indirectly blamed Hoytie Wiborg for the Murphys' tragedies. When Hoytie made some ill-advised business ventures during the Depression years, she lost most of her money and petitioned Sara to help her out by buying her portion of the Wiborg estate. This quickly led to serious misunderstandings and a breach in the relationship.

67. STELLA CAMPBELL TO SARA MURPHY, Beverly Hills, 23 March 1935

My beloved Sarah.

I am almost afraid to write to you, perhaps letters are a trouble to you to read. They said you might come here—now I hear little Patrick is better and that you feel you must stay with him until he is well enough to be moved. Mrs Phil Barry spoke to me on the telephone this morning. . . . we are all so stunned we are almost afraid to think or speak to each other of what you and Gerald are suffering.

Darling Sarah dont let anything *anything* have the chance of happening that might in anyway get on your nerves—that are now strained to their very limit. . . . I allude to poor Hoytie. Olga tells me she is on the water. . . . Gerald will be wise and protect you . . . I am nervous about you—and I love you and cannot endure that at this time there should be a word spoken, or a look passed—or even a teasing memory near you.

Protect yourself—you are so wise and so brave—our nerves are nothing to do with our character . . . protect them dearest. The unspeakable unbelievable tragedy that has befallen you both, demands that nothing this world can put upon you that could be avoided should be endured.

Forgive my writing like this you are so dear to me

Your ever loving

Stella

HMD

68. ELLEN BARRY to SARA MURPHY, Los Angeles [c. 24 March 1935]

My darling Sara—

I am heartbroken for you and Dow Dow—all week I have thought of you and your terrible agony and anxious watching—what awful suffering you have known—I only hope my darling you can find some physical relaxation—some rest for your poor exhausted nerves—There is nothing else that can be done for the spirit—Please please try dear Sara to come away as soon as possible—I think you would like it here—it is so close to the Riviera in feeling—we are reminded of your Antibes every day—and your loving friends Dottie Doug Bee Bobby Mrs. Pat Campbell are all longing to see you so— Please please come to us we have a little separate guest house across the garden where you could rest well—and we love you so much I think we could help—

Words are no use now—You know what I feel for you—I wish I could be closer to you to-day—

Your devoted

Ellen

HMD

69. JOHN and KATY DOS PASSOS and ERNEST and PAULINE HEMINGWAY to GERALD and SARA MURPHY, Key West, 26 March 1935

DEAR SARA AND GERALD WE WISH WE WERE THERE WITH YOU OR YOU WERE HERE WITH US WE MUST ALL HOLD TOGETHER WE ARE YOUR

FAITHFUL FRIENDS AND YOU ARE PART OF OUR LIVES YOUR WAY IS OUR
WAY WE SEND LOVE AND ARE WRITING SOON=

DOS   KATY   ERNEST   PAULINE.

HMD

70. JOHN and KATY DOS PASSOS and ERNEST and PAULINE HEMINGWAY
to GERALD and SARA MURPHY,
Key West, 29 March 1935

WE WILL COME SINGLE OR IN SWARM AT ANYTIME TO LAKE PLACID OR
WHEREVER YOU GO HOW ABOUT COMING DOWN HERE FIRST OR TO BI-
MINI ANYTIME DURING APRIL MUCH LOVE=

KATY   DOS   PAULINE   ERNEST.

HMD

*MacLeish had been with the Murphys in Massachusetts during Baoth's
illness and was now en route to England, where he would prepare a* Fortune *magazine story on King George V.*

71. ARCHIBALD MACLEISH to GERALD and SARA MURPHY,
On board S.S. *Majestic* [29 March 1935]

My dears:

For some things in this world one must give words to one's admiration—
for courage & grace & nobility such as yours. It is hard that people must suffer so to raise these memorials to the greatness of the human spirit. It is hard:
but also just. Because the human spirit is not often great—because the greatness of the human spirit is the only enduring beauty—because it would not be
fitting to achieve greatness without pain. All this is of no comfort to you. You
did not wish for that cruel marble tearing the palms of your hands. You
wished for your son. But for the rest of us, who have not suffered as you have
suffered, a new justification of all suffering, a new explanation of the eternal
mystery of pain, has been created. It is the heart of the irony of our lives that
this justification—this explanation—should be apparent not to you who
need it but to us. For the symbol of the irony of our lives is the phoenix which
must die to live.

No one can give you comfort—only time whose comfort (until, like unwanted sleep, it is given) we reject. Those who love you can only ask you to believe that you have not suffered in vain. It is true.

I love you both

Archie

HMD

72. STELLA CAMPBELL to SARA MURPHY,
Beverly Hills [c. late March 1935]

Beloved Sara.

I have just come from the Phil Barry's. It was so comforting to talk with them . . . they have such a wealth of love for you both, and such a passionate desire to be of service to you both.

They showed me the Guest-house where they long for you and Gerald and Honoria to be. It is peaceful, and very very comfortable and very sunny. Just the amount of rooms you would want. A verandah and a pretty garden in front of the house and then quite a large space—a gravelled court between the Guest-house and the house. Lovely mountains covered with green trees—the early spring green and grass. And flowers everywhere. . . . A nice verandah outside the bedrooms too. A comfortable kitchen and a room and bathroom for your maid. . . . You would have no trouble whatever with housekeeping . . . and you would see only those you wished to see.

At a little distance there are fine golf links. "Bel-Air" is a very beautiful place and Los Angeles and Hollywood a thousand miles away. . . .

Oh darlings they want you so much to come . . . there is healing in the air . . . perhaps a fortnight or a month—may give you the rest you *must* have.

Think of it dearest—it has the same serene spirit of the Ferme des Orangers" . . . it is a lovely place and seems to me to call for you both. . . . I wanted to tell you that there is such a place as you would wish for ready for you to come to—if suddenly you felt you and Gerald would like it. . . . The sun is divine. Their desire to be of service to you will help a little—if anything can help you darling.

Stella

HMD

73. PHILIP BARRY to SARA and GERALD MURPHY,
Los Angeles [c. spring 1935]

Dearest Sara and Gerald:

Fifty times in the last weeks I've tried to write you, and couldn't, and I can't now. But I love you Dearly, as you know, and always will. Ellen will give you the news, such as it is. I wish to heaven you were here with us, because it is all right here, but we don't like it quite as much as we say we do. We are Easterners, and we will be back early in June with a lot of dough and a sense of having had a change.

My Ellen is a darling and I love her best of all. I did even when I had my Mary Ellen—whom I still love, just as you still have Baoth. But these things are tough and I will have some questions to ask some time.

God love you both. We will see you soon. From your loving,

Phil—

HMD

74. PAULINE HEMINGWAY to SARA and GERALD MURPHY,
Key West, 4 April [1935]

Dear Sara and Dowdow,

We tried to get Patrick's serenade [on Alexander Woollcott's "The Town Crier" radio show] Sunday night but failed. The static starts in earnest—I believe that ernest is spelled with an a—here about the end of March. We had tried all afternoon to get the Symphony and we did get one but it turned out to be Cuban. Anyway, come around seven o'clock Katie Dos Ernest and I settled down to hear Patrick's serenade and we were pretty disappointed not to get it. Was it pretty fine?

Sunday morning at an early hour, Dos, Mike [Strater] and Ernest are setting out for Bimini. Ernest has been hoping all week that maybe one of you would join them. It won't be a very long trip—about two weeks, and a fine life on the water. Maybe you could fly down and over and stay a few days and come back with them. Either sex would be MOST welcome, and we are having new slip covers put on all the cushions to give satisfaction to the most fastidious taste. I would have gone but am going through ordeal by porch with carpenters, gutter snipes and I am afraid even riviters—cutting two stone wall windows into doors. Dowdow, you will come down here to Key West, won't you sometime—soon sometime—and tell me about my talent for remodeling? NOBUDY can do as much for my self esteem as you can. And a house-worker often gets discouraged.

Dos and Katy are so happy in their house and cistern. They are very comfortable and Dos is getting a lot of work done despite some days not feeling too well. He still has those sweating spells but they are coming less frequently and lasting shorter. Katie is blooming and beautiful, gaining beyond all her dresses, with her weight at 130 and her headaches practically a thing of the past. I think their only real personal problem at the moment is getting rid of a cat named Scat who has the mange. They keep taking the cat out on the keys to lose it—not liking to deprive the cat of its life outright which comes I suppose from reading the Nation and the Masses—but so far the cat is in Scotland before them every time and we met them only yesterday out near Pirates' Cove looking for a likely spot to set Scat out. They are getting a little frenzied as the cat Scat is about to have kittens.

I WISH you were down here, both of you. And we are surely coming to Lake Placid [New York] if you will leave us know when you want us. We feel we MUST see you very soon. You are such lovely people. Dear Sara and Dowdow.

Your loving friend,

Pauline

HMD

75. ALEXANDER WOOLLCOTT to PATRICK MURPHY,
New York, 5 April 1935

My dear Patrick,

I am glad to hear that you enjoyed the serenade. I feel I was lucky that no storm or static played mischief with my well-laid plans.

I had to save up the last word of the broadcast for an old woman named Susan, even if I could not be sure she would be listening. I think you might like to know that luck, or whatever you want to call it, was with us in that matter, too. I have had a letter from Susan. She got the message all right and it pleased her for many reasons, including the fact that it came on her eighty-seventh birthday.

I hope I shall see you soon.

A. Woollcott

[On the reverse side of this card was the Woollcott caricature by William Auerbach Levy which came to identify him. A few quickly-sketched lines capture well Woollcott's round, owlish glasses, his dark cropped mustache, his heavy jowls and thick neck. Woollcott liked the sketch so much that he had it engraved on his stationery. Beneath this caricature Woollcott had written to Patrick:] "With my Compliments."

HMD

76. ERNEST HEMINGWAY to PATRICK MURPHY,
Key West, 5 April 1935

Dear Patrick:

I was awfully glad to get your letter today and am writing right away because tomorrow we will be packing to leave on a trip. And if I don't write now I will spend several weeks intending to write you—and won't do it. You know how hard it is to write on a boat.

We have been trying to make you a movie of sailfishing—but the minute I took the camera on board the sailfish refused to bite and we haven't seen one since. But now we are going from here up along the coast for about a hundred and fifty miles and then cut across the Gulf Stream to Gun Cay and Bimini in the Bahama Islands to see what it is like there for fishing this next May and June.

We plan to go up well out in the current of the stream and troll up for two days, putting in inside of the reef to anchor at night. Then cut across early in the morning of the third day taking a bearing from Carysfort Lighthouse (you can find that on the Chart) and steering East North East for Gun Key.

I have gotten my camera that I had in Africa cleaned up for taking movies and we are going to take the film your mother brought down and try to get you some good exciting pictures of Marlin and tuna fishing. I will send the films from Miami with your address on them. So you will be the first to see them. Then we can get copies from them later. Will try to get some very good shots.

If your father will order the chart showing Florida and the Bahamas you can tell just where we are and where the places are that I will refer to.

Dos is going on the trip and so is Mike Strarter. He is the President of the Maine Tuna Club and we kid him about this a good deal and always refer to him as The President. When he hooks a big fish we plan to put I Don't Want To Be President on the Phonograph. He takes his fishing very seriously. But he is a good fellow and a good clown too. The other people on the trip will be Old Bread who is engineer on the boat. Your mother can tell you about him. He is

fat and a good man with engines and also a good sailor. His real name is Albert Pinder. For cook we are carrying a man named Hamilton Adams who is
very tall and thin and is a good friend of Bread's. He is known in Key West as
Saca Ham. Here everybody has goofy nicknames which they get as kids and
then have all their lives. I don't know what kind of a cook Saca is. If he isn't
good on this trip we will get somebody else for the next one.

This way you will know who is who in the pictures. Saca is tall and thin
with a lean face. Mike has a wide grin and very wide shoulders and looks a
little like Abraham Lincoln as a young man if he had gone to Princeton. You
know what the great Portuguese Marriner and line breaker Honest Jack
Passos looks like. I look much the same as always except a little bloated. Will
hope to get thinner.

We are going to try to catch Wahoo, Tuna, Marlin and sailfish. We plan to
take two weeks for this first trip to look things over. The Giant tuna aren't due
until the middle of May. Nobody has been able to catch one yet. They run off
all their line and break it at the reel. I have gotten a new reel to hold 1000 yards
of 39 thread line and have another ordered to hold 1500 yards. The first is a
14/0 VomHofe. The other big one is a Hardy Zane-Grey model. (I suppose
you know their catalogue) I have been using that model in a 5 1/2 and 6 inch
for three years now. They are fine reels.

I have two hickory 23 oz. tips for the big Marlin and two Hardy No. 5 (20
Oz tips) 2 Hardy No. 4 16 oz tips and regular medium tackle rods for wahoo
etc.

Because nobody has been able to catch one of those huge (2000 lb) tunas
yet I have rigged up one of our regular fishing chairs in my 13 foot Lyman Sea
Skiff that I plan to tow behind the Pilar. When we hook a big tuna we are going
to get into the little sea skiff and shut down on the drag and see if they can
really go sixty miles an hour the way they say they can. The President has said
that this is Madness and that the tuna will tow us up to Nova Scotia. But between ourselves I think the President is slightly Goofy and that the Tuna will
tow himself to death in a short time. Anyway I hope we can get you some
movies of it. With a chair to brace in I can give the tuna or the marlin the devil
pulling.

The difficulty will be to get Dos to take the movies with the camera pointed
away from him and toward the tuna instead of away from the tuna and toward
him. But he is full of confidence and already thinks of himself as a big camera
man and is starting to wear his cap with the visor on backwards. But if you get
any closeups of Dos's eye instead of the tuna don't say I didn't warn you.

The skiff is clinker built, very light and beautifully sea-worthy. She is about
half as broad as she is long and I hope we can get her to go faster with a big fish
than a racing outboard ever pushed her.

I have been feeling very gloomy with too many visitors and haveing to take

127

the treatment for my amoebic dysentery that makes me over three quarters goofy. But now am cured, I think, and want to wash myself out clean with the Gulf Stream and the best soap I know—which is excitement or whatever you call it. Anyway we will try to can some of it on the films and send it up to you. Really good jumping fish pictures are swell and I hope we can get some.

I'll take some of the boat and the people on the first reel so you will know who is who even if not why.

Now about the animals. I have either a Grant's Gazelle or an Oryx that you can have for whenever your last birthday was. Which do you prefer? I would have had it mounted before but have been half goofy with my lousy treatment. Let me know will you.

Will you give my love to your mother and your father and tell them the reason I don't write is because I can't write. But that I would like to see them. If they would like to fish; come to Bimini. You can fly it in less than an hour from Miami. If you go to the country this summer we will come up to see you wherever you go. We are putting an outrigger on the boat to make a big baitxs skip. Will let you know how it comes out. We never found them necessary off Cuba but they say they are good. Mike Strater is giving it to the boat for a present.

Well Bo if there is anything you want to know about the trip write me to Bimini and ask. The address will be On Board Yacht Pilar, Bimini, Bahama Islands. B.W.I. Dos and I will write you from there.

We clear from here tomorrow.

We leave here early Sunday morning. Run out to the stream past the Sea Bouy to about twenty miles outside of the reef—then take the stream up until it is time to run in to anchor that night. We should be up beyond Sombrero light. Next day troll up the stream again, saving gas by going way out for the big current, then come inside of Carysfort. The next day head across the Gulf for Gun Cay and go on up on the other side to Bimini where we will enter. We plan to run across the gulf trolling so will steer about 70 degrees after leaving Carysfort light to allow for the set of the big current.

Would like to find some place over there with just as good fishing as Bimini but not so many boats. We'll fish it together sometime.

Am taking the 6.5 mannlicher and 100 rounds, the 22 Colt Woodsman (with the long barrell. Have never tried the short barrell yet) with 1000 rounds, and my 12 Guage pump you all gave me and 200 rounds. We carry 300 gal gas, 150 water and will carry extra water. Always have canned goods for 2 months on board in case of ever being broken down and drifting and have the top deck rigged to catch water and run it into the water tanks whenever it rains. There is ice and gas (expensive) at Bimini.

Well So Long old Timer. Write me to Bimini will you?

With best love from us all. Our Patrick caught a big barracuda yesterday

128

without any help (on 6oz. tip, i5 thread line, 4/0 reel) barracuda of about twenty eight pounds. Hooked him in the channel and thought he was a small tarpon. He was jumping in the sun. Jumped eight times. By the third jump we could see he was a barracuda. He made a fine fight.

Well, So Long again.
Your friend

Ernest

HMD

77. JOHN DOS PASSOS to PATRICK MURPHY,
Key West [April 1935]

Dear Patrick—

Well we started out to Bimini but we didn't get very far. About five miles outside of American Shoal we ran into an enormous school of dolphins. Immediately everybody was hooked into great big dolphins (about 20 lbs) that looked very silvery as they jumped. When you get them near the boat their fins look bright blue and they have peacock colored spots on them. Then when you bring them up out of the water they turn green and yellow and finally die a greyish yellow. We'd been catching dolphins for about ten minutes when two huge sharks appeared—a deep sea kind of shark with a tail like a mackerel shark and very large tails and fins. In Cuba they call them galanos, but I dont know what their name is actually in English—anyway they were mean looking customers. Mike Strarter got one on his light rod and Ernest got his in first (he'd previously popped two lines and the shark had the hooks and leaders hanging from his maw—but they didn't seem to discourage him) and shot him once with a rifle. Then they gaffed him with a very heavy gaff and were holding him up out of the water for me to photograph with the movie camera when an odd thing happened. Ernest had out his small colt automatic (.22) and was just going to finish the shark off with a final shot to get his hooks and leaders back when the shark went into a tremendous spiral convulsion and broke the pole of the gaff. The broken piece hit the pistol which went off. We didn't hear the shot on account of the great snapping noise the gaff made breaking. The bullet (a softnosed lead bullet) hit the brass edging of the boat's rail and splattered into both calves of Ernest's legs. Fortunately the wounds were not very bad, but we thought it was wiser to turn back to get a doctor to dress them. So we are not in Bimini yet. As soon as we finish taking the movie reel we'll send it up. I think it shows the gaff breaking. I hope it came out all right but I'm afraid it wont be very good because it's the first time I've ever tried to use a movie camera. Give everybody my love and Katy's

We'll take a lot of reels and send them up as we take them.

You be good and dont kick the covers off too often

love

Dos

HMD

78. JOHN DOS PASSOS to GERALD and SARA MURPHY, Key West, 30 April [1935]

Dear Gerald and Sara—

Just back from Bimini where I left Ernest struggling with the gigantic furries—I am sending a couple more reels of film to Patrick tomorrow. Dont bother to write—but if somebody should happen to feel like it I'd certainly be pleased to get a word. I'm wondering just how good no news is.

Katy had to go up to Baltimore to interview a physician—she's staying with the Gantts—Her address is care Dr Wm. Horsely Gantt, 632 North Washington Street, Balt. Md—I hope she will only be there for a week or so and then she may get to New York before coming down here to pick up yr. humble servant who is working rather hard at this business—I hated to let Katy go on up there alone but we decided I'd better inhale the fetid air of the tropics for another month at least—You'll certainly see her as one of the things she wants to go over to New York for is to take a look at you gents, and to see if there's anything she could possibly do that could be of any use to you—Dont forget that we are both inordinately fond of you

Dos

HMD

The Dos Passoses and Hemingway had returned to Bimini after their first aborted trip, but they were not there long when both the Dos Passoses had to return to Key West. Dos Passos needed further rest, and Katy suffered from further internal disorders. While seeking medical help in Baltimore and then New York, she also saw the Murphys. Dur-

*ing May, there would be a memorial service for Baoth at St. George's
School, where MacLeish would read his poem "Words to Be Spoken."*

79. GERALD MURPHY to ADA MACLEISH
[New York] [c. May 1935]

Dear Ada:—

Twice I have tried to write Archie of what it meant to Sara and me,—and to
Baoth, for him to have done and felt as he did last Sunday,—on that clear open
May morning—but I cannot. It's all *too* incommunicable,—It's depth more
than it's mystery. I cannot blast it out of my heart, try as I do. I could stand
telling him were I able. I tried to speak of it but my words sounded like pebbles
falling. I *heard* them. But I must write you. For beauty for grace and strength
of thought I shall never see human creature equal Archie that day. I have never
known simplicity before. You deserve so to have seen and heard him.

Since he spoke we know that Baoth is lost to us,—but we know that the
supreme thing has been done in his name. It is all one with Sara's and my love
for you and for Archie—and the joy we feel in knowing that Peter is our
godchild.

                                                    Gerald.

LC

*Katy had returned from the East to rejoin Dos Passos in Key West in
mid-May. At the end of that month, they left for Havana and then a
week in Bimini, following which they headed north by car. Katy's letter
is written en route to Provincetown after a sustained period in the
tropics due to Dos Passos's ill health. The Murphys had just moved
Patrick to Saranac Lake, New York, where he would begin treatments at
the Trudeau Institute.*

80. KATY DOS PASSOS to GERALD MURPHY,
Fort Pierce, Florida, 20 June 1935

Dearest Gerald,

We're on our way home from Bimini, still dizzy with sun, water, guns,
champagne, marine monsters and tropical desolation. How many times we
wished you were there—it is always so much more fun when you are there,
and easier to see things—just as if you had turned on better lighting—And
you would have been entertained too—It's a fantastic place—a crazy mixture

of luxury, indigence, good liquor, bad food, heat, flies, land apathy and sea magnificance, social snoot, money, sport, big fish, big fisherman, and competitive passion. The big fishermen work over catching the big fish like Russians on a subway—they've got it all charted and organized and they're all out for records, and madly jealous of each other—The fish are huge—a thousand pound tuna—800 pound sharks—600 pound marlin—We had the tuna on the line eight hours—Ernest finally brought him up, alive and almost landed, when five sharks rushed him at once. They come like express trains and hit the fish like a planing mill—shearing off twenty-five and thirty pounds at a bite. Ernest shoots them with a machine gun, *rrr*—but it won't stop them—It's terrific to see the bullets ripping into them—the shark thrashing in blood and foam—the white bellies and fearful jaws—the pale cold eyes— I was really aghast but it's very exciting. I'm writing Patrick all about it, but not certain where to send it, or Sara either. Just Saranac N.Y.?

Dear Gerald, I can never thank or repay you and Sara for your kindness and goodness to me. I haven't the words or the wit, and can only tell you lamely how I can't tell you what I feel. It is a very true feeling, though, and goes down deep. Dos and I want you to know that—

I've been wanting to write you, but there are no mails from Bimini, and before we went there, I didn't seem able to write at all—felt quite goofy and no account for a long time. I'm writing Sara, and will just chance the address—

We are anxious to hear about Patrick—how he fares at Saranac—how he likes it—I'm glad we're coming back, and can see you and talk—Dos is crazy to be home again. He's very bored with the tropics, poor animal. We'll see how he does—I hope it's all right, but feel a little cautious. He's going to see the doctor Chester Arthur told us about in New York, and I think we'll stay there for a while, if Dos wants to consult him for any length of time.

Oh I hope you are well—I hate you to have that poltergeist in your back—I would rather Bernarr MacFadden had it, we must exorcise it right away. Oh Mr. Parsons and I are pretty crazy to see you. We are hitting it up along the dreary ashfalt of Florida, tearing along through the tin cans and poisonous reptiles—almost scalded with sun and washed away by the rainy season, but pressing on. We haven't had a thing to eat for three days except tourist meals, and are thinking of going on milk and raw fish till we get home. We're awfully tired and damp—No way to get dry—except steaming in the sun. The hotels are all closed and the whole state of Florida is like the vacant lot when the circus has gone—

Forgive a dull letter—I'm a dull dog tonight, but the dog's name is

Tray

Your loving

Katy

We're bringing records and shaker—Love to Mrs. Puss. Dos sends love We hated to miss staying with you at 439—but Dos wasn't quite well enough to come North, and we kept delaying till too late—

UVA

81. F. Scott Fitzgerald to Gerald Murphy,
Baltimore, 24 June 1935

CAN YOU WIRE ME APPROXIMATELY WHAT ROSEMARY HALL COSTS AND IF YOU THINK ITS WORTH WHILE MY TRYING TO ENTER SCOTTY THERE THIS FALL ADDRESS HOTEL STAFFORD MUCH AFFECTION=

SCOTT.

HMD

82. Gerald Murphy to F. Scott Fitzgerald
[New York] 25 June 1935[1]

School sixteen hundred yearly entrance easily arranged Honoria not returning former headmistress aged in harness now lacks organizational director policy antiquated merely monument to era of rather snobbish eastern finishing schools catering to untamed daughters of pretentious western parents suggest considering Ethel Walkers school Simsbury Connecticut love all.

Gerald

HMD

---

1. This is taken from Gerald's typed copy of the prepaid day letter sent to Fitzgerald.

83. Ernest Hemingway to Sara Murphy,
Bimini, British West Indies, 10 July 1935

Dearest Sara:

It's a crime that we had the kids all settled here before we got your letter [inviting them to the Murphys' new "camp"]. It would have been marvellous to be together up there. But they are so crazy about it here that I dont see how we could take them away now. Patrick has gained 2 lbs and is brown as a real Mexican. Gregory [born 12 November 1932] is learning to swim and Bumby is out all day in an outboard with his black friends. They have the real ocean and a perfectly safe seven mile long surf bathing clear sand beach at the back door. Have built a cabaña on the beach out of thatched palms. No insects there and the water is absolutely clear Gulf Stream and always cool but never cold. Their house is on a ridge that overlooks the ocean and the lagoon and is only $20.00 a month! It blows a big breeze every day and they swim all morning and fish all afternoon. They are crazy about it and I dont know where in the world we could get such a beach or such water. You'll have to come here. Before we knew you and Patrick had gone to the Adirondacks Pauline and I thought maybe you could come. What you write about the woods makes me want to go there very much. When we come north Pauline and I will come up to see you and Patrick and Honoria. We havent any dates yet. When we finish here I want to go somewhere to write for 3 months.

Lately the fish havent been here. They've gone to Cuba and if they dont show up here in the next 3 weeks they've gone for this year. May go to Cuba for 2 weeks to see. Then north. Have to find some place to put the boat so she will be safe in hurricane months.

You would love this place Sara. It's in the middle of the Gulf Stream and every breeze is a cool one. The water is so clear you think you will strike bottom when you have 10 fathoms under your keel. There is every kind of fish, altho the big marlin and tuna seem to have passed. There is a pretty good hotel and we have a room there now because there have been rain squalls at night lately and so I cant sleep on the roof of the boat. That's not a very nautical term but a fine cool place to sleep. Dos and Katy will tell you about it.

Tell Patrick I have a Thompson Sub Machine gun and we shoot sharks with it. Shot 27 in two weeks. All over ten feet long. As soon as they put their heads out we give them a burst. We caught a Mako shark within 12 lbs of the Worlds Record in 35 minutes. 786 pounds. Dos will tell you about the big tuna and the marlin. We fought one tuna of about 1000 lbs with another man who had him first for 9 hrs and 50 minutes. Then just when we had him whipped and on the surface showing terribly big in the searchlight at 9 o'clock at night 17 miles from where he was hooked the sharks hit him. 5 hit him at once. I shot 3 with the Mannlicher but they cut him up like a log in a planing mill. The head alone weighed 249 lbs. It was a dirty shame. Cook had him 6 1/2 hrs. I had him 3 hrs 20 minutes after Cook's hands gave out.

I dont know any more news. Patrick would love this place. You can catch snappers, tarpon, and 25 kinds of small fish right from the dock here. About 400 people live in the town. Mostly turtling boats and spongers. Bonefish are common as grunts.

134

We bring our drinking water and ice and fresh vegetables on the pilot boat that comes once a week from Miami. There is no kind of sickness on the island and the average age of people in the cemetery is 85. About 2/3 of population is black. It is under the British flag and there is only one policeman who was gone to Nassau for 2 weeks. We have celebrated the Queen's Birthday, the Jubilee, The Prince of Wales Birthday, the 4th of July, and will celebrate the 14th of July, getting drunk on all of these. We miss you on these occassions as well as all the rest of the time and send you <u>much</u> love and hope to see you soon. Best to Patrick and Honoria, much love again from Poor Old Pappa.

How you write here is Capt. George D. Kreidt, 1437 S.W. 5th Street, Miami, Florida, For E. Hemingway, Capt. "Pilar" Bimini, BWI. That way it saves 2 weeks as [it] comes over on the pilot boat every Tuesday.

Ernest.

We got another bunch of wonderful discs from Gerald. Dos and Kate forgot to take your camera. Can I send it?

HMD

John Dos Passos and the MacLeishes visited the Murphys in July and then returned together to Conway, where Dos Passos stayed briefly before returning to Provincetown. Katy had remained in New York to find outlets for her writing. Before marrying Dos Passos, she had worked as an editor for a trade magazine in Chicago and then writing copy for an advertising agency. She was now writing human interest travel accounts, sometimes in collaboration with her Provincetown neighbor and good friend Edith Shay. They had discussed some ideas for a magazine series and would later collaborate on a guidebook to Cape Cod.

84. KATY DOS PASSOS TO SARA MURPHY,
Provincetown, 26 July 1935

Mrs. Puss Dear

How I hated not to see you when Dos and Archie and Ada did, but they told me all about the trip. Dos very delighted with the aquatics. I stayed in New York quietly scorching, and trying to awaken the magazine world to the real value of some notions I had but don't yet know what will come of it.

Of course we think of you practically around the clock, and at seven when Gerald calls our ears prick up—I wish we were over the fence neighbors is what I wish.

We have the most absurd neighbors here, by the way. They are pansies—not the bohemian intellectual or even theatrical kind, but purely home-keeping and domestic—two young men of thirty-five or forty I should say, constant readers of Esquire, which they regard as high-brow but worth the effort. They spend all day in house-hold tasks, and all day long they keep up a little tattle and chatter about their doings. "Now where did you put those rags, Jim? Oh dear me these windows are dirty—How *could* that scratch have got on the car?—Dickie, did you sweep those rugs?—Is'nt it lucky the sun's so hot—now Lucy can dry the laundry—Oh look—that geranium pot's cracked—" It goes on every minute, till Dos really looks quite black at times, but it's funny too. They follow our movements with the most intense interest, and we can't poke our noses out, but they start a shrill twitter of talk—They were in Cuba last winter—"not the old part—a nice quiet suburb." Their housekeeping puts all the rest of the street to shame, and Susan Glaspell, who is rather slack about such matters, is nearly crazy because in an excess of zeal they sweep the pavement in front of her house every morning at six—thus waking her up three hours early with their squeaking.[1]

We are having a good time here with Charley and Adelaide Walker, who are visiting us and are up to their necks with Theater Union affairs, also left deviations from the Communist Party. It's a known fact that they are inclined toward Trotskyism and this is regarded by the Party as the blackest heresy of which a Communist is capable, but the C.P. shuts its eyes to it in the Walkers, because of their value to the Workers Theater so it's all very exciting and underground, and we all feel something like a gang of counterfeiters. I keep thinking it's just like my childhood days when we used to play Robin Hood, and we had a secret organization called "The Ten Terrors of the Black Crook Cave."[2]

Oh Mrs. Puss, I do miss you so. I suppose you know you are my Ideal. I wish you were here to give help and advice about our garden and new curtains in the living room. Our house in Wellfleet is now overgrown with lilacs and vegetation so that it's a pioneer job to clear it, and it looks so pretty and far away, but I'm afraid to do anything about it till we see how Dos fares in this

---

1. Susan Glaspell was an American novelist and dramatist who had helped to organize the Provincetown Players, the experimental theater group that included John Dos Passos.

2. Charles and Adelaide Walker lived near the Dos Passoses in Wellfleet, Massachusetts. Their friendship stemmed from a mutual involvement in politics during the 1930s. They had joined with Dos Passos and other American writers in support of the striking Harlan County coal miners in Kentucky, and they remained committed to leftist causes during this time when many writers flirted with Communism.

climate. So far he's doing very well, and working every minute. I'm going back to New York Wednesday, and then I can see Gerald, and hear about you and about Patrick, and maybe even hear your voice over the telephone. Do you remember the orange dress you gave me. It's being fitted over my fattened outlines and looks wonderful. It's such a lovely dress and I expect to wear it for key interviews with big executives in New York.

Dos sends his best love and I send mine. We are writing to Patrick today. I certainly do love you—

Katy

UVA

Zelda Fitzgerald remained unimproved at Sheppard-Pratt Hospital in Baltimore, and Scott Fitzgerald shuttled back and forth between Baltimore and North Carolina, where he began to seek relief during 1935 for his own physical and psychological ills. Gerald Murphy urged Fitzgerald to visit them at Saranac Lake, where Gerald commuted from the city to join the family for weekends.

85. GERALD MURPHY to F. SCOTT FITZGERALD,
[New York] 11 August 1935

Dear Scott:—

If at any time during this late summer or Fall you are to be free for a weekend (one during which I am going to Saranac Lake) I'd like so much to take you up with me. I go every 2 weeks. A train leaves at 10:15p.m. (daylight),—one reaches here at 7:30 Monday a.m.

It has occurred to me in all this that you alone have always—known shall I say—or felt?—that Sara was—that there was about Sara—something infinitely touching,—something infinitely sad. Life begins to mark her for a kind of cumulous tragedy, I sometimes think. Surely only those who have been as honest and trusting with life as she has really suffer. What irony! She needs nourishment—from adults—from those who are fond of her.

(Patrick's temperature and pulse remain where they descended. His appetite is falling. The poison causes this, the doctors say. He has lost 7 pounds since he went to Saranac Lake.) This drains Sara. I can tell from her voice.

I wonder so much how Zelda is.—It has been worrying us too,—your health. Be careful, Scott,—about everything!

Your affectionate admonisher,

Gerald.

I'd like to feel I know where you are from time to time.   G.
PUL

86. F. Scott Fitzgerald to Sara Murphy, Asheville, North Carolina, 15 August 1935

Dearest Sara:

Today a letter from Gerald, a week old, telling me this & that about the awful organ music around us, made me think of you, and I mean *think* of you (of all people in the world you know the distinction). In my theory, utterly opposite to Ernest's, about fiction i.e. that it takes half a dozen people to make a synthesis strong enough to create a fiction character—in that theory, or rather in despite of it, I used you again and again in *Tender*:
"Her face was hard & lovely & pitiful"
and again
"He had been heavy, belly-frightened with love of her for years"
—in those and in a hundred other places I tried to evoke not *you* but the effect that you produce on men—the echoes and reverberations—a poor return for what you have given by your living presence, but nevertheless an artist's (what a word!) sincere attempt to preserve a true fragment rather than a "portrait" by Mr. Sargent. And someday in spite of all the affectionate skepticism you felt toward the brash young man you met on the Riviera eleven years ago, you'll let me have my little corner of you where I know you better than anybody—yes, even better than Gerald. And if it should perhaps be your left ear (you hate anyone to examine any single part of your person, no matter how appreciatively—that's why you wore bright clothes) on June evenings on Thursday from 11:00 to 11:15 here's what I'd say.

That not one thing you've done is for nothing. If you lost everything you brought into the world—if your works were burnt in the public square the law of compensation would still act (I am too moved by what I am saying to write it as well as I'd like). You are part of our times, part of the history of our race. The people whose lives you've touched directly or indirectly have reacted to the corporate bundle of atoms that's you in a *good* way. *I have seen you again*

& again at a time of confusion take the <u>hard</u> course almost blindly because long after your powers of ratiocination were exhausted you clung to the idea of dauntless courage. You were the one who said:

"All right, I'll take the black checker men."

I know that you & Gerald are one & it is hard to separate one of you from the other, in such a matter for example as the love & encouragement you chose to give to people who were full of life rather than to others, equally interesting and less exigent, who were frozen into rigid names. I don't praise you for *this*—it was the little more, the little immeasurable portion of a millimeter, the thing at the absolute top that makes the difference between a World's Champion and an also-ran, the little glance when you were sitting with Archie on the sofa that you threw at me and said:

"And—Scott!"

taking me in too, and with a heart so milked of compassion by your dearest ones that no person in the world but you would have that little more to spare.

Well—I got somewhat excited there. The point is: I rather like you, & I *think* that perhaps you have the makings of a good woman.

Gerald had invited me to come up for a weekend in the fall, probably Sept.

It's odd that when I read over this letter it seems to convey no particular point, yet I'm going to send it. Like Cole [Porter]'s eloquent little song.

"I think it'll tell you how *great* you are."

From your everlasting friend,

Scott

HMD

87. SARA MURPHY to F. SCOTT FITZGERALD,
Saranac Lake, 20 August [1935]

My Dearest Scott,—I was (& am) touched beyond words at your sweet letter—it did me a lot of good too—*thank* you for wanting to,—& writing it—(I so often want to do things & then don't) It *is* a moment when I am raw to the feelings toward me of my friends (like the man who scraped his fingers to feel the combinations of safes.)—So that any demonstration of affection,—not to mention a regular "letter of recommendation" such as you sent me,—throws me into a comfortable state of basking—

I don't think the world is a very nice place—And all there seems to be left to do is to make the best of it while we are here, & be *very* <u>very</u> grateful for one's friends—because they are the best there *is,*—& make up for many another thing that is lacking—and it seems not to matter *nearly* so much what one thinks of things—as what one feels about them.

I hope you *are* coming up to see us in Sept.? Gerald said he thought you would & we are all delighted. Would you like to bring Scotty? There isn't the least danger, as the guesthouse is separate—and all Patrick's dishes, silver, & laundry even are done apart. And we have had lots of guest-children & so take infinite precautions. We should love to see her again. I should love to see Zelda too—I think of her face so often, & so wish it had been *drawn* (not painted, drawn). It is rather like a young Indian's face, except for the smouldering eyes. At night, I remember, if she was excited, they turned black—& impenetrable— but always full of impatience—at *something*—, the world I think. She wasn't of it anyhow—not really. I loved her. & felt a sympathetic vibration to her violence. But she *wasn't throttled,*—you mustn't ever think she was except by herself—She had an inward life & feelings that I don't suppose anyone ever touched—not even you.—She probably thought terribly dangerous secret thoughts—& had pent-in rebellions. Some of it showed through her eyes,—but only to those who loved her. Why do I use the past tense?—Because she may *very well* be all right yet. I have been thinking about her a great deal lately—I read a Christian Science book the other day—(to please a C. Scientist friend)— and it said the easiest people (for them) to cure were those who were out of their minds. Why don't you try it? It might very well be true. *Anything* might be true, Scott. I will for you, if you like. Because God knows we have all of us tried every material aid we or anybody else could *think* of—It might be a good thing to turn to the spiritual & hope the bon Dieu won't notice that it is a last resort!

We all send love, & hope to see you sometime soon. And thank you for the comforting letter—I needed it—

> Your old halfbaked but affectionate
> friend—for good, as you must
> know.
>
> *Sara*

How *are* you?

PUL

88. KATY DOS PASSOS TO SARA MURPHY, Provincetown, 26 August 1935

Dear Mrs. Puss

It's like early autumn here, and are you shivering in Saranac, I wonder. Dos and I feel very migratory here—it's so nice too, it makes me rather mournful to be here so seldom. My house seemed mousy and mildewed when I got back [from New York] and Dos howled out loud when he saw other people's gardens, full of green peas and striped squashes, and tomatoes and corn, while ours was a waste of sand and weeds. In fact agriculture is impossible at this date, so we have turned to aquatics, and have a fine sailboat and small dory. Sea-going Sadie is greatly missed on board. The Herb-woman is missed in the garden—We miss Madame Murphy the talented decorator all over the house and oh if we only had Sarah the cook in the Kitchen.

I've been running and barking ever since I got home as company arrived the same day, and I have a maid whose mental powers and capacity for learning are well below those of the average laboratory (or Yale) rat. Also Dos has not been so awfully well—though much better now. He has been taking vaccines and they have a slight reaction sometimes. The New York doctor wants him to spend three months in New York under treatment, which can't very well be given at long distances, so we will have to go to Manhattan about the fifteenth of September, and find a small flop of some kind to stay in. I'll be pleased to be in New York, but really do hate to leave home so soon again. It's lovely here. I'd forgotten how pleasant it can be on the Cape—the water and the woods, the blue sea and sweet-tasting air.

It's been some time since we heard about Patrick. I called Gerald up before I left New York but the merchant prince could not be reached at the moment. I love to see the prince in his office, and would like to see him President of the United States or what is left of them in 1936.

Oh Mrs. Puss I hope you are well and wish so for good news from Saranac. Dos sends his best love. Love to Patrick, and Honoria. Love to you, and to Gerald.

With love

Katy

UVA

When Sara heard that almost one thousand war veterans had died in a hurricane which tipped Key West and then landed its most devastating blows at Islamorada and the Upper and Lower Matecumbe Keys on 2 September, she was worried about the Hemingways and wired for news, following which she wrote this letter. The "February last night" she refers to is the evening Hemingway rushed her and Ada by boat to the Florida mainland prior to Baoth's death. Sara was in the midst of reading Hemingway's Green Hills of Africa, *which was serialized in*

Scribner's *magazine before it came out in book form that October. Sara
had also read Hemingway's "Notes on the Next War: A Serious Letter"
(Esquire, July) in which he denounced war as the product of man's greed
and propaganda. Hemingway predicted that World War II would come
in 1937 or 1938.*

89. SARA MURPHY to ERNEST and PAULINE HEMINGWAY,
Saranac Lake, 11 September [1935]

My *Dearest* Hemingways,—

Oh how we didn't like your storm the other day! And so after Patrick & I
had worried for a couple of days I sent off the wire & we were all greatly relieved to hear from Pauline that you had had no worse dégât [damage] than
trees—What P. & I feared for was the boat—of course we knew you-all were
all right. We imagined Ernest *would* be in—or go into—the thick of things—
& how awful it must have been! Won't it take quite a time to get over the
horror of it all? I noticed by the map how much of the storm was over the very
route you rushed me over that February last night that seems so many aeons
ago, now—yet it seems like yesterday—Too.—we are much the same here—
but I do feel that my Patrick is on the mend,—definitely. Of course he's thin, &
doesn't eat too well,—& still has temperature—but last 2 x-rays show that
the cavity is closing—& pulse & respiration etc are all better & dr is pleased.
Patrick is pleased too—He is very gay—& looks forward to fishing again,—
(although still abed of course)—& perhaps shooting—very soon. He continually asks for news of you, because in an unguarded moment I told him you
might be coming North. What *about* the Northern-minded Hemingways? We
have had a sort of Adirondack summer. Boats, bathing, quite some rain,
friends to visit,—a great many of them Honoria's school friends—I love
them—they are all so pretty, & they giggle & love *everything*—we also picnic
& camp once in a while—girlies of the Wood (like B. Lillie) are we. The Merchant Prince [Gerald] comes to us les 15 jours—He is as busy as a birddog—
& is doing *awfully* well, & it is good he had it to do this summer. Now it
seems it [work for Mark Cross] has to go on most of the winter too—perhaps
for years—So we've taken a small non-housekeeping apt. for him (& me
when I go down)—in N.Y. city. Honoria is going to boarding-school there—
and I've taken a house up here for the winter (Big enough, good Lord, for lots
of guests who want to help me out & come—& I hope to have a lot of nice
clean snow to offer. We'll be in this camp, however, till 15 Oct.—unless frozen
out—*Is* there any chance of your coming up to these parts? Really? Because I
am pining to see you. I have *such* a good wine cellar, & a good cook, & lots of
new music—Room for the children too, if you want to bring them—Our
guests are in a guest-house apart—& all Patrick's dishes—silver laundry etc

etc are separate so there isn't the slightest danger about that, & people have confided their children to me all summer—oh we sleep under piles of blankets and have a roaring wood fire most of the time—and we love you very much. (and always will,—if I'm not being fulsome?)

I am still enjoying Green Hills of a.—piecemeal—& we all loved Ernest's article in Esquire. If that doesn't keep us out of war what will—Dos has been up—with the MacLeishes but Katy hasn't been yet—we hope for her later— She is terribly busy—They are to be in N.Y.C. they write for the next few months—& I *hope* Dos keeps well In any case I shall hope against hope to see you soon—And in the meantime—family all send much love,—& so does yr obliged devoted old shipmate

Sara

& I *persist* in saying à bientôt!
JFK

90. ERNEST HEMINGWAY to SARA MURPHY,
Key West, 12 September 1935

Dearest Sara;

Am sending you duplicates of the galleys [*Green Hills of Africa*] I've just corrected. Wish I could carry them up there instead of send them.

How are you and Patrick and all of you? We are fine but it is dreadfully hot now and maybe we will see you pretty soon. I was up at Matecumbe when you wired. Things were too bad there to write about. I wrote a piece for the New Masses, by request, (I'm calling it Panic) think of being tapped for the new masses when I had never even thought I'd make literary digest, and it should be out this week [*New Masses*, 17 September]. That gives what little news there was of the blow here, we only had the edge, and what it was like on the keys when we got up there as a relief expedition. It was as bad as the war. Worse really because so stupid and avoidable.

With the piece sent a letter to the new masses saying that they would know from reading their own columns what sort of a bastard I was so they had best print this disclaimer, "We disapprove of Mr. H. and do not want anyone to ever be sucked in by anything else he may ever write but he is a very expensive reporter who happened to be on the spot and because he does not believe in making money out of murder he has written this for us for nothing."

How are you, dear Sara? This is a hell of a year or maybe it is just that they are always as bad but your numbers only come up on the wheel all in one

143

season. I've gotten the feeling that maybe I am bad luck and that I should not have to do with people. The last thing that gave me a shock was finding three hundred men drowned at that lower matecumbe where you and Ada and I landed that night when you were going up to Miami to get the plane.

I have such a goddamned good time and enjoy my life so that it seems wicked and unbelievable that where you go such things happen to toe other people. Maybe there is an answer but I do not know it. I don't mean this goofy. But it gives you the horrrorous.

You're lucky you are in a cool place now. It's most bloody hot now. Have had to stay here to look after the boat (would probably have lost it if hadn't) and we've been you know off and on broke but now looks as tho could get off pretty soon. Have been working hard and have one long story that I think is maybe or will be pretty good. Have written some pieces for Esquire and started another story. Green Hills comes out as a book in October. Pauline and all the kids are fine. Am going somewhere cool and write a book.

Give my love to Patrick. Tell him the reason the movies gave out was because I was alone and couldn't take them. We caught 14 marlin from 540 lbs down. One mako shark 786, two tuna 381 and 340 I think. Bimini was lovely all summer. Key west was fine when we first came home then very hot. We were too broke to move but so hot now move anyway. This long story should bring in pleny cash. What do hear from Dos and Katy? Ada and Archie? I've had cards but haven't written anybody in months.

Goodbye and very much love

Ernest

HMD

91. JOHN DOS PASSOS TO SARA MURPHY,
Provincetown [16 September 1935]

Oh Sara your letter arrived in the form of a raven. How naughty, as Honoria used to say. I dont know what we can do about you and Gerald. That raven by the way arrived at an almost embarrassingly convenient moment. Oh but Sara you hadn't ought to.[1]

I'm still struggling with some things I'd scheduled to finish on September one—that's still the date for me. When I've finished this particular section (in

---

1. Sara sent the Dos Passoses money from her mother's estate. See her letter to Hemingway following.

two weeks?) I think we'll stir about a little—anxious to take a peep at you in the fall at Saranac. I bet it'll be wonderful in winter.

It's lovely up here now. We go sailing every afternoon and are beginning (feebly) to put our houses in order. Dont you think maybe you and Gerald could hop into a closed or closeable machine and get on the boat and drive out here from Fall River or Providence? We'd so love to see you and show you the magnificent growth of poison ivy that is the main feature of our new estate. And the Cape is remarkably handsome in the fall and very empty and quiet, dogstands closed, shore dinners boarded up for the season—beach plums on the hills and wonderful pale autumn light through the clouds and across the flats. But if it's too difficult we'll see you right away anyway in New York or Saranac—I suppose Patrick will stay up there all winter—I suspect that winter will turn out the best time there.

Oh Sara consider yourself thoroughly hugged—and we're both so wishing we could set eyes on you.

By the way yrs. truly seems to be holding up remarkably well. I think there's something wrong with the rheumatics; they come back from time to time, but in the feeblest form imaginable.

Love to Patrick and Honoria and yourself

Dos ben Elijah

That raven, whose name is Hadn'toughto sure is a glossy boy

Sara darling I'm speechless but writing
xxx

Love Katy

HMD

92. SARA MURPHY to ERNEST HEMINGWAY, Saranac Lake, 18 September [1935]

My dearest Ernest,——

Just by a curious coincidence—Some of my mother's estate has *just*, this month,—been settled up. (She died 18 yrs ago) and so I have some *Cash*. Quite a lot of cash—(It nearly *never* happens!) Before it is re-invested—ugh Will you (& I *hope* you aren't furious?)—do me the greatest compliment one friend can do another, & take some?

Please, *please* don't say no right off like that without thinking—now *listen*: we have plenty—we don't need it.—We have no boy to put through school—

It is cheaper than n.y. to live at Saranac. Gerald has a good salary—Our friends are the dearest things we have (after the daughter, & she is fixed up)—and you know where you come on the list of friends! So I don't see how you *could* refuse,—especially as it would give such *pleasure.*

I enclose a small amount which would get you all North & if you want any more it is yours for the asking—(I sent some to Dos & Katy too) I swear I would take it from you if I needed it—It is just a short cut, if you really want to start your book & get settled, where it is cool.—

I know you can make the money, but why wait? And it would give an old & devoted friend such immense pleasure! So you can't refuse—Say you are won over. (and it should be much more, only I am afraid of making you mad.)

And please don't say that again about being bad luck—It isn't true—It's a lie—When have you been anything but good for people? I have been thinking that perhaps I was a jinx for my family—or worse still that I was negligent in not seeing they were ill in time—or how ill they were.)

But we mustn't any of us think those thoughts—because that is destructive—any more.—I won't if you won't—You are a stimulant & an ideal for your friends, that is what you are—You are something living, in a dead or dying world, to hold to—You are generous, & warm-hearted & you *know* more than anyone I can think of Am I being fulsome? Because I could go on for *such* a long time! Give my *very* best love to Pauline I am writing her too,—about coming up here till you can look around & see where you want to be—Is it New England?—or Canada? We are only an hour's motoring from the border—3 hours from Montreal—

I'll take you around, if you like—And it would do me a lot of good to see you all.—

With *much* love

Yr Sara

JFK

93. SARA MURPHY TO PAULINE HEMINGWAY,
Saranac Lake, 18 September [1935]

My Dearest Pauline,—

I sent you off a wire today to please all come—I got the feeling that you *must* have had enough for the moment of tropics (with that storm as a coup-de-grâce) & that the best thing for you all would be a northern autumn—(the best thing U.S.A. has to offer) (am I meddling again?)—My dears, <u>do do</u> come here—and just *sit* for a spell until you can find & arrange what & where you want to be—& I shall,—& it will be my pleasure—to cozen & feed you & make you little drinks & what not (& wrap up your feet in a red blanket)—I am fixed up *so* well here! With a good cook, a heated camp, a licenced guide (*how* that man talks!)—all alone mind you, all alone—Honoria is off to school on the 30th & my Merchant Prince Dowdow only comes every 2 wks & sometimes not that—Here Patrick & his nurse & I live in solitary state & he P. is off in isolated quarters & on his porch, so I roam the place in desolate grandeur

I can't go away to New York to live too—P. counts on me to be here & tell him jokes & bully him—So you see, it would be a kindness, & besides I think you would like it & the children would like it. The guest-house is apart—& is well-warmed & lots of hot water in the bathroom. I have a *good* cook, & my Ernestine & a waitress besides my chauffeur guide—do you think I would make a good saleswoman? So please darlings, come along, & cheer me up & I have such a lot of new music & wines & spirituous liquors, & a boat & hunting—just a boaster, not a saleslady—

It is awfully cold you need sweaters—but lovely & hot in the middle of the day & the trees are turning all colours & we have a huge roaring fire at night & for breakfast & waffles & syrup & sausages!

So I don't see how you can not come, unless it was just wilful—& God knows you aren't that—

<u>Much</u> love, & a bientot—

Your Sara—

I hope mentioning the sausages wasn't a mistake—Shooting season Oct 15— deer, duck everything And a lovely 3 day canoe trip I like to take—What do you say? (Yes, please)

JFK

Sara was anxious for friends to visit her at Saranac since she felt so isolated. As it turned out, Hemingway did come north, first for the Joe Louis/Max Baer fight in New York on 24 September, and then in mid-October for the publication of The Green Hills of Africa. *Both Hemingway and Pauline probably stayed at Saranac during the September visit; and Hemingway may have stayed there as well during October. He definitely saw Sara, and no doubt Gerald, in New York City that month.*

Sidney Franklin was the American bullfighter Hemingway met in Spain in 1929 and apparently later introduced to the Murphys.

94. SARA MURPHY to PAULINE HEMINGWAY,
Saranac Lake, 18 October [1935]

(Patrick's birthday)

Dearest Pauline—

This is not the start of that to-be-famous Sarapauline Correspondence for which museums will be grappling at some future time—Just a line to say that *any* time you & yours wish to come back for hunting—or even health reasons: (sleep & nibble-a-biscuit) or any reasons *whatever*—there is place in our house & heart, & a candle in every window for you all—and I send a cutting to show Ernest how some awful woman has shot the biggest buck so far & how are we to stand it? (Ruth Hallenbeck indeed! and from Albany too, to add insult to injury).

Patrick is fine. He had the start of a 2-day celebration today Telegrams, cards, some presents & a small glass of champagne—Tomorrow Dowdow & Honoria arrive, & there will be a lot more of the same—only more & bigger & better—He *loves* it—& he looks well. Dr came today & seemed satisfied—
Goodbye dears—. I still miss you *dreadfully*—

Yr old friend—with much love
Biguine
(shall we biguine?)

I am so glad S. Franklin is getting on so well—He sent *such* a sweet telegram to P. I shall drop him a line to say thankyou
JFK

Following the October publication of The Green Hills of Africa *in New York, Hemingway had returned to Key West embittered over the book's ambivalent critical reception and fed up with New York literary circles. Having just seen Sara, he was aware of her intense loneliness at Saranac and regretted he could not act on her invitation to return for Thanksgiving. He urged the Dos Passoses to do all possible to get there, and they did. When Hemingway wrote Sara in December, he had just completed the second of his Harry Morgan stories, "The Tradesman's Return," which he mailed to Arnold Gingrich at* Esquire *on 10 December. Hemingway had seen Gingrich in New York in October, and Sara was with him then on at least one occasion. Although Sara had talked about not coming for the 1936 spring to Key West, she ended up traveling down by car with the Dos Passoses. Ada MacLeish could not join her this year since the MacLeishes would be in Japan, where MacLeish was writing the articles for the September 1936 issue of* Fortune *devoted to Japan.*

95. ERNEST HEMINGWAY to SARA MURPHY,
Key West, 8 December [1935]

Dearest Sara;

The mince meat was marvellous. Our jig made it into a fine pie and there is plenty more for more pies. I'm glad the Dosses were with you for Thanksgiving. We miss them here. There's nobody but the [Charles] Thompson's and Sully [J. B. Sullivan], Bra [Saunders] and Mr. Josie [Russell] too of course but I had just enough (too much) of N.Y. to spoil me for Mr. Josie's place [Sloppy Joe's Bar] as a substitute for the hotspots for just a little while. Had just enough of N.Y. to spoil hell out of plenty for a little while.

Seem, at this late age, to be made up of two people. One can stay out all night, drink like a fish, and sleep anywhere provided not alone, and keep a moderately even disposition. Other has to work like a sonofabitch, has a puritan conscience about work and everything that interferes and has to get to bed by at least ten o'clock. Only place these rival skyzophreniacs agree is do not like to sleep alone. Szchyzo number two or the Moneyproducer rather than He Who Gets Slopped (Sczyzo Number I) also likes to read in bed and would kick Miriam Hopkins out if she objected.

Anyhow haveing been working like a horse trying to make lots of money we've spent and writing bloody what shall we call it surely s--t is not the word and dumping it into the wastebasket. Have written two long and very tiresome stories.

Just heard from Mr. Gingrich that he saw you again in N.Y. He tells me that it has been published that I now own Esquire and that insiders have it that they owed me so much dough that Jock Whitney had to take them over to get his mine and jumbos money back. Mr. G. says this is all too jolly to deny and says My Publisher I salute you.

What is all this nonsense about you not coming down? Let Mr. MacLeish go over to see his Geisha girls alone tell Mrs. MacLeish. Why should they both bluff each other about going on this plane? Tell Mr. MacLeish Bill Leeds flew around the world on the first trip of the Graf Zeppelin and it still proves nothing. Keep Mr. MacLeish on Terrus Firmum. Quote him the example of Bill Leeds. Does he want to follow in the flysteps or hoofwingbeats of Bill Leeds with Mrs. MacLeish on his traces like the Hounds of Springwheel wagondry? No. Over a thousand times no. Tell Mr. MacLeish to get Mrs. MacLeish and

You and fly down here where the people will understand what he is saying. Not just a lot of slot eyed orientales who will bring him to no good end. Or is he going over to see his Ballet[1] or to get Material for a new Ballet. In that case. OK Cast off MacLeish. Contact.

The plane is now leaving in less than five minutes so bring this to a hurried conclusion. Tell Patrick to keep on gaining weight. Tell him in the effort to find out how to gain weight best I am now as fat as a hog. Our Patrick and I went out shooting yesterday and never saw a dove nor snipe nor plover so finally shot 2 buzzard, 1 chicken hawk and a large crane. There is a great supply of buzzards here but just two offered softened the market so that we had to unload our offerings by burying them.

Will write you again and very soon. With very much love much love and love also with love,

Ernest

HMD

---

1. *Union Pacific*, with story by MacLeish, music by Nicholas Nabokoff, and choreography by Léonide Massine, was first performed by the Ballet Russe de Monte Carlo in New York City on 25 April 1934.

96. SCOTT and ZELDA FITZGERALD to GERALD and SARA MURPHY, Baltimore, 26 December 1935

WE THREE WERE TOGETHER TODAY AND WE THOUGHT OF ALL FIVE OF YOU AS ALWAYS TOGETHER=[1]

SCOTT AND ZELDA

HMD

---

1. Although Zelda seemed well enough to join Scott and Scottie for Christmas at the Cambridge Arms Apartments in Baltimore, she soon grew worse again and had to return to the hospital.

97. GERALD MURPHY to F. SCOTT FITZGERALD, Saranac Lake, 31 December 1935

Dear Scott:—

I have been here since the 24th. Honoria was here also with us & went to the Myers at Bedford Village for New Year's day. To-morrow I return to New York.

We have thought of you very much these days and wondered if our wire would reach you. It was good to hear from you and that you were able to be together. Thank you for that message, Scott. Of all our friends, it seems to me that you alone knew how we felt these days—still feel. You are the only person to whom I can ever tell the bleak truth of what I feel. Sara's courage and the amazing job which she is doing for Patrick make unbearably poignant the tragedy of what has happened—what life has tried to do to her. I know now that what you said in "Tender is the Night" is true. Only the invented part of our life,—the unreal part—has had any scheme any beauty. Life itself has stepped in now and blundered, scarred and destroyed. In my heart I dreaded the moment when our youth and invention would be attacked in our only vulnerable spot,—the children, their growth, their health, their future. How ugly and blasting it can be,—and how idly ruthless.

When you come North let me talk to you. I am probably going to England to the factories late this month. "Trade" has proven an efficient drug,—harmful but efficient.

Our love to you all,

Gerald

I suppose that we are two blatherskites living in stone huts in some distant Irish valley. You and I, I mean. I count so on my rare dish of talk with you. I guess we are Irish.

PUL

Gerald began to make almost yearly trips to England, where the Mark Cross Company had owned factories. His buying trips often included other countries such as France, Belgium, Germany, Austria, and Czechoslovakia. On this trip he planned to keep a daily journal for Patrick to read.

Fernand Léger had made his second trip to America in September 1935. He traveled with Le Corbusier, and he participated in exhibitions of his works at the Museum of Modern Art in New York and the Art Institute of Chicago.

98. GERALD MURPHY to SARA MURPHY,
On board *Europa*, 5 February 1936

Dearest Sal:—

My calender-journal will give you (what I fear he'll find) the dull facts of our crossing. For a moment the first morning I felt that drama stalked the ship as I read in the passenger-list the (last alphabetically listed) name of: Mrs. Thornton Woodbury. But nothing has materialized. She might be anybody. She is. They *all* are, aboard, nothing but, and from the same mould. In space for 600,—160 voyagers rattle around. Distances and perspectives seem infinite. It is all sufficiently spectral—for many reasons. I hadn't allowed for that. Our first crossing years ago with Lillie and Ella Nyberg is in my mind constantly. Memory is odd—what boat was it: a Cunarder, I think, beginning with "C",—the "Cedric" or some such name?

The [Christian] Science Lessons I like very much. I'm grateful, first, for real contact with the Bible, which Catholocism had neglected for me,—but further I have the feeling of learning a new language with which I find myself sympathetic and vaguely familiar tho' I've felt myself not adapted to such by nature. I shall see to it that I was wrong! (Father was much interested on his own and studied. Why I do not recall, but I *remember* his belief in Science.) I have not yet learned where one's sense of worldly (or material) responsibility ends and fear begins. You might ask Mrs. Norton what one does about one's concern about *other's* welfare and *feelings*,—to keep it from becoming fear. Wm James' "Varieties of Religious Experience" would interest you in synchrony. His is such an open, humourous point of view of man's need for a religion. Only man's *personal* religion interests him.

As I shall doubtless have cabled you my address is to be the Savoy, London. I'll advise you of every move beforehand: dates, whereabouts, etc. I have no idea what the trip holds. It's strange retracing the steps made first by Father when he was twenty-one: 50 or 60 years ago! I've been reading a report of the first founding of the Factories in Walsall, when I was 2 yrs. old.

I'm writing from the boat to Violet and to Talbot even, telling the former to prepare for the 12th–15th and the latter to be *thinking of* something you'd like. Then, in case my stay is short, they'll be no scramble. My general plan is:

London until about *Feb. 12th or 15th*
>   with overnight Walsall trips 2 1/2 hrs. away. (I'll leave the Savoy my address each time)

Brussels: for 1 day
Paris: " 2 or 3 days
Leipsig: on Mch. 1st or 2nd (will send you address there)
>   then

Dresden ⎫
Prague ⎬ dates, addresses later
Wien   ⎭
Berlin
Bremen   where I embark this boat again on the morning of March 10th

arriving in NYC USA the 16th of March. Where you'll meet me, I hope.

———————

I hope I didn't leave Fernand [Léger] too suspended. Naturally if we bought toiles [paintings] from him as patrons it might be easier to pay him 2 thousand dollars outright,—but we don't buy pictures to own and I'd rather *give* him what we can afford. This amount he can only know by our telling him,—which I did. He is *giving* us in return a toile, which is all right.[1] At least we've been the means of his getting over *when* he wanted to to put himself in the way of what the USA had to offer. Of course he's too much to stomach to be a comfortably *recognized* painter like Van Gogh,—even Picasso and decorative Chirico. Where does one *put* a Léger—where one puts a garage or an ice-plant, I suppose.

I hope Stella [Campbell] unravels her snarl, poor dear. Should I try to see her friends in London, I wonder? I'd like to talk to her lawyer, Guedella, his name was. I think I may.

You are *bringing to* Patrick all that these Lessons *show* us is true in the Bible. I see it very clearly. You must *believe* that you *are* as strongly as I *feel* that you are. For I do.

I've been so short with Honoria lately. But I get impatient at the fact she is not being exposed to the same valuable influences which we seemed to be searching for at her age,—or did it come later with us. Your mother, of course, insisted. Too much, perhaps,—I wonder. Naturally times are different. She is different,—and a late-bloomer,—so I guess I'm wrong.

All my love to you, to Patrick and to
Honoria when you see her,

daou.

P.S. Lina and Betjeman [family lawyers] will take care of everything for you. Alice Lee [Myers] when she is away. I spoke to Maher about the stock-clerk dismissal. He's a tough little accountant,—and I guess more like the business world than such as we are.

d.

HMD

———————

1. Probably at a second exhibit of his works at the Museum of Modern Art ("Cubist and Abstract Art," 1936), the Murphys picked out their painting, one done in a brown tone rather than Léger's usual bold colors. Léger anticipated their choice of *Composition à un Profil* and had already inscribed it to Gerald and Sara.

99. GERALD MURPHY to SARA MURPHY,
London, 11 February 1936

Dearest Sal:—

My "journal" to Patrick will serve a little as a source of facts, I hope. The crossing was most comfortable,—but not gay. There is a peculiar nostalgic grimness about all those strangers living in such proximity for a little stretch of time and yet on their separate voyages. Frankly I found it extremely depressing—or, could have. Not once did I go on deck,—didn't even have a chair. I had much information to absorb regarding what lay before me: and found that I could sleep quite well. As I wirelessed you the Lessons have been a source of great gratification. A little upheaving at first,—but nourishing. I find it a language I seem always to have known, and believe unhesitatingly in all its claims. Life moves to another level. Something happens to perspective and vision. Horizons get larger. I enjoy it so much. Thanks, Sal, for the Lesson Book and Reader. On Sunday I was walking up Half-Moon Street & found at the end the 2nd Church of Christ Scientist,—with a Reading Room inside and the day's lesson opened to view in a glass case on the sidewalk. All seemed so calm and peaceful.

It was bad on the boat and I missed you all terribly. It seemed so strange to be going off on a journey alone. I got pretty spooked. Here it's better. I am rushing from 9 a.m. till 6. Then we plan the 90 things to be done the next day. It's all very necessary & should have been done years ago,—as Father must have done it originally. To-morrow I go to Walsall for the night and Thursday. Then back here for another week. On the 23rd I expect to go to Paris for 5 or 6 days, one day in Brussels, then to Offenbach and Leipsig, Prague, Dresden, Vienna, Berlin and Bremen. I'll keep you posted of every move.

The reports of the cold and blizzards at home have been worrying. I hope the pipes didn't freeze at Saranac. This whole continent is in the grip of it,— and Asia too. Also Birmingham, Ala.!

Ruby I called up. She was taken every eve. for a wk.—what with la semaine anglaise [five-day work week]! She's so sweet and affectionate and deeply adores you. How *lasting* real affection is! Mrs Shepherd has been so sweet on account of Dick's [Richard Myers] letter and I'm dining there Fri. night. London has not changed one jot, in aspect or *feeling*,—something is absent, tho'. I don't know London well enough to know why.

The war menace seems very real, tho' they all take it dumbly or coolly.

The cold here seems typical. One expects it. How is Honoria? Well I hope. Pook's [Patrick] gain is good. How wonderful the persistence of the rise.

Much love to you, dearest Sal, and to P. and to Daughter. I hope you're having friends and going to Farmington

daou.

Is Judy well? I've written to France. V. [Vladimir Orloff] will meet me. I'll see Noel [Murphy]. Mmes Groult, Talbot etc. have all answered so cordially my notes from the boat.

HMD

Hemingway had recently read the first two of Fitzgerald's three "Crack Up" articles in Esquire, *which got him angry again over Fitzgerald's failure, as Hemingway saw it, to use his talent well. He saw "Mr. FitzGerald" as one lacking in courage, too easily defeated by life. Hemingway and Sara had talked about Fitzgerald at length in Saranac that fall.*

100. ERNEST HEMINGWAY to SARA MURPHY,
Key West, 11 February 1936

Dearest Sara:

Damn I wish we could come up there for the winters sporting but I have to work like the devil the rest of the winter. If we could only keep the visooters away. If and if only. I thought that piece I wrote last year would keep some of them off but it only keeps the nice ones away. They've been here every day for last ten days and bringing their women and their movie stars with them. I *have* to do my work in the winter and here there is only two months of winter left and the last twelve days have been solid with the brain sucking time eating bastards thick as grunts.

Well well just got that off the chest. How are you dear beautiful Sara? Is Patrick still holding it and I'll bet you're frozen cold in that cold. Anyway its dry there and its cold as hell everywhere else too. The records were grand. Burris Jenkins who was down sent a new phonograph for the boat and it came just right for those last swell records. Mama don't allow it is lovely.

I had a gigantic dream about you about ten days ago and woke up determined to write you a long letter (much longer than this one) and tell you how highly I thought of you and instead here were sixty trained visitors scuffing the paint off the porch. Now you know how to handle a visitor. How to cool them with a dirty look, how to say Mrs. Murphy don't live here anymore, how to put the boots to a visitor in short (look at the way you kicked us out of Lake Placid) (joke) but I was brought up where never less than fourteen people sat down to the table at a time, often fifty four, and as I look back I realize there were probably people visiting at [our] house ever since the civil war who came for the war and hadn't heard it was over and my family liked it. But I hate it. Fornicate a visitor say I. Only most of them aren't worth a quick one even.

Last week we had oh hell why go into it.

But the fishing is wonderful. It's lousy with sailfish. Caught seven last week in four times out. Hooked and landed a triple header tell Patrick. Two on the outriggers and hooked a third on a straight line. Seven feet five, seven feet two, six feet ten tell Patrick. And the biggest one I had on light tackle and a pack of ambaerjacks started to chase him, about twenty five of them, and he jumped like crazy. They just chased him because he ran. Make a note of that for Mr. FitzGerald. Then a white shark started to chase him too. The same white shark that finally chased Mr. FitzGerald I think. And I gave him absolutely free line and he ran away from all of them and then like a dirty son of a bitch that I am I ran up on him and caught him. But we cut him up at the dock and gave him away along with 250 pounds of kingfish. Every time out we catch three or four hundred pounds of fish for the poor. The cold has driven all the fish in the gulf stream down here. You would love it. So would Patrick.

That was a wonderful whiskey you sent for Christmas. Simply grand. Best Scotch I ever drank. Along before Christmas I had gotten gloomy as a bastard but started going out in the stream and fishing again and in no time was swell. Thought was faceing impotence, inability to write, insomnia and was going to blow my lousy head off and all I was was overworking and not getting exercise. So now am feeling swell and all am facing is hunger and gigantic thirst and visitors interrupting work. Why goddamn it we are only supposed to do so much work and it is just as important to keep in shape and have fun and it is a perversion to do anything else really. Why go nuts just to please the people who would like to see you nuts? What you have to have is confidence and not be spooked every time you need a new set of spark plugs every twenty thousand miles if not ten. Only I have to get my work done to enjoy my fun and that is what am up against now. May go over to Cuba if they get too thick.

I wish we could see you but at that I remember you very well. There are about three records that I never hear without think of you. I wish you were here, Sara.

Good bye, God bless you, take good care yourself, give my love to Patrick.

Ernest

HMD

Depressed over Patrick's condition and feeling increasingly isolated at Saranac, Sara may have written to Hemingway about the strains in her relationship with Gerald. Although Sara's letter has not survived, Hemingway may have made some personal remarks in response to Sara's remarks; somebody—probably Sara—has torn off the bottom portion of

Hemingway's letter. Hemingway refers in this letter to the evening in spring 1934 when Wallace Stevens barged in on the Hemingways to tell Hemingway that he was a "cad." After leaving the Hemingways' home, Stevens then went to the Waddell Avenue home which the Dos Passoses, Sara, and Ada MacLeish were renting.

101. ERNEST HEMINGWAY to SARA MURPHY,
Key West [c. 27 February 1936]

Dearest Sara:

Just got your letter today along with a giant hangover like all the tents of Ringling. So this is letter out of the hangover into the snow. Hangover came about through visit of my lawyer Mr. [Maurice] Speiser whom I cannot see without the aid and abettment of alcohol plus seeing off in southern farewell the Judge [Arthur Powell] of the Wallace Stevens evening? Remember that Judge and Mr. Stevens? Nice Mr. Stevens. This year he came again sort of pleasant like the cholera and first I knew of it my nice sister Ura was coming into the house crying because she had been at a cocktail party at which Mr. Stevens had made her cry by telling her forcefully what a sap I was, no man etc. So I said, this was a week ago, "All right, that's the third time we've had enough of Mr. Stevens." So headed out into the rainy past twilight and met Mr. Stevens who was just issuing from the door haveing just said, I learned later, "By God I wish I had that Hemingway here now I'd knock him out with a single punch." So who should show up but poor old Papa and Mr. Stevens swung that same fabled punch but fertunatly missed and I knocked all of him down several times and gave him a good beating. Only trouble was that first three times put him down I still had my glasses on. Then took them off at the insistance of the judge who wanted to see a good clean fight without glasses in it and after I took them off Mr. Stevens hit me flush on the jaw with his Sunday punch bam like that. And this is very funny. Broke his hand in two places. Didn't harm my jaw at all and so put him down again and then fixed him good so he was in his room for five days with a nurse and Dr. working on him. But you mustn't tell this to anybody. Not even Ada. Because he is very worried about his respectable insurance standing and I have promised not to tell anybody and the official story is that Mr. Stevens fell down a stairs. I agreed to that and said it was o.k. with me if he fell down the lighthouse stairs. So please promise not to tell anybody. But Pauline who hates me to fight was delighted. Ura had never seen a fight before and couldn't sleep for fear Mr. Stevens was going to die. Anyway last night Mr. Stevens comes over to make up and we are made up. But on mature reflection I don't know any body needed to be hit worse than Mr. S. Was very pleased last night to see how large Mr. Stevens was and am sure that if I had had a good look at him before it all started would not

157

have felt up to hitting him. But can assure you that there is no one like Mr. Stevens to go down in a spectacular fashion especially into a large puddle of water in the street in front of your old waddel street home where all took place. So I shouldn't write you this but news being scarce your way and I know you really won't tell anybody will you really absolutely seriously. Because otherwise I am a bastard to write it. He apologised to Ura very handsomely and has gone up to Pirates Cove to rest his face for another week before going north. I think he is really one of those mirror fighters who swells his muscles and practices lethal punches in the bathroom while he hates his betters. But maybe I am wrong. Anyway I think Gertrude Stein ought to give all these people who pick fights with poor old papa at least their money back. I am getting damned tired of it but not nearly as tired of it as Mr. Stevens got. It was really awfully funny to have a man just declaring how he was going to annihilate you and show up just at that moment. Then have him land his awful punch on your jaw and nothing happen except his hand break. You can tell Patrick. It might amuse him. But don't tell anybody else. Tell Patrick for statistics sake Mr. Stevens is 6 feet 2 weighs 225 lbs and that when he hits the ground it is highly spectaculous. I told the Judge, the day after, to Tell Mr. S. I thought he was a damned fine poet but to tell him he couldn't fight. The Judge said, "Oh but your wrong there. He is a very good fighter. Why I saw him hit a man once and knock him the length of this room." And I said, "Yes, Judge. But you didn't catch the man's name did you?" I think it was a waiter. Nice dear good Mr. Stevens. I hope he doesn't brood about this and take up archery or machine gunnery. But you promise you won't tell anybody.

Poor Sara. I'm sorry you had such a bad time. These are the bad times. It is sort of like the retreat from Moscow and Scott is gone the first week of the retreat. But we might as well fight the best goddamned rear guard action in the history and God knows you have been fighting it.

Weather has been lousy for fishing the last ten days or so. Put the boat on the ways and scraped and sanded her and repainted. Also copperpainted the bottom with a new paint called murcop that has murcury in it and is supposed to be very good. Have it looking swell. Now must write an Esquire piece, do my income tax, and then get back to my book. Hope to God the people will be gone.

Waldo [Peirce] is here with his kids like untrained hyenas and him as domesticated as a cow.[1] Lives only for the children and with the time he puts on them they should have good manners and be well trained but instead they never obey, destroy everything, don't even answer when spoken to and he is like an old hen with a litter of apehyeanas. I doubt if he will go out in the boat

---

1. Waldo Peirce graduated from Harvard and then drove ambulances in France during the war. He became a painter and met Hemingway in Paris in 1927.

while he is here. Can't leave the children. They have a nurse and a housekeeper too but he is only really happy when trying to paint with one setting fire to his beard and the other rubbing mashed potato into his canvasses. That represents fatherhood.

[Rest of letter missing]

HMD

Nora Flynn and her husband Lefty befriended Fitzgerald during a difficult time. Worried about his lungs as well as his general physical and mental health, Fitzgerald moved to the Oak Hall Hotel while Scottie boarded with the Flynns in Tryon, North Carolina. Fitzgerald would place Zelda in Highland Hospital in Asheville, North Carolina. The first of his three "Crack-Up" essays had just come out the previous month in Esquire.

102. F. SCOTT FITZGERALD to SARA MURPHY, Baltimore [30 March 1936]

Dearest Sara (and Gerald too, if he's not in London)

I want news of you. The winter has presented too many problems here for me to come north, even as far as New York & my last word of you was by kindness of Archie—and not too encouraging.

If you read the little trilogy I wrote for *Esquire* you know I went through a sort of "dark night of the soul" last autumn, and again and again my thoughts reverted to you and Gerald, and I reminded myself that nothing had happened to me with the awful *suddenness* of your tragedy of a year ago, nothing so utterly conclusive and irreparable. I saw your face, Sara, as I saw it a year ago this month, and Gerald's face last fall when I met him in the Ritz Bar, and I felt very close to you—and correspondingly detached from Ernest, who has managed to escape the great thunderbolts, and Nora Flinn whom the Gods haven't even shot at with much seriousness. She would probably deny that and she helped me over one black week when I thought this was probably as good a time to quit as any, but as I said to her the love of life is essentially as incommunicable as grief.

I am moving Zelda to a sanitarium in Ashville—she is no better, though the suicidal cloud was lifted—I thought over your Christian Science idea & finally decided to try it but the practitioner I hit on wanted to begin with "absent treatments," which seemed about as effectual to me as the candles my mother keeps constantly burning to bring me back to Holy Church—so I abandoned it. Especially as Zelda now claims to be in direct contact with Christ, William the Conqueror, Mary Stuart, Appollo and all the stock paraphanalea of insane asylum jokes. Of course it isn't a bit funny but after the awful strangulation episode of last spring I sometimes take refuge in an unsmiling irony about the present *exterior* phases of her illness. For what she has really suffered there is never a sober night that I do not pay a stark tribute of an hour to in the darkness. In an odd way, perhaps incredible to you, she was always my child (it was not reciprocal as it often is in marriages), my child in a sense that Scotty isn't, because I've brought Scotty up hard as nails (Perhaps that's fatuous, but I *think* I have.) Outside of the realm of what you called Zelda's "terribly dangerous secret thoughts" I was her great reality, often the only liason agent who could make the world tangible to her—

The only way to show me you forgive this great outpouring is to write me about yourselves. Some night when you're not too tired, take yourself a glass of sherry and write me as lovely and revealing letter as you did before. Willynilly we are still in the midst of life and all true correspondence is nessessarily sporadic but a letter from you or Gerald always pulls at something awfully deep in me. I want the best news, but in any case I want to know

With Dearest Affection to You All

Scott

HMD

103. Sara Murphy to F. Scott Fitzgerald,
Saranac Lake, 3 April [1936]

Dearest Scott,—

I <u>was</u> so glad to get your news—we have wondered so often, Gerald and I,—and Dos & Katy and I—and Alice-Lee Myers and I, *where* you were & how Zelda is doing & how big Scotty is—& how *you* were. Gerald is back— since the 16th March—he was gone 6 weeks—and though according to himself he had a dull & terribly busy time it must have been good for him, as change always is, as he came back looking 100% better or at least 100% more interested in the world—(which I suppose means the same thing & is the best we have.) Is that the worthwhile school of thought? (If so, I take it back—) Anyhow he is back in harness in Mark Cross Co—& looks awfully nice, & *better*. A little too thin perhaps—but he says I always say that. We here on the Magic Mountain are really doing better too. I am *really encouraged* about Patrick,—you will be glad to hear, I know. He is still in bed (a year & a half!)

& still has temperature—if that went down he could get up—And though he has his ups & downs which we expect, & scared us to death by having grippe about 5 or 6 weeks ago—he looks & acts—& the symptoms are *better*,—& from weighing 59 lbs last Sept. now weighs *80*—So you see that is concrete evidence, even if one couldn't see & feel the change. I am sure, Scott, he is going to be allright & will yet have a good life, quiet perhaps, without violence, & yet maybe better than any of ours—in the end. I hope so indeed.

I did indeed read your trilogy in Esquire—& think you must feel better for it—as it seemed to me to accomplish that,—get something off your chest,—if not much more not more for anybody else, I mean. *Do* you feel better? Do you know, I never realized, till I read those pieces (of course you won't care what your "half-baked" old friend thinks,—but you can tell me so in yr. next letter.) I never realized to what *extent* you thought you could run things & control your life by just wanting to—(Even I knew that much.) Do you *really* mean to say you honestly thought "life was something you dominated if you were any good—?" Even if you meant your *own* life it is arrogant enough,—but life! well if you thought *that*,—out of college, married, a father, travelled, seen life, etc etc—I give up. I can't fight you on paper, but there are several very loose stones in your basement, rocking the house. Let us have another argument—sometime—(proving nothing & neither side giving way an inch!!) Oh how wrong you are,—Scott, about so many things—but nevertheless go on,—I hope you *do*?—regarding Gerald & me—as your "inalienable friends"—But I *do* think [William Ernest] Henley's man who said [in "Invictus"] "my head is bloody but unbowed" is better than you on your old rifle range—They are both heroics if you like,—but the first is cheerfuller.[1] If you just *won't* admit a thing it doesn't exist (as much)—Even not admitting,—rebelling, dragging one's feet & fighting every inch of the way, one must admit one can't *control* it—one has to *take* it,—& as well as possible—that is all I know—I remember once your saying to me—in Montana [-Vermala, Switzerland], at Harry's Bar, you & Dotty [Parker] were talking about your disappointments, & you turned to me & said: I don't suppose you have ever known despair? I remember it so well as I was furious, & thought my god the man thinks no one knows despair who isn't a writer & can describe it. This is my feeling about your articles.—You mustn't think from this that I can't know & feel what you have been through—& I *do* think & feel about it oftener than you think—You have been cheated (as we all have been in one way or another)

---

1. Sara directly refers to Fitzgerald's essays. In "Handle with Care" Fitzgerald speaks of the feeling that he "was standing at twilight on a deserted range, with an empty rifle in my hands and the targets down." And in "Pasting It Together," he picks up on this theme of desolation and "of the necessity of going on, but without benefit of Henley's familiar heroics, 'my head is bloody but unbowed.' "

but to have Zelda's wisdom taken away,—which would have meant *every-thing* to you,— is crueller even than death. She would have felt all the right things through the bad times—and found the words to help,—for you, & for her real friends—I miss her too—You have had a *horrible* time—worse than any of us, I think—and it has gone on for so long—*that* is what gets us, & saps our vitality—your spirit, & courage are an example to us all—(Even though I do think your thinking processes are faulty!) And we will always have a warm spot in the heart, & a lighted candle for you—that is forever.—

> With love—your old & very devoted
> (though irritating) friend—
>
> *Sara*

I didn't know I was going to write such a long letter! And no writer either. When are you coming up to see us? And you never said how you were *yourself?*
PUL

The Murphys sometimes wrote to each other when Gerald stayed on in the city. The letters from Sara mentioned by Gerald have not survived.

104. GERALD MURPHY to SARA MURPHY, New York, 16 April 1936

Dear Sal,—

In answer to yr. 2 type-written and rare semi-philosophical letters:
It isn't surprising that Miss Sanderson thinks Honoria's "training" "differ-ent." Her experience has not been the average American one,—and the result is an *absence* of the American training,—which is interpreted as "different." Honoria's process of mind is not *thorough*. This she gets from both of us: my lack of mathematical sense your lack of mechanical or practical (in the mate-rial sense) aptness. I was a downright bad scholar. We are both irresponsible in the material sense. So is she. We were (and probably still are) ingenuous and unworldly to a fault. So is she. It's a logical result. Her sense of responsibility will have to come from *herself*,—and this will occur, to my mind only if she's left to fend for herself over a period. She doesn't even know how to pack. It's been done for her too much. I think she should be left to find her own solution of her summer, without her feeling that someone is worrying and wondering about her. I think even her tendency to want to telephone in order to "know if everything is all right."

Scott's letter: his answer to yrs. (if one comes) will indicate how much he is in a frame of mind to understand.

There is one thing that has always surprised me and that is one's tendency to feel that just because two people have been married for 20 years that they should need the same thing of life or of people. You are surprised anew periodically that "warm human relationship" should be so necessary to you and less to me. Yet nothing is more natural under the circumstances. You believe in it (as you do in life), you are capable of it, you command it. I am less of a believer (I don't *admire* human animals as much), I am not as capable (for a fundamental sexual deficiency, like poor eyesight), I lack the confidence (quite naturally) to command it,—or to keep it in its proper relationship to me. Certainly feeling exists in people or it doesn't. No two people show it in the same *degree* or *manner*. Hence the inadequacy of most relationships which are supposed to be kept at *constant* emotional pressure. It is hard to believe in the ultimate value of Love if one has always questioned the real value of Life (as one knows it limitedly). One must believe *fully.* You are luckier than I am. I *fear* Life. You don't.

d.

HMD

105. Gerald Murphy to Sara Murphy,
New York, 18 April 1936

Dear Sal:—

Addenda: I suppose it's downright tragic (if things in life *are* tragic,—or just life—) when one person who *lives by communicated* affection should have chosen a mate who is (damn it) deficient. I have always had (as early as I can remember) the *knowledge* (conviction, feeling) that I lacked something that other people had,—emotionally. Whether this is due to the absence of degree and depth of feeling, or the result of trained suppression of feelings, distrust and fear of them,—I don't know. Possibly both. I do recall my attitude toward feeling being warped by mothers influence. Suffice it to say that now whenever I think to myself "this is the moment that I should like to give my feelings play, this is when I should be feeling something, etc.—" then I feel a constriction at the source and a choked sensation. Is it dread of emotional attachment or is it that one must be sufficient (as opposed to deficient) fundamentally—basically,—in order to feel fully.

There is nothing which I *believe* in that should cause this lack;—nothing against Nature. God knows she's right for this world. There's no use denying that. Outside of a man and a woman, and children and a house and a garden,—there's nothing much.

One thing: I certainly am not afraid of feeling because of having that feeling hurt.

Not a day has ever passed that I haven't thought of how rotten it's been for you. Especially as I've known you to be crediting my deficiency to a *personal* lack of affection. You naturally *feel* it personally. Why shouldn't you! I hope all in all it hasn't been too awful for you. I wonder if anyone who wants as much feeling of life as you do,—ever really gets it. Very rarely from one person, don't you think? You certainly have always given it to people. People talk of you with emotional gratitude as having been made to feel something you gave them for which they're glad. I can tell it from what Dos, Katy, Alice, James, Pauline, Jinny,—even Mr. Maher, Mr. Hopkins spoke of it. You certainly have done that. [Illegible name] & Ginnie felt it. Pauline told me about it. Even Ada. Archie strongly and Phil and Ellen. Certainly above all Bob. (Don't think I'm trying to make you feel all puffed up. You *know* this.)

Love

d.d.

HMD

Shortly after receiving Gerald's last letter, Sara drove with John and Katy Dos Passos to Florida. They spent a week in Havana with Ernest Hemingway, which Pauline missed because she had already planned a trip to Piggot, Arkansas, to see her family. The Dos Passoses and Sara were back in Florida by 12 May, and Sara flew back to New York on 15 May from Jacksonville.

106. SARA MURPHY to PAULINE HEMINGWAY,
Havana [11 May 1936]

Dearest Pauline—

Another line to say what a *beautiful* week we had, & how much we missed you—progressively more every day. Your not being here was a huge mistake,—& we can't get over it,—& we *can't* stay longer, (as I explained in Key West letter)—I *love* Havana, & you know how much going out on the boat meant to me—as an old shipmate!! Out of the 8 days we were here—6 were at sea!! And 2 of them busily catching marlin—I am going back with an entirely new line of conversation for Patrick:—(all about fish, & boats, &

tackle--& Cuban sailors &, most of all, his adored Ernest)—and a beaming new face & lots of little packages of iodine against the mountain air—for myself.

Will you tell the Gros Patron again how much I am in his debt, forever, & with deepest & muchest love to you both,—and please—à bientôt! Yr

Sara

P.S. Gerald sent you so many messages.

JFK

107. Sara Murphy to Ernest Hemingway, Saranac Lake, 20 May [1936]

Dearest Ernest,

This is the first moment I can sit down to write you about what a LOVELY time I had down at Havana with you on the Pilar. I only got back here to Patrick yesterday as Gerald and Honoria and I went to Easthampton over Sunday. My plane got in about 6 (Newark) Friday night. I left from Jacksonville, you know, after 2 days motoring and flânering with the Dosses up through Florida. We had the greatest fun, stopped everywhere to look at whatever caught the eye: views, clouds, plantes grasses, old men selling grapefruit, jungle gardens, the Barrys new house at Hobe Sound [Florida], & some very funny places to eat. We drank some too, & all missed you so much we could hardly stand it. Specially when it came to saying good-bye to all that beautiful blue-green water.

Oh Ernest, what wonderful places you live in and what a good life you have made for yourself and Pauline, and what a lot of people you have made love you dearly! Perhaps that doesnt mean so much to you, (although I think it probably must) but it IS very remarkable and very extraordinary, & now I have no more adjectives, & you will think I want to borrow money, but it is all very true and a more generous and warming and understanding friend doesn't exist (I know because I have seen them all, being very old & extensively travelled) So pride yourself a little (& don't take wood nickels).

And thank you, HOW many times, thousands, for all this, and your accueil [welcome] & your hospitality, & the general healing and 'back to normalcy' effect, you are able to produce, so that there have been many favorable comments on all sides upon my alleged improved appearance. It certainly did us all good too to see Pauline, although it didnt last long enough. I really HAVE to see her face every so often, then I feel better & can go on. She went onto the Havana plane looking like a delicious, and rather wicked little piece of brown toast, & the opinion was unanimous that she, & her hair, had *never* looked better, & that she is a divine woman. I HOPE she didn't feel that we had made her rush away from Key West too soon,—afterwards? We did get sort of insistent, we wanted so to see her, & the feeling got much worse when we arrived in Miami. So we got to telephoning, & couldn't stop. Please say thank you & excuse it and much love.[1]

Why should this machine write uphill? I can make nothing of it?[2]

Patrick is VERY proud and happy with his marlin bills. He was really leaning out of bed to see me and hear all your news, and I have described EVERYTHING about the fishing in full detail, from leaving Havana Harbor in the morning, (not quite) ahead of the garbage scow, (through no fault of our own) to the triumphant return in the evening, with the fish flag flying. In the cases where I was slightly hazy about the technical details of what rods & threads were used and those swaying bamboo outriggers, I would simply point;—with trembling finger,—to your marlin article in his treasured fish-book that you gave him.

Please tell Carlos [Gutiérrez] too, how much he likes, and how frightfully interested he is in the paper-cutter made out of a bill. It is his favorite possession.

Patrick and I are awfully well together. Much better than we ever were before his illness. You cant imagine how glad I was to see him, & he seemed so glad to see me too. And we had missed each other. I found him very well, you will be glad to hear. He had gained another lb. last Thursday. I'll keep this letter over tomorrow, weigh-day, in case there should be another pound to add!

Speaking of pounds, Heavens! How well we ate chex vous! In one way it was good for the figger, as one cant ever eat afterwards, again, everything seems so awful by contrast. I've got quite thin since. Did your discs come finally? I'm not sure how good they were; although Love is a Dancing Thing is quite good, I think. Do you remember Face the Music, Dobatz? And the Small Hotel? I have tried everywhere to get No Hubo Barrera, it can't be recorded

---

1. On their stopover in Miami en route home, the Dos Passoses and Sara had apparently contacted Pauline, who had just arrived back in Key West from Arkansas. She probably came to see them in Miami and then flew from there to rejoin Hemingway in Havana.

2. This is one of the few letters Sara typed. The lining is uneven, and some of the keys had jammed, causing letters to overlap.

yet. They have the order when it is. Will you sometime, when you think of it, give those 3 men that always played for us at the Ambos Mundos cafe, something for me? I can see them standing in a row under the lit "Ambos Mundos" sign. One with a round face, & a straw sailor, another with a Panama & always a coat over his arm.

It was really a lovely time. Seems so funny to be back hearing "Mees Otis regrette de ne pouvoir venir diner" (Madame), & Yvonne Printemps, & a funny one called "La Baignoire" do you know it? And SNOW, of all things, on the lilac buds! And 34 temperature, although it was warm when I first got back. The camp is being fixed up & will be very nice (I think) Are you all coming to see us in it? We move around 1st June & then Ill set about making plans. How are yours?

About being snooty: You dont REALLY think I am snooty do you? Please dont. It isnt snooty to choose.

Choice, and one's affections, are about all there are.

And I am rather savage, like you, about first-best everything: best painting, best music, best friends Id rather spend a few hours a year with the friends I love than hundreds with indifferents.

(If I hadn't decided that *yrs.* ago, I'd have been another Mrs Astor by now, what with my wealth? position & Conversational Powers!!)

There isnt the faintest doubt, however, that I've grown to talk (& write) too much. Will everybody please stop me? This will be like one of Dos' galleries. Do you know they still had a whole day's work to do in Miami [on the galleys for *The Big Money*]??

Give my *very best* love to Pauline, and please say to Mr Josie [Russell] that it was a great pleasure to meet him & I hope it will happen again soon. What a friend to have to "stand by for a crash"! The very most reassuring person I have met for yrs. I do hope he liked me.

I admire and love Pauline more than I can say, & do so hope to really SEE her soon. And I love you too, Sir, and am yr. obliged &

very devoted friend
& old shipmate

Sara

PS Weight stationary: 83 lbs
our operatives tell us that the MacLeishes are on their way home [from Japan] & I hope its true. The children have had chicken pox.
JFK

The Murphys moved from the house in town at 29 Church Street, Saranac, where they had spent the winter, to another summer "camp" at Paul Smith's, New York, in June. They christened it "Camp Adeline" and remained throughout the summer. Patrick described the camp in a diary he kept. "It is lovely," he wrote on 11 July, "with about eight different cottages, including guest, servants', dining and cooking, main, playhouse, and another cottage for Honoria, my nurse, and myself. Also boathouse and dock, with a launch, rowboat and canoe." As before, Gerald Murphy continued to commute from the city whenever possible.

108. GERALD MURPHY to SARA MURPHY,
New York, 26 June 1936

Dearest Sal:—

Your last missive was a poser. I've thought about it much,—but didn't feel up to answering it. My ideas on topic A are so bad, that even I think so. I'm afraid I've always skulked the question. Wanted to and was aided and abetted, I guess, by family and education. (In the Last Puritan there are some good side-lights on this . . . "he had been brought up to believe that all women were ladies but not that ladies were women—" etc. I'm not looking for alibis. Too late, too late. People are defective. Life is defective. My defect though not openly ruinous effects life and people very fundamentally. You say that I think about it a great deal. Well, it *is* a thing that one cannot disregard. It effects everything, I suppose. Unfortunately it gives one a feeling of inferiority. No, dear Sal, *my* quarrel is not with life or with you or with my antecedents. I'm not angry—just terribly, terribly disappointed that I'm as I am. As for changing: either it's impossible to change anything so elementary,—or I'm too weak. It sounds as if I were thinking like this all the time,—I mean about myself,—but I don't. I naturally think about it often because I think about you,—and about what I wish I could do for you. It's kind of sad. I sometimes think that it must be someone else it's happened to—not you. It's unlike you. Unlikely things happen. I wonder if *life is* unlikely. What *is* likely? What happened to Baoth to me is so *unlike* what one could think of for him, for us. I find myself uncomprehending—and I may say chastened by one thing and another. It does not leave one defiant. I hope it isn't scorn I feel. There's no comfort *there*. About myself my nerve has been taken,—and above all I am very bored with the kind of person I'm like. It doesn't sound so to hear me talk but I am. I wish I could talk about what we have to talk about,—without mentioning myself;—but it doesn't seem possible.

I suppose it sounds as if I were talking in circles;—no just out loud is what I mean to do. Something might come out of it. God knows I can't talk to anyone else about it (were I able to!)

Don't think of me as churning and worrying. I know that doesn't help,—but I *must* think. I feel responsible,—and always will,—and should.

Only one thing would be awful and that is that you might not know that I love only you. We both know it's inadequate (that's where "life" comes in);—but such as it is it certainly is the best this poor fish can offer,—and it's the realest thing I know. Who knows but that the good Lord may let it make up for its great defect in some other way?

G.

HMD

Around the time that the Murphys were planning their summer move to Camp Adeline, the MacLeishes were returning from Japan. As MacLeish worked over the final drafts of his Fortune *articles on Japan, he moved into the New Weston with Gerald, who had taken an apartment there. Dorothy Parker and Alan Campbell had grown to hate Hollywood and had purchased a farm in Bucks County, Pennsylvania, which they would begin to restore, commuting back and forth from California. Gerald had helped Woollcott pick out some briefcases, which he had monogrammed—a Mark Cross specialty. Woollcott would come into New York City from his home at Neshobe Island, in the middle of a lake near Bomoseen, Vermont.*

109. GERALD MURPHY to ALEXANDER WOOLLCOTT,
New York, 14 July 1935 [1936]

Dear Alec:—

It's a relief to know that the brief-cases ("attaché cases," the British prefer) were suitable. I had been tempted to convince Mr. Brown at some later date that his was a little voluminous *if* practical,—and to choose another. He may, at any time, if inclined. The [Charles] Lederer confection had a proper insolence about it, bearing out yr. insult. There is something chiselled in granite about the words burned and gilded in leather. The shipping-room was baffled.

The next week or two is to be given over to a dual meet with my tonsils. After that Sara and I hope to junket a little in Vermont (to Charlotte, for instance) and we shall ask permission (in advance) to take shelter with you. It

169

will be part of a scheme to be undertaken with Archie and Ada and the Dos Passoi to bundle up through Maine to the Gaspé Peninsula. We shall want you (and need you) for some time in Sara's Camp,—later,—when you will.

Archie is at the New Weston with me in mortal combat with his article on Nippon. What *is* the ultimate thing to be said of Japan? I would dread to try. He has been almost all the time on Cricket Hill,—and looks it. Mrs. Alan Campbell has wired someone from Kansas (bound East) that the next time she crosses this Continent it will be in a coffin covered with the American flag. There are threats of a farm in Pennsylvania and of not returning *ever* to Hollywood,—"except to make money."

Recently I have sat lightly-clad playing Brahms' quintets and quartets and trios, reading Le Rouge et Noir, The Last Puritan and The Return of the Native. The result has been very Brahman;—while you hang between earth and sky in yr. liquid lake.

Love from us,

Gerald.

Patrick holds his own and loves the camp.

HL

110. PAULINE HEMINGWAY to GERALD MURPHY, [Key West], 17 July [1936]

Dear Dowdow,

I wonder if you think about me as often as I do about you. I guess not. Anyway, you'd probably be surprised—and it isn't on account of the records which go with us everywhere on the boat. No, I think it must be because you stand for something to me—one against will-o-the wisp, or something like that. Says the original Mother Mudlum.

Patrick Gregory and I have been here for two weeks after Bimini, waiting for Ernest and Bumbi to join us so we can go on I think it's a trip—though every place we think of going, principally out West, seems to be in the grip of some scourge. Ernest and Bumbi stayed on in the now vanished hope, as they get back tomorrow, of catching a really big marlin. Our Bimini venture wasn't a great fishing success, though from the point of view of human contact it was terrific. Fishermen (and what strange bedfellows *they* are) arrived daily by plane and boat, and what talk there was of 6 o reels and 7 o reels and 39, 54, and 72 thread line—but never the kind of line that give a man enough of it he would hang himself, oh no, just stay up all night talking about it line. Ernest and I decided before I left that we would get an old coloured man and put him at the front gate with a Mannlicher with instructions to shoot at every Salt Water Anglers of America badge he sees—which, fortunately, every Salt Water Angler of America wears over his heart. But so far I have not been able to find any old coloured man who isn't working on relief.

I was going to write to you about two months ago, just after I saw Sara in Miami, and tell you how beautiful your wife looked. She met me in the Pan-American station in pearls and one of her hats, and I thought who or whom is that lovely woman expecting, and it turned out to be me . . . So it turns out I've made myself the heroine of the story again. Ernest says I do it all the time. But there is certainly no doubt about who was the beauty. Did she go over for the boat ride? I think we would have been much better situated if we had gone with her. But the children were the problem, and we did get to see a lot of all three of them—Patrick set the house on fire, Bumbi kept four birds at large in his room, and we couldn't get Gigi to swim out over his head. Said he was just a timid rabbit. That's children for you.

How are your Honoria and Patrick? We don't seem to have heard about any one of you for a long time. And may I before I stop this cult writing, acknowledge those lovely records you sent us before we left for Bimini? Our Murphy record collection is our great pleasure. NOBODY has records like we got. Thank you Dowdow for every one of them. And love to all of you.

Pauline

Tell Patrick Mark Cross seems to be getting a lot of preferred position in our World-Telegram.
HMD

Although the Hemingways were spending another late summer at the Nordquist Ranch in Wyoming, where they received Sara's letter, many of the Murphy's friends remained on the east coast for "a delirious roller-coaster kind of summer—all up and down, fast, yelling and out of control," and a fall filled with "a round of State Fairs with Gerald and Sara." John Dos Passos had written Hemingway earlier that the Murphys had "just discovered that you can have a good time on the American continent and that it's fun riding around in a car." The car, as Gerald described it to Woollcott, was "a black and chromium mechanical panther" which he had purchased for the purpose of "junketing." Although Sara began this letter in longhand, she completed it on the typewriter as her "hand tired."

111. SARA MURPHY to ERNEST and PAULINE HEMINGWAY,
Camp Adeline, 29 July [1936]

My dear Hemingways,—

This will have to follow you as I don't know (& hope to god you haven't told anybody!) where you are. If it *should* be the L-T [Ranch]—please tell Mr Nordquist that that summer [1932] was one of our best,—will you? How the boys will *love* it!

We are all fine here. I am just back from n.y.—where Gerald had his tonsils out at Harbor Hospital. He *loved* your letter Pauline. I also rec'd yrs., on my return, Ernest, & thank you.

Gerald has been having such a lot of arthritis & other disagreeables, they thought tonsils might be poisoning him. We hope he will feel a *lot* better now,—he is to take a vacation at last too. This Camp is a great success. The house is much nicer than last year—the Lakes remain the same. Fortunately friends come to see us—& I hope you will too on your way back from the West. Patrick still runs his temp. & eats badly, but looks, & feels I think, better. He has had 2 transfusions for his rather bad anemia,—the last, & most beneficial one about 10 days ago—The donor was a handsome Hebrew woman, so we tease him a lot about Jewish Blood—He doesn't mind a bit. Lately, in an effort to improve his appetite, (which seems to resist everything) we push him all around outdoors in a reclining wheelchair, even down to the dock where he holds a fishline. He is simply *ravished*, as he catches bullheads, perch, & sometimes little trout. It has really made his life over. Of course he is surrounded by his treasures—in his room. Ernest's impalla & bushbuck, his guns, & Baoth's guns, & all his fishing paraphanalia—He simply loves the camp, which is such a comfort. How awful if he didn't. He is a really remarkable person, & it's a pleasure to know him.

Honoria is getting older, & is very stiff with me when I make so bold as to correct her. She has had 4 or 5 girls visiting her, & they seem to have a lovely time. They are all darlings, & mostly terribly pretty. They squeal, giggle, bicycle in shorts,—rush in & out of the lake with the most incredible yellings, then suddenly become Women of the World & loll about—smoking cigarettes (quite badly) & assuring each other how much they prefer Older Men (about 26) to College boys—Boys are beginning to drop in, too—Honoria has a nice deep speaking-voice, & lovely coloring, & a be-au-ti-ful figure—am I being fatuous? Certainly. As doting as hell. She has also learned to drive the car this Summer.

Shall I now tell you about all our friends? (although I could go on about H.!) Well, we danced with Archie & Ada on their 20th wedding anniversary [21 June]—in their big barn. It was Midsummer night & the greatest fun & very gay. They had a country orchestra with a man who called out directions:

"Salute yr opp'site partner Salute the ladies all. Something something something and promenade the hall." We did it *all*, & Virginia Reels & Pop the Weasel too amid gen'l disorder & drinking. We were all in sort o invented peasant costume made up of whatever there was; Ada made a picture I shall *never* forget—blue overalls, with a flying wedding veil, & wreath of syringa, & her small pink feet, (which hardly ever touched the ground) *packed* into string sandals. She never stopped, & felt fine next morning. Ada looks, & seems wonderful. Archie is dead-tired, as he works night & day on his Japanese article—Finished soon, & he is to take a holiday. We are all planning to take a (hand tired) small motor trip with them, & with the Dosses, about middle Aug.—around the Gaspé Pen. Next: well, at last we got to Provincetown after all these yrs. & simply loved it. It was only 2 days, like most of our trips, but we lost no time. Their house [John and Katy Dos Passos] is LOVELY just my favorite kind of house, where you can reach out of the window & touch a ship. And we ate Superlatively, the LOBSTER!! Oh heavens the lobster. They are both fine. Dos' book [*The Big Money*] will be out soon. Perhaps you have it already? & his picture is to be on TIME that wk. Katy has written a book, with Mrs. Edith Shay, about Cape Cod [*Down the Cape*]. She calls it a guidebook. It's awfully good. Purdon me if I tell you all things you already know Just Zeal. Also we went over to DENNIS (Mass) where Phil Barry's new play *The Bright Star* was being tried out at the theatre there. It is really VERY funny & about the youngest sort of people. It is said to be going to be a BDY (Broadway not bloody) success. Jed Harris manager, & what an awful man HE is.

Dotty & Alan Campbell are East. They have bought, we hear, a stone house in Penn. They are coming up to stay over Sunday with Don & Bee [Stewart], who have bought a house (stone) at Ausable Forks, quite near here, I hope they will come here to stay too. I really love Dotty. Do you see, there is quite a Migration away from the stucco of Hollywood. Not for good, I suspect, but encouraging even as a tendency, don't you think? Our beloved Mr Benchley is still in that hellhole, I *hope* making a LOT of dollars.

Well, my dears, I am glad that you are all getting away from the frantic atmosphere of tropics for awhile. We all need CHANGE for our health & nerves. AND we all need some time to ourselves, & I hope you get a *lot* of it (old aunt stuff). It will seem wonderful to ride your horses again over those lovely trails, specially with the children,—and come back at night to sit about & have those Dainties Pauline used to whip up with the moon cocktails. And how one slept in that good air! (We always got sciroccoish when we stayed at ANTIBES too long, why shouldn't you? (Old Song)

The Weatherbird was suddenly rented for July & Aug. so I never got my sailing trip. (If you had of come it wouldn't have been rented) So I may go over (Spaniards willing) to Paris in Sept. I want new clothes & new ideas (in order named) & Hellstern shoes, & perfumery & trick hats, & linge [linen], not to mention THE eve. dress & to sit hours with Léger & his friends in cafés, & haunt rue la Boetie, & see every good new play & all music if any, & be back here in about 3 days & ll hrs. 27 mins. I WISH Jinny Pfeiffer would go too. (I'm sure you all couldn't). I think, (& hope she thinks so too,) that we would get on rather well on a trip. I should *love* it. I'd also like (how I do run on) to dance late at Boeuf or somewhere & go to the Halles. Dark dawn in Sept. What's in season? Des chouxfleurs [cauliflower], ma petite dame, des reines-marguerites [China asters]. Do you like it? I bet Pauline does. And it all SMELLS so different,—from the Adirondacks shall we say? (It all sounds like the gibson girl's 5-year Plan)

Goodbye dears, it's a great world.

Think of us sometimes, because we really love you. And now how do *you* do?

Much love—from Sara.

JFK

112. GERALD MURPHY to F. SCOTT FITZGERALD, Harbor Hospital, New York, 30 July 1936

Dear Scott:—

I find that I can go just so long without knowing how you all are,—where you all are. Just so long is at an end now. Send me a card or something. I leave the hospital to-morrow without my tonsils,—and go to camp for most of August. Sara has taken—or rather bought very advantageously—a well-built one of Edith Wharton's era which she has somehow transformed into something outside of New Orleans—gay, light, colored rooms, white rugs, a small jungle of indoor exotic palms and plants,—mexican metalware partout, etc. The old guard of Upper St. Regis is fluttered in the dovecote. We are on a quiet remote lake. Patrick likes it very much and is holding his own. It is Sara who needs attention now. I want to get her to Europe for a month. Her inconsolability,—and her present anxiety over Patrick begin to tell on her. She refuses to release her tense grip and is burning white. The same pride in not sparing herself that her mother had,—has come to her now. There is little one can do for her. Even her loneliness I cannot reach. She is gay,—energetic,—but is not well.

One day riding down alone through Vermont I had a long conversation with you and asked you many questions,—abstract, they were. I wish I might know yr. answers one day.

We have seen Dos & Katy often. They are so fond of you as we are. Please send us some word. We *wonder* so and somehow must know,—soon. Just a telegram or card,

Aff'y.

Gerald

PUL

Shortly after Fitzgerald moved to Asheville, near the sanitarium where he had placed Zelda in April, he tore the muscles of his shoulder during an awkward dive into a swimming pool. Although the shoulder had started to heal, he fell on it again and was bedridden for weeks thereafter. Fitzgerald had apparently written Gerald in response to his 30 July letter, detailing his accident and reacting in alarm to Gerald's account of Sara's despair, but his letter has not survived.

113. GERALD MURPHY to F. SCOTT FITZGERALD, Camp Adeline [c. August 1936]

Dear Scott:—

The mood of my letter must have been wrong. I feel a kind of disloyalty to Sara in giving you the impression that she admits to herself even remotely the fact of what she is withstanding. Her resilience is formidable,—when one considers that she faces squarely the truth about everything every minute of the day. I do not know what goes on in her mind. I doubt if two human creatures ultimately succeed in sharing grief. But I should never have made you think that she *shows* the slightest sign of what she's undergoing. Indeed everyone remarks her gayety and becomingness. She's never looked prettier. This camp is a bower.

Your article [the Crack-Up trilogy] I have not read due to an oath I took with myself upon returning here from Europe last March that I would no longer read the newspapers and magazines.[1] As a result I've lived with "Le Rouge et le Noir," "The Return of the Native," "The Last Puritan," "Arctic

---

1. Although Gerald had not read the *Esquire* articles in August, he did read them that fall, commenting on them to Woollcott: "Scott's article moved me unduly,—I suppose. He deserves to speak of what has happened to him. More people should—or *must* one be Irish and unbecoming in order to?"

Adventure," "Barchester Towers," "Le Crime de Sylvestre Bonnard,"—and now Dos' new book [*Big Money*],—which I admire very much. It has all recreated a kind of distant region in which I enjoy living,—and I find my mind freed.

As for life (as they call it) I find it turning out to be the very thing that I'd always suspected it to be: a very badly-schemed and wasteful process. Having felt it to be such, I find that I don't mind it as much. For those who believe in it (and believe in being in it and of it) (such as Sara,—and you, I suppose) it must be a very painful experience. I find that my only fear is what *other* people may be suffering. Sometimes the thought is well-nigh intolerable. However, I find myself learning *again* not to take life at *its own* tragical value.

Your shoulder sounds painful. I hope it doesn't continue so long. Thank you for your letter. It brought much with it. Santayana describes his man at the end as an "ascetic without belief,"—I find that I have inadvertently been enjoying a kind of self-imposed incredulous self-denial for more than a year. It's insulation, at least against idle wear and tear. It's not what we do but what we do with our minds that counts. Our greatest affection to you,

                                                            Gerald

Cummings says:—
"We live for that which dies, and die for that which lives." Is it true?
PUL

114. KATY DOS PASSOS to SARA MURPHY, Truro, 18 September 1936

My Dearest Mrs. Puss

Ouch what a storm is whipping around Truro, and we are thinking of you among your pines and spruces, and what do your palms and potted Florida exiles think of the weather up there? I'm sure they're pale green with fright. We are planning to leave for Conway tomorrow on the way to New York and will probably take off in a tremendous gale—

Oh Mrs. Puss we are getting quite homesick for you—and will have to arrange something—saw Gerald for a short time in New York and heard about you, but hearing isn't seeing—I have been pricked with the little thorny thought that we never told you how lovely the white glass lamp you sent us appeared. It was a beauty and I put it away till it could be properly enthroned in the restored living room. We have the white rug out here and see it every

176

day—also the screens which make a suite of rooms out of our small guest barn. And oh Mrs. Puss how I do thank you for the samples, which are so pretty and inspiring—no one but you could have collected such a showing—

We've suffered a great but comical shock in relation to our house in Provincetown. You know Edmund Wilson rented it for the summer. He brought with him his colored maid and a small picaninny of eight months—the child of the maid (Hattie's) daughter, who had unfortunately lost her mind (what a sentence!)—I was a little uneasy about this, but thought poor Bunny [Edmund Wilson] had to have Hattie, so could not avert the baby—its name is Delores—and after all it was *his* funeral, which it seems to have been, as it howled every minute all summer long. Bunny left a few days ago, telling me he was leaving Hattie to clean the house—Dos and I went in yesterday, to see if it was ready, but as we entered the living room we heard the most alarming uproar in the basement—a minute later Hattie floundered upstairs with a strange look on her face, and said she was 'cleaning'—the next minute three coal black negro children burst out of the basement, and two more from the bedroom—they actually seemed to be coming through the floor. "Hattie!" I shrieked, "What does this mean?" And Hattie fell into a chair and began to wring her hands and cry—"Them's my daughters chillin—" she groaned, "an I aint got no place to put em—Their pa just brought em here and left em with me he aint got no way to care for 'em—I aint got no money to take em nowhere—and Mista Wilson he don't know what to do neither."

Mrs. Puss, I was flabbergasted. I looked out the window and the yard was full of Harlem laundry—diapers and towels, shirts, underwear—pillowslip's sheets, blankets—a lot of rusty tin, garbage, and most of my best kitchen things in terrible condition—a strange rich smell began to make itself felt more and more—The black faces were everywhere. Mrs. Puss I learned from the neighbors (who are almost crazy) they've been there since Labor Day—Mrs. Puss—what would you do? Mrs. Puss—the oldest (15) is half-witted, and the neighbors say he spent days on the back porch beating on my pots and pans with forks and spoons. Mrs. Puss, I ran out to look at the blankets all wet on the lawn and what do you think I saw hopping on one of them? Fleas. Mrs. Puss—I knew no more. Harlem fleas. Mrs. Puss what shall I do now? The neighbors are all wild but not so much as I am. I'm putting poor Hattie right out but what then? Mrs. Puss, do you think Mr. Wilson did right?

I'm sending Patrick a little note. We were so pleased to hear his X-rays looked improved. Do write us about him and the camp and what you are doing, and please how do you feel? Dos sends his love, and I send mine

With love to you all

Katy

P.S. Such a cute note from Honoria the other day. Has she had fun this summer? Give her my love with pink ruffles on it—
P.S. Love to Gerald with whipped cream and sherry—
P.S. Love to Patrick in port wine
UVA

115. KATY DOS PASSOS to SARA MURPHY,
Provincetown, 2 November 1936

My Dearest Mrs. Puss,

What a wrench it was to go away from you and your house, as it always is. I wish we lived where we could see you every day, it would be just like fine weather. We had such a good time with you and Gerald, and the feeling followed us home. We never got to Boston as planned, because a great storm of wind and rain came up and drove us into a farm house in Vermont where we spent a very comical night with a lot of Vermonters who were raising canaries. We had flannel cakes for breakfast, doughnuts, ham, eggs, biscuits, cottage cheese, jelly, maple syrup, honey toast, peaches, baked apples and pie. As a result Mr. Dos Passos gave a kind of gasp just as we were going through Conway, and said he felt just the least mite squamish, so we stopped there for a restorative. They [Archie and Ada] were both looking well, and Kenney [MacLeish] was there with his girl-friend who seemed very nice. I hope Mrs. Puss dear that you had a good time in New York—and how did Honoria like Hamlet? I suppose she said, "Oh the poor thing." Wish I could have been with you. We saw Midsummer Nights Dream at the local theater last night. Yards and yards of cheesecloth and high-school fairies in soft focus with General Electric glow worms and stuffed owls and actors and all the hams in Hollywood except the Barrymores. I wish they had put in the Barrymores. I would love to see John as Oberon. Though Oberon was really rather good—he had a sad, spiteful, unhuman look that was quite nice, and Titania was very silky and shiny— They all floated wonderfully on wires.

We're just settling into Provincetown now and soon will be settled enough to go away. We've got the screens up as Gerald suggested and they are wonderful. White rug down and priceless Mrs. Puss lamp in full view—The name of the room is now "The Old and the New"—like Einsenstein's [1929] film— and we're having a lovely time moving furniture around in it. Weather has been delicious, with a winey fall flavor and sun all day long. Now a big gale coming through. The town is so quiet I'm a little lonesome; all my friends have been smoked out by the depression, and only a few are left to go to see in the

1. Sara, Garoupe Beach, Cap d'Antibes, c. 1925.

2. Sara sunning pearls and Ada MacLeish knitting, Garoupe Beach, Cap d'Antibes, c. 1925.

3. Gerald raking Garoupe Beach, Cap d'Antibes, c. 1925.

4. Gerald giving Murphy children lunch, Garoupe Beach, Cap d'Antibes, c. 1925.

5. Scott and Zelda Fitzgerald with Scottie, Garoupe Beach, Cap d'Antibes, c. 1925.

6. Ernest Hemingway with Bumby, Garoupe Beach, Cap d'Antibes, c. summer 1926.

7. Hadley Hemingway with Bumby, Garoupe Beach, Cap d'Antibes, c. summer 1926.

8. Dorothy Parker, Robert Benchley, Honoria Murphy and Gerald, Garoupe Beach, Cap d'Antibes, c. summer 1926.

9. Villa America as viewed from the terrace.

10. Gerald on Villa America terrace, c. 1926.

11. John Dos Passos, Ernest and Hadley Hemingway, and Gerald and Sara (center), Austria, March 1926.

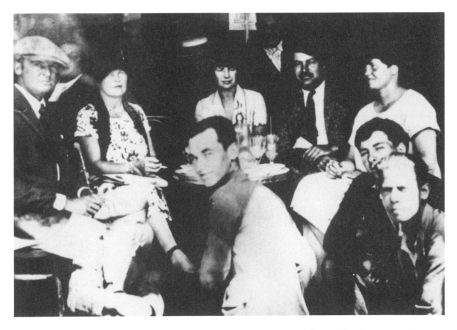

12. Gerald and Sara, Pauline, Ernest, Hadley, and bootblacks, Pamplona, Spain, summer 1926.

13. The Murphys on board oceanliner, returning from America, early 1929.

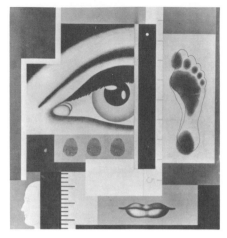

14. Gerald Murphy's *Portrait*, c. 1928 (destroyed).

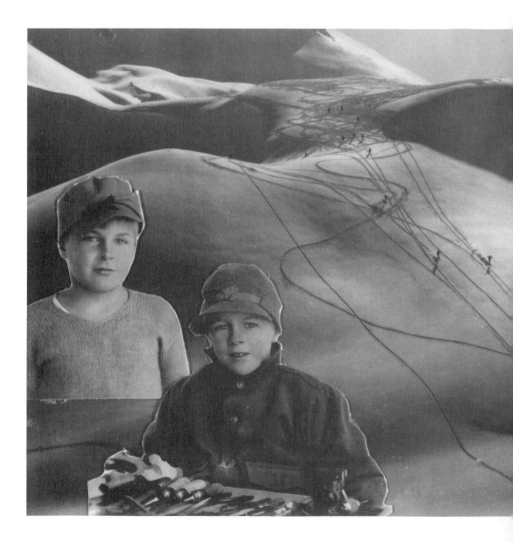

15. Patrick Murphy with etching tools, Palace Hotel balcony, Montana-Vermala, Switzerland, 1929.

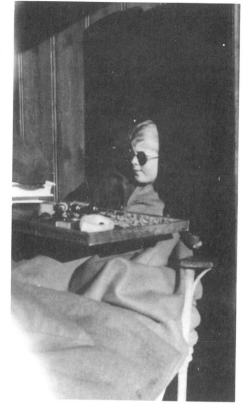

16. Family collage designed by Sara: Baoth, Patrick (with tools), and Honoria, c. 1930, Montana-Vermala, Switzerland.

17. Ernest and Honoria, Montana-Vermala, Switzerland, c. 1929–1930.

18. Ada and Archie MacLeish with Honoria, Montana-Vermala, Switzerland, c. 1930.

19. Ernest and Pauline, c. 1930.

20. John and Katy Dos Passos, Key West, Florida, c. 1932.

21. Pauline, Sara, and Gerald, top; and Baoth, Ernest, and guide, Wyoming, fall 1932.

22. Pauline, Ernest, and Gerald, Nordquist L-T Ranch, Wyoming, fall 1932.

23. Gerald Murphy, the "Merchant Prince," Saranac Lake, New York, c. 1935.

24. Archibald MacLeish, Librarian of Congress, c. 1939.

25. F. Scott Fitzgerald in Hollywood, late 1930s.

afternoons. We have had a great many strange visitors, however. Most of them seemed to be crazy, like Mr. Stevens was that night in Key West [See letter 101]. We got really rather worried. Three came in one day—one came especially to tell Dos that he was "a babe in the wood," and another to complain that his brother was persecuting him by camping in his front yard with a tent—it seemed to be some dispute over property, and the third was a pale young man from Harvard who was preparing himself for a diplomatic career in communism (when it comes). They were all very fanatical and hard to get rid of. I hope if I go nuts it will be in a nice way, with feathers in my hair and a fixed notion that I'm able to make myself invisible, or can fly, or anything that will make me feel cheerful and agreeable.

Dos and I are off for Boston this morning (election)—then we come back tomorrow, and may go to New York the last of the week. We haven't any plans we could blue print yet. I wonder if you'll be in New York? Of course we're all the time thinking about Patrick, and send him our very best love—And to Gerald and you, our most faithful high-powered devotion

Katy

UVA

116. GERALD MURPHY to ALEXANDER WOOLLCOTT, Saranac [c. November 1936]

Alexis lunaire:—

You and Dos Passos are the only two people I've ever met who know what people are *going* to think about!

My dear boy, when we planned to have you come a day in September or October that you were free (we always think of you as having so *many* demands made upon yr. time!)—our plan—as very often—was erased by Patrick's two or three weeks of rechute [relapse]. Then we moved and Sara said: "I think Alec will enjoy coming when there's snow and we're in Winter Quarters." It has come and we are ready for you. Let's you and I entrain [from New York] on the 3rd or 4th, 7 p.m., dinner on the Water Level Route, arriving at Saranac at the timeless hour of 6:30 a.m. Sara is always up and awake with the *Best* Coffee:—for our arrival, I mean.

As to why we want you to come: 1) We've loved you since the moment we met you. 2) The thought of you's been a comfort often; seeing you, asylum. 3) You've been a kind of talisman in our minds for Patrick: the things you've done for him and said! 4) It would be wrong somehow if you didn't come to us before the year has passed. 5) We want you.

179

I can understand your feeling about youngsters. Patrick is an adult. Eight years have made him so. He is not precocious. He expects and demands little in the way of communication. His exchange is as I told you yours was: one that acts by its presence and without visible means.

Ernest Hemingway was afraid of him for years,—said he'd been "born tough," mentally: incorruptible, I think he meant. You will find him removed from what goes on about him,—yet incisively clear in mind. One of the reasons we'd love to have you here is that Patrick would love to see you. He's always wanted to,—quite naturally. You've taken a place in his life. He will expect nothing of you, but will get a great deal. I know him. Nothing of value escapes him.

For years we've shared with Patrick the things we cherish. They belong to him naturally. He is not a remarkable child, he is a remarkable person. When he was five Picasso said of him: "C'est un monsieur qui est par hasard un enfant" [He is a man who is by chance a child].

Here are things that would interest me in New York to see: Johnny Johnson, Son of Mongolia, Garden of Allah, Yellow Cruise, Song of China, Les Miserables. Would any one of them you? Shall I get 2 seats for the 1st mentioned? I'll telephone you.

Why isn't Hamlet depressing,—when you consider what happens? At the 4th seance it occurred to me that Hamlet when all had gone against him and life was too much for him,—found himself *on the side* of destiny itself. I'd like to believe that this can happen. Tell me.

Aff'y.

Gerald.

HL

117. GERALD MURPHY to ARCHIBALD MACLEISH,
[Saranac Lake] 7 January 1937

Archie:—

Your *wish* to write me—as you did—will walk with me always.

Whenever I have realized that I really *loved* anyone—as I do you and Ada,—at once the spectre of my inadequacy has forced itself into my mind. In the past there have been times when I have dreaded the risk of your finding me unsatisfactory. Once during a ten-day visit here from Europe I avoided seeing you,—fearing I might somehow destroy a thing so perfect as our feelings for each other. Always I knew this to be selfish of me. I am no longer afraid.

What I feel—what your letter brought me—is as incommunicable as what you have wished to say.

Think of me as having a gift from you beyond price. I now feel within me the thing for which I have always longed,—some secret region—unexplored—to which I can go and find more than gold,—for you've marked the spot.

These last months and weeks I had tried to teach myself that I dare not again hope for a kind of happiness for us in the time to come. Your letter has helped to prove me wrong; thank God.

I shall say to you now that during these last days we have told your names over and over to ourselves. It is of course that we need you, but how clear, how clear it is at such a time that we love you.

Gerald.

LC

Hemingway came to New York to collaborate on the documentary film, Spain in Flames, *which was to premiere at the Cameo Theatre on 28 January. In mid-January he stopped in Saranac to see the Murphys. Pauline had remained in Key West.*

118. GERALD MURPHY to ERNEST HEMINGWAY, Saranac Lake, 8 January 1937

Dear E.:—

The name of the tailor is Gray and Lampel, 18 E. 53rd. I have spoken to them about you. Very good reliable old N.Y. house, no chi-chi. Sensible cut, *best* materials. Would suggest Hotel New Weston, 50th St. & Madison with Brevoort's old cuisine and chef. Fine bar where you can eat. Subsidized by French & English Chamber of Commerce. Croissants for bkfst. Around corner from Jinny. Do you *know* N.Y.?—Am here now indefinitely so wanted you to have tailor's address. Use my name with Miss Humphries at hotel.

Aff'y all.

G.

Conditions same here. P. certainly no better. Au contraire, I'm afraid.

G.

JFK

119. GERALD MURPHY to PAULINE HEMINGWAY,
Saranac Lake, 22 January 1937

Dear Paolina:—

Your letter brought so much of what was needed. Sara and I backed up and took on a load. It has helped, I can tell you. In a moment of boastful expansion with Ernest I referred to certain passages in the letter which were "not uncomplimentary" to me. Drunk with success I gave it to him to read. It is now confiscate,—so I must answer you at random.

Ginnie, Ernest and Sidney [Franklin] motored up from New York a few days ago in the latter's pulsing motor. It *was* nice,—you'll admit, of people to do *that*. We were delighted. It was mother's milk to Sara. There was, it seems, a certain amount of conversational sniping going on between Ernest and Ginnie. Both were in the pink of condition. Someone won on points, I suppose.

Ernest looked fine, I thought,—and hardened down. He seems to be accomplishing everything he wanted to about the book [*To Have and Have Not*, 1937]. Sidney seems all repaired,—and is certainly an angel for disposition. He's less like the popular idea of a bull-fighter every day.

Ginnie has stayed on until today. Sara has been so happy to have her. We *love* that girl. There's no one *like* her. She not only says things that no one else does, she *feels* different things than any one else,—and what's more she has learned the most endearing way of communicating them to people. She's in better health, too,—and has never been so handsome. There's too much drawing packed into that face to get it down on paper or canvas.

We talked so much of you, Pauline! We missed you. We said so often. There were no dissenting votes. We wish we saw you more, and we wonder what you think about. Your young cousin, Ward Werner, came last night in Ginnie's car from New York, after a hair-raising trip thro' blizzards, over glaire-ice, onto railroad tracks (where flares were lighted to warn the approaching trains that he had skidded down a bank onto the tracks—only the first train didn't stop and the car was dragged off 60 seconds before, etc.) He had not driven a car for fifteen years. He's a bright boy and we enjoyed so having him. They've gone off (Ginnie driving, at his request) up to Quebec for some *really good* ski-ing. They had been headed for Woodstock, but Quebec is only 40 miles further by road, so I re-routed them. They wore very Kitzbuhl clothes, and the plan is that they should stop wherever they find snow as they roll along, and get out and ski,—then get in and drive along. They're stopping here on their way back through for a visit.

I just heard Sara tell someone: "Ginnie's such a cozy creature. I love to feel she's in the house."

Your general deduction from this letter should be that if your family ever needs to be convinced that they have a couple of Grade A daughters out on the Atlantic Seaboard, that we'll be ready with our argument.

Dos and Katy are up on the Cape trying to keep Neptune away from our door. Their bulkhead's gone out to sea. Headed for Mexico or Jamaica after. The good little other Waddell Avenue sister [Ada MacLeish] is here with Sara and it's a joy to have her. Archie begins his lectures at Princeton next month.

Ginnie's stories of Patrick and Gregory do one's heart good. Take care of yourself, Pauline,

Aff'y.

Gerald.

JFK

120. GERALD MURPHY to ALEXANDER WOOLLCOTT, Saranac Lake, 29 January 1937

Alexis:—

Wednesday I was in town planning—in the midst of insect vexations—to talk to you by telephone . . . when word came that I should return. Patrick's decline comes in periodic drops from one level of vitality to a lower . . . each time he seems to withdraw a little . . . his mind is clearer and more detached . . . his horizon larger. We seem to have been able to stay any apprehension . . . his sense of the future is painfully clear. I feel as if we were all caught in some vacuum of timelessness . . . the days are like the tick of a clock. We feel you thinking of us and it's warming. Sara loved so talking to you. I shall keep in touch with you. You are a haven of thought. I wish that I might make you feel it,—sufficiently,

Gerald.

p.s. Thank Dorothy [Parker] for her kind messages to us the other day. I was inadequate, I'm sure. Sara asks how she is—always.

G.

HL

121. GERALD and SARA MURPHY to F. SCOTT FITZGERALD, Saranac Lake, 30 January 1937

PATRICK DIED PEACEFULLY THIS MORNING   LOVE

SARA GERALD

445 PM

PUJ.

122. F. SCOTT FITZGERALD to GERALD and SARA MURPHY, Tryon, N.C., 31 January 1937

Dearest Gerald & Sara:

The telegram came today and the whole afternoon was so sad with thoughts of you and the past and the happy times we had once. Another link binding you to life is broken and with such insensate cruelty that is hard to say which of the two blows was concieved with more malice. I can see the silence in which you hover now after this seven years of struggle and it would take words like Lincoln's in his letter to the mother who had lost four sons in the war to write you anything fitting at the moment. The sympathy you will get will be what you have had from each other already and for a long, long time you will be inconsolable.

But I can see another generation growing up around Honoria and an eventual peace somewhere, an occasional port of call as we all sail deathward. Fate can't have any more arrows in its quiver for you that will wound like these. Who was it said that it was astounding how the deepest of griefs can change in time to a sort of joy. The golden bowl is broken indeed but it *was* golden; nothing can ever take those boys away from you now

Scott

HMD

123. ALEXANDER WOOLLCOTT to SARA MURPHY, New York, 1 February [1937]

Dear Sara

When I was talking to Saranac on Saturday—was it only Saturday?—Alice Lee [Myers] gave me your message to the effect that you were glad I had come up. Sara, I have no words emphatic enough to tell you how glad *I* am, how thankful I am, that I made that trip to Saranac early in December. It scares me—it makes me seasick—when I think how easily I might have postponed that week-end, how casually I might have gone off instead to some flossy engagement I thought important.

I count it one of the great privileges of my life to have known Patrick—just as I am thankful I knew Father Duffy and Mrs. Fiske and that I know and can sometimes go to see Edward Sheldon. I hoard every memory I have of Patrick. I suppose that really, in some confused, unconfessed, frightened way, I am counting on him to put in a good word for me on Judgment Day, or—if thats asking too much—I'm planning myself to put forth in my defence before the throne of grace the fact that anyway Patrick thought well of me. It ought to count. I think it ought to count.

Sara, among the few things I'm sure of is this—as long as I live, as long as I remember anything at all, I shall remember Patrick—not hazily, no perfume growing fainter and fainter with time, no mere formless glow like the setting sun shining on the snow, but sharp and clear forever, like some precise and perfect masterpiece, a Vermeer, changeless as long as paint and canvas last. And years from now, Sara, when you are old and I am so feeble I can just about walk and chance brings us together in some town, you will be glad to see me and wont even have to talk to me because you'll know without any word from me that I'm still thinking of Patrick with undiminished respect—indeed that I cannot, cannot forget him.

A. W.

HMD

124. Gerald and Sara Murphy to Archibald and Ada MacLeish, Saranac Lake, 3 February 1937

THE RARE THING YOUR MESSAGE BROUGHT IS SURELY THE ANSWER TO WHATEVER CIRCUMSTANCES LIFE CAN DEVISE=

GERALD SARA.

LC

125. Ellen Barry to Gerald and Sara Murphy, Hobe Sound, Florida [February 1937]

My Dearest Sara & Gerald—

My heart aches for you and I wish I could be with you now. All day I have thought of Patrick and I realize more and more what a vivid person he was and what a privilege it was to know him—I can think of very few of my older friends that I feel are as valuable in their persons as he—from the first time I saw him in his yellow bathing suit at Antibes I felt how remarkable he was—and I remember him so well and think of what he said and how he said it on all those happy occasions I was lucky enough to know him. I wish he might have had a longer life—

Dear Sara I think of how tired you must be—and of how strong and brave you are—I love you very much—my love to you dear Gerald too—for ever and ever—

Ellen

HMD

126. PHILIP BARRY to GERALD and SARA MURPHY, Hobe Sound, Florida [February 1937]

Dearest Sara and Gerald:

I can't help feeling that Patrick has at last escaped a thousand million enemies who singled him out for attack for no other reason than that he was so plainly and shiningly a child of Light. You know what I believe about the survival of the individual who has earned it, and never have I known any one of any age who so clearly earned his as did Patrick. I do believe that now he is free to wander examine inquire and enjoy, and that he will do so.

I should like some way to celebrate his victory, and inasmuch as in these last two days he has seemed to me to become closer and closer identified with this spirit of the individual I am trying to exhibit in my new play, and with his struggles, I would like to write it for him, and when it is finished to dedicate it to Sara and Gerald's son, Patrick Murphy.[1]

Ellen and I send all our love. You will never find any two people who love you more.

Phil

HMD

---

1. Philip Barry's *War in Heaven*, adapted as the play *Here Come the Clowns* and produced on Broadway in December 1938, was dedicated "To Patrick Francis Murphy II. There was in him something that was fierce and imperishable."

Alice Lee and Richard Myers had met the Murphys in France in 1929 and had continued to see them in New York during the 1930s. Richard Myers was an aspiring composer and musician.

127. ALICE LEE MYERS to ERNEST HEMINGWAY, Saranac Lake [6 February 1937]

Dear Ernest—

Perhaps the reason for possessions is to give one something to do when one can't grieve and remember. Sara and Gerald are courageous and resigned. In going over Patrick's possessions, they asked me to send you his gun racks and for your boys, two engines that he loved. He had not played with them so that they are quite safe. Sara also wished me to ask you if you would like the mounted heads that you sent him, for your trophy room. Since their plans are indefinite—except that the camp is for sale or for rent, Sara felt that it would be so much better for you to have them than for her to store them.

In a day or two, we shall be going to New York. Probably Sara will take a furnished apartment for the next two months so that Honoria can be with her. Beyond that, she hasn't decided anything.

Patrick loved seeing you so—the last work he did were a few little scratches that he made on his etching of you. When he was so weak that no one else could have lifted a finger, he insisted on doing everything for himself.

Sara sends you her love—
Very cordially

Alice Lee Myers

JFK

128. PAULINE HEMINGWAY to GERALD and SARA MURPHY, Key West, 8 February [1937]

Dear Sara and Gerald,

I have been praying for Patrick all week and I know that you do not believe in prayer, but I cannot help feeling that when a little boy goes alone to another place it is good to have prayers follow him. And I am having some masses said too. I hope you do not mind—these are the only things I know to do for him now.

As for understanding why a boy so richly and uniquely endowed to live in this world happily should have been taken from it, I don't. And I do not know what to say to comfort you for a loss like yours and I do not know why such things happen to two people like you who did not need to be refined by suffering.

Dear Sara and Gerald, I am thinking about you all the time and loving you and wishing, wishing, wishing I could do something to help you pass the time a little.

Your loving friend

Pauline

HMD

Gerald had asked Woollcott if he would speak to the "assembled tiny Employment Group of the Personnel Division of the Retail Dry Goods Association in the Loft's Tea Room." If Woollcott would tell them a story, Gerald wrote on 17 May 1937, he would "buy a life membership to the Seeing Eye." Because Woollcott's poor eyesight made him feel vulnerable to potential blindness, his favorite charity was Seeing Eye, devoted to training and supplying guide dogs to the blind.

129. GERALD MURPHY to ALEXANDER WOOLLCOTT,
en route to Saranac [c. spring 1937]

Alexis, Prince of the Heavenly Flocks:—

You were superb Wednesday night. The National Retail Dry Goods Association is reverberating in every corridor with your sudden appearance. They appear to be quite unseated. I wanted to call you the next day to tell you this,—but I knew you'd growl at me and make me feel that when I try to tell you how nice you are that I am being transparently perfunctory.

I am on my way to Saranac to bring down to the City Patricks urn— containing his ashes. Later we shall place them at Easthampton beside Baoth's in the old cemetary (1653) where lies Sir Lion Gardiner in armour,—nearby.

To-morrow I shall be passing down thro' my paradise—the Rutland Valley and shall incline toward your Island Home,—quaffing at the "Castle."

I am taking out a membership in Baoth's name to the "Seeing Eye." May I make this use of what is rightfully yours? He would have loved to know about it. What an *expansive* heart he had. *All* generosity, he was;—and so must have been happy.

Some day I should like to be assured of a life membership to Alexander Woollcott. What are the dues?

Affectionately,

Gerald.

p.s. I love 12 hr. day trips in day coaches. Is this wrong? G.

HL

Shortly after the Murphys sold Camp Adeline and moved into a penthouse in the Hotel New Weston, Sara began suffering from neck spasms for which doctors prescribed bedrest. Dorothy Parker's and Alan Campbell's Bucks County farm, Fox House, was ready for occupancy the same spring. As they commuted between their farm and California, where Parker was working on her second David Selznick script, Nothing Sacred, *they sometimes saw the Murphys, usually in New York. Hale Walker and Harold Heller, the Murphys' long-time decorators, evidently helped to plan the house's decor, which not everyone found tasteful. Dorothy had decided to do the living room in nine shades of red, to which she added mirrors and fancy fixtures, which scandalized the more traditional neighbors who also did not like the lack of window coverings.*

130. DOROTHY PARKER to SARA MURPHY, Pipersville, Pennsylvania [c. spring 1937]

Dearest Sara,

I'm afraid I must ask you to get right up out of that bed, and come see the mirror. There are no words to tell you how lovely it is. You simply never have seen anything like it. It arrived yesterday, in an ordinary package and by ordinary delivery just as if it were not one of the most beautiful objects in the world, and Alan and I have been shedding soft tears ever since. Nice tears. Tears that make you feel good.

Now it is on a wall of the red room, and the red room promptly has become a dream. We have to keep running up to it all day, to believe it. This is raising hell with the completion of that play; but there are more important things.

It's beginning to look a little bit hopeful outdoors. There are robins, and even a crocus here and there—hideous little yellow things, but you get so grateful—and the whole effect is considerably less Constance Spry than it has been for such a long time. Yesterday I saw in the woods a group of five grown-up deer and two baby deer with them. I never saw a thing like that before. Between that and the mirror, I never want to leave this place.

It was so lovely to see you the other day, and particularly to see you looking like that. Will you kindly stop that cheating, and come down here where you're needed? The puppies are all out of hand, they're so insolent. And one of the cats is going to have kittens. Sometimes I wonder if we're not overdoing things, in the animal line.

I've got to come in to town next week to speak—if I can wrench myself out of the red room—and will you let me see you then? You'll be back home, won't you, and done with all this damn nuisance?

Oh, Sara, there's no good trying to thank you and Gerald. All I can say is, wait till you see it—and please don't wait long.

Dorothy

Would you tell Hale and Harold how truly we admire and love what they've made?

HMD

In support of the Spanish Loyalist cause that spring, Hemingway had collaborated with Dos Passos and others on the film documentary The Spanish Earth. *The Contemporary Historians—a corporation which included Lillian Hellman, Hemingway, Dos Passos, MacLeish, and Gerald Murphy—helped to promote and distribute the film during the summer, with Hemingway acting as its major spokesman. He talked before the Second American Writers' Congress in New York in early June, and the Murphys were there at Carnegie Hall, which was filled to capacity. Hemingway surprised his fellow writers with his new social commitment, and his speech, along with the first showing of* The Spanish Earth, *was enthusiastically received. Acting as chairman and master of ceremonies MacLeish introduced him, and Fitzgerald watched the performance from the sidelines. Following the Congress, Hemingway went to the Bahamas with his family before returning to Spain late in the summer. The Murphys would also go to Europe that summer, Sara and Honoria sailing on 16 June and Gerald meeting up with them later in July.*

131. Sara Murphy to Pauline Hemingway,
on board R.M.S. *Aquitania*, 22 June [1937]

Dearest Pauline,

I meant to write you before sailing, but things piled up so, & the air was so full of tissue paper & to top all Honoria & I took to our beds with socalled Summer Colds, just to make the confusion complete.

And Ernestine [Leray, who had worked for the Murphys in Europe] decided she would rather stay & be an American god help her, so our packing was very temperamental indeed, in fact Honoria and I, who are rooming together, haven't found anything YET, although I suppose its all there to the last belt, if one had the courage to look.

We have had a flatcalm passage, and land tomorrow. Beyond staying a few days in Paris, & then to London for the same, we have no plans as yet, all the future is a clear jelly, & about as interesting. However I persist in believing that this impression is just post-cold (post-heavy-cold) cafard [depression], & that all will seem better in the deceptive light of Europe. Lights OUGHT to be deceptive, and, by god, mine shall be.

Some things still seem important, and even more very funny, so I imagine with this equipment one can still hobble along. What do you think? So lets all laugh a great deal, (just short of being irritating) & drink, of course, and see a lot of our friends.

It was lovely to see Ernest in N.Y., we all wished you had come back again too. I suppose it was hardly worth it as he was working like fury on the film. I DO wish you could have heard the speaking, though, specially E's. If there was a fascist hair in the hall it must have not only have whitened, but singed as well. It was a terribly interesting meeting, & a most intelligent audience. The speaking, with just a tiny false note or 2 by Muriel Draper etc, was wonderful, we thought. So full of conviction, honesty, dignity, & overwhelming proof of what they were saying, that the papers hardly dared print a word about the meeting.

Where and how is Jinny?

And how are the children? And how are YOU, madam? We all three send you such a lot of love.

Did you finally get the records, and were they all right? DO&DO&DO send us a line as to yr plans (Guaranty Trust Co is always the address)

And how is BIMINI this year?

And if and when you do come over, remember that if Spain gets too hot, and Ernest wont let you stay there with him, (and it IS sort of getting hotter, isnt it?) that there is always Antibes. The villa after Oct. 1 (rented till then) and the Ferme always. And Joseph to look after you. So dont forget. Its a lovely place, but I somehow dont think there is a possibility of our going there this year.

Remember too that we love you both, and count on you, always. And a Paulinish sort of letter to make us all laugh would be sort of cheering.

Much, MUCH love again to you all
That old horror

SARA

cant even write straight
JFK

132. ROBERT BENCHLEY to GERALD and SARA MURPHY,
Los Angeles, 1 July 1937

Dear People:

I am writing for no other reason than that I wanted to establish contact. It also happens to be the day when all the original Benchley clan stay indoors and cower until sundown, for, as you may remember, July 1st. has already marked San Juan Hill (1898), my mother's encounter with a moving automobile (1927) and my own dear *coup de soleil* [sunstroke] at the Cap [d'Antibes] in 1929, making it a date evidently set aside for the Benchleys. Gertrude and the boys are on the high seas aboard the "Lafayette" and I received a radiogram just now reading: "*Prenez garde premier juillet*, [be careful July 1]" which will show you how little hold superstition has on us. Anyway, I am prenezing garde, and having a very pleasant time at it, too.

I still have one hazzard to face, however, as this evening is to mark what is supposed to be a reconciliation between the Campbell clan and Benchley, one of the minor feuds of the early summer season. I wasn't a party to it, so I don't suppose you could call it a feud. It seems that one night just before I left New York I assailed Dottie in "21" on some labor issue and, in the course of my tirade, told her not to make those ingenue eyes at me as she was no longer ingenue. (I am told that I said that) Dottie didn't mind my views on her labor activities, but the "ingenue" line (so I am told) cut her to the quick, and, during the month that they have been out here, they have refused to answer the telephone, although I have tried six or seven times. Finally, last Saturday, I paid a personal call at their hotel and left a note, saying that I had just dropped by for a swim. Mysterious underground forces have been at work since then, and tonight I am asked to dinner at the Wells Roots, and, I understand, am to be seated at the same table with the Campbells. It almost seems as if I were back at Rosemary Hall and I am sure that we will all end up making fudge up in Alan's room later in the evening.

Things out here are "unutterably un-gay", as the young lady says in Punch this week. I am going off on a yacht for over the Fourth with the [David] Selznicks and Joan Bennett, which will mark my first appearance in society during the "Little Season". I am doing all kinds of odd jobs, making shorts, acting in a full-length picture with Robert Montgomery and Rosalind Russell, taking a small part in "Tom Sawyer", making up funny jokes to go into other people's scripts, and staring at the swimming pool. I get up to Santa Barbara once in a while for a week-end, but without Louie or the Ludingtons it isn't much fun. The Ludingtons get out here in August and Louie not until September. She is working very hard, I understand, on her new job at Harper's Bazaar, and, I also understand, making a big hit at it.

There are ugly rumors out here about Don and Bea [Stewart] but, as they are at the Paysons for Joan's Fourth of July party, at least the old form seems to be being kept up. Liz Dupont just arrived here and had lunch with them in New York just before she left and said that they were in very good form. I certainly hope so. I was afraid, when Don decided on the farm last year, that some sort of show-down would result. I never hear from him, but then, we have never corresponded anyway. I had one letter from Bea a few months ago, asking for advice about going into radio-writing, which sounded a little grim at the time, but Phil Carr tells me that she didn't land the job, a fact which may have given her pause about striking out on her own. Liz has married an Englishman named Govett who knows Capt. ("Lunch is Impossible") Gullen, which endears him to me already.

It looks now as if I should be out here until Fall, although, if things should let up a little, I might sneak off early in September and pick the folks up in England. They have taken the car and eleven suitcases and don't know where they are going from Havre. The idea was for the boys to see some parts of Europe that they had never seen, but at last reports, they wanted first to go back to the Cap, "just to see what it looks like". They will probably end up at the Villa a Vendre for the summer and sail home from Villefranche without so much as peeking at new lands.

It is the strangest feeling—this writing a letter. I haven't written one for years, except the routine reports. I guess that I really wanted to write this one. And that is a nice feeling, too.

I do hope that you are well and enjoying the pent-house. (That's the way one ends a letter, isn't it? I see no other way to end this one, otherwise I might run on forever).

I love you all very much.

                                                        Bob

193

Miss Lewis is supposed to be tending to "L'Illustration." I subscribed through New York Brentano's, which means the greatest confusion at the greatest possible effort.

[written at the top of this letter, which is typed on both sides of thin paper]: Never get stationary that shows through.

HMD

133. PAULINE HEMINGWAY to SARA MURPHY, Cat Cay, Bahamas [8 July 1937]

My dearest Sara,

Imagine my surprise and delight at getting a letter from you from a big ocean liner—delight mixed with dismay for I shall be in New York Saturday, where where shall I go to help arrange flowers? I'll probably find myself dining with Ernestine, both crying into our soup. Ernest is dining with P. Roosevelt tonight and showing the film [*The Spanish Earth*] after—can't wait to hear what the president does to him. Do you think he will say "Not Hemingway the boxer!" Then Ernest and I are making quick trips to Hollywood and San Francisco. Then back here for a few weeks and THEN I don't know what. I'm thinking some of taking Bumbi and Patrick to a ranch. They are so crazy pour le ranch, and Ernest seems to feel he'd worry less about me in this country than in another, and maybe I'd be happier here, too. I don't know. Anyway, will keep you informed, and thank you for Antibes, and do please write me about Sweden. You wouldn't like to go to Russia with me, would you? Ernest has something like 100,000 dollars in royalties there, and we could come back in sables and cavier, and find out, incidently, what the Russians really are doing. I don't believe a word of it.

Jinny is here trying to make up her mind when to leave, and where to go when she decides. I think it will be Aquapulco, but in my absence all will doubtless be changed. She went to Nassau the other day and brought back three fighting cocks (one of them is a hen, I'm pretty sure) and the children are completely happy finding them lizards and bugs to eat and deciding to let them loose and letting them loose and then deciding to not let them loose and catching them. I don't know just how much longer we shall be able to stand it. We may have to eat them.

Will you thank Dowdow for the magnificent records? We play them every day while we are on the boat having really abismal fishing—days without a strike—and they keep up the optimism. Where the optimism would be now without those records I hesitate to say. I am taking Ada [the children's governess] and the children out today to see if Ada can get anything. It seems to catch a big fish is her dream. It is very nice here and comfortable. I think you might like it if you don't mind an island. It IS an island, with bicycles and wheelchairs and no sharecroppers. Swiming outside the door, sandflies, I'm afraid, inside. Although the management says they CAN'T be inside when there's oil on the screens, and maybe it's right, as most of the oil is now on my clothes. Dirty pauline.

And the war is always there like a dirty backdrop. Ernest is going sometime in August. Will you be in Paris then? He asked me especially to ask. His address is the same as yours there. The incognito luggage tag for Ernest arrived, tell Dowdow, and I am taking it up to him. He will love the air of mystery and royalty and will now probably travel the rest of his life. He bought me some beautiful airplane luggage at Mark Cross, so I shall probably travel with him the rest of *my* life. Unless we go to Africa if things get TOO thick, which they are always apt to do. Would you visit us there? And bring Honoria and she could have fauns to play with. Tell her that.

In my next letter I shall tell you all about Hollywood and how I found it, and how the stars are and if they have improved any, but I'm sure they are just the same only older. I do hope they are older. I'm sick of getting old by myself in the middle of the night with fools just being born every minute. Also, do not be discouraged for my NEXT letter will—shall—be a lot better, full of racy anecdote, written in a room by myself instead of with three children dashing in and out with roosters and fish and asking for apples. And Mother what is the difference between a clipper plane and a Douglas Amphibian and how do you feel about the Chick razer. Bumbi is going to have a red or blonde mustache and wear it with points on the end and practices quite a lot on the twirl.

Well, good*bye Mrs. Murphy and Mr. Murphy and Honoria and love to all of you from all of us. Don't forget about Sweden. How is the drinking water?

[no signature]

HMD

134. GERALD and SARA MURPHY to JOHN and KATY DOS PASSOS, Karlsbad, Czechoslovakia, 11 August 1937

Dear K. & D.:—

This card [with its floral bouquet against a mountain backdrop] seems to me to deny and include much. I'm grateful for the spirit of it,—and it's frankly lacking in Perth Amboy, N.J. Our minds turn constantly to the date next March with Vova and the Wbird at Genoa. It might make us believe in a lot of things to see antique Sicily. We've sold a bit of Antibes and bought *new* sails. Do start to-*morrow* planning for it. Things hurl about us here as Pershing in a series of one night stands has unveiled Five American War Monuments in a row within a week!

Aff'y. Gerald.

We get up at dawn, drink warmish ugh water—jiggle on machines— Perfect health or our money back—we say—Looking forward to Province-town in the autumn *Best* love

Sara

[on side of card] Sara in spite of certain amt. sales-resistance is benefitting by the cure! G.

UVA

Prior to Gerald Murphy's leaving for America on 3 September, the Murphys had spent time in Paris with Hemingway when he arrived in late August. Gerald sailed from Le Havre and kept an ongoing letter on board for Sara and Honoria. As Gerald began this letter, he was thinking about his brother Fred, who had died in May 1924 as a result of injuries received in World War I.

135. GERALD MURPHY to SARA and HONORIA MURPHY, Journal de bord S.S. *Ile de France*, 4–9 September 1937

(Fred's birthday)

Dearest Sal and Daughter:—

This is a pleasant ship: spacious, not too big. The cabins are compact but comfortable. All the grandes salles are light and airy and mercifully free of decoration. (This makes the people look quite dowdy. I wish people had gay plummage or a shiny red coat like the puppy or manes and tails. There is so little to look at tho' the boat is packed.) The food is excellent, varied and not overpowering.

Gertrude Benchley and the boys are on board. Bobbie is almost as large as Nat. They're nice boys tho' both their complexions are poor. G., I must say, was most solicitous about you and wished so that Honoria was on board. Nat is 21!

The Brittanic has no telephone so I'm wiring A. L. [Alice Lee Myers] (This is being written in a high wind on the rear deck where I intend bivouacing away from all those E. Arden faces and trick Park Avenue accents.)

Next to my table is that of the returning Harvard crew,—and for moronic, humorless conversations I've never heard the like! Daughter you may be right!

Sunday, Sept. 5th

The Benchleys had cocktails with me (I take a champagne one,—works very well) last night. She has got quite handsome. Nat is too,—tho' he has her humorless run of chatter. Bobbie is sweet—and much the most original,—tho' swamped by the other two. They all have the most inordinate curiosity about Honoria. Bob (the E. Rabbit) had a motor accident 3 weeks ago. His chauffeur was hurt but he got away with an "upholstery burn" on his forehead. He has apparently primed G. & the boys to find us and ask if there was anything that you wanted done at Antibes. They searched London and Paris for us. We were away. Each is head of the humorous paper at College & Exeter,—both sketch and write. Both "George & Margaret" and "French without Tears" are coming to America, they say. Bob would have come abroad but for the accident.

A strange passenger list: when Morris Gest travels incognito! I spoke to Carol (Mrs. H. Guggenheim) a pale replica of herself with eyes too wide apart and only empty chambers behind them. She says Pauline sits up in bed and paints all morning and is collecting (as we heard) for a Washington Modern Museum. I'm going to write her and see if she can stomach Léger. I doubt it. Mr. Lee A. Ault and Mrs. Lee A. Ault are on board. *Where,* I don't know. Mrs. C. D. Gibson too;—also Mrs. and Master D. F. Malone. How *dull* people are! There's a Mr. W. BLUH, also;—and a Mrs. H. BEVERIDGE, Prof. A. L. CRU, too. Mr. and Mrs. W. A. GLICK, Mrs. L. GREIF, Miss Y. GUEGO, Mrs. Z. M. ROUNSAVILLE, Dr. A. SELTZER, Mr. A. SOFAER, Mrs. M. SUGARMAN, and Mr. Sidney ZIPSER (whom Honoria *must* marry.)

11.30 a.m. I am wakened at 7, take my waters, breakfast at 8, work in the gym from 10 to 10:30, massage. So you see the cure goes on.

The weather is fair,—a wind yesterday but they expect a calm crossing,—some movement to-day,—but she seems steady. Madeleine Carrol and Clargable in "I'm Yours Truly" or some such was the attraction yesterday. I am not yet ready to stomach the American idiom so didn't go. (Excuse me Daughter!)

Alexander Korda cabled for Bob to come to London for an important part and Metro wouldn't release him.

2. p.m. Sal, your roses are blooming. I've cut the stems and changed the water daily and generally made a mess in the cabin the way you do,—and they thrive.

I've *started* "War and Peace" finally,—but find the inconsequential actions of the endless stream of characters (all of the most mysterious source and relationship) very misleading. It's like trying to divine Vova's motives and plans. The parts read at meals to the *unavoidable* accompaniment of the young collegians nearby talking about how much they drank and how little sleep they had—do not tend to advance my progress. . . .

My chair is on the upper deck. There's a high headwind to-day and no sun,—and a small dog who started a hysterical bursting bark at Le Havre—continues—in the kennels . . .

(What *does* the ocean mean? I peer at it and wonder. Possibly the Inventor's reminder of infinity,—made more obvious than the sky.) *Seven-eighths* of the globe is water!

6 p.m. I stopped and talked a while with Carol. Her Guggenheim daughter (Diane!) is 13 and being allowed to major in music at Brearley. They've both just been to Salzburg. The Potter daughters like to shoot! C. is very sweet. She has always, she says, cherished such a warm memory of you, and heard about Patrick in Salzburg from Sally Scaife. She also saw Hoytie there whom she failed to recognize on account of a spotted veil and new coiffure.

There's now a heavy fog and heavier siren. It seems like Autumn. I've made

good use of my Hermann Handweber Jacke und Biedermeyer $\left.\begin{array}{l} \text{eir} \\ \\ \text{ayer} \end{array}\right\}$ mantel,—

not without scandalizing the passengers somewhat, tho'.

I sent Dick's [Myers] friends the Russel Kelleys a note asking them for cocktails (as she suggested it to Dick) at 7 (as I dine on the gong at 7:45 getting up at 7 a.m.) they riposted with an invitation to join them and dinner guests for *8 o'clock* cocktails. I begged off pleading Karlsbad Nachkur and mysterious 8:30 electrical treatments, etc. (You'd *hate* such reasons).

Thursday
9:30 a.m. The high damp wind from the south with its fog kept up all thro' the day yesterday. This morning we have it following. We have had sun only the first day. I hope you have better luck. Even if not, you're faster and it's over sooner. The film yesterday was "Mlle. Ma Mere" with Danielle D[arrieux]. and Pierre Brasseur. I went hopefully and was obliged to leave. They have her in a broad comedy part, terrible white French slacks short tight checked jacket and yachting cap, screaming like a cockatoo all over the lovely peaceful port at Monte Carlo, asking men on different yachts to marry her, etc. in order to avoid an enforced marriage to her father's choice, etc. Awful!! She is *not* a comedienne. Sorry Daughter!

My pen has run dry. The Russel Kelley man called up last night and I'm having a drink with them before luncheon. They're confirmed diners-out (like Dick & A.L.) even on board. He sounds very nice.

Zaidee Bliss and her son are not on board, as far as I can see. There is something very false about this 600 strange people in confined quarters for 6 days. I don't know what it's like except the attitude of people toward each other as they sit waiting in a doctor's waiting-room. Possibly it's more unreal if you're alone.

The Ringleader of the Collegians said last night, "I liked England, but couldn't stand London. Never been so bored. We saw 3 movies in the two days we were there. That was our sight-seeing." (Poor Daughter!)

Went down and filled my pen. . . . Your roses are *still* booming. Did flowers keep more *or* less in the Deckhouse on the Weatherbird? I can't remember. More at Montana [-Vermala], I know. Less at sea, I think.

For the first time I feel that I do not know what is ahead of me in America. There's a strange impermanence about it . . . and all thro' the world if one reads the papers. I'd like once to be long enough in a place to see hay around the house taken in, fruit and vegetables grow and pumpkins and apples ripen. Not to speak of flowers. The Légers enjoy the Ferme so, he originates all his pictures there now as he told us.

I've been thinking a lot about Ernest. He dreads life becoming soft for him (or anyone he likes),—and if it threatens to he takes it in hand. The Crusades would have given him his chance. To-day he must make his own. Never being in his field (as Archie and Dos have been—are . . .) he has never done anything violent to me (and tho' I've been terribly critical and think that at times he's been pretty nearly a cheap sport) I find it easy to revive my affection for him. Don't worry about what I'll say about him to Dos and Archie. I'd like to try (as I did with E.) to fan the embers of an old affection even if it comes to nothing. It seems to me an impertinence to try to negotiate an understanding. It's all gone on *between them*. I only hope they haven't destroyed everything for each other the way Cole [Porter] did for me, (—tho' he did nothing to me directly.) Possibly it will be all right itself,—with Dos, anyway. But Ernest's altered feelings about Jinny are not encouraging. He may be unreasonable in his own right,—and critical and unforgiving. For me he has the violence and excess of genius. . . . (He may be wrong, but what he represents is doubtless life all right)

We are due in to-morrow (Thursday) at 4 or 6 p.m. possibly sooner. I'll be in the office all Friday and go down to E. H. [East Hampton] for the wedding, Saturday, at 4 p.m. If H. & H. [Hale Walker and Harold Heller] are there I'll stay overnight at the Hodges or somewhere near (Montauk, I think) and report to you.

I've been thinking I'd order from some Iron Works two not too large iron urns and have them carefully red-leaded and *painted a thick white* for the Cemetery at E. H. (with zinc linings.) That way there'll *always* be something to put flowers or branches in. Randolph can keep repainting them from time to time.

199

(Gaytrüd just passed and said she almost called me as I passed their table in the baahr yestudday and had I noticed that Nayutt was pale, because he keeps breaking out in a culd sweyutt and refusing his fur . . . She got him to go to bed,— and thinks he ate something or maybe it's his cabin, etc. etc. . . . So you see the Mother Hen and Chicks principle does not defeat itself! I must say they're very sweet with her. They all talk constantly of Bob, the Absent,—and she sends skittish cables reading: "How's tricks?" and he replies: "Peachy Thank you." I guess he's the lonelier of the two. No date of return to New York. Apparent he has to make his money *there*.

A girl on board they know tells me that the Sarah Lawrence College is very difficult to get into. Apparently you have to have some professional intent, and apply long in advance, as it's become very popular. It's at Bronxville and one can go as a day scholar. I feel that Honoria is not yet ready to attack any special interest as hard as that. It might just serve to put her off it. She has loads of time for her *ultimate* studies. This girl has been majoring in music. Apparently the girls there have all that the New York Stage and Concert Hall has to offer put at their disposal.

I hope you've been able to adjust the hotel rooms comfortably. Do go to see Bombois with Léger.

Daughter do find me a black collar with big imitation turquoises or something for the "Duchess", Alec's [Woollcott's] black police dog.

In 2 wks. from to-day you sail! Love to you both. Take care of yourselves is the wish of

Yr. loving

daou.

Never said good-bye to the "Puppy." Sorry! Hope's he's fine.

p.s. Ernest will have given his life *one* thing and *that is—scale*. The lives of some of us will seem, I suppose, by comparison, piddling.

p.p.s. Daughter: possibly it would be best to leave the popular records we held out for Romey Hill. Write him a note (since he entertained you at Salzburg) and give them with it to Dick to leave in his apartment.

d.

Tues. not Wed.

Dear Sal & Daughter:—

Certainly that mammoth contraption the Daou-Daou Mind went thoroughly askew to-day. In spite of my Journal de Bord, the daily paper, dates on letters, etc. calendars, I went briskly to my cabin opened all packages, repacked them, packed everything carefully, tagged trunks, had a surprised but pleased steward remove my luggage, eschewed even my "smokeen", changed

200

money, arranged tips, generally bustled about and taking on a virtuous air of finality went down to clever, early dinner in mufti (to be rested for the big morrow's arrival—and found the dining saloon filled with screaming passengers in paper caps at the gala dinner. We don't land for two days,—and everyone on board knew it except me!

What an interminable trip with its featureless ocean screened in fog! Six days is too long!

Wed. *surely*

Tolstoi has hurled me into the midst of War and Peace and I find myself carried along by this violent disorderly book. "Quelle Toile" [what a painting] as Fernand [Léger] would say. And so *various*.

2:30 p.m.

This noon the sun returned and there is ideal Weatherbird weather with a burnished blue steel ocean and squadrons of clouds all shaped like sleeping camels lying on some invisible flat floor above. The mood of the ship has changed after 3 days imprisonment in fog.

Sal: I've written Dick about the people whom we listed in the Arts Decoratifs catalogue. You may not find it worth while to track them down. Possibly the Chez Pavilion will offer more.

Daughter: be sure to go to O'Rossen and get a perfect fit!

Daughter: Dick might try Primavera for the "pestle-and-mortar" cendriers, white lined with gold, not as small as the Trois Quartiers ones we saw. Make Mother rest *sometime* during the day. Love to you both. I land to-day— and hate facing it without you two

daou.

HMD

136. SARA MURPHY to ERNEST HEMINGWAY, Paris, 20 September [1937]

Dear Ernest,

Here is a receipt from this hotel [Elysée Park] for your 3 pieces of luggage. Honoria and I are sailing Wednesday [22 September]. I cant tell you how glad I was to get your wire this A.M. & know everything is all right. Thank you, and see you soon. Dotty and Alan Campbell are leaving tomorrow, Tues. night for Valencia, and will surely see you. I'm sending a FEW more foodstuffs, as you will find someone who needs them if you & yr friends dont quite yet. I *wish* I knew what you needed most. This is just a guess. I hope you have plenty of warm clothes, if your weather is anything like ours here.

We had a letter from Jinny a couple of days ago. Everything fine. She was at Piggott, and expected Pauline & the boys there when they left Sidney's ranch 15th. Jinny is coming back to her apartment, so will be near us at the NEW Weston again, which is so nice. But you are of course au courant of all this. I do hope Pauline will come on to N.Y. for a visit, when everything is settled, & the boys at school. Baoth would have gone to college this autumn.

Honoria looks ravishing in her new clothes. She sends much love.

Come back soon, and in the meantime take care of yourself.

Bless you. with love

Sara

Please get the war over soon.

This address [c/o Rubio Hidalog, Prensa y Censura Extranjera, Valencia] looks *very* strange to me. Hope it's all right!

Sent by Dorothy Campbell   Sept 20
3 poulet roti, a la gelee
1 confit d' oie
2 jambonneau
1 jambon, a la gelee
2 saumon
1 truite saumonee
2 boeuf aux haricots
1 tripe a la mode de Caen
1 viandox (40)   ⎫
1 bouillon Kub (20)   ⎬   for bouillon
1 poule au pot (50)   ⎭
3 Kraft welsh rabbit
2 mixed antipasto
2 Washington coffee
2 pkges cut sugar
1 Horlicks malted milk (good mixed with cocoa)

JFK

137. Katy Dos Passos to Sara Murphy, Provincetown, 12 November 1937

Dearest Mrs. Puss,

There's a fierce gale blowing and a terrific sea smashing against the bulkhead—and rain pouring down, and the whole house shakes with the waves—I hope the seawall holds up because otherwise we will be pushed back onto Commercial Street, where we will certainly be run over. Oh Mrs Puss we did so enjoy seeing you—I wish we were all having a drink together here or there this afternoon. Dos is getting a little metropolitan itch, I think, but the weather has been so fine we couldn't bear to leave it and haven't even gone to Boston. I wonder what Miss Puss is doing and if she likes her job and think she's a smart puss to walk right on the boards like that.[1] Please give her my love—Do you suppose Hoity is having those little family suppers right along now with [Ambassador William] Bullit and the Windsors?

We are very quiet here—tranquil would be the literary word—A neighbor was robbed of $400 yesterday, but the criminal just took the money and walked up and down the back shore where he was instantly apprehended— He apologized and said he just wanted to see how it felt to have $400 on him—cash. So nothing was done—

Have you heard anything of the Monster of Mt. Kisco [Hemingway]? Pauline's visit was a great pleasure to us, but she seemed worried about Ernest, and no wonder—she was very cute and nervy, I thought—but could'nt sleep, and said she found it a little dull in Key West, though she has her great swimming pool project on hand—There's something consoling about carpenters, I have always found—I've practically given up reading the newspapers, as can't do anything about the Japanese or Mussolini or Hitler and realized that I was thinking a lot more about them than they are about me—so I won't give them the satisfaction—

Oh Mrs. Puss—lookit—this is now Nov 17—and I never got this finished—events closed in on me so—And now we're coming to New York tomorrow, arriving Friday morning, so I may as well bring this letter in my hand. But I won't—will mail it anyway to show intention—My very best love to you all—with extras—

Devotedly

Katy

Hello Sara

Isn't Katy awful about her letters? Wish you'd been here to superintend dragging privet into our yard. We continue to plant in spite of the fact that the codfish swim around the roots of the bushes during high tide

Love to Gerald & Honoria

Dos

UVA

---

1. Honoria had begun to work for the French Theatre of New York and had landed some small Broadway parts.

138. PAULINE HEMINGWAY to GERALD and SARA MURPHY,
on board *Europa*, 18 December [1937]

My dears—

This is just a little note written on very large stationary to tell you (at the risk of personal popularity, I'm sure) how wonderful you are—You are my ideals—What are your ideals? But really, Sara and Dowdow, I know now what suffering and tribulation are for—to make such people as you to make other people try not to be such sons of bitches

Sorry if I offend—Seems like I had to say it—

The boat is very nice, no vibration, and my cabin, except for some little birds in the plumbing, is quiet and full of repose—I have read all but one of the magazines Honoria and you, Sara, brought me—Ernest will *love* the picture of an actress that Honoria sent him—the last one I am saving to read tomorrow—The records I have not even unwrapped and shall play them with Ernest in Paris—I am doing just what Dowdow said to do, not stuffing my face, and seeing *nobody* but my masseuse, Mrs. Tiffany and the Duchess of Westminister—They are all wonderful—perhaps the first is just a shade the most stimulating—

Two cables from Ernest, both from Barcelona, saying he is at the front working hard and that he hopes to get to Paris Wednesday—I shall write you from Paris after he arrives—Thank you for being so lovely in New York and love to all of you

Your devoted friend

Pauline

HMD

139. JOHN DOS PASSOS to SARA MURPHY,
Provincetown [14 January 1938]

Dear Sara—

We'd have been down in the big city before this except that we've been having trouble with the weather, which has been much too fine for January, and I've been having trouble with my work of a literary nature, alas—trying to get some stuff finished that doesn't even seem to want to get begun. So we just might not get down till next week—we have to take a couple of hurdles round Boston first. I'm afraid we'll have to hunch up in the Lafayette because I'll be working and not fit to be seen by daylight. Towards evening, however, you'll continually be having to sweep us out of the penthouse; in fact I'm afraid we'll be underfoot a good deal—Speaking of underfoot, your rugs are remarkably cosy in our living room, and did I ever thank Gerald for his neckties that are remarkably easy to wear? Just as you threatened it's snowing over the sea—so maybe we wont have any more trouble with the weather.

I wish we were all in Jamaica right now—

Much love

Dos

HMD

140. KATY DOS PASSOS to SARA MURPHY,
Provincetown, 15 January 1938

Dearest Mrs. Puss,

Oh Mrs. Puss your hooked rugs are down on our floor and we are walking on them proud as princes on plush. They look wonderful and feel as fine underfoot—have a cosey warm look too, very grateful in this weather. There's a deep snow and the sea is a clear black with little crisps of ice at the edges. Lots of ducks and gulls, and a three-masted schooner in the harbor—Oh I wish you were here. We are crazy to know how you liked the tropical isle [Jamaica?]. Your cards sounded as if you did like it. Did you notice the Indian cattle—of course you did, and I'm sure that Mr. Puss saw more than anyone ever did—he always does. I often wish Mr. Puss were President. "Mr. Puss for President!" Make a fine election slogan, would'nt it? He could go right in and straighten out the State Department. I am sure they are in a terrible way with their files. Darling we miss you both, and Miss Puss too—hope to see you about the middle of next week—We're coming down for a protracted stay of two or three weeks—Have to hole up at the Lafayette, as Dos is working like a mule train—But we can come in every day and nag you.

I hate to leave—it's been so lovely here—we take great walks on the sunny hills every day—it's been like Spring till this snow—Then we come in for a drink at five oclock—and there are the hooked rugs, simply glowing on the floor—Mrs. Puss-cat dear, thank you so much. I don't think I managed to tell you how we enjoyed the little Arabian nights house in East Hampton—My, that's a lovely house—Gee we had a lovely time. Gosh we certainly do love you—

We have Charley Kaeselau's little boy staying here. He's just out of the hospital—an operation on his leg, and is still in a plaster cast. An attractive clever child, but very spoiled and bad—He has two favorite replies—One is No. The other is I hope you choke. I have broken him of the last retort which was really rather trying. But what do you do when you tell a child to do something and he looks at you darkly and says No. He kicks when he's put to bed. What do you do then?

Have you heard from Pauline? I suppose Ernest is in Spain now, with the big Teruel fight going on.[1] It's a sensational victory—the greatest of the whole war, and must mean that Franco is badly crippled, as now he can't push his offensive except under terrific difficulties.

We laffed at your wire—and now the snow *is* on the sea. But melting. We had two great Xmas parties, much larger than we intended. We gave two, so we would not have too many people at a time, but all the people we didn't invite came anyway, both times, so nothing was gained by it. Dos made his old father's rum punch the first time but that turned out to be a mistake, as it went to people's heads, so we made egg-nog the second time, but that was a mistake too as they just got into the cellar and drank straight whiskey. They had the oddest reasons for asking for the whiskey. One boy said he had appendicitis—Another said he could'nt touch egg-nog because of his diabetes, another claimed he was allergic to cream and eggs—

We are blue at missing Archie and Ada. I hope they get a good bite of South America. Dos and I don't know where we are going. Maybe to Texas. But first to New York where we'll see you and that's the best of the New Year to date.

1938 Love

Katy

UVA

---

1. The Hemingways were at sea en route home.

Although Fitzgerald lived in California during the last years of his life, he occasionally traveled East to see Scottie, who attended the Ethel Walker School and then Vassar College, and to visit Zelda, still hospitalized in Asheville. During the Christmas of 1937, Scott took Zelda on a trip to Miami, and he had asked the Murphys to meet Sheilah Graham in New York City during her own visit to the East Coast.

141. GERALD MURPHY to F. SCOTT FITZGERALD,
New York, 29 January 1937 [1938]

Dear Scott:—

Since we are being so scrupulous about such matters, I insist upon repaying you for the 2 tickets I bought for Ginnie and Honoria,—who were our guests! This is authentic. I have the bill.

Sara was sorry not to be up to calling Miss Graham. She's felt this week sadly, I notice. Tomorrow a year ago Patrick died. We go to Easthampton this afternoon, as Sara wants to go to the cemetery. . . .

I shall call you next [illegible word] Dos and Katy are at the Hotel Lafayette,

Aff'y.

Gerald.

PUL

142. GERALD MURPHY to F. SCOTT FITZGERALD, New York, 1 March [1938]

Dear Scott:—

For some time I've felt constrained to write you. Not for any special reason . . . It is too bad we didn't see you again. I'm sorry that Sara was not up to calling Miss Graham just for a talk. Of course she's inarticulate anyway,— and actually *dislikes* the effort to communicate by voice. Moreover, her mind was far afield, all those days after you left. I doubt if she'd have attempted anything. All this I say (quite unnecessarily, no doubt),—in order to dispel any strange reasons which you might have given yourself for her silence. You know you have been inventive at times in imputing motives! I naturally hesitated to call Miss Graham myself. I enjoyed so seeing her and she left me such a souvenir of a delicately porcelainlike transparency of nature. . . . restful, I find . . .

We hope you're well. Sara goes with Honoria and a girl friend to Europe in May. I shall remain here. There's a longing to go somewhere remote and to read and read. I feel the need of nourishment and solitude. Rare, the latter. Rarer to want it I suppose. Dos and Katy were with us for two wks.—on to Biloxi, Miss. and Texas. Ernest and Pauline are not coming North. Jed Harris flew down for conference re the play. Difficult to cast,—and not yet revised.[1] Archie and Ada and Peter are in Chile.

I had thought you like Pushkin but I suppose only the Russians are like Russians. You are possibly Celtic by nature. I wonder? Or is it American?

We went to Boston lately. Teddy Chandler was there. His music is being

---

1. The adaptation of Hemingway's Spanish Civil War play, *The Fifth Column*, was never enacted to his satisfaction.

very seriously considered these days. It's excellent tho'—I feel—extremely intellectual. A comfortable distraction has descended upon him—enriching in effect—and he stands cloudcapt in whatever commotion surrounds him. We spoke long of you. He has great affection for you. So have we all,—and I beg you not to forget it.

Gerald.

p.s. If the "Weatherbird" is not rented (it rarely is *now*) Sara, Dos & Katy will meet it near Sicily and look upon the antique world a while. She cannot return, she says, to Antibes. In the meantime, houses and gardens there and here, devised for a life that's been telescoped, stand breathing.

G.

PUL

143. F. Scott Fitzgerald to Gerald Murphy, [Culver City, California] 11 March 1938

Dear Gerald:

Your letter was a most pleasant surprise. The telegram I sent you was prompted by one of those moments when you see people as terribly alone—a moment in the Newark airport. It was entirely a piece of sentimentality because, of course, Sheila has lots of friends in New York; and I realize now that it was a bad time to ask anything. You were awfully damn kind, in any case, and as a friend, you have never failed me.

Alas, I wish I could say the same for myself. I don't gather from your letter whether you were going to look upon the antique world with Sarah, Doss and Katy. I wish I was, but with the sort of wishing that is remote and academic. I don't care much where I am any more, nor expect very much from places. You will understand this. To me, it is a new phase, or rather, a development of something that began long ago in my writing—to try to dig up the relevant, the essential, and especially the dramatic and glamorous from whatever life is around. I used to think that my sensory impression of the world came from outside. I used to actually believe that it was as objective as blue skies or a piece of music. Now I know it was within, and emphatically cherish what little is left.

I am writing a picture called "Infidelity" for Joan Crawford. Writing for her is difficult. She can't change her motions in the middle of a scene without going through a sort of Jekyll and Hyde contortion of the face, so that when one wants to indicate that she is going from joy to sorrow, one must cut away and then cut back. Also, you can never give her such a stage direction as "telling a lie," because if you did, she would practically give a representation of Benedict Arnold selling West Point to the British. I live a quiet life here, keeping regular hours, trying to get away every couple of weeks for days in the sun at La Jolla, Santa Barbara. King Vidor appeared for a day or so, asked about you and is off for England. Eddie [Edwin Knopf] and I talk of you. Sheila, of course, was fascinated by you both, and I looked up old pictures in old scrapbooks for her. "Tender Is the Night" has been dramatized and may go on the stage next fall.[1] I shall obtain you gallery seats for the first night where you can blush unseen.

[Scott]

PUL

---

1. The play never made it to Broadway, although the novel did become a movie in 1962.

144. KATY DOS PASSOS to SARA MURPHY,
Warm Springs, Virginia, 20 March 1938

Dearest Mrs. Puss,

Here we are in a very early chilly Virginia Spring with daffodils, blue birds, pussy willows and smoky black mountains. The famous Warm Springs Pools are just a step down the hill—and Dos and I swim for hours in the clear pale green water, which is like dipping in gallons of Warm White Rock—It makes me twitter as I go round the pool and Dos gay like a bull—If we only had you and Gerald paddling around in the magic spring with us we would be as early gods, but it's rather solitary, as there is no one in this Inn but the Innkeeper and his wife. She is a dour, incompetent woman from New England who belongs to the school that thinks housekeeping is Pie. Two kinds of heavy pale pie. Everything else like salads or dusting is Frills. But we take our lunch out by a brook or river, and have broiled steak and wine, and watch the lambs frisking, and it's lovely—

We had a fine high-speed trip through Alabama, down to New Orleans, slogging up the Mississippi delta through seas of mud—visited all the old River Towns, Natchez, Vicksburg, Memphis, Cairo, saw the Noriss Dam and T.V.A—towns—Cumberland Resettlement and had a funny good time in New Orleans—Mrs. Puss, you would love New Orleans—it's such an easy, cheerful comical city—with more internationally known celebrities known locally there then anywhere else in the world. I sent you a few local items from there which I hope arrived safely—Couldn't send the best things, like crawfish fresh boiled and a wonderful thing called a "poor boy," which is a hot loaf of French bread filled with some sort of Creole mixture.

Well—I see your poor Austrians are Nazified now—and the Versailles Treaty, says Dos, has got for Germany what the Kaiser tried to get in the last war—We get the papers a day late, but at that everything goes too fast. Saw in the paper that Ernest had left for Spain without hat or overcoat—Did you see him in New York? How is he? And Pauline? We've had no mail for weeks—Just arrived here, very tired, and expect to stay about a week or ten days—Then back to New York and so home—Mrs. Puss dear, I can't thank you for your delicious kindness to a couple of pretty spidery incumbents. I did so enjoy being with you—it was on the Heavenly Side, and so are you—And how are you and Mr. and Miss Puss, and are you going to Paris as planned? Pears like nobody gits to carry out his plans but that ole Hitler.

Dos sends his love, and double, and I send mine (multiply by five, add kisses) How is my Favorite Dog? There is a very nice dog here that smiles, like Judy. Also a lot of guinea hens and plenty of horses to ride, and watercress grows thick in all the brooks—We are always mushing it like cows—Saw an old man in the mountains yesterday with snow-white whiskers like Emperor Josef, chewing snuff. All the women wear pink calico and everybody has the same hound dog—

Oh my goodness Mrs. Puss we certainly think a heap of you all. Never will forget that delightful stay at the Murphy Arms—Hope now to see you soon—and maybe you'll come down the Cape and help us get the crops in—

Yours Ever so much,
Your loving

Katy

UVA

145. KATY DOS PASSOS to SARA MURPHY, Warm Springs, Virginia, 25 March 1938

Oh Mrs. Catkin,

I hope you don't mind being written to all over again but we miss you down here, and Dos and I never go in the carbonated sparkling pool without wishing you were in it too. Spring in these mountains is so sharp and fresh, and the whole country is humming and rustling with brooks, and everywhere in the pale green fields the black and white lambs "is hoppin—" We were so pleased to get your telegram—I wonder if you and Miss Puss are already in a packing fit, getting ready for Paris Paris—I have a sneaking wish to be there myself—but want to be in so many places at once that it's confusing. I wonder if Archie and Ada are back yet from their South American invasion. We are going to leave here Wednesday and set off to New York by degrees—Our travels are so mild that they make me think of what the Reverend Sydney Smith wrote to a friend about a journey he took in England—"Few are the adventures of a curate traveling gently over good roads to his benefice—"

Did I tell you that in Illinois we had wonderful food? Great thick beefsteaks and hog jowl and turnip-greens and cornbread. We've been traveling on our stomachs, like Napoleon's army, all the way. Almost entirely without alcoholic stimulants except beer. In Virginia you can't advertize beer openly—you call it A.B.C. I don't know why. If you take a glass of whiskey in a public restaurant it's fifty dollars fine and disgrace, but you can sit in your car drunk as an owl and pour it down—which people do a good deal—They then throw the bottle revengfully on the road which gives a strangely dissolate air to the highway.

I am quite heart-broken over the pitiful list of Mr. Whitney's assets and investments. Florida mud to cure sores, and applejack. There's something very touching about the whole collection. He was really just an old-fashioned sucker. Oh dear.

Dos sends his love. Love to Mr. Puss and Honoria. We'll see you soon—I hope you're all well and rosy—Easthampton and Swan House must be lovely now. Compliments of the season and year-around love

from

Katy

UVA

146. GERALD MURPHY to HALE WALKER AND HAROLD HELLER, East Hampton, 16 May 1938

Dear Hale and Harold:—

When we left the house this morning Sara and I went to the cemetery and visited the graves of Baoth and Patrick for the last time before she goes abroad.

As you two know better than almost any of her friends she is—and will always be—hopelessly inconsolable. As time goes on she feels her bereavement more and understands less why the two boys were taken away,—both of them.

We have both felt that our life was definitely stopped before it was finished and that nothing that we do further has much meaning except as it can possibly be of service to Honoria and our friends.

For some time I have wanted you two to know what an oasis of comfort all that you have done at Easthampton means to Sara. She has made you feel it I know,—but I do want to tell you so. She speaks to me often of your solicitude and thoughtfulness and of the many things you devise to amuse and please her. God knows she deserves it, poor dear! Life will never be able to make up to her what she has been deprived of: her two boys. She who lives and *has* lived for her children. It is incomprehensible that it should have happened.

She is so deeply fond of you both and so grateful for all you have done. I do not mean the house *only*,—but the so much which you have brought her *with* it.

I'm afraid in my zeal and anxiety for Swan Cove that I have been unpleasant at times. I'm sorry. The spectacle of her enjoyment *for the first time* has been somewhat emotional to me. I had not thought she could forget for a moment what haunts her continually. There is nothing that I can do for her. I serve rather to remind her of what has passed. Moreover one cannot share one's grief,—only one's pleasure—with another. I never knew this until three years ago. It becomes more true all the time,

Affectionately,

Gerald.

HMD

---

147. Alexander Woollcott to Sara Murphy, Bomoseen, Vermont, 17 May 1938

Dear Sara,

In December there was a faint sprinkle of snow like powdered sugar on apple pie and this was enough to discourage two such campfire girls as you and Ada. I am still a little bitter about this, but I want you to know that I expect you both here for a penitential week between now and the end of the year.

I hope everyone who goes abroad this year has a terrible time and wishes he (or she) were on the island with kind old

Mr. W.

HMD

Sara and Honoria sailed on 22 May and Gerald met them in Paris on 6 June. The Murphys stayed in Paris until they met up with John and Katy Dos Passos for a cruise down the Italian coast on the Weatherbird *in July. The Murphys returned to Paris in late August and sailed for America on 3 September, Honoria remaining in Paris throughout the fall with her good friend Fanny Myers, daughter of Richard and Alice Lee Myers. Back in the States, MacLeish had accepted a post at Harvard University as curator of the Nieman Foundation, and Pauline had seen Ernest off for Europe once again in early September. Stella Campbell had left California and was living in New York at the Hotel Sevillia. She had recently traveled to Italy. On 21 September, a storm struck the Long Island coast, seriously damaging the Murphys' East Hampton property.*

148. GERALD MURPHY to ALEXANDER WOOLLCOTT, New York, 28 September 1938

Dear Alec:

The fifth to seventh I am due to be out of town, but I shall call to see if you are still here upon re-entry. . . . As for enstrangement: what does one wear? I feel very *strange*, though.

Archie begins at Cambridge this week on his chair of Journalism: Ernest went to the wars in advance: Pauline is here: Stella I finally extricated from West 58th Street and got to the Lago di Garda, whence she writes: "I can breathe here, the air has oil in it . . ." Her mother was born in Brescia nearby. [John] Gielgud wanted her to play with him in London,—but Moonbeam [Stella's dog] objected.

As for Fall visits: I'm afraid they're out: we shall be picking among the ruins of our house and garden at Easthampton these coming weekends. We had returned to find it glowing with tuberoses, bamboo, elephant ear, white heliotrope, nicotiana,—and Sara's brocades inside the house. She left it that Wednesday having arranged her linen and lace closet and placed what we had dragged from abroad to perfect it: when the elements annihilated it . . . water two to five feet in the house . . . no trace of garden . . . 5 inch bass in the orchard. But in the Village only 12 of the 72 elms are standing. Some were 200 years old.

Did your island drag anchor? I hope not. Your letter never spoke of wind or water.

Love from 2 dispossessed,

HL

Gerald.

149. Katy Dos Passos to Sara Murphy, Provincetown, 8 October 1938

Dearest Mrs. Puss,

Ach! we were so aghast about your garden—Gerald gave such a visible description of before and after. We're sorry all over—Our garden was simply razed, but everything else was all right, and the planting was pretty sketchy anyway. But yours *was* a garden—I'm distressed specially about the pear tree? Was it lost too? And I have house worry too—did it damage floors and walls? Oh dear. Mrs Puss, do you think these convulsions of nature are accompanying political disturbances like they used to in Sartonius—Remember all the phenomena that surrounded Caesar and Augustus? Lightenings and statues hurled down and all those augurs? Well, I don't know—but it's funny we have a hurricane just while Hitler is starting to march—

Not a word from Mister Puss about where is Miss Puss and how—Please reply. We're getting anxious to see you. When we do see you watch out—as you will be violently hugged. Sara dear, I can't possibly thank you for that wonderful squeeze of orange juice—we were absolutely out of vitamins and it was like an angelic intervention—which it was. Tell Mr. Puss he found us brick and left us marble like Augustus.

We have a Prowler in Provincetown. A mysterious face appears at windows after midnight—the Prowler is known locally as The Black Flash, because he is said to wear a black cape and jumps over hedges—My maid said "Oh Mrs. Dos Passos, he's a great Leaper!"

Dos is working hard, and the weather is beautiful and so are you—We'll be coming to New York in a couple of weeks I think—We're still swimming in the Bay. Saw a tobacco dove yesterday in the woods—a rarity here. Looked a little like Honoria, I thought.

Well darling—wasn't that sailing-trip [the July Italian cruise] a fairy-story? I want to talk about it with you and Gerald all over again—We're the only ones that know about it—like people who've been Back of the Moon—

True love from Katy

UVA

150. Katy Dos Passos to Sara Murphy, Provincetown, 15 December 1938

Dearest Mrs. Puss,

I've had it in my mind to write you daily, but nothing in my mind to write. We sit here modestly on the harbor like wooden ducks in a pond and not even

214

a quack to distinguish us from the scenery. Dos and I have given up conversation and communicate by signs—shivering when the furnace is low, pointing at the door to go walking. Dos rubs his stomach to show he's hungry, and raises an imaginary bottle at five oclock—I occasionally pretend to be a train to indicate that I want to go to New York and Dos then passes the hat in dumb show—We were momentarily enlivened last week by a visit from Léger and Simone and the Lowndes[1]—it was fun; and Léger very comical—but now we've gone back into torpor again—We have one friend whom we go to see in the afternoons but he is always busy with his stamp-collection and cutting out paper-dolls—

Isn't this the day Honoria arrives. If she does, she's home—Give her a fur-trimmed welcome from us—Wish we had been there at the dock to wave flags and holler—How is she? If she looked terribly pretty I wouldn't be surprized. How are you, my dearest Sara? Oh I hope you're feeling improved—Can't bear for you to have the smallest little sick. We miss you mighty bad, and hardly got a look at you last time—Maybe we'll get to New York before Christmas—if Christmas doesn't come too quick. I think they're running it off faster this year than last and we're even worse prepared for it—

Mrs. Puss, the rugs you gave us are such a pleasure—greatly admired by all, and so warm and luscious on the floor. You'd admire to see them—I'm putting up new curtains of that flowered stuff we got so long ago in [illegible]—they look fine—We've planted ten little cedar trees in the back yard, and lots of tulips—all at the mercy of a South-east gale of course—Dos is working like mad but claims to tear up most of the web he spins, like Penelope—I wish I could see Mark Cross' Christmas windows—Wish we were seeing you all—Dos wants to know if you know the address of that old wag and social-revolutionary Don Stewart—

Did I tell you that we had no cold turkey for Thanksgiving because Eliza Poodle ate it? It was an act of sheer hooliganism, as she got it down from a high shelf and had obviously been planning the whole thing while under the table at dinner—She must have been reading the papers about the Munich pact—as she never did such a thing before—Dos went simply wild and shrieked out "That dog's for sale!" He says men feel more intensely about food than women because women have a layer of subcutaneous fat and never get really hungry, while men have only a little skin and bone and are hungry practically all the time in a way no woman can ever understand—

Aren't the papers awful? They simply blow up in your hands—People with

---

1. Fernand Léger was in America from September 1938 to March 1939. He traveled throughout the United States, spending some time with the Dos Passoses in Provincetown, and also with the Murphys. Lloyd and Marion Lowndes were good friends of both the Dos Passoses and the Murphys.

social consciousness keep sending us the most frightful Christmas cards—of bombings and barbed-wire and trains de-railed and sinking vessels. I'm getting quite cross about it as none of it is our fault but they make you feel you're responsible—Jay Allen [*Chicago Tribune* reporter covering the Spanish Civil War] writes that there's a chance for the Loyalists now and we're working to get the embargo lifted with better hope of success—What did Franklin D. [Roosevelt] say to Archie?

Well dearest Mrs. Puss dear, I will now go down town for a fresh flounder and wish you were coming for lunch—Dos sends his love—very special from us both to Honoria, and you and Gerald mit keeses

Katy

UVA

151. SARA MURPHY to KATY and JOHN DOS PASSOS, New York, 17 December [1938]

Dearest Dos & Katy

Honoria is home, and I feel much better, so I think I shall write youall on my teetering typewriter (unusually so today, what DO I do?) H. is looking ravishing (we think) and so do other intelligent people. She is keeping one of her new Photographs for you. She is fine, had a marvellous time in Paris, & has gone instantly to rehearse with the French Theatre, who have been clamoring over the telephone to me for her. She seems to have a large speaking part this time, and reports herself terrified, which I doubt. The play is something by Merimée. Also a gentleman on the boat, the French playwright who wrote "A Tovarích" (than which there was never anything worse in my opinion, but that not shared by Hollywood apparently,) nagged her incessantly across a very rough ocean to be the lead in his new play, in French. So you see she is not boring herself.

Dowdow and I are the same.

And how are YOU both?? Mrs Lowndes said you were coming right back but you haven't. We are counting on that "day or two before Xmas," that Dos speaks of in yesterday's postcard. We shall be right here it seems, in spite of many half made plans. Could you go to Easth. with us for New Year? We are planning to go, & if fine weather it might be nice, will you? All picked up there—

A sort of a thunderbolt has struck. Well its a strange world, as you may have noticed. A letter comes from Vladimir saying he is awfully sorry, but can't help it, that he is in love with Louise Dowdney, & stranger still that she is too. Well what do you know! We DID notice SOMETHING, do you remember, it

216

crossed my mind several times that V. might be amouraching himself of L., (a born gentleman-killer) who always turns on the Charm, in the presence of the least of the male sex, but it didn't occur to *any* of us that she is bowled over, and will wait indefinitely until the divorce goes through. Of course G. & I aren't any too delighted about it, as V., nice as he is, is not awfully healthy, is 18 or 19 yrs older than L. besides being married to his mistress, so we can't help thinking he would get more out of it than a very young girl, used to quite other ways of living. We are frankly baffled, and would like your advice, I wouldn't blame her parents if they considered us responsible, although I don't see really what we could have done, do you? After this *no*one but adults will be allowed on the boat. So you see you must come right down to N.Y. and not leave us. What WOULD the child's life be? V. must have a job outdoors, on account of health. Well I shant go on about it any more, it will, as those things must, settle itself.[1]

Dow called up awhile ago to say that there were 3300 people in the shop, all milling. All the shops are like that, so I stay quietly in the home, and will send presents for New Year, like the French. It is all impossible, but people seem to like it. Christmas, I mean. G. is very elated that all the things he bought last summer are going so well, they are being snapped up like hotcakes, it seems, so that none of us will even see them.

Jinny was here last night for dinner, & said one of her friends in Wall St. said that Coster shot himself because he couldn't face the musica.[2] She, nor anyone else, has heard from the Hems, since they left. Ernest was in fine shape, very gay, but so busy that we only saw him about 2ce. He said, several times, he wished he could see you—He was trying to get his play [*The Fifth Column*] back from where Capt Dart got it to. Phil Barry's play [*Here Come the Clowns*] is out, & seems to be a succès d'estime. We have seen Dotty & Allan several times and Lillian Hellman. We went to a very amusing dinner the other night at the Museum of Natural History, all the food brought in served in a committee room. (Black tie.) Several of the professors spoke—& told us about catching the gorillas and finding meteorites, & all about humming birds, and Mexican sculpture. And we were allow[ed] to handle everything, and wander through the Museum, I haven't had such a nice time since I was a child and went to the Zoo with my father on Sundays. It looked so nice too.

---

1. The Louise Dowdney–Vladimir Orloff affair did "settle itself" over time by quietly dissipating. Louise was the daughter of the Murphys' friends, and she had sailed with them that summer and then stayed on in France with Fanny Myers and Honoria.

2. F. Donald Coster, president of McKesson & Robbins, a drug company, killed himself on 17 December 1938 after he was exposed as an ex-convict and swindler. Jinny Pfeiffer was making a pun on Coster's real name, Philip Musica.

Lovely ladies floating through those tall empty rooms, at immense distances, (and just as good near-to)

I feel I shall see you both soon, I hope not baselessly, so will get this wandering news bulletin off to Provincetown. Dos, is your book coming on? And Katy, are you taking your calcium?

I send my highest regard and <u>much</u> <u>love</u>. Pay no attention to my typewriting, it doesn't deserve it. A Bientôt

yr

Sara

Ends of words get me [Sara has handwritten this note on the right margin of the first page. The typewriter's pre-set right-hand margin caused Sara to cut off the end letters of some words, each of which she has then completed by hand.]

UVA

152. DOROTHY PARKER to GERALD and SARA MURPHY, Fox House Farm, Pipersville, Bucks County, Pennsylvania, 25 December 1938

Dear kids, I was afraid that a certain newspaper item might have slipped your attention, and so I am taking the liberty of repeating it to you, in the hope that it will set you, as it has me, an all-time standard of swank. I found it in a society column, devoted to reports of the various ways in which the high-born observe the birth of Christ. Some of them were pretty good. But this is the one:

"On Christmas Eve, Mr. J. P. Morgan gathers his children and grandchildren about him in his house on Murray Hill, and reads aloud Dickens's Christmas Carol, FROM THE ORIGINAL MANUSCRIPT."

There is no other seasonable news, save that our heating apparatus ceased to function just as the Christmas bells rang out, and we are all wrapped in swaddling clothes and lying in mangers; trying to keep warm.

Your loving aunt,

Dorothy.

HMD

During the fall, while Hemingway was in Europe, the Murphys saw Pauline and the two Hemingway boys, Patrick and Gregory. Pauline had rented an apartment near the Murphys' New Weston penthouse, and

*Gerald devoted much attention to the boys, who perhaps reminded him
of his own lost sons. Hemingway had seen Honoria in France on at least
two occasions during the fall. He would make several trips to New York
for further revisions on* The Fifth Column.

153. PAULINE HEMINGWAY to GERALD and SARA MURPHY, Key West [December 1938]

Dearest Sara and Dowdow,

Is it true you aren't coming down here for New Year's? People have intimated that you aren't but it is only today that I have come possibly to believe them. I'm evidently a sucker for wish fulfillment. All I can say is I am very sorry and it certainly is nice down here, with the orchid trees in full bloom and the ocean sparkling like starlings. The weather is lovely, though some say it is too cool, but it is ideal for bicycling and the sun is shining.

My I have missed you two and puppy and the New Weston. The beautiful sailboat you gave Gregory sails all day in the pool—just like man and life, going so smoothly, then veering and turning around, making for the side of the pool, bow out of water against the side and thinking it is going to get out, and go on a larger body of water, then setting out smoothly into the pool again and doing it all over. But the little dog [Gerald had given Patrick] we have lost. It went out of the garden one day and never came back. We advertised and got a lot of little white and little black boys interested in a reward for its return, but no one has ever seen it since. I think one of those TOURISTS who drive down to Key West, creep through the streets and turn around again to make Miami by dinner time, must have taken it. We miss him and his little deer hoofs. Wish you were here.

Ernest is home from New York very relaxed and contented, although we are not sure very much has been accomplished about the play—which reminds me Clifford Odetts is here, and what a dull citizen he turns out to be, and I am afraid he is going to be with us for some time as he is looking for a house here and plans to do some WORK. If he will just work that will be fine, but the danger is that he may decide to play, and he has no talent for that. Mr. Hemingway came home full of praises for your daughter Honoria But she is charming, charming, he keeps saying.

Please write to me. Please write to me and say you are coming down here and when. You won't have to fish Dowdow. You can just lie in the sun. How are your [gall] stones, Mrs. Murphy? I think you could probably swim them right out of you. And as for Miss Honoria, there are sixty naval officers here in clean white suits, with, so far as I can discover, nothing to distinguish one from another. I will find you a small house with a Bahama black to take care of it. Come soon. Much love,

Pauline

HMD

154. KATY DOS PASSOS to GERALD and SARA MURPHY, Provincetown, 11 January 1939

Oh Mrs. Puss darling and Gerald al Raschid,

I screamed steadily all through Christmas as the puss packages arrived in a star-sprinkled razzle-dazzle of fun and surprizes—Oh you *are* Christmas—and New Years, Easter, The Feast of Saint Swithen and the Fourth of July—You are also the Flame of Life and May Day and the Governor's Pardon—I would like to list the arrivals (Know them every one, though some have been eaten) but feel ashamed to put down in black and white the magnificent catalogue of what you Santa Clauses sent us damnable miserables. Oh it was wonderful. It was twice wonderful because we were very blue and down with chest colds and too enfeebled to make much cheer for ourselves between pills and sneezes. And we were missing you very bad—Then came the golden rain. Oh Sara—that beautiful linen—the exquisite delicacies—the heart-warming wine. And then when already groggy with excitement we were completely knocked over by the amazing life-saving Xmas-making Xmas-money—Please forgive me for not writing our thanks and delirious feelings before this—but I've been laid up in bed with a terrific cold, and my coughs laid end to end would read from here to the Mayo Clinic and a hospital cot. We had a lot of Christmas company—Charlie Kaeselau and his two little boys, and guests for New Years, and more guests, and a final great triumph of guests when Archie and Ada came, and I couldn't organize myself between sneezing and cooking so as to write you properly and when I finally had time to write I went to bed instead—*Never* had such a cold. It has wrapped itself all around me like the dragon of Wentley, and I have an iron dog sitting on my chest and a rough growling voice and I sit all scrouched up looking meanly around me out of my little red eyes.

The Christmas season here was a strange thing surely and if anything were wanting to complete the disillusion of Munich it was Noel in Provincetown. It started out very beautiful and heilege [solemn] with candle-light and wreaths and eggnog parties and music and everybody kissing and presents and good wishes and compliments exchanged on all sides and this kept up for a couple of parties and then on Christmas Day at a goodwill gathering at Phyllis Duganne's a man and wife fight suddenly broke out and Bud Beauchamp a young writer from the West struck his wife Sally Sousa (grand-daughter of Sousa's band) and then Eben Given knocked Bud down and they fought like wildcats in the kitchen till reconciled by Charley Kaeselau and then they all had a loving cup together but as soon as he drank it Eben knocked Bud Beauchamp down again and then his brother knocked Eben down and then for no reason at all a quiet man who hadn't said a word all evening rushed over and struck *his* wife and the whole party rose up in the wildest disorder and now Sally Beauchamp is suing for divorce and there are black eyes and broken friendships all over town. I am sure this is the fruit of Chamberlin's appeasment policy.

And that's not all because Eliza Poodle got in heat and our house has been picketed by hundreds of dogs all fighting and howling all night till last night at four in the morning one of the neighbors called up the police and at four-thirty a.m. the police and the Board of Health came down with guns and flash-lights, but while chasing a dog the Board of Health (Frank Flores is his name) fell off our bulk head and sprained his knee and broke his search light and the police had to carry him home. So now *he's* in bed and the dogs are simply terrific. Poor Eliza has been sent away to Chatham, but that does no good because Susan's dog Tucker, across the street, is carrying the torch now. The chief of police is nearly crazy because there's a civil war on our street between dog and bitch owners and both sides call him up in the middle of the night demanding that the other side take away his dogs. Dos is very calm and makes everybody mad by quoting Lucretius about Venus Genetrix.

We ate all the caviar alone and were very very happy. Love you forever— and always more—Ring out Wild Bells—

Your devoted Katy

UVA

Hemingway had spent a month in Cuba prior to returning to Key West on 14 March. He stayed until 10 April, in time to see Sara, who decided to join Jinny Pfeiffer for the Key West visit in early April. Hemingway returned to Cuba, where Martha Gellhorn joined him. His marriage to Pauline was clearly over, although Pauline continued to keep up a front.

155. PAULINE HEMINGWAY to SARA MURPHY,
Key West [10 March 1939]

Dear Darling Sara,

I talked to Jinny last night and she said you had your [gall bladder] operation yesterday and that hard riding Sara had taken it in her stride—with no complications (that hydra monster). I am SO glad! What a weight off all our minds! I am sure MR. Mark Cross is standing on his head. Dear Dowdow. And certainly I am unusually light-hearted this morning. No stones about anybody's neck now.

Jinny also said she thought seriously of driving down here the first of April, and of course I know you are much too lying down now to think of motor trips, but when you get a little stronger, *please* consider coming with her. I think lying in the sun might be just what you will want, and in April the sun here is at its best. We would have a wonderful time. Ernest will be here and life will be VERY nice. Keep this in mind.

I am enclosing an old letter I wrote you and Dowdow a long time ago which got lost and just turned up. Ordinarily I wouldn't send it, but in hospital a person will read anything and try to like it—also shows Mrs. Hemingway is not such a swine as was at first supposed by people who never heard a word from her.

Also, am enclosing a bracelet for hospital wear. Twenty one turtles were butchered to make it. They were all very proud.

Is Honoria there? Perhaps she would like to come to Key West too. Hope so. Dear Sara, I'm so relieved you have had this thing over. Much love to all three of you.

Your most devoted

Pauline

Please send health bulletins!
HMD

Alexander Woollcott and Gerald often had dinner together in New York, and also attended the latest films and plays. It seems likely that Murphy saw Thornton Wilder in New York, since Wilder was there that spring and socialized with Woollcott.

156. GERALD MURPHY to ALEXANDER WOOLLCOTT,
New York, 21 April 1939

Alexis, Liberator of the North:—

A whisper of gratitude to you . . . just on principle . . . It's nourishment to see you so well and so *galvinized*: Thanks for the film . . . what shadows passed thro' it . . . and what a strange reecho of a night years ago when an unguided voice said to me "What are you doing now?" . . . as I sat and waited for further news of Baoth . . . before starting out. From that moment on—as I've come to a corner—I've felt the thing which you give by your presence *somewhere*. In a world in which almost no communication between human creatures is possible it is *strange* to feel as I do—and to know—that I owe you so much,

Aff'y.

Gerald.

p.s. What a visit to some secret valley Wilder is: the torment of his thought that is *thrust* through the surface like Excalibur.

What a clarity the Lady has . . . and what a lovely light comes out of her. Who lit it and how long ago?   G.

HL

157. SARA MURPHY to JOHN and KATY DOS PASSOS,
à bord, *le Champlain*, 29 May [1939]

Dearest Katy and Dos,—

We *hated* to go without seeing you—but Honoria got to champing & pulling toward Paris, & there doesn't seem to be any war momentarily, my great excuse for delay—I hope you had a most *wonderful* trip [throughout the West]?—We loved your postcards & notes (you never said where to answer them)—and I hope you both feel fine now? I do, since all those Foreign Bodies [gallstones] were removed—I haven't felt so well in years—and hope you are the same. I suppose you went (or are going) right to Provincetown?— I *wish* I could have gone (better luck next year) and I hope you will go to East-hampton—Gerald will be going every weekend—We have no very definite plans—except Honoria wants 2 weeks in England (last half of June) and a month on the boat—starting toward middle July—& the rest of the time, before & after, Paris floating—I shall have two girls, as Fanny Myers is joining us, but I hope no love, for the moment—Romance, yes,—the tall handsome type, mostly dark, Honoria likes—but no love, please god—We are still hung over from last summer—Vladimir will probably come up to Paris to plan our cruise with me—Either loafing around Corsica,—or else what I would really like to do—get Weatherbird *out* of the Mediterranean, & into Portugal—This may however be too complicated, with a passel of girls. We shall see. (Louise D. [Dowdney]—*fortunately,* is in USA with a stock company, for the summer. Sigh of relief.) So far, this is Monday—we are having a lovely crossing—Coldish, clear & smooth and the French being very charming—There are a lot of names on board, mostly the Women-Without-Men type—Ruth Draper, Eve Curie, Alice Marble the Paul Kochansky widow—Kirsten Flagstad (*She* has a fat man,—probably husband)—also there is Brancusi, & several other minor celebrities—Honoria considers, (and I do too) that the rest of the passengers are definitely unattractive,—But we are having a lot of air & sleep—& make merry each evening with a pint of champagne a relative sent us to the boat—And an attentive super steward plies H. with crêpes Suzette & god knows what. The Puppy, too is well & happy—So we shall (I hope) spring off the boat Fri morning,—ready to go—Honoria has a little Chevrolet too, I forgot to mention, with her, which she now drives beautifully—I shall write you again later, this is just regrets, & how *many,* at having missed you!!—and only just! I would have liked to go to the [New York] World's Fair more than my once,—I thought it quite pretty—*Much* love to you both—Do write me—(c/o Guaranty Trust Co, always—) Gerald is noncommittal about coming over, except to say he isn't coming—However, something may change his mind,—one never knows—hope so

Very much love again—

Your Sara

Honoria sends love
Scuse pencil
I am starting Dos' book [*Adventures of a Young Man*, published Spring 1939]
UVA

158. JOHN DOS PASSOS to SARA MURPHY, Provincetown, 12 June [1939]

Dear Sara—

Your letter came just as I was starting to write you to complain about having missed you in New York—I'm sure you are driving the gendarmerie wild skating around Paris in Honoria's Chevey. It must be a very fine sight. Katy and I have been rowing and gardening and complaining about the weather ever since we got home, and that's about all. Its been chilly as the dickens— P'town although hot everywhere else. Spent two evenings at the World's Fair with Gerald. It's dandy there at night. We had a very good time. I'm anxious to go again. It's just the place everybody has always been looking for around New York in summer. Cool and not crowded, and with nice places to sit and drink beer—We kept going back to see the giant panda and the twoheaded cow. Gosh its too bad you couldn't get up to the cape this spring—maybe in the fall—Have a good time send us lots of postal cards and letters . . . London and Paris ought to be kind of interesting this summer

> love to Honoria and to the Weatherbird—
> yrs Dos

HMD

During the spring, Archibald MacLeish had agonized over whether to accept the appointment as the Librarian of Congress. He had come to discuss it with the Murphys, who encouraged him to act on his desire to write poems. He knew that public service would take over should he assume this position, and he declined until President Roosevelt assured him he would still have time to write. Roosevelt announced the nomination on 6 June, and MacLeish took office in October. He served as Librarian of Congress for the next five years.

159. GERALD MURPHY to ALEXANDER WOOLLCOTT, New York, 13 June 1939

Alexis:—

Archie came to us from the White House lunch table [on 23 May] He was against accepting so were we his doing so. I am still haunted by his reasons in support of non-acceptance. He alone—by now—must know what the position calls for . . . but 4,000,000 volumes! (and *all* sons of bitches) He'll *never* get thro' his dusting mornings.

The next 48 hrs are opague, but I shall call you for a slice of time,

> Aff'y
>
> Gerald.

And *how* are you O Green Mountain boy?

HL

Although Hemingway was using the Ambos Mundos Hotel as his mailing address, Martha Gellhorn had purchased and begun to renovate the Finca Vigía, about fifteen miles outside of downtown Havana. This would soon become his main residence in Cuba. As Hemingway thought about the dissolution of his marriage to Pauline, he was concerned about bringing in extra money from the movie rights to his work. He had talked with Shipwreck Kelly that spring in Key West about making "The Short Happy Life of Francis Macomber" into a movie. Hemingway's typewriter skips occasionally (primarily omitting letters in the middle of words), which makes this letter even "rougher" than usual.

160. ERNEST HEMINGWAY to SARA MURPHY,
Havana, 13 June [1939]

Dearest Sara—

How are you and goes everything and all of it? Here it's blowing a huge storm—close to a hurricane—and the royal palms are bent over in it and the branches clashing all out in one direction and the mangoes are scattering down and trees are going down in the gusts and it's been raining two days and two nights with me in bed with a bad head and chest cold. But that's the first that have felt bad since been here and came from getting caught in a huge rain-squall and soaked through and then sitting in the ambos mundos bar afterwards without changeing. It's nothing and now have gotten up to let the maid change the sheets and gotten dressed, full of quine, bromo-quinine-aspirin and pergante and write to you.

Dear Sara how are you and how is everything? It must be lovely there now and where are you and Honoria and how do you feel and how is everybody?

I have worked like very hell and gone good, better almost than I ever have, and better than I ever did in years. Have 243 pages done on my book [*For Whom the Bell Tolls*] and am way over half—maybe 2/3 through and think I have had very good luck. Have swam and played tennis almost every day and fished two days a week. Weigh 202 pounds and have slept good and worked hard. We caught 10 marlin and a very big wahoo and about a dozen tuna but haven't fished so much. Have been to the pelota (Jai-Alai) a lot and won quite a little money. It has been very good because all the best players are here because being basques they cannot go back to Spain and Mexico is closed too because of some trouble there and so it is very fine. I know them all, or most, and we go out on the boat and make paella at the cove (remember where we went for lunch and when you breakfasted me on bromoseltzer and whiskey sours) and we had such a fine day that time. Otherwise I work and work until I am too dead to think or write or anything and am happy doing it because that is what I am meant to do. But when I finish will certainly like to raise hell and do a lot of other things.

The last I heard from you was from after leaving the girls at Maine-Land. Probably you've heard from them. But Pauline and Jinny went to Piggott then K.C. [Kansas City] Infantile turned up in K.W. and I shipped the kids north by telephone in one day (with great aid of sully [J. B. Sullivan] and considerable financial agility) and now Pauline and Jinny are in N.Y. from Piggott. The kids go to camp [in Connecticut]. (I agreed to it but don't think it's too smart) Had a fine letter from Pauline about five days ago when they got to N.Y. But since imagine the gay times have commenced. Jinny is awfully awfully nice but an utterly irresponsable rummy and has done me great harm in my life but what the hell. Irresponasability around N.Y. is suposed to be the most admirable trait a person can have so let us join in admiring it.

I [illegible] the deal selling the Have and Have Not to pictures and the Ship-wreck deal is going marvellously well and smoothly and as it should so that everybody will have much or anyhow some money. Mr. Josie [Russell] hasn't come over yet because I have been working so bloody hard didn't see how I could entertain him. But will get him later when the big fish run. I've only been drunk once which was last Friday on purpose when eight of the Pelota players and three of us made a paella at the cove and drank 19 bottles of wine, two dozen beer, four bottles whiskey and just a little mansanilla and sang and swam far into the night and also ocean. Had worked so hard that week that was going get drunk so as not to think about it and certainly achieved that result. It was a fine party and many times and all the time I wish you were here for the fine good jolly times

I never did thank you for the lovely records and I never could thank you for how loyal and lovely and also beautiful and attractive and lovely you have been always ever since always. I hope you are haveing a good time dearest Sara. Give my love to Honoria and much love to you. I wish we were killing this rainy afternoon together. It is a beautiful storm.

Do not see how I can finish this book under two months more. Then want to go somewhere with the boys to fish. Then to Europe. How late will you be there? Were the Gallaghers on the same boat going over?

Would like to shoot there this fall. Please tell me about everything and about your plans. I love you always and please always count on it.

Ernest

HMD

227

161. JINNY PFEIFFER to SARA MURPHY,
New York, 14 June [1939]

Dear Sara,

We have got this far on the summer and I am beginning to be glad that only seven more days will see winter setting in. Theres one thing to be said about winter. It handles you, whereas you have to handle summer. My I admire the way you tackle plans and seasons! I am so weary of them all! However I am just about to sign up with a gland specialist and hope when I am sixteen everything will be different.

New York is rather sweet with the fair gay people from the country and they make it look so much healthier, by reducing the number of subway grown faces fifty fifty, at least. Also the provincial ease of handling what to wear in the heat is refreshing.

I have a window full of dirt and pots and implements and my yellow thumb keeps me busy throwing out dead plants. The little stuffinose is a marvel, keeps shedding its leaves and putting out more and I have a silly Rhododendron that is going to bloom on chemicals.

Pauline is going to Nantucket this week to see if thats what she wants to do. I think Ruth Allen (no one ever knows about an Allen) is going too, as she is out for a summer solution too. The children are on a farm in Connecticut and seem to love it. Ernest is still plodding hard at the novel in Cuba. I think he had his last bit of fun when we were there in Key West.

Did you hear about Archie getting appointed by the President to be Congressional Librarian? The P. spoke very highly of him, but the appointment is not yet confirmed as there is some opposition from all the Librarians in the country who think a Librarian ought to be chosen.

Dos was here but we missed him. His new book [*Adventures of a Young Man*, 1939] has not made him popular with his old friends. (Not including me and you) I mean all the Spanish epoc ones. I have never been a great Dos reader but I think I will have to read this as seeing people go back on Cummunism is one of my favorite sports. (Have read the book and find it very interesting sample of objectivity.)

We havent seen Gerald either although he has telephoned. I always think it takes at least one Murphy to make a summer.

I went to the Village Fair with Dawn [Powell] and Ruth [Allen] the other day. It was seething with people you knew. Don Stewart was master of ceremonies, and Dorothy [Parker] chief hostess. Your old pal Gypsy Rose Lee was there too as so was Marc Blickstein. The Mirror asked Gypsy Rose if she would raise her skirts a little higher for the Mirror which she did but refused to take them off for anybody but the Daily Worker. It doesnt sound so good but it was rather funny. She has very spontaneous comebacks for some one with so much leg power. Helen Hays auctioned off a bouquet given by mrs Rosevelt and it was very embarassing for nobody bid at all, untill to save the day Don bid $25. and got it. I met the much discussed Ella Winters but its very odd that I cant remember what my impression was. It must have been those Champagne cocktales plus the mint Julep. I only remember that she turned a full powered graciousness and warmth on me that didnt seem warranted by the occasion.[1]

How is Miss Honoria and what lead has she been chosen for? Please give me all news of her along with any Mother Murphy scandals fitten to tell. How is your beautiful rickety neck and all it stands for? I miss the whole thing and toy with the idea of hopeing maybe to come see it and Paris a month in the better part of fall. Tell me just how pretty Paris is Miss Clara.

Much love

Jinny

P.S. Have definitely given up Photography Love to the Barries and tell them have written regularly.

HMD

---

1. Donald Ogden Stewart was now divorced from Beatrice and had recently married Ella Winters, widow of muckracker Lincoln Steffens.

162. GERALD MURPHY to ALEXANDER WOOLLCOTT, New York, 22 June 1939

Alexis:—

Thought you'd enjoy this excerpt from Sara's letter,

G.

[Gerald had typed Sara's letter, as follows. This account (referred to in succeeding letters as the "Oxford Adventure") entertained the Murphys' friends as Gerald repeated the story, often reading Sara's letter directly. The original of Sara's letter has not survived.]

We arrived in England in fine shape in H's car (I cabled). Left Paris about 7 a.m. (What slave driving *that* took!)—put the car on the "Auto carrier", Calais, at Dover—Honoria turned smartly to the left—like an old Britisher, and only boggled at the London busses, "they are so high" she said—And how narrow the streets!! That was last Thursday 15th—On Sunday a.m. we went to Oxford—arriving for lunch. The boys *very* nice—the inviter, Lloyd Bowers (Yale) about 23 years, like a better-looking Ned Trudeau—a really nice, well-brought-up boy, with *manners*—and also the Friend—[Alan] Jarvis, very tall blond, nice-looking—sculps and likes the stage,—but very attractive and no feathers anywhere—The girls seemed to hit it off very well with them both—So much so, that I invited Bowers to go to Corsica with us for a couple of wks anyhow—He seemed such a *relief* after the Cafe characters the girls were seeing in Paris, piano players, hangers on at Joinville and the like—(me no like) So, the weather luckily being fine, we went all over the countryside in Honoria's car; around Oxford Sunday p.m. and Monday— sightseeing in the colleges and teas and lunches at old *old* pubs, with names like "The Trout", the "Wedge & Beetle"—my favorite "The Rose Revived", and others. The big dance night was Monday—(no mothers, but I was sent flowers and treated like glass!) The girls looking *too ravishing* in their organza dresses,—went out to the ball (through the hotel lobby and all the employees lined up to see the ball-goers) with escorts in white ties in a *high* state of excitement—We stayed at the old "Mitre"—and the University College was almost across the street. The dance was in a big pale blue and white striped tent, filling one of the courts of the College, and the buffet in a tent in the second court—all *lined* with flowers—Never was there so much food or champagne, the girls reported afterwards—and the boys took them also around to various parties in Rooms—It all seemed most gay and hospitable—They all went out on the river for breakfast about 6 or 7 a.m. afterward—and we went back to London after lunch, no one having been to bed at all. But I think they had *great* fun, and it was an enormous success,—and Oxford is such a lovely old Town—one of the young men bit Honoria, apparently momentarily maddened by her appearance and champagne—which caused a little scene of fury—otherwise everything went off most smoothly—I told her she must consider it a compliment. No one ever bit me, even in my heyday,—that I can remember. She is still angry and has teeth marks near the elbow! London is pleasant, but if possible, even more "muddy" than ever—the daily papers are driving me mad—and am sending you some examples of what they consider hot news (in case you have forgotten the English). I can find *nothing*—but cricket, spin-bowling and the speeches at grammar schools, and *anything* may have happened in the world.

HL

163. SARA MURPHY to JOHN and KATY DOS PASSOS, on way to Corsica, 18 July [1939]

Dearest Dos & Katy,—

It seems *so* strange to be starting out without youall—we so seldom have (and I wouldn't like to have it happen again.) *There* is the cushion on top the

claire-voie [sky-light], & no Katy on it—& there is the old Riviera outline of
coast with no Dos in a little linen hat peering, oh dear—We have Honoria, &
Fanny [Myers], & what I *must* call a worthwhile young man [Lloyd Bowers],
in a spirit of fun,—as no one over 25 will *ever* be as serious again—(although
very nice & all that,—& keeps the girls in order)—not an adult in a carload,
as you see—However, it is worth it to me, even with like conditions, to be
sliding along over these blue waters,—Vladimir is *exactly* the same—He
bears no marks of Love, at any rate,—& is certainly not pensive or pining, at
least visibly—The Crew is all Russian, or nearly,—nobody, except Antoine,
that we ever saw before—but all nice, lean, middleaged wary-looking
sailors—Our cook (a very good one) is 70 & nearly stonedeaf,—but spry &
clean with a round pink face under his chefs hat—we thought we had lost him
a few days ago—He didn't like Popoff—a saturnine man who waited on
table—There was a loud Russian quarrel in the kitchen & Vladimir came out,
breathing rather quickly—followed by our waiter with his hat on. Now we
have another waiter, cheerfuller—named Anatol—& sweetness & light
reigns in the kitchen, & chef is staying—Such good coffee!—And what Russian dishes!—Oh dear, & I meant to get so thin—It will be hopeless now. The
Puppy, you will be glad to hear, is in full charge of everything again—
including Vladimir's dog—A Sealyham,—(Judy's grandson, in fact)—I can't
believe his name is Jowlty, but that is what Vladimir *seems* to call him. Each
dog has his own side of the deck,—& what growlings & mutterings go on if
one of them forgets! No real fighting, just an armed neutrality. However on
shore they rush along together, looking for other dogs to fight,—in the greatest camaraderie—I think it is that each wants to be captain—We were held up
in Montecarlo, for several days by mistral, & grosse mer—& are just now
starting—with a long day & night ahead, & beautiful sea & sun. The girls, I
hope, are enjoying themselves—They chatter along & play the Victrola, &
read endless movie magazines with some light manicuring in between,—so
think they'll be allright—although Honoria always wishes the boat were run
more along the lines of the Ritz,—& it is *all* that I—& the W.W. young man
Lloyd—can do to get her up in the morning—I am looking forward to
Corsica—It may be crowded,—as everyone considers it about the only place
safe or pleasant to go to in these times—(I hope we wont all have to run home
like rabbits next month) no one speaks much of War here—They only look
rather tired when you mention it, as though they were—and why not—quite
bored with the malevolences of an old world—& would rather think of something else when possible. The newspapers are *all* partisan & worthless for
news—So we really know nothing (—& are just as well off probably.)

Gerald sounds well & cheerful in his letters—I think he is having a fine
time,—as he loves Easthampton—He said he might be going to see you
later—May I come in the Fall?—as I missed so not going last Spring—I hope

all our illnesses are past & gone. I certainly feel spryer—(although at the moment expect I am turning into one of the nastier variety of schoolmistresses! Where *are* all the adults?

We have just seen a *huge* yellowish cachalot, meandering along, & not hurrying on acc't of us—All sails set & a little breeze—which dies down at times & we have motor—It is very pleasant, & I *wish* you was here.

Very much love, and please agree my most distinguished considerations—Write me what you are doing. I *loved* Dos' book [*Adventures of a Young Man*]. Vladimir is learning English & he wants to read it, so am leaving it with him. How are those MacLeishes? Very best love again

Sadie—

UVA

164. JOHN DOS PASSOS to SARA MURPHY,
East Hampton, 21 July [1939]

Oh Sara—here Gerald and I are rattling around in Swan's Cove—that looks very charming—and who do you think we miss most damnably? our Sadie. Gerald says you are already on the high seas—hope you are having nice weather. The summer on the cape has been definitely chilly but fine. Katy's been in fine shape—we've gardened and boated and I've been working like a nigger. Gerald looks well—he's out pruning fruit trees and in a moment we are going in bathing—love to Honoria—My that was a funny letter about England. Frankly there are going to be a lot of people very much delighted when you get home to these shores. Have a nice time—Give my best to Vladimir—Tell him I'll yet send him pictures of American clipperships—

love

Dos

HMD

165. GERALD MURPHY to SARA MURPHY,
New York, 26 July 1939

Dear Sal:—

I'm not sure where this will reach you as you said nothing about having your mail forwarded to you by the bank during the cruise.

I hope it's turning out fine. I'm sure it is. What luck that we had the boat for you to do it, as the Continent doesn't sound any too attractive. How can it with such spirit of aggression in the air. Now the English have sold China down the river to the Japanese! There seems to be no *principle* left.

I think you'll find Paris more attractive when you go back to it. Avoid the August pall. Stay somewhere on the Riviera and take short trips in the boat.

We are in the midst of the most cruel drought. No rain for six weeks and the thermometer around 90°! The wells have run dry and all the fruit and vegetable crops are blasted. I've been able to hold on to a bit of the garden, but the heat has made even the chrysanthemums bloom in advance! All lawns are brown. The worst in 73 years.

Dos has just been with me for a few days. We went down to EH [East Hampton]. Esther stayed over two days to see him. He's fine, but they've had no sun at the Cape. Katy except for a slight relapse has been well. She goes down to Johns Hopkins next week and possibly they'll come down to EH for the week-end. The Lloyd Lowndes are coming. We are in the midst of painting the interior. The ceilings have been leaking until recently. McGuirk says that the house was badly strained by the hurricane and that it is now settling.

Did I tell you that Don [Stewart] passed through town with his new wife. She strikes me as being formidable and far from alluring although she is reputed as having been able to do anything she wanted with the opposite sex (Steffens was already much older when they married),—and even Mr. James Cagney is on the roster. Grimly socio-politico-economic in her interests (as they all seem to be these days). He said he hoped I'd give a good report of her to you. As I said good-bye to her I said. "Take care of him for us",—at which she gave me a steely look and said "I *will*" . . . and she should have added . . . "but I have other things to do as well which are possibly more important . . ."

It was a strange crew we were. Dorothy had asked me for luncheon with Alan. He had a date and I found that we were to meet Don and his wife and one of the editors of the New Masses at the "Bayberry Club" (née Elbow Room) where we sat in a black light with giant jade bayberry *trees* in the corners at black glass tables in gold leather chairs. The talk was violent and technical and the check very high. Being a guest I did not pay, but Don insisted on paying himself and everyone told him he should save his money for his children, etc. etc. Why didn't we go to Schraft's then? I have luncheon there every day.

The enclosures give you most of the news. Much love to you all. I hope that you got my cable to Ajaccio,

Dev'td'l'y

Gerald

HMD

166. JOHN DOS PASSOS to SARA MURPHY,
Baltimore, 3 August [1939]

Dear Sara—just before we left Provincetown we got the finest letter from you bound for Corsica—it did make us Weatherbird-sick—there certainly ought to be more adults aboard—Katy's just been at Hopkins to be checked and passed with flying colors—stool negative—so the amoeba really has been kicked—We feel awfully good about it—We wish you and Gerald were here to drink a champagne cocktail in the dandy Belvedere bar on the subject— Gerald we'll see in East Hampton on the way home, but there wont be a glimpse of our Sadie—except that everything in the house always makes me miss our Sadie most dreadfully—We all converged at the MacLeishs last week—Ada and Archie are fine. Archie's going to get a little vandyke false beard to wear with his alpaca coat when he works in the library—Otherwise he'll be unchanged. It's certainly going to be a fulltime job for a couple of years—Mrs Murphy's absence at Conway caused unfavorable comment on all sides—plenty adults but no Sadie.

lots of love

Dos

HMD

Pauline Hemingway had arrived in Europe and was trying to meet up with Sara, who had already left Paris to cruise on the Weatherbird. *Dick Myers had arrived in France on a wine-buying trip and saw Pauline in Paris and also for a weekend at Harry Woodruff's country home in Fontainebleau.*

167. PAULINE HEMINGWAY to SARA MURPHY,
Paris [17 August 1939]

Dearest Sara—

Dick just called-up and said you are sailing on the Normandie on the 7th— In that event, why dont you come or wont you *be* coming up here earlier? Dick says he couldn't go down there [French Riviera] before next week and that would just complicate your plans, I'm afraid.

Paris is lovely now, full of fun and charm—*Please come up earlier*—Why dont you come to this hotel—*Very* nice rooms—inexpensive, quiet, near the round point *and* the etoile.

Am sending this off in great haste to get to you—*Do* write back and say you are coming—We could have such a good time here—Have gained seven pounds over weekend in the country with Dick—Look like enlarged Strasbourg *liver,* bon liver—

Dearest Sara, please hurry up—Am dying to see you—Write or telegraph on dotted line you will not regret it—

Much love to all

Pauline

HMD

Richard Myers took the night train from Paris on 18 August so as to meet up with Sara and the girls in Monaco the next morning. He returned by train to Paris on the twenty-first, and Sara and the girls joined up with him three days later as war rumors intensified.

168. RICHARD MYERS to GERALD MURPHY,
Paris, 27 August 1939

Dear Gerald;

What days! Ever since last Wednesday, we have been living in a state of tension that is a definite test of nerves. Rumors fly thick and fast—planes fly over Paris, soldiers go off to their posts—and every day somebody you know is missing—and you know they have left for their regiment. Many women with tears coursing down their cheeks—and everywhere a state of calm dignity on the part of the French that is admirable and impressive. Last night we spent in a darkened Paris.—and it brought back memories of the night Alice Lee and I arrived in Paris on Nov. 10th 1918—only this time it seemed more poignant, for then we were used to war—and now the mere thought of it nauseates most sensible people.

Sara hastened up from Monte Carlo with the girls—and we held a counsel and decided to try and advance our sailing—which is well-nigh impossible—for the frantic Americans have grabbed everything in sight until Sept. 15th but we fortunately have reservations on the Normandie—(Tourist)—in very good (first-class) cabins on the 6th. And we are praying that the Normandie will sail. If there is war—we will go to Normandie—within easy reach of Havre—which is the best plan according to all—keep H's car and use it to get to a boat quickly—(trains already demoralized). Then if we cannot get the car on a boat—we will leave it here—until it can be claimed later. Sara even thinks she might give it to the French Government. So far we are alright—Sara and the girls have excellent rooms and salon in the Hotel de la Trémoille—(at half the price of the Plaza-Athenee and for twice as much space)—and I moved from the Woodruffs and came here to be near them—best we all stick together.

Last night Fanny and I went over to the Flores to see Guitou Knoop and her beau—and he will shortly be mobilized. Fanny received a blow when she found her playmates and friends all on the eve of departure for the front—and she sobbed bitterly all the way home and long after she got there. But Sara mothered her and we gave her a sleeping pill and she soon dropped off to slumber. But her young heart was breaking—her first acquaintance with what war can do. Neither of the girls have realized until now, what the situation is—but they do now.

Janet [Flanner] and Noel [Murphy] have offered us shelter in case of trouble—but we think we will go to a spot nearer a port. Everybody is helpful. Mme. Helene is facing the prospect of both son and husband going. Your nice friends at O'Rossen have been mobilized—and they are going to send most of their stocks down to Tours—and everywhere you go—you find gaps. Paris is deserted—except at night when you will find people huddled at a café where they can discuss and hope.

Nobody knows what the outcome will be—but everybody hopes.

Many Americans have signified their intention to remain and join the French army—and even Sara says she will stay and start a canteen—and I am sure that Alice Lee would want to do so too if she were here—The French are so grand about this. Not one complaint. Sara's declaration, however, brought a terrific outburst from Honoria, who protested vigorously—and said she would then stay too.

We may get on the Manhattan—the 7th—but if there is no war by the 6th—I dont see why we cannot take the Normandie which is fast—and on which we have definite bookings. Furthermore, I do not believe the French would allow her to sail if there were any danger.

The franc has fallen to 40—the pound to $4.35—but nobody here is interested in taking advantage.

I am registering all of us tomorrow at the American Embassy—and in case of any real trouble—I have a letter to [William C.] Bullitt. Also many friends at the French Foreign Office. So I am not worried yet.

To-day is Alice Lee's birthday—we have cabled her—and we will celebrate it by lunching at Orgeval with Janet and Noel.

I cant tell you how marvelous the three day sail on the Weatherbird was—but here are some pictures to look at. Keep them—I have others for A.L.

I am still hopeful—for I think nobody wants war—not even the Germans—although everything is being done by the Hitler regime to stimulate them—military marches being blatted all the time—day and night—but

Mrs. von Rath says, (who has just returned from Germany) that they are all secretly listening to the English broadcasts. Roosevelt's moves have been met with approval—and America could stop the war now if she would just say definitely that she stands with Britain and France.

I asked Jo Davidson the other day what he would do about all his statues here—and he said—"Well—if there is a war—I am not interested in preserving any of my work for a civilization that has gone to pot". Not the point of view of the French who have closed all the Museums and are safeguarding the pictures etc. There are 400,00 men on the Italian front. Everything is ready—they have been preparing and have done a good job.

Will you send this on to Alice Lee—and tell her not to worry—she has been so helpful and not sent us cables etc—which everybody else is doing—we will get home alright.

Sidney [Howard]'s death so shocked me—I was sunk—what a terrible tragedy—he was so talented—and such a fine fellow. I cannot forget it.

America will look good to me—I can hardly wait to see you all—and if we move we will wire you.

Yours—

Dick

My new suit is magnificent.
HMD

Although they had earlier reservations on the Normandie, *they booked passage instead on a neutral ship, the* George Washington, *scheduled to sail from Le Havre on September 9. As Sara recorded it in her travel log, they had spent all day in port. "Airplanes around us. Alerte this* A.M., 5 A.M. *Four in cabin. Very stuffy. All coughing. Sailed about 7* P.M.*" In Southampton, England, the next morning, the ship took on more passengers. "Now over two thousand. Left Southampton late, about 5:30. Watched mines laid across mouth of harbor, after we were through in angry sunset." Gerald Murphy's reference to their arriving on the S. S.* Manhattan, *rather than the* Washington, *probably reflects his earlier confusion as to what ship, if any, they were on. As Richard Myers had reported to to Alice Lee on 27 August, they waited daily to hear of cancellations on other boats sailing home. Their goal, not unlike that of other Americans caught in the mad scramble, was to get the first boat out.*

169. GERALD MURPHY to JOHN and KATY DOS PASSOS,
New York, 21 September 1939

D & K:—

Sara and Honoria look splendid. Full of praise for the superb job done on the S.S. Manhattan despite 1754 in space for 950. Dick Myers slept in the swimming pool and—among others—slid from the shallow to the deep end every night. Honoria danced all day. Food delicious, etc. They are filled with tales of high adventure in France. . . . I feel like sitting under a tree in the sun and holding someone's thumb . . . Sara anxious to come to Cape. I think we'll really try to as soon as she's seen Swan Cove. We move on Oct. 1st over to 54th St. back of the Modern Museum. Guess it'll have to be in mid-Oct. if you're still there. Archie and Ada are passing thro' next Mon. & Tues. He was here yesterday looking noticeably young. Sara says yr. letters during the summer were a Godsend. She did love getting them.

Yrs.

G.

UVA

170. F. SCOTT FITZGERALD to GERALD MURPHY,
Encino, California, 21 September 1939

WAS TAKEN ILL OUT HERE LAST APRIL AND CONFINED TO BED FIVE MONTHS AND NOW UP AND WORKING BUT COMPLETELY CLEANED OUT FINANCIALLY WANT DESPERATELY TO CONTINUE DAUGHTER AT VASSAR CAN YOU LEND 360 DOLLARS FOR ONE MONTH IF THIS IS POSSIBLE PLEASE WIRE ME 5521 AMESTOY AVENUE ENCINO CALIF=

SCOTT FITZGERALD

HMD

171. GERALD MURPHY to F. SCOTT FITZGERALD,
New York, 22 September 1939

DISTRESSED YOU HAVE BEEN ILL WE HAD BEEN WONDERING ABOUT YOU MONEY READY WHERE SHALL I SEND IT PLEASE TAKE CARE OF YOURSELF NOW SARA HONORIA JUST LANDED WE ALL SEND YOU MUCH LOVE.

GERALD

PUL

238

172. F. SCOTT FITZGERALD to GERALD and SARA MURPHY,
Encino, California, 22 September 1939

THANK YOU STOP THIS WAS THE FIRST EXPERIENCE OF PERSONAL LOAN
YOUR WIRE TOOK THE CUTTING EDGE OFF IT WOULD IT BE POSSIBLE TO
TELEGRAPH THE SUM TO BANK OF AMERICA CULVER CITY CALIFORNIA
TODAY OR TOMORROW LOVE TO ALL AM WRITING=

SCOTT.

HMD

173. F. SCOTT FITZGERALD to GERALD AND SARA MURPHY,
Encino, California [c. September 1939]

Gerald & Sara:

What a strange thing that after asking every other concievable favor of you
at one time or another I should be driven to turn to you for money! The story is
too foolish, too dreary to go into—I was ill when I saw you in February and
for a week had been going along on drink. Like a fool—for I had plenty of
money then—I took two more jobs and worked myself up to a daily temperature of 102° & then just broke & lay in bed four months without much ability
to do anything except lie to the world that I was "fine." I couldn't even reduce
costs—there were the doctors and the government & the insurance, and the
"face."

Well, I'm up now. I've even worked two weeks & tomorrow may find the
financial crisis over—an idea at Metro—but the way all our personal prides,
vanities melt down in the face of a situation like not being able to continue a
child's education is astonishing. Not having any credit, What a thing! When
credit was exactly what one thought one had.

Last year for example I payed my Eastern agent $12,000 which he had ad-
vanced me over two years plus 10% of my gains (of about $68,000). Would he
back me again—for $1000—$500? No—in spite of the $70,000 in commis-
sions one paid him in the past. All this may interest you, Gerald, as an indication of the fluctuation of talent value—I can see Sara yawn & I don't blame
her. Anyhow it has been frightening and lost & strange. One's own reaction
was:—I couldn't call on the impecunious, and eternally so, to whom I had
"lent," or rather given many thousands—not only because they didn't have
it—but because some relation established at the time of the lending forbade it.
There were the bores I have tolerated because they have been nice to Zelda or
some such reason, but once in a faintly similar situation years ago I sounded
out one—& buttoned up my overcoat quickly at the chill in the air.

Then there were relatives & friends. My relatives are all poor now, except my sister whom I detest, and, as Gerald once remarked, your friends are the people you see. Forty-eight hours went into worry as to whether or not to ask you to help me. And then I wired, knowing somehow that if you were in America it would be all right, presuming on your grace. Next day came your wire—telephoned, but I went down and got a copy of it.

You had probably been going thru hell yourselves with Honoria on the high seas. And how easy too, in these times, to have been irritated by the intrusion of this preposterously personal problem—how can that Idiot, who has such abilities to be solvent, get himself in such a hole? Let it teach him a lesson!

You went a good deal further than that—you helped me perhaps because I would *never* learn—or "for help's sake itself," to paraphrase E. Browning. Anyhow it made me feel much too sentimental than is proper to one of our age & experience. And it is nice to know that when I send it back to you it will in time probably go to aid some other "unworthy case" (—do you remember Ernest's passage in "The Sun Also Rises" about being sorry for the wrong types, unsuccessful whores, ect.?)

You saved me—Scottie and me—in spite of our small deserts. I don't think I could have asked anyone else & kept what pride it is nessessary to keep.

Scott

HMD

174. GERALD MURPHY to F. SCOTT FITZGERALD,
New York, 29 September 1939

Scott:—

Sara and I appreciated so much your letter and all that it brought with it. We were distressed to hear you'd been ill. I wish we'd known. Please don't keep us ignorant ever again. Please take care of yourself. Please don't worry about the money. If you knew how *fond* we are of you I think you'd believe this. One is fond of so few people. Our love to you

Gerald.

Sara and Honoria landed a week ago.
PUL

175. GERALD MURPHY to JOHN and KATY DOS PASSOS,
New York, 30 September 1939

K & D:—

For yrs. I've tried to recall what my feeling at P'town (especially *in* the town and out that long wharf!) made me think of,—and now I've just run across it in the first act of the Tempest, Sc. 1 on the ship he says: "A very ancient and fish like smell." Thought I'd let you know. Sara is tending Puppy who picked up something on the steamer so I'm going down to breast the October surf. What weather these days and how I chafe at it in the office! Archie & Ada passed thro' [en route to Washington and The Library of Congress], the latter off her feed (too much moving) and Archie feeling as if he were going *away* to school for the first time. Really so anxious, concerned and young! Sara is bending toward you this month and I'm going to try to join her. Love from all,

G.

UVA

The Murphys had just attended the Broadway opening of The Man Who Came to Dinner, *the Moss Hart and George S. Kaufman play wherein Sheridan Whiteside is modeled on Woollcott. Most playgoers recognized Woollcott's sharp wit and prima donna qualities in White-side, and the play became an immediate hit. Woollcott liked the play, maintaining that it brought out his best and worst qualities.*

Gerald Murphy was helping Woollcott to landscape the area directly surrounding his Lake Bomaseen home, which Woollcott wanted to make less primitive. In order to get to the island from the mainland, visitors had to be ferried over—a service provided over the years by William Bull and his son Howard, who operated an inn at the lake.

176. GERALD MURPHY to ALEXANDER WOOLLCOTT,
New York, 17 October 1939

O, Eastern star:—

It is my fervent hope to come to the Island on and during the day of the 26th of October. I shall have stopped at the nurseries on the way and prepared to order the material in case you are not affronted. Were I to spend the night could I roll you back here on the 27th in my barouche which is very comfortable and runs silkenly? The top slides back too and one sees "up above what wind-walks, what lovely behaviour of silk-sack clouds . . ." It would all be such a nice October junket.

Should your dates change, don't bother;—but do leave word at that boat-landing place on the mainland (Buell or Bull the name as I recall) that I am permitted to go over and make a topographic plan of the terrain surrounding the house. If you have a plan of the island (especially the built part) would you please bring it to New York, should we not connect!

Last night we saw the play—and were with Dorothy [Parker] and Alan [Campbell] afterwards. The audience (I hate first-nights) had that greedy sense of being included at the only spectacle worth going to. Norma Shearer (who sat by) wore a travesty of the Medici mourning cap and streamers. The play depressed me . . . it doesn't even succeed in being incisive . . . such good values were passed up in the name of general unworthiness. I wonder if any of all those people you know know what you're like. I'm not saying I do,—but I am saying that the play showed me (by what it lacks essentially) how fond I am of you,

Aff'y.

Gerald.

HL

During the winter of 1939–1940, the Dos Passoses were caring for Christopher "Beanie" Kaeselau, the ten-year-old son of Marguerite and Charles Kaeselau. Following the death of Marguerite in 1936, friends from Truro and Provincetown, including the Dos Passoses, took turns with Beanie and also Jean Kaeselau.

177. KATY DOS PASSOS to SARA MURPHY,
Provincetown, 10 December 1939

Oh Mrs Puss,

I was floored by the windbreaker for Beanie, but just coming up to thank you when knocked into the ropes by the expressman complete with furnishings. Saw stars for days but rallied and was just staggering toward the typewriter when the mailman handed me a wrapped package with both hands and I went down for the count.

Now Mrs. Puss you know we can't love you any more—have already exceeded the legal limit, so what are you trying to do, you naughty kitten? Are you trying to corrupt and undermine a nature never strong and already tending toward the deadly vices of pride and gluttony? If I was to go to the devil it would be due to your sinful indulgences—feel like a pampered infink right now. And M. Fish the same. Oh Mrs Pusser the chairs are so pretty and the baskets too and in your wicked goodness you remembered exactly what was most needed and oh gee the lovely stool with that sweet parrot—he is wonderful. Beanie was simply delighted with his jacket—he wrote you a letter but I don't know if he mailed it. He's constantly asking when are the Murphys coming back. And then those beautiful clothes—all fitting amazingly—I was never so delighted in my life as was down to bare poles and only one tattered nightgown left. I don't see how Honoria could part with them. Please thank her for me and I will thank her myself too. The gloves are a delicious tidbit too. Oh Mrs Puss, Mrs Puss.

Your room looks mighty nice right now and you know why and when are you coming back—we miss you terribly all the time. Weather has been wonderful. Dos and I have taken up dancing and go down every night with the [Charles] Walkers to a little class known as Duffy's Dance Hall where we practise the new steps with real hand made music. I wish you could see Dos doing the polka. He unites to all the skill and variety of step the most joyous and liberal grace of the head and arms.

Now here's your tillitating wire and we are crazy to come and will come if can find someone to take care of Beanie who is indeed a handful. I have finally managed to clean him up though it's a terrific struggle to get him to wash, and most of his clothes were beyond help and almost a menace to health. I bought him a new suit and underthings and some shirts and now the house no longer has the rich and spicy fragrance of a Morman emigrant train. If can find a keeper for him we'll try to get off Saturday or Sunday. Would have liked to attend the Barry's party for the radiant movie star, but saw no way to make it by Thursday.

Gerald's post card said Pauline was coming—please give her my love. How long is she staying? And you aren't going south for Christmas—what is Honoria's party to be like? A Dance? We are dance crazy and planning to give a Ball. Couldn't you come? I don't suppose it would be possible to snatch Honoria from New York at such a season. Is she having a good time? Do tell me what she's doing. Give her my love again.

And Dos sends his love Sara darling, and I send mine and endless thanks and please recommend me to Mr. Pusser, dearest and best beloved of all earthly pussers.

Your affectionate

Katy

UVA

The Fifth Column was produced in late 1939, after Hemingway had re-worked Hollywood scriptwriter Benjamin F. Glazer's version of it. Hemingway began to tell people thereafter that "he ought to have written The Fifth Column *as a novel." He had spent part of the 1939 fall with Martha Gellhorn in Sun Valley, Idaho, and when he decided he would come to Key West for Christmas, Pauline told him not to come if he planned to rejoin Martha thereafter. In mid-December she left for New York to spend Christmas with Jinny and the Murphys. When Hemingway arrived in Key West to an empty house, he left for Cuba. Martha Gellhorn was in Finland covering the war and would not return to Cuba until mid-January 1940. The book Hemingway was still working on was* For Whom the Bell Tolls, *which would be published in 1940.*

178. ERNEST HEMINGWAY to SARA MURPHY,
Havana, 27 December [1939]

Dearest Sara;

Thank you for the lovely letter. I had kept your other letter from France with me always to answer. Had hoped we would all be in France this fall. Then the war—and book still unfinished. Now I will go in the spring when this is done. Am in the last part now.

Weren't you my Sara to write! Do you know it was the only Christmas greeting or present or anything of any kind I had for Christmas? I think that was a little drastic. People ought not to be afraid they would compromise their financial position by saying Merry Christmas to people they got along with all right for many years. You gave me some good advice once about 14 years ago that I didn't take.

But Patrick and Otto [Bruce] and I had a fine Christmas with great wheel-barrow loads of suckling pig being trundled by the old Ambos Mundos and everybody happy and jolly and I had that orchestra play No Hubo Barrera en El Mundo for you.

I don't think it is my play they are doing but some re-jewing of a jewed version of it. Let's all give it a miss.

Must finish this book. With a little luck and a little less being slugged over the head (it's a good tough head though and people liable to find they broke something hitting it) it can be the best one that I have written. I put a couple of things in it for you that you may find sometime.

The Ambos Mundos will always get me. Will come to N.Y. and will see you when the book is finished. Take good care of yourself.

Give my love to Honoria and to Gerald. I hope you didn't get the impression from Pauline and Virginia that I was away from Christmas anyway of my choice or of my own free will. I think it was a sort of a frame-up designed to get me to commit suicide. One can get gloomy if absolutely alone on one of those festive occasions and I think usual procedure is to kick people out of their homes the day *after* Christmas. But refused to get gloomy, or drunk, or suicidal. Just got jolly the way we used to get jolly when things were too bloody bad to be born.

Cut the last part of this letter off and burn it and forget what it says. Am always unjust. But have to talk to someone sometime.

Much love always from your old friend who will be your good and old friend as long as he lives and afterwards will think of you with considerable affection. good kind beautiful lovely Sara

                                                            Ernest

HMD

In early 1940, the Dos Passoses moved to northern Virginia, near Washington, so that Dos Passos could do research at the Library of Congress. They put Beanie Kaeselau in a school there and remained until the end of the school year.

179. GERALD MURPHY to JOHN and KATY DOS PASSOS, New York, 21 February 1940

K & D:

We *enjoyed* so luncheon with you: and seeing Alexandria. How is the school working out? We'd sort of like to keep track, if you don't mind. Last night Joris Ivens showed the [Spanish] Earth and his new Chinese picture [*The Four Hundred Million*]. The E. holds up and the Chinese one is superb. Masses of Mongoloid Bees. Splendid,—but crushing to the spirits. Promise not to get official-minded in & about Washn. The papers and the world seem so full of it. That faulty instrument of precision the heart is becoming rarer. One seldom hears its voice any more. I'm sick of opinions for the moment, and opinions for the sake of having them. Sara's *pretty* well.—Such a surprising number of old wounds were opened by the Puppy's going. He was the last tie to the boys. It's a rotten unnecessary shame. We went to the Dog Show and saw again the Lhasa Terriers. They're awfully nice. Thibetan and dignified. We dream of leaving mid-March. We may send the car to Charleston, pick it up there and ride to Marineland and Hobe Sound. S. would go on to Key W. Is there a chance of our joining up any place. Keep us in mind. We miss & need you.

G.

Much love from all.
UVA

180. PAULINE HEMINGWAY to SARA MURPHY,
Key West [1 March 1940]

Dearest Mrs. Murphy,

Just ran across your husband's picture in Time and am inclosing it, although you have doubtless seen it yourself. Also, would like to be a little bitter about the way you haven't come down here. Wallace Stevens is here and Martha Dodd is coming tomorrow and John L. Lewis was here yesterday, but no Murphys. Lately it hasn't seem[ed] so bad to me here. I dont know why unless it makes me happy to see how miserable the northers make the tourists. And we have a new green snake, crisp and cool as a lettuce leaf, and he lives in a brown lunch basket on the bench in the front hall.

* * * * *

Dots denote the passage of SOME time. I was evidently writing you at the same time you were writing me. Since then the Dodds have come and are pretty bad, and the green snake escaped, so there is nothing left except rollar skating. Do you like that? I am so eager to have you come down here and so loath to urge you because by the end of March it's going to be pretty dull down here I'm afraid. Also, about then (just between you and Dowdow and me) I hope to be in the throes of the divorce. So far it is being held up by Ernest wanting to finish his book [For Whom the Bell Tolls]. Of course I can understand his wanting to finish it first, but the interim is a little nervous making to one not writing a book. And it keeps me from making any very definite plans, such as suggesting that we pop down to Mexico and see Jinny in, if her letters are an indication, her far from ideal situation. She says Mexico is full of the most terrible Americans, all of them with disentry. But she has doubtless told you all I know, as she wrote she had written you. But it might be fun to go down. Mexico IS something to see. Maybe you would go down, and stop by and see me on the way.

Or maybe you and G. would come down to Miami and I could come up and we could drink quietly in our rooms, or take in a race. So please keep me

246

informed of your plans and mine may be all changed by then. Would LOVE to see you. I felt terrible about Puppy and so did the children. I was surprised to find they had such a realization of what Puppy was and meant. You're certainly right about this life. But what can we do about it? I thought the Hudnut Success Course might help but when I dipped into it I couldn't answer the questions. Here are some of them:

Do you awaken mornings feeling "alive" and eager for what the day may bring?

Can you enter a room quietly and still get the attention of people in the room?

Do you feel confident and composed when the center of attention? !! (ANS. Wouldn't know)

Do men who see you casually ask to be introduced to you?

Do you find that you can awaken fresh interest in people who have known you for a long time?????????

So I am just going on muddling. The flower show opens today.

Love,

Pauline

HMD

181. KATY DOS PASSOS to SARA MURPHY, Alexandria, Virginia, 1 March 1940

Dearest Madam Puss,

Almost too dumb-smitten with suprize and pleasure to answer your letter. And the check for the boy Nero is the last straw that breaks this camel all up, loaded down as this camel is with Murphy favors. Mrs. Puss you are *too* good, and are keeping the angels up nights putting stars in your crown. I am keeping an Angel Book myself, where your name leads all the rest. Mrs. Scantified-Puss, thank you forever. I have bought the boy Tiberius a new hat, which he keeps on his head all day long, also gloves and pair of pants. He is actually *improving*. The Boy is behaving like a human and has for two days—Washed his face of his own free will yesterday; today said several polite things, such as "May I," "Please," and "All right, if you say so—"

Mrs. Puss, we've been struggling with plans, because crazy to make trip with youse, and after a little scene-shifting have arranged everything and Mrs. Puss we *can* meet you in Charleston March 23 on Plan Day, as planned, and proceed as indicated—at least to Marineland—I hope Honoria comes—

We'll arrive in the morning, complete with poodle and Plymouth—then "Shame on the false Etruscan who lingers in his home—when Porsena of Elusium is on the March to Rome—" We'll sniff every camellia in de ole souf—they don't smell, though, and put vine-leaves in our hair and brown up and slow down—You won't mind if I doze most of the time Ah hope. Ah do declare honey chile, Ah feels sleepy as a houn dawg most all day long—I would just love to lie out on a beach and drowse for *hours*. And hours. Perhaps a few dips in the sunny foam and then another refreshing nap—I think I've been talking too much for the past week—World events, war, politics, elections, the life history of the oyster, Hitler, Stalin, republicans, democrats, the delinquent child, whither are we drifting,—Just drift is all I want—You can't enjoy drifting if you try to find out whither—Think I will let Archie find out whither—I know it's somewhere in the stacks of the Congressional Library, and when Archie finds out he can send us a wire to Beaufort.

Dear Sara, I know so well how you must miss your sweet dog—He was such a delightful animal—I can't bear for you not to have him—darling, we're so sorry—he was the purest form of Pet, wasn't he—simply *made* to please, and yet a fine fellow in his own right—There never was such a little dog, and that's the only comfort I can think of, darling—You really had the dearest little dog in the world.

I went to see Ada today and she was sick in bed with the flu, looking very pale in her white fur jacket, and sniffing a croup kettle—She had a temperature and wouldn't go to bed but kept trotting around till really laid low. I'm going to call tomorrow and hope she's better—She said to give you her best love. Archie is now working nights. He appeared before the Senate and *wowed* them, Ada said. I'm sure he did—now he's putting crosses opposite his favorite appropriations, which will undoubtedly go through (Archie for President!) He admits he wants to be a Senator. He'd make a lovely Senator and once a Senator—! But says it would take a lot of back-work in Conn. Ada could sing for him at meetings—she could certainly sing him into the White House don't you think?—

Sara, thank you again—I loved your letter. Dos is writing too—We'll be there like flies. Watch for the Gordons!

So much Love

Katy

Tell Gerald Dos says he doesn't know much about places to stop, but the gardens will be very fine.

We are just finishing up the Ham—a perfectly *wonderful* ham—I never thanked you enough when they appeared—all those good things—it took us days to *realize*. More delicacies kept coming out of wrappings, like a fairy-tale table—We were as belly-gods, enjoying all things—

Love to Mr. Puss and 'Noria—X X X

UVA

The Murphys apparently met up with the Dos Passoses in Charleston as planned, after which they spent some time traveling in Florida—some of that time with Pauline Hemingway. Shortly after this trip, the Dos Passoses left for Ecuador. John Dos Passos was acting as secretary for the New World Resettlement Fund, an agency which was helping Spanish refugees resettle in South America.

182. GERALD and SARA MURPHY to JOHN and KATY DOS PASSOS, New York, 13 April 1940

D & K.:

Diagonally opposite Gluck's Bar on the St. A. [Augustine] square is a cigar store with a cigaritos selection. Try some 'K-Z!' Splendid. I love St. A. Superb stretch just N. May settle there. The Carolinas delapidated but handsome: the tobacco silos of logs: with shed around, outside oven, etc. Wilmington lovely. Had an oyster roast en route. 33° drop in 8 hrs. in Norfolk temperature with snow,—and us in tin-foil pants. Exciting 7 a.m. ferry. Love G.

Back in NY tonight. Such a lovely trip—Do you know a nice little house in (or near) provincetown for August?

Best love

Sara.

UVA

183. PAULINE HEMINGWAY to GERALD and SARA MURPHY, Key West [23 April 1940]

Dearest Mr. and Mrs. Murphy,

I hope you feel as fine after your Florida trip (you are in a cage, the monkeys are free) as I do. Fun with friends is just as good as blood letting—why do you suppose I almost wrote BED WETTING?—in that it seems to introduce a great calmness into the brain. I have gone around with quiet repose ever since I got back getting Things Done, with all the time in the back of my brain a pleasant feeling of excitement and adventures to come. I hope I am not just a victim of delusion. Anyway THEY can't take the feeling away. But we had a lovely time, and how well we ate and drank and swam, even in spite of the war, and I'm glad we did. It seems that Death in the Dardenelles is about to raise its hydra head. What about Honoria? Has she shaved off those long red nails? Or was that just young girls plotting over their kirsch?

Hoyningen-Huene and Horst came down here the day I got back and took a lot of pictures of Key West and caught me up with the gossip of the big world. Now Ernest's mother is here for a few days, painting a picture of Rest Beach. And it is blowing a rather nasty southeast breeze—there's a tropical disturbance out at sea.

Good-bye dear Sarah and Dowdow and thank you for taking me into the Florida jungles, including that little lukewarm dream of the South Seas. And seeing Katy and Dos. I am thinking of building you a little house down here to be already for you next year. Do you believe in the after world? My mother-in-law has a cousin who does automatic writing—has written ninety books by dead famous people—says we all have a guide, each his own personal guide, so that we can feel we are somehow linked with the beyond. All I can say is, mine has done a damn poor job. GUIDE. I'll take the Murphys.

Yours,

Pauline

HMD

184. GERALD MURPHY to F. SCOTT FITZGERALD, New York, 24 April 1940

Scott:—

On September 21st we got a wire from you which—to say the least—was disturbing. We answered it on the 22nd. You wrote us also on that day, but only to enlarge on your telegram. . . .

Since then no word.

Sara long ago convinced Celtic me that it's kinder (and more honest) to *tell* friends when you feel they're being a little unfriendly.

So I thought I'd write you.

And have.

You must *know* how long we've been fond of you and for how many reasons. . . .

*   *   *   *   *

We've just had three splendid weeks in the back-country of Florida (fabulous state!) with certain days at the amazing (deserted) giudeccas that are Palm and Miami Beach. Dos and Katy were with us till they set off for Ecuador. (Dos is arranging for farming space for the Spanish dispossessed.) We went to see Pauline and brought her away with us for a while. She seems to me forlorn. Few women are *capable* of *just* that. I guess women who really love have always been. Think back over great loves. . . .

Love from us all. . . .

Gerald.

PUL

Earlier in 1940 Woollcott had been acting in the West Coast touring company of The Man Who Came to Dinner *when he suffered a severe heart attack. After being hospitalized in California, he had returned to Lake Neshobee by June for a slow recuperation. Guinsburg was co-founder of the Viking Press, and he and his wife Alice summered at Antibes during the 1920s, at which time they met the Murphys.*

185. GERALD MURPHY TO ALEXANDER WOOLLCOTT, New York, 24 June 1940

Great White Heron (habitat N.A.):—

Don't let them make you breathe hard over the bushes' growing. Neshobee may not be *meant* to be a bosky dell. . . . Shrubbery's a gamble.

Les Guinzbourgs have given us your news. I wonder what feeling rested feels like to you. I'm glad you're being amenable. You are *not* glad. The Binghams, Les Guinze, Sara and I sat beside a pond (ours) in horizontal sun-light yesterday p.m. and talked of you with affection. Such things should be nourishment to one.

*   *   *   *   *

Archie is being pulled thin over what he calls "this blood and disaster". . . . His skull shows through and his eyes are farther away. . . .

For weeks I have waked up to the old nightmare that first Baoth and now

251

Patrick is dying. Will one's heart never touch bottom? Is there a point beyond which impotent rage can carry you? By noon of every day the brain has reached saturation. . . .

The Committee started by Wm Allen White has been some relief to one's sense of helplessness. Sara has procured and all but rolled up the loading plank onto the boats nine tons of Dried Milk. It has been received. Now the money (more) she's raised festers in a bank.

Noel (my brother's widow) was at Amiens and did a great job with the American Ambulance. She relayed supplies to a *mobile* Field Station.

I probably shouldn't have written this letter,—but I wanted to talk to you,

Aff'y.

Gerald.

HL

186. SARA MURPHY to ERNEST HEMINGWAY, East Hampton [29 July 1940]

Dearest Ernest,—I hear you are in N.Y.—& it would give us *such* pleasure if you would come down here to spend a few days. There is just us 3—& its very peaceful, & cool seabathing—There are a few of your friends nearby: the J. Allens, & Luis Q [Quintanilla] & his wife—& we would *so* love to see you again!—We are all fine, & hope you are? And I bet the book is magnificent— *Do* come for a couple of days anyway, if you can, possibly.

The MacLeishes are at Conway—Dos & Katy at Provincetown, Jinny in Mexico, & has Pauline gone to California? It's been *so* long since I heard from her.

We are going to N.Y. tomorrow (Tues—) but are coming down again by car *Thursday*—about 5 P.M. If you can come telephone me at our new apt *25 W. 54th St*. Columbus 5-0198 (we are in the phone book if you lose this)—and we can all motor down together—

We all so want to see you. (Honoria sends special love.) A bientôt—we hope—with love

Yr old shipmate

Sara.

JFK

187. F. SCOTT FITZGERALD to GERALD and SARA MURPHY, Encino, California [c. summer 1940]

Honey—that goes for Sara too:

I have written a dozen people since who mean nothing to me—writing you I was saving for good news. I suppose pride was concerned—in that personally and publicly dreary month of Sept. last about everything went to pieces all at once and it was a long uphill pull.

To summarize: I don't have to tell you anything about the awful lapses and sudden reverses and apparent cures and thorough poisoning effect of lung trouble. Suffice to say there were months with a high of 99.8, months at 99.6 and then up & down and a stabilization at 99.2 every afternoon when I could write in bed—and now for 2 1/2 months and one short week that may have been grip—nothing at all. With it went a psychic depression over the finances and the effect on Scotty and Zelda. There was many a day when the fact that you and Sara did help me at a desperate moment (and remember it was the *first* time I'd ever borrowed money in my life except for business borrowings like Scribners) seemed the only pleasant human thing that had happened in a world where I felt prematurely passed by and forgotten. The thousands that I'd given and loaned—well, after the first attempts I didn't even worry about that. There seem to be the givers & the takers and that doesn't change. So you were never out of my mind—but even so no more present than always because this was only one of so many things.

In the land of the living again I function rather well. My great dreams about this place are shattered and I have written half a novel [*The Last Tycoon*] and a score of satiric pieces that are appearing in the current Esquires about it. After having to turn down a bunch of well paid jobs while I was ill there was a period when no one seemed to want me for duck soup—then a month ago a producer asked me to do a piece of my own for a small sum ($2000) and a share in the profits. The piece is *Babylon Revisited*, an old and not bad Post story of which the child heroine was named Honoria! I'm keeping the name.

It looks good. I have stopped being a prophet (3rd attempt at spelling this) but I think I may be solvent in a month or so if the fever keeps subservient to what the doctors think is an exceptional resistance. Thank heaven I was able to keep Scottie at Vassar (She came twice to the New Weston to call but found you gone) because there was no other place for her. I think she will go on now for the four years.

Zelda is home since this week Tuesday—at her mothers in Montgomery. She has a poor pitiful life, reading the Bible in the old fashioned manner walking tight lipped and correct through a world she can no longer understand—playing with the pieces of old things as if a man a thousand years hence tried to reconstruct our civilization from a baroque cornice, a figurine from Trojans columns, an aeroplane wing and a page of Petrarch all picked up in the Roman forum. Part of her mind is washed clean & she is no one I ever knew (—This is all from letters and observations of over a year ago—I haven't been East since Spring.)

So now you're up to date on me and it wont be so long again. I might say by way of counter reproach that there's no word of any of *you* in your letter. It is sad about Pauline. Writing you today has brought back so much and I could weep very easily.

With Dearest Love,

Scott

HMD

188. GERALD MURPHY to F. SCOTT FITZGERALD, New York, 26 August 1940

Dear Scott:—

It was good to hear from you,—but I do not like to feel that you *consider* yrself ill. I can't believe you *are*. Don't think me without heart:—but just as you—so have I—seen much illness around me. Your account of your condition for some reason recalled to me my own surprise the day you came to see us in New York wearing rubbers—which you removed and *remembered* to put on again when you left. It seemed so unlike my idea of you. It still is.

No, but I *do* feel that Yeats (in his last letters) was probably right. " 'Bitter and gay' that is the heroic mood. When there is despair, public or private, when settled order seems lost, people look for strength within or without. So many young writers who seem the new movement *look* for strength in Marxian socialism, or in Major Douglas. They want marching feet. I think that the true poetic movement of our time is towards some heroic discipline. People much occupied with health or morality lose their heroic ecstasy.

Wine and women and song
To us they belong
To us the bitter and gay."

What cruel sad days in Europe!
I'm glad Zelda has been well enough to be at home. There's probably some

unrecognized comfort for her in it . . . like Ernest's feeling of being sick as a child and being put to bed by his mother . . .

Aff'y—

Gerald.

PUL

189. F. Scott Fitzgerald to Gerald Murphy, Hollywood, 14 September 1940

Dear Gerald:

I suppose anybody our age suspects what is emphasized—so let it go. But I was flat in bed from April to July last year with day and night nurses. Anyhow as you see from the letterhead [Twentieth Century-Fox Film Corporation], I am now in official health.

I find, after a long time out here, that one develops new attitudes. It is, for example, such a slack *soft* place—even its pleasure lacking the fierceness or excitement of Provence—that withdrawal is practically a condition of safety. The sin is to upset anyone else, and much of what is known as "progress" is attained by more or less delicately poking and prodding other people. This is an unhealthy condition of affairs. Except for the stage-struck young girls people come here for negative reasons—all gold rushes are essentially negative— and the young girls soon join the vicious circle. There is no group, however small, interesting as such. Everywhere there is, after a moment, either corruption or indifference. The heroes are the great corruptionists or the supremely indifferent—by whom I mean the spoiled writers, [Ben] Hecht, Nunnally Johnson, Dotty, Dash Hammet etc. That Dotty has embraced the church and reads her office faithfully every day does not affect her indifference. She is one type of commy Malraux didn't list among his categories in *Man's Hope*—but nothing would disappoint her so vehemently as success.

I have a novel [*The Last Tycoon*] pretty well on the road. I think it will baffle and in some ways irritate what readers I have left. But it is as detached from me as *Gatsby* was, in intent anyhow. The new Armegeddon, far from making everything unimportant, gives me a certain lust for life again. This is undoubtedly an immature throw-back, but it's the truth. The gloom of all causes does not affect it—I feel a certain rebirth of kinetic impulses—however misdirected.

Zelda dozes—her letters are clear enough—she doesn't want to leave

255

Montgomery for a year, so she says. Scottie continues at Vassar—she is nicer now than she has been since she was a little girl. I haven't seen her for a year but she writes long letters and I feel closer to her than I have since she was little.

I *would* like to have some days with you and Sara. I hear distant thunder about Ernest and Archie and their doings but about you I know not a tenth of what I want to know.

With affection,

Scott

HMD

190. F. Scott Fitzgerald to Gerald and Sara Murphy, Hollywood, 14 September 1940

Dear Gerald and Sara—

I can't tell you how this has worried me. This is the first *personal* debt I've ever owed and I'm glad to be able to pay back $150 out of the $350.

Your generosity made me able to send Scottie back to Vassar last Fall. This year she is the Harper's Bazaar representative and has sold stories to various magazines and things are in every way easier. But she *was* the type to whom a higher education meant everything and it would have been heartbreaking not to give it to her.

With love to you both and *so much*
gratitude,

Scott

HMD

191. Gerald Murphy to F. Scott Fitzgerald, New York, 3 October 1940

Scott:—

Yr. letter was such a pleasure to receive. We miss not being able to talk to you these days. There are so few people who are capable of ruminating all that now happens to us in this reeling world. As Yeats says: "We have no longer reverie . . ." Conversation becomes discussion, then argument and you find yr-self aligned—suddenly—against an array of someone else's sacred cows. . . .

We share in retrospect yr. feelings about Hollywood. We stood alone in a community made of tight little sets all of whom distrusted each other. Their insecurity and fear of official disfavour was depressing. With a veneer of cosmopolitanism they are hopelessly provincial & dread any risk. . . .

Unluckily we missed Scottie the last time she was here. Please ask her to call us the next time if she has a moment. We really want to see her. She'll do remarkable things one day.

Sara joins me in love to you—and Honoria too. You are one of the people of whom we are very fond. We think of you much.

Gerald.

p.s. Yr. cheque gave me a turn somehow. I wish we could feel that we'd done you a service instead of making you feel some kind of torment. Please dismiss the *thought!* G.

PUL

192. GERALD MURPHY to JOHN and KATY DOS PASSOS,
New York, 3 December 1940

D & K—

How well I remember the day we passed all that [Italian] coast. How strangely far-off and inaccessible it seems now. (The Greeks are the highest paid soldiers in the world. Why? Because some of them get as high as 20 guineas a day.) Tin-green with envy I was at the report of yr. bathing. We had hoped to steal up there but Sara got to putting Swan Cove & its garden to rest for the winter and Honoria trying for a part. She got it & opens Jan. 6th. There are 6 girls who play a chorus. Guild production so she'll learn a lot. [John] Houseman is directing. She really wanted a job and just *went out* for this one.[1] How complete the formula already was for making up the legend of Jesu. I'd forgotten all those Oriental & Greek gods that died, were buried and rose again. . . . How limited imagination is really. We are certainly back in the groove to-day,—but one senses a long arc of undercurrent which is progressively revolutionary. We miss you. Work hard.

G.

UVA

---

1. Honoria had a part in Philip Barry's play, *Liberty Jones*, which had a brief run on Broadway in early 1941.

193. KATY DOS PASSOS to SARA MURPHY,
Provincetown, 6 December 1940

Dearest Mrs. Puss,

The seagulls are blowing around this house in the wildest disorder and the woods are full of hunters blazing away at everything that moves, so it's as much as your life is worth to go out. Dos and I were nearly bagged yesterday. We couldn't bear to stay in so went for a walk but in the effort to keep out of the woods we got into a terrible half-frozen marsh and lost our way and found ourselves as dusk drew on wallowing in the mire *on all fours,* looking more like a couple of escaping deer than if we had dressed for it. We could hear the shots fired in the woods all around us but there was nothing to do but plunge on and ascend a sand-hill, still on our hands and knees, waiting every moment for the fatal bullet. When we finally got back on the road we'd practically been through the whole Albanian campaign. I kept thinking how Mr. Puss would never have let this happen if he had been along as I cannot imagine him losing his head to the extent of going several miles on all fours in a frozen marsh in the deer season. It was like that day we rowed up the Inland Waterway in the rain and were beached—there was nothing to do but go on under increasing hardship to an unknown goal.

We "kepen in solitariness" here as every one who can has pulled out for Florida or Manhattan. The only news is that I had a new colored maid to whom all our ways were a continual astonishment so she never addressed me without adding Oh my Gawd. "Mrs Dos Passos oh my Gawd does the dawg drink coffee? Mrs Dos Passos Oh my Gawd is that the way you does the oysters? Mrs Dos Passos oh my Gawd did you say *sour* cream?" So everyone in town has taken to calling me "MrsDosPassosOh MY GAWD."

We are so delighted about Honoria. I'm sure she will be very telling in the role. We've been missing you all mighty bad. Missed you terrible on the day of election [President Roosevelt won his third term]. I never saw the town in such a ferment. There was weeping and gnashing of teeth among the Wilkie men and Mr. Hallett the banker practically got down on his bended knees to all the bank's minor customers to beg for Wilkie. Now that his great tragedy has overwhelmed the country he seems more cheerful about his chance of survival, but the Wilkieites still meet on Tuesday in the Truro Town Hall to keep democracy alive.

Darlings we are coming to New York Tuesday and will be at the Lafayette and will call you up immediately as won't last much longer without seeing you. Dos has been working awfully hard and longs for the bright lights and gabble in bars.

Aren't the Greeks a wonderful little people? Well I must go out now and help Dos put up the storm windows as the sea is coming over the bulkhead in great sloshes. It's really wonderful weather and very bright and exciting.

Much love of the very best quality to you and Miss and Mister Puss and Dos says the same.

Always as ever your devoted

Katy

UVA

194. GERALD MURPHY to ALEXANDER WOOLLCOTT,
New York, 26 December 1940

Alexis:—

I thought of you at once when news about Scott came . . . You had spoken so *affectionately* of him the other night . . . His letters to me recently have been so sad and so beautiful . . . Sara and I are flying to Maryland to-morrow to the funeral . . . Little Scottie is tragic and bewildered tho' she says that she has thought for so long that *every* day he would die for some reason . . . I thought of him as imperishable somehow . . . Zelda seized upon his death as the only reality that had pierced the membrane since they separated . . . gave weird orders for the disposition of the body . . . then collapsed. She is not allowed to come to the funeral . . . Sheila Graham has wired that she wants to see us and she arrives by plane Saturday . . . Scott is being refused burial in the Frances Scott Key family plot because of his excommunication from the Church at the time of the publication of "This Side of Paradise." In *this* day and age!!

I wonder if he wanted to die. I fear. . . . How cruelly the world needs the beauty of his mind . . . and its tenderness . . . He was a poet . . . and looked like one . . .

Affectionately,

Gerald.

He was so fearless . . .
HL

Hemingway and Martha Gellhorn were married on 21 November in Cheyenne, Wyoming. They honeymooned in New York City at the Hotel Barclay and then left to have Christmas at Finca Vigía in Cuba. Gellhorn had agreed to cover the war in China for Collier's magazine, so Hemingway got his own assignment with Ralph Ingersoll's PM tabloid.

195. ERNEST HEMINGWAY to SARA MURPHY,
Havana [c. late December 1940]

Dearest Sara;

It was lovely to get your letter. New York was a madhouse while we were there but in any kind of a madhouse I would find plenty of room to go and see you and Gerald but I felt sort of strange about the honeymoon business too and the rush of people anxious to shift their allegiance from Pauline to Martha had me sort of disgusted too. So I didn't go to see Ruth Allen nor you nor other oldest friends (I have no closer friend than you) because it seemed sort of vulgar. Am writing this about as clearly as I talk. Which as you know can be very unclear when dealing with subtle things. I mean I didn't want to strain your loyalties altho I always marry good wives as you know. But I think you and me felt about the same and I love you the same as always and will see you in New York this time toward the end of January.

We are very happy and have a fine time. And it is something too to not just be on the run and to be so that Jinny cannot harm you and to be able to tell everybody to go to hell again. Not to mention how jolly it is to have some money after long time no money although I never noticed it when didn't have it except that it wasn't there.

Although the only things I care about really like caviar and France and Africa you can't go to anymore. Goddamn it don't you wish we were this nigger rich before they locked up all those things?

Anyway we are going out to the East just like Somerset Maugham only between man and woman and they say it is very fine. Marty is going two weeks ahead of me because she has to do some work in Manila and then I will meet her in Hong Kong I have always wanted to smoke opium and have sing song girls clustered around and I think it is now too late for me to be corrupted by these vices and life seems very short so am going to have very good very bad time before they lock up the east on us too. Maybe I can find something as good as caviar. I wish there was some vice that tastes as good.

Wasn't it a hell of a book? [*For Whom the Bell Tolls*] It is just about three times as good a book as I can write so am in no particular hurry to write another and maybe after I get into my opium epoch I won't even have to. Although they say it ties up your bowells so I may have to cut it out.

How are you my Sara? It will be fine to see you. I guess we must be the only two non serious people left. I am so serious in my work that cannot be serious in life anymore. Was explaining to Patrick that everytime I sell hundred thousand copies I forgive some son of a bitch and when sell one million would forgive Max Eastman. But Patrick said, "No Papa. I would prefer that we leave it as it is and that our ancestors fight his ancestors."

The kids are fine. I will give you a good picture of them in N.Y. Give my best love to Honoria and love to Gerald and to you.

We will have big party and I will break in my opium pipe

Much love

Ernest

I feel as you do about Scott. Poor Scott. Yes Scotty is the one to help now. No one could ever help Scott but you and Gerald did more than anyone.

HMD

196. ZELDA FITZGERALD to GERALD and SARA MURPHY, Montgomery, Alabama [c. late December 1940–January 1941]

Dear Sara and Gerald—

Your devoted remembrance of Scott means so much to me. He cared so deeply for his friends and always had plans for better happinesses and more auspicious rendez-vous, that were to bring them closer to him; he is somewhere grateful to you for this last tribute.

Those tragicly ecstatic years when the pockets of the world were filled with pleasant surprises and people still thought of life in terms of their right to a good time are now about to wane. Maybe Times pass into less eclectic, more imperative, easier (in that they are more definite) yet more exacting category and we will be better able to live for the more rigorous rules to live by. Scott, as exponent of the school of bitter necessities that followed the last world war, gave the era a tempo and a plot from which it might dramatize itself (or even let things go) with as good a grace as could be salvaged. Maybe, this time, we'll all be more righteous.

I grieve for his brilliant talent, his faithful effort to keep me under the best of very expensive care and Scottie in school; his devotion to those that he felt were contributing to the aesthetic and spiritual purposes of life—and for his generous and vibrant soul that never spared itself, and never found anything too much trouble save the fundamentals of life itself.

That he wont be there to arrange nice things and tell us what to do is grievous to envisage. Though we have not been much together of recent years, he was as comprehensive and intelligent and gratifying a friend as I could ever have found—

and he loved you dearly

Thanks again—

Devotedly

Zelda

P.S. Also, I am most grateful to [you] for remembering Scottie so thoughtfully and generously at Christmas. She will find more uses than one would care to itemize for the money, I know; and was most appreciative.

HMD

PART THREE
1941 — 1964

Back There
Where We Were

The trouble with life is that about the time you begin to think what the
trouble with life is you begin to find out. And about the time you begin
to find out you find out that life has lost interest in *you*. Turned its back
on you. Like this day of off-shore wind with the sounds of the rail-road
yard and the faint yelping of dogs and Ada's voice high and pure and
sweet singing the chant Dissident of Stravinsky all blown out and away
from me out to the sea and the shoulders of the little waves running
backward up the slope of the sea away from me with their bundles of
white in their arms leaving nothing behind but me here at this table and
an empty page and a white butterfly falling falling falling toward the sea.
Turns its back on you!

      ARCHIBALD MACLEISH, *Freedom Is the Right to Choose*

The Dos Passoses continued to travel throughout the United States during
the 1940s as John Dos Passos reported on the American wartime scene for his
"People at War" series in *Harpers* magazine. He and Katy continued to enjoy
both their Provincetown home and their friendship with the Murphys during
these years, and their mutual correspondence dwells upon both the "undercurrent . . . progressively revolutionary" and simple domestic concerns. The
Murphys and Dos Passoses traveled together, often south, and they visited
together in New York City, East Hampton, or Provincetown. Sara especially
loved the Dos Passoses' Provincetown home, which had a large glassed-in
room overlooking the water. "More people speak of that room of yours,"
Gerald wrote Katy on 26 January 1942. "It has—or leaves—an indelible

memory. It's the light from the windows and that joint feeling of nearness to the water and a cabin'd feeling of protection from it." Gerald Murphy never overcame his disenchantment with New York City, and his talk of the seasons' changes and of activities there often underscored his desire to get away. Occasionally, his thoughts turned to the Riviera, his heart " 'sick for the palms and the sweet rain' as Mr. MacLeish, the Poet, says."[1]

By the 1940s, Mr. MacLeish, "the Poet," had become more of the public man than the artist. When he had left his editorial post with *Fortune* magazine in 1939 to become the Librarian of Congress, he reorganized the administrative structure of the Library to make it more accessible to the public. As Van Wyck Brooks wrote Lewis Mumford on 2 March 1941, "MacLeish seems to be doing wonders at the Library, in the way of making it an active center."[2] Simultaneous with the librarianship, MacLeish served as Director of the Office of Facts and Figures (1941–1942) and then Assistant Director of the Office of War Information (1942), posts established by Roosevelt to aid in the American war effort. When MacLeish left the Library of Congress in 1944, he became Assistant Secretary of State until 1945, and then he became involved with the United Nations Educational Scientific and Cultural Organization (UNESCO). Throughout these years of public service, MacLeish was subjected to criticism by his fellow writers, particularly those who felt that an artist betrayed his art when he turned to public speech. Some never forgave MacLeish for shifting his political and artistic stance during the 1930s and 1940s and labeled him an opportunist.

MacLeish's ideas regarding the artist's role in society did indeed undergo a radical change, reflected in two key works, "The Invocation to the Social Muse" (1932) and "The Irresponsibles" (1940). "The Invocation to the Social Muse," which emphasized that poetry is too intimate for causes, became the grounds for both Marxist criticism and artistic praise. John Peale Bishop, for one, applauded MacLeish for this stand taken at a time when so many had "deserted literature to engage in polemics." "It is too often assumed that if a poet does not mix in politics," Bishop wrote, "he is refusing in some cowardly fashion to face life." "The truth is," Bishop concluded, "a poet has shown enough courage if he can face his own life. And it requires a great ignorance of literary history not to be aware that politics is the besetting sin of poets and one which has done them and their craft more harm than all forms of drunkenness and debauchery put together."[3]

When MacLeish published *Public Speech* in 1936, however, he no longer deserved Bishop's categorical praise. He had become an open spokesman for American democracy because he believed the events of the 1930s made it imperative for the artist, and particularly the poet, to act. Poetry best ordered and made recognizable to man his political world, and it was up to the artists and the intellectuals of America to respond through their art to a time of crisis.

"The Irresponsibles" expressed this idea unequivocably, and writers throughout the war years continued to accuse MacLeish of both rigidity and literary
irresponsibility. As Edmund Wilson argued, a good writer cannot choose his
moods "as if they were suits from a well-stocked wardrobe."[4]

MacLeish never fully outlived this image of the artist corrupted by too close
an identification with public issues, although he came to understand the accu-
sation. "It was not that the artist was Communist, or 'a clerical fascist,' or a
New Dealer," he said in 1958, it was that "he had proven himself 'aesthet-
ically unreliable.' Having violated 'the American mystique,' he was not a pure
artist. He was, instead, a political man."[5] As a political man then, and a man
of public service, MacLeish had little time for either his art or his friends during the war years. His hours became consumed by the administrative burdens
under which he sometimes chafed, and with endless rounds of public speaking. When he did see his friends, including the Murphys, it was often at one of
his own lectures or for a brief dinner or concert in either New York City or
Washington. As the correspondence between the Dos Passoses and the Murphys during 1940–1946 centered upon domestic concerns, the letters between Gerald Murphy and MacLeish during these same years confronted the
war's presence and questioned what best to do about it. Murphy had become
involved with an Emergency Rescue Mission which tried to help artists such
as Picasso and Léger get visas for America, and he tried to use Mark Cross to
arouse public awareness by way of window posters and displays. When
Vladimir Orloff needed authority to leave Monaco in early 1945, he cabled
Murphy hoping that MacLeish in Washington could make the necessary connections. Murphy's follow-up letter to MacLeish (21 February 1945) provides
an interesting glimpse of the French Riviera during wartime. As the war in
Europe and the Pacific intensified, life at the Villa America apparently continued quietly under the loyal care of Joseph Revello and his family.

When the war ended in 1945, MacLeish contemplated a return to the East.
He had tired of the hassles of life in Washington and sometimes regretted his
departure from the purer literary life of his cohorts. Yet as his letters during
those war years reveal, he had felt a commitment to his government work as
long as the country remained at war. It was his own form of service, just as
Gerald Murphy had finally settled for doing what he could through his connections in New York. As for John Dos Passos, he continued his American
wartime reporting by going overseas to the Pacific front in late 1944. He wrote
Gerald and Sara on 21 February 1945 from "a ruined sugar plantation set
among big trees draped with Bougainvillea and an immense growth of philodendron" in the Phillipines, and his letter conveys despair over the inevitable
carnage of war. Dos Passos continued to report on the war's bleak aftermath
in Europe until he returned home in the fall of 1947. Back in America, on a
Massachusetts highway, he would confront his own personal devastation

when a truck he failed to see off to the right of the road sheared off the top of the car, killing Katy immediately and leaving Dos Passos without the sight of one eye. The day following the accident, Gerald Murphy had to leave for a Mark Cross buying trip in England, but he kept thinking about Dos Passos throughout the trip, as Sara back home tried to be with Dos Passos as much as possible. She and Honoria, and also the Lloyd Lowndeses, traveled with Dos Passos to Virginia and then also out west in October. Dos Passos looked to travel for solace. By the following fall, he would be in Havana, where he saw Hemingway briefly on the day Hemingway was leaving for his first trip back to Europe since covering the war during 1944. Dos Passos left Havana himself shortly thereafter and spent some time in Brazil and Argentina in order to report for *Life* magazine on his travels. He described to Sara (7 November 1948) the "large synthetic city" of Buenos Aires which reminded Dos Passos of "the Paris of the Parc Monceau region," and he thanked her for remembering the one-year anniversary of Katy's death by placing flowers on her grave in Truro, Massachussetts: "After a year the void is as deep as ever."

Following Katy's death, Dos Passos moved in with Lloyd and Marion Lowndes at Snedens, an exclusive New York community on the Hudson River. The Murphys soon joined him there when they bought a house adjoining the Lowndeses' property. Gerald Murphy spent several years and much of the remaining family money on the restoration of Cheer Hall, the former home of New York Mayor William Merrit. Merrit had built Cheer Hall in 1700, and it later served briefly as the capital while certain state papers awaited transfer to Kingston. Gerald Murphy researched the house's history, and his desire to restructure it became a preoccupation. He seemed bent on finding a home for Sara and himself which might give them a sense of place. By the end of World War II, Gerald continued to believe what he had told Sara a decade earlier (18 April 1936) that "outside of a man and a woman, and children and a house and a garden—there's nothing much." As Murphy continued to commute from the city, this small Rockland County community would become home until 1963.

In the summer of 1949, Dos Passos would marry Elizabeth ("Betty") Holdridge, whose husband had been killed in an automobile accident in 1946. She had one son Christopher ("Kiffy"), and she and Dos Passos had met in Snedens Landing. As the Dos Passoses were settling into the farming life at Spence's Point, Virginia, where Dos Passos had inherited property, Archibald MacLeish was toying with the idea of going into academic life. He and his family had returned to Conway in 1947, and MacLeish was in the midst of planning some winter lectures when he heard from Hemingway, who had been traveling through Italy showing his new wife, Mary Welsh, his old haunts. He had met her in Europe in 1944, and they had married in 1946, after Martha Gellhorn had granted him a divorce. In a reminiscent mood,

Hemingway wrote MacLeish a surprise letter. It was good to hear from Hemingway "in the old voice with the old kick in it," MacLeish wrote on 1 December 1948, and it seemed to him that Hemingway was "damn well married and no horrors the way you used to have them in all that empty sun at Antibes that summer [1926]." MacLeish reported that Conway was "still wonderful," but he regretted not being able to "see the water and its water I want. Somehow I seem to have buggered my life up that way and I don't see what I can do about it." MacLeish reemphasized in his postscript to Hemingway that getting his letter was "grand." "I feel fine about a lot of the best years of my life now. Formerly I didn't. I'm obleeged to you—more than that."6

Often now these friends would feel a strong nostalgia about the past and a recognition of time's passing; and for Gerald Murphy, the feeling became the most poignant during the fall months. As Murphy reflected upon a strange feeling of time suspended, MacLeish would write him to say that while "October is the time for change . . . the change had not come. . . . We await it, our hearts beating faster than the season." Murphy would write Dos Passos to say how grateful he felt to MacLeish "for his ability to think and write about the feelings one has in relation to nature in the American scene. So few poets today are willing to or can do so." For Murphy, and for the others as well, the nostalgia gradually became associated with an American more than a European past, underscoring the fact that none of these expatriates could have escaped an American identification even had they wanted to. Every artist "interested in living inside" himself, Gertrude Stein once said, has two countries—the one where he belongs and the one in which he lives really.7 Each of these artists, to varying degrees, lived inwardly, but each finally belonged to America.

Gerald Murphy elaborated on this idea in his 31 October 1951 letter to Dos Passos. As he flew the width of the American continent from New York to California, he reflected on the vast landscape passing underneath and on his own American identity. Murphy's "American Letter," written over two decades after MacLeish's "American Letter" to him, may have been prompted by his finally laying Europe to rest the previous year. With the war over, and Sara vowing she could not go back, Gerald had decided he would sell Villa America, and that he would have to return alone. He did not think he wanted to see the Villa again, he confessed to Sara (23 May 1950) "especially if it's sold. . . . I guess it's right to preserve a memory if one can." Essentially he kept seeing "Patrick at his little garden." When Gerald did get to the Villa by late June, it was in many ways just as he had remembered it, and he was not sorry he had come. The place with its "compelling beauty" overcame all his senses, as it had the very first time the Murphys had seen it.

Throughout Murphy's stay that summer, he would be struck by the way the war had defaced Europe and by how radically different all that was coming in the place of what they had known was from what they and their friends had experienced. He also came to feel that despite change there was also changelessness. Writing to Sara from Paris on a calm summer evening (26 June 1950), alone "among begonias and geraniums as of yore" with the moon "just over the roof tops," Gerald Murphy would feel again the power of Paris, "for which there is no substitute." "I see you here," he told Sara, "not in the past but in the future. You will come and find what was always here and will continue to be. Nothing changes." He would reiterate this idea two years later when he told Ellen Barry (14 November 1952): "By and large what we did had a kind of personal style. I don't see its like around anywhere to-day."

Throughout the 1950s, some of this nostalgia for the past would be quickened as the death of old friends reminded them of life's passing and of relationships which, for one reason or another, had become strained. Gerald Murphy's relationship with Archibald MacLeish had cooled during the 1950s, primarily because, as MacLeish saw it, he had given Murphy good cause to write him off. "I didn't behave well," he told Hemingway in 1958. "Numerous occasions, as you know, I haven't."[8] The particular occasion which caused a breach in the relationship seemed to have occurred in late 1953. The Murphys and MacLeishes had been vacationing together in Antigua when Sara took ill with bronchial flu and had to cancel their planned activities. Archibald MacLeish apparently felt that the Murphys had overreacted to the illness, and a quarrel developed which would not be resolved until after 1958, despite MacLeish's attempts to overlook it in 1956. He wrote Gerald Murphy on 3 June: "Perhaps the time will come when you will find it possible again [to see me]."

As it turned out, they did see each other again in 1958 when they both attended Richard Myers's funeral. MacLeish described to Hemingway that September how he had sat "between Gerald and Sarah whom haven't seen for maybe two years. . . . I felt very sad and far off somehow sitting between them with no relationship anymore except of Sarah's warmth and generosity and thinking about the years when I knew Dick and everything off at the back of those years. The only friends you make really are the ones you make when you are young—or so, anyway, of my life—and you keep them but don't keep them. I mean they are always anyway your friends because they once were but only in memory. When you see them again you go back there where they were."[9]

Ironically, Hemingway was at work at this time on the memoirs which would implicate several friends from the younger days in his later unhappiness. In *A Moveable Feast*, written during late 1957 and 1958, years when he felt both physically weak and psychologically vulnerable, Hemingway devoted a chapter to the "nightmare winter" which preceded his divorce from Hadley, speaking in no uncertain terms of Dos Passos—the "sort of pilot fish who goes ahead of" the rich—and of the Murphys. Dos Passos, "sometimes a little deaf, sometimes a little blind, but always smelling affable," had talked up the Murphys to the then skeptical Hemingway as "the good, the attractive, the charming, the soon-beloved, the generous, the understanding rich who have no bad qualities" until "they have passed and taken the nourishment they needed." They came, said Hemingway, only when there was a certainty of linking up with success. "They never wasted their time nor their charm on something that was not sure. Why should they? Picasso was sure and of course had been before they had ever heard of painting. They were sure of another painter [Léger]. Many others." And this year they became sure about Hemingway's future greatness because they had the word of the pilot fish whom they "loved and trusted . . . because he was shy, comic, elusive, already in production, and because he was an unerring pilot fish." Hemingway himself trusted him, "as I would trust the Corrected Hydrographic Office Sailing Directions for the Mediterranean, say, or the tables in *Brown's Nautical Almanac.*"

> The pilot fish leaves of course. He is always going somewhere, or coming from somewhere, and he is never around for very long. He enters and leaves politics or the theater in the same way he enters and leaves countries and people's lives in his early days. He is never caught and he is not caught by the rich. Nothing ever catches him and it is only those who trust him who are caught and killed. He has the irreplaceable early training of the bastard and a latent and long denied love of money. He ends up rich himself, having moved one dollar's width to the right with every dollar that he made.

When Hemingway met the Murphys, he became immediately taken by them,

> as trusting and as stupid as a bird dog who wants to go out with any man with a gun, or a trained pig in a circus who has finally found someone who loves and appreciates him for himself alone. That every day should be a fiesta seemed to me a marvelous discovery. I even read aloud the part of the novel that I had rewritten [*The Sun Also Rises*], which is about as low as a writer can get and much more dangerous for him as a writer than glacier skiing unroped before the full winter snowfall has set over the crevices.
>
> When they said, 'It's great, Ernest. Truly it's great. You cannot know the thing it has,' I wagged my tail in pleasure and plunged into the fiesta concept of life to see if I could not bring some fine attractive stick back, instead of thinking, 'If these bastards like it what is wrong with it?'[10]

While it is difficult to determine why Hemingway would turn so brutally and so publicly against his friends, it had been a conscious break with Dos

Passos, and perhaps Hemingway felt his slurs against Dos Passos's character were just vindication for what he saw as Dos Passos's treason. Just months before his first break with Dos Passos over the situation in Spain, Hemingway had modeled the novelist Richard Gordon in *To Have and Have Not* (1937) after him, even though Arnold Gingrich had warned him that he "clearly libeled" Dos Passos accordingly. Hemingway argued then that this was no problem as he could always get around Dos. But when Hemingway read Dos Passos's *Chosen Country* (1951), based upon both Dos Passos's and Katy's early lives, the tables had turned. The character of George Elbert Warner, an "Indian-like boy with dirty fingernails" who joins the Marine Corps, was drawn from Katy's description to Dos Passos of her childhood days with Hemingway in Michigan, and Hemingway was outraged. He wrote Katy's brother Bill Smith that his Cuban residence housed "a pack of fierce dogs and cats trained to attack one-eyed Portuguese bastards who write lies about their friends." By 1958, Hemingway felt he had just cause to destroy his one-time friend in print.[11]

With the Murphys, Hemingway seemed to feel both that they had taken a proprietary interest in him and that they had misdirected him. In a portion of *A Moveable Feast* deleted from final publication, he elaborated upon and somewhat softened his outright attack. They had failed him, finally, in not telling him when he was doing wrong, particularly in leaving Hadley.

> It wasn't that the decisions were wrong although they all turned out badly finally from the same fault of character that made them. If you deceive and lie with one person against another you will eventually do it again. *I had hated these rich because they had backed me and encouraged me when I was doing wrong.* But how could they know it was wrong and had to turn out badly when they had never known all the circumstances? It was not their fault. It was only their fault for coming into other people's lives. They were bad luck for people but they were worse luck to themselves and they lived to have all their bad luck finally; to the very worst end that all bad luck could go.[12]

When Sara Murphy heard of Hemingway's illness and hospitalization in the spring of 1961, she wrote him one last letter which ironically reinforced the virile image of Hemingway the man and the writer that he could no longer sustain. Almost one month earlier, Dos Passos had sent a similar note after years of scant communication. He hoped that Hemingway's series of hospital stays was not going to become "a habit," and urged him to "take it easy there."[13] The brevity of these notes reveals the void which had formed over the years between these once-close friends. When Dos Passos had written Hemingway upon hearing of Pauline's sudden death in 1951 from a tumor of the adrenal medulla, he underscored that sense of a time and of a friendship no longer vital. "Lord it seems longer than half a lifetime ago, when I first met the darkhaired Pfeiffer girls with you in Paris," he wrote. "October's a month when everything seems far away and long ago."[14] It seemed fitting that when Dos Passos read of Hemingway's death, he was traveling in the country which both drew together and separated these two authors. Dos Passos wrote Sara from Bailen, Spain, in August 1961: "Until I read of his poor death I didn't realize how fond I'd been of the old Master of Mt. Kisco. In Madrid I found myself in places I'd been with him."[15]

When Sara learned that Hemingway was dead, she did not take it well. "Sara is repairing slowly," Gerald told Calvin Tomkins, "but it's been a wretched business. Ernest's death affected her deeply. She had written him ten days before assuring him that his illness would pass and that it was unlike him to be ill. Apparently he decided he wouldn't wait to find out."[16] Just as Sara had tried to will away the sickness of her sons (chanting "Breathe, Baoth, Breathe," as he lay dying), she tried to do the same for Hemingway. By his death, as with the other deaths, she felt betrayed.

In the spring of 1963, the Murphys sold Cheer Hall and retired to East Hampton to enjoy the late spring and summer months. They had their regrets about selling the house, but it had become burdensome of late. Its "slippery road, remoteness,—little or no help," along with the home's oppressiveness during the summer months, all conspired to make the move seem inevitable.[17] "We like Sneden's better when the leaves are off the trees," Sara told Dos Passos during their last fall there. "The house is so *dark* with all that foliage." Having always believed it good to "leave a place before it leaves you," they sorted through their belongings—"a fearful accumulation of *stuff*"—and shipped most of their furniture to Honoria's new home outside of Washington, D. C.[18] "Screening the accumulated possessions of 48 mortal years of marriage," the Murphys discovered a box of "remarkable letters" from "all those of our era Sara had saved."[19]

Added to those letters, and rounding out this book, are the letters written between Archie MacLeish and Gerald Murphy during the last two years of Gerald's life. Following their reunion at Richard Meyers's funeral, they would bury their hurts to realize anew the enduring value of this relationship—a relationship which continued to intensify as Gerald Murphy's death drew closer. "I have a constant and urgent need to talk to you—hear you talk," MacLeish wrote on 26 June [1964]. "The process of getting older throws one more & more, in one's deepest self, on the friends (& how few they are) with whom one has lived through this curious journey (to nowhere? somewhere? where?). Again & again as I feel the loss of myself I find myself thinking that you would understand this—perhaps only you—& whether you know the loss in yourself or not." As these last letters compellingly demonstrate, Murphy did know this loss as he also knew the inestimable value of the relationship.

When MacLeish brought him a copy of his play, *J.B.* (a modern version of the Job story written with Gerald Murphy in mind), he hoped that its message regarding grace under pressure would lend Murphy additional inner strength. Murphy saw the irony implicit in MacLeish's giving him this work at this time, his life so close to its finish, and he wished "it were not so late."

The *New York Times* on 18 October 1964 noted Gerald Murphy's death with a long obituary. He had given up "a promising career as a painter" in order to clear the Mark Cross Company of debt, it stated, and while he set up innovative trends for the company, he never found the work congenial and retired with relief in the late 1950s.[20] He had not really ended his painting career in obscurity, however. "His few paintings existed and were beginning to make their existence felt," MacLeish said. The Dallas Museum for Contemporary Arts exhibited five of Murphy's paintings in 1960 in a show called "American Genius in Review," and from this showing along with the recognition of art critics Rudi Blesh and Douglas MacAgy, the Museum of Modern Art in New York learned of Murphy's work, regretting they had not heard about it sooner. MacLeish gave to the museum Murphy's *Wasp and Pear*, and it was soon hanging "alongside paintings by Léger and Picasso." Ten years following Murphy's death, the Museum of Modern Art staged a one-man show of his surviving works, "establishing Gerald Murphy as what he really was and always had been, a painter of his time." Gerald Murphy was interesting, MacLeish has stated, not because of his "irrelevant fame as a character in contemporary fiction," or because he and Sara were "patrons of the arts and supporters of artists," but because "he was himself an artist of major importance."[21]

If Gerald Murphy in later years tried to justify his artistic renunciation by virtue of life's injustices, what he really believed about his art he did not say openly. He did confess at one point: "I was never happy until I started painting, and I have never been thoroughly so since I was obliged to give it up." He wondered "how many aspiring American artists have been claimed by the harmful belief that if a business is your 'inheritance' that it is heresy not to give up all in favor of it." He hoped that not too many were. He believed there was a need for "real American artists." "There is something to be painted by us that only we should do," he said.[22]

When Murphy did say that nothing really prevents a first-rate painter from emerging, he implied by indirection that he was only second-rate. Murphy never rid himself completely of the self-doubts which interfered with his personal relationships and which finally scared him from his art. His pronouncement to Fitzgerald that "what we do with our minds" counts more than "what we do" almost seemed a rationalization for not painting. Friends and family soon learned that two subjects in the Murphy household were taboo: the deaths of Baoth and Patrick, and Murphy's art. MacLeish revealed his understanding of the issue and of Gerald when he described how the statement attributed to Murphy, "Living well is the best revenge," has been misinterpreted. Rather than justifying a Fitzgerald universe, it instead reflects the bitterness which only "a very serious painter" who has turned from his art can understand. "To any artist, and to a painter above all, the best revenge upon life, or more precisely upon death, is not living either well or badly but creating works of art, and Gerald Murphy, whatever he may have said upon the subject, knew it. His life, though he and Sara lived as bravely and as gracefully as humans can, was far from constituting a revenge on anything."[23]

When Gerald Murphy reread *Tender Is the Night* prior to his death, he was surprised to realize how many details Fitzgerald had drawn from real life during the years (1924–1929) spent together in Paris and on the Riviera. Murphy became aware that almost every incident and conversation in the opening section of the book had some basis in an actual event or conversation "although it was often altered or distorted in detail."[24] Hemingway too was stunned by the evocative accuracy of the book when he reread it in 1939, and he changed his mind about it, having previously disliked it. The book seems most accurate in those moments when the reader first sees the beach, the Villa, and the Divers through the innocent and unsuspecting eyes of Rosemary Hoyt. To Rosemary, "it seemed that there was no life anywhere in all this expanse of coast except under the filtered sunlight of those umbrellas, where something went on amid the color and the murmur." When Rosemary and her mother approach the Villa Diana for the evening festivities to which Diver has invited them, Rosemary feels that here "was the centre of the world" wherein "some memorable thing was sure to happen."

> There were fireflies riding on the dark air and a dog baying on some low and far-away ledge of the cliff. The table seemed to have risen a little toward the sky like a mechanical dancing platform, giving the people around it a sense of being alone with each other in the dark universe, nourished by its only food, warmed by its only lights. . . . The two Divers began suddenly to warm and glow and expand, as if to make up to their guests, already so subtly assured of their importance, so flattered with politeness, for anything they might still miss from that country well left behind. Just for a moment they seemed to speak to every one at the table, singly and together, assuring them of their friendliness, their affection. And for a moment the faces turned up toward them were like the faces of poor children at a Christmas tree. . . .
>
> The diffused magic of the hot sweet South had withdrawn into them—the soft-pawed night and the ghostly wash of the Mediterranean far below—the magic left these things and melted into the two Divers and became part of them.[25]

273

Archibald MacLeish would say years later that the Murphys' life together had seemed almost "intentionally tragic, as though an enemy had planned it. And those luncheons on the thick blue plates under the linden tree at the Villa America were not a compensation for the suffering but almost an aggravation."[26] Honoria likewise recalled the linden tree and its happier associations. Childhood on the Riviera was "instructive," "warm," and "fun," largely because her parents and their friends had always seemed so interested in them and put great effort and imagination into making their lives "enchanting and educational." Zelda and Scott "would always invent some fascinating and imaginative new tale or game which they demonstrated by getting down on their hands and knees, if necessary," and Ernest would explain "the structure of the innards of a certain fish" making it "sound like a jewel out of the sea." The MacLeishes would come with their own "beautiful children" and Archie would read his poetry "in his resonant voice." John Dos Passos, "a modest, gentle man, was always the long awaited traveller." Honoria and her brothers knew all of this "amidst the mysterious trees to climb in the garden . . . the scent of mimosa, lemon verbena, and rope peaches; the sight of the 'burnished blue steel' Mediterranean."[27]

As Sara and Gerald were completing their move from Snedens Landing in the spring of 1963, Edmund Wilson came to visit them there. "They lived up to their tradition of gracious living," he told Dos Passos, "by providing an incredible lunch—for which a special chef had been procured—with the menu, à la francaise, on little porcelain tablets." Wilson added that they always spoke of Dos Passos "with a toast and a tear," but that since Dos Passos had just received a citation from Goldwater, he was probably "insensible to such humble tributes."[28]

During these years when Dos Passos received several citations for his cumulative years of work as a writer, he remarked that writing did have its hazards, particularly in the personal sphere: "The spiteful reviews, the pained expostulations, the angry letters of disappointed readers, the people who were once your friends who cross the street to avoid you."[29] When an artist utilizes his experiences and his friendships to stimulate or enrich his art, it does not make for easy relationships. MacLeish recognized this. His friendship with Dos Passos, Hemingway, Fitzgerald, and Murphy during the 1920s and 1930s had little to do with their art, he said, and when art entered the picture, difficulties sometimes arose. "Sooner or later" artists who band together as artists "lose a great deal." They "lose themselves, their identities, and become part of the echoes that they hear, part of the shadows that fall across their pages."[30]

Because the relationships between this particular group of artists took on such human dimensions, the friendships continued to matter to each of them even throughout the difficult times. Hemingway always regretted having severed relations with Dos Passos, although *A Moveable Feast* seems to belie this, and he felt saddened by his strained relations with the MacLeishes. "I think I am at very worst in a war in which interested," he told Ada in 1941. "Am very charming at a war or during a war in which take little interest." Essentially he regretted his self-righteousness during that "so un-belle epoque" and hoped that the MacLeishes would "try to love Poppy again and forget horrible past."[31] When he told Archie two years later that it felt good to be friends with him again, he reconfirmed what he had told Ada, that the "self-righteous bastardry" of his Spanish Civil War period continued to haunt him. "He had managed to alienate all the old pals that he had failed to alienate during his 'son-of-a-bitching' epoch of 1934," and he "had missed them all— 'like hell' ever since, including Dos Passos as he had used to be before the Loyalists shot his skilled but worthless translator Robles." Hemingway had concluded his 1941 letter to Ada with the comment that Scott Fitzgerald's recent death made him feel the loss of his friendship also. "As Bra [Saunders] put it people are dying this year that never died before."[32]

By 1964, Fitzgerald, Hemingway, then Murphy, had died, and just a few remained of the original group. Dos Passos told Ada MacLeish that he would "love to spend another couple hours with the MacLeishes" before they were "all delivered over to the men in white and the men in black." "About all my old friends are dead and it makes me value the few survivors more," he concluded.[33] Since Dos Passos could not be at Gerald's funeral, his friend Dawn Powell described for him how it was "all carefully organized by Gerald I'm sure including the brief church service—poignant & perfect." Powell added: "It was—as you might know—a lesson in courage disguised as *taste.*" Archibald MacLeish would later underscore the beauty of a funeral such as Gerald's when he told Ellen Barry that at a funeral you "see life whole."[34]

Upon learning of Gerald's death, Dorothy Parker, who was living at the Volney Hotel in New York, sent Sara a telegram: "DEAREST SARA, DEAREST SARA." Sara Murphy would soon take her own apartment at the Volney where she and Dorothy Parker spent many evenings together prior to Parker's death in 1967.[35] Sara continued to see Dos Passos, and she enjoyed reading his memoirs, *The Best Times*, when they came out in 1966. "Oh *how* I am enjoying your book!!" she wrote on 2 April. "It is such fun to read that I dread finishing it!!! *So* I reward myself (when I've been a good girl, & often finished the Soup!—) I do wish I could *see you all.*"[36]

John Dos Passos died in 1970, and Sara Murphy died five years later. On 17 October 1975, the eleven-year anniversary of Gerald's death, MacLeish attended the memorial service held for Sara in East Hampton, New York. There he presented Honoria Murphy Donnelly with an inscribed copy of his *The*

Human Season: "For Honoria/on Sara's day/with my love/Archie." Mac-Leish died seven years later, followed shortly thereafter by the death of Ada. It was MacLeish who chose the inscription for Gerald's grave: "Ripeness Is All," because Gerald "achieved the most complete maturity I have ever seen," said MacLeish. Gerald had earlier chosen Sara's inscription: "And She Made All of Light." MacLeish felt that the inscriptions complemented each other in the same way that Gerald and Sara had complemented each other in real life during the years they had all known them.

197. Pauline Hemingway to Gerald and Sara Murphy
San Francisco, 4 August [1941]

Dear Mr. and Mrs. Murphy,

I ran into Monsieur Léger the other afternoon and he was speaking perfect English. I thought you might be interested to know. Also, (I am psychic) I have been thinking for several weeks now that YOU are just around the corner. Consequently I go around each corner con cuidado (I'm taking Spanish) but so far, as I have heard a lot of people say, NO SOAP. Is it true what my control (she is Chinese and her name is Ping) tells me, i.e., that you *are* coming out here? I won't make this a long letter as you may be packing right now. Altho I have a great incentive to keep writing on and on as I have a tough grapple ahead of me this afternoon with the Spanish subjunctive, which no matter what you hear, the Spanish people do use practically constantly, the old Iberian savages.

I got a letter from Mrs. MacLeish today (the Mrs. MacLeish who has been married twenty-five years and who is going to be a grandmother, what small ears you have) and she said you were there to see the twenty-sixth year in and it started me thinking how time flies and how there are no friends like the old friends, and just for a minute I was *sick* of now. But I went into the bathroom and threw it all up and now is—am—wonderful again. Anyway, it's all we have, and I'm sure that out here it is better than any other place. The weather alone is worth a lot—under blankets every night and the fire lighted at five-thirty every afternoon. And such good food. Had a superb meal the other day down on the dock with the ocean thrown in for thirty-five cents. And then there is the Chinese Bubble Girl in the neon gilded cage and Finoccios (the best female impersonators' show in the world) and always the tuberous begonia.

The young boys, Patrick and Gregory, are in camp at the moment, but will be here in two weeks for a while, after which they are joining Ernest in Sun Valley. I get very short hurried notes from them which I suppose is a good sign. They seem to be having a very exciting time. [Fashion designer] Murial King's child is at the same camp, I hear. Didn't know she had one.

I hope you will answer this in the affirmative.

Your loving friend,

Pauline

HMD

198. ERNEST HEMINGWAY to SARA MURPHY
Havana, 14 August 1941

Dearest Sara,

Thank you for the lovely letter about Mr. Josie [Joe Russell, owner of Sloppy Joe's Bar in Key West]. He was terribly fond of you too and we had been talking about you just before he died. It was just too bloody awful for that to happen to him just when he made enough money so that he could turn the place over to his boy and his son-in-law, and was figuring on buying a boat again. We had tickets to go to the Billy Conn fight and one of the things he had looked forward to was seeing you in New York. We had planned to all go out together on the town. There's nothing ever to say about anything. But your letter says all the things that I never can and I read it over many times.

Each time we have been in New York it has been like a mad-house of work on last-minute preparation for getting off. First, going to China and then having to write my stuff that I'd carried in my head to avoid the censor when we came back. But the next time we will have fun together. I wanted so much to see Ada but when I went to Washington and saw Archie, she had just gone. Archie was fine. I made all up with him because what are people doing nursing old rows at our age? I don't think we ought to be nursing anything. It isnt dignified. But certainly not old rows.

Marty is fine and so are all the children, although Bumbie is a rat about not writing but when you see him he feels so contrite and it never occurs to him that he's six months without sending a letter. I'll try to bring him around this fall to see you and Gerald and Honoria.

Last fall we had a lot of fun with Dotty and Alan. In the old days I was an awful dope not to appreciate how truly funny and what very good company Alan was. We went on very comic trips into the heart of the primitive area of the middle fork of the Salmon River in Idaho and Dotty was in as good form as in the best of the old days. Dotty in the heart of a primitive area is pretty wonderful anyway. But when we had finished the second quart since lunch and Alan began to say, "How marvelous the air was up there in the primitive area, so that you didn't need to drink anything in order to be exhilarated"—(and he really meant it, not having noticed either quart because the top of the car was down—if you understand this). We soon moved on from there into primitive and more primitive areas and had a wonderful time. I think that one bond that holds them together is what bad housekeepers they are and a hatred of cleanly measures of any kind. I think if we could have found some very expensive place in the heart of the primitive area where they would never have to wash, especially Dotty never wash her hair, they would have settled down and homesteaded. Anyway, let's have some fun this fall. I always figure we will have the last fun there is long after it's become a state's prison offense.

Take care of yourself, Sara, you certainly take care of all of us. Much love to you, and Gerald, and Honoria.

I love you very much

Ernest.

HMD

199. GERALD MURPHY to ARCHIBALD MACLEISH
New York [c. October 1941]

Archie:

It was a relief for me to hear from Ada that The Back hadn't turned wicked. She should *keep* at her exercises. They make all the difference to me. Possibly we're only as young as our spines.

Whoever said that 'the best prose becomes poetic, that the sublimest speech is a poem'—would bear me out in finding Time to Speak [a collection of MacLeish's political essays, 1941]—which I have just finished—ineffably beautiful in form, spirit and content. Here's laurels to you, Archino. I mean it—indeed.

*   *   *   *   *

Weeks ago I started a losing fight to get the Fifth Avenue Merchants to devote their windows for one poor week to displays of their own choosing calculated to stop the passer-by in his tracks and make him *think* about what he stands to lose *right now*. They all begged off, but I learned that the real reason was they would not risk offending *their* clients whose 'sentiments might be opposed to intervention.' (Can you *beat* it?!)

So I had my own windows alone (of which I forward you photographs to be peered at and slipped into the same envelope and mailed back to me).

During one week our doorman clocked the results accurately. An average of 3000 people a day *stopped* and *read* every one of the six posters, with a maximum of 5000 daily and at times 70 to 80 readers at two 11 foot windows. We had requests beyond count in person, by mail and telephone (some from bus-riders) for copies of the wording on the posters. Twice as I passed I heard foreigners translating them word for word to friends who didn't understand English. The posters stood five feet high, and the print was Canterbury Roman blown up on white background. The letters, words and lines were double spaced and could be read at 30 feet.

I've never been more moved by anything than the public reaction to them, and some of the comments of the people were downright heartbreaking. [1]

The idea occurred to me after the success of our several 'Blackout' windows in which I showed scenes of what has gone on in our factory and air-raid shelter at Walsall (4 miles out of Birmingham) since the beginning. You see Father established this factory in 1892 which since has never ceased to make goods according to our models and uniquely for export to America. We are the last outpost of British manufacture of Leather Goods and the only firm I know of with an American owned factory in England which manufactures for American consumption.

The posters I am sending out to the various representatives of ours throughout the country. We have 1800 such, now as opposed to 2300 before the war. We can't produce sufficiently under the circumstances of conditions abroad and our factory here is already overtaxed, what with government orders.

Recently I've had an outcropping of my sophomore predilection for readings from Ralph Waldo and Thoreau. The former has said something that strikes me as having the mood of so much that one is thinking these days: "Of every storied bay and cliff and plain we will make something infinitely nobler

---

1. MacLeish responded to Murphy's letter with a brief paragraph. The original has not survived, but a typed carbon copy (without a heading or signature but dated 23 October 1941) is appended to Murphy's letter in the MacLeish Papers: "This is one paragraph to say what it would take a whole book *to* say—that the beginning of your letter did a very great deal for my spirit and the rest of it did a lot for my backbone. I think it was a wonderful thing you did and the selections of language are, as of course they would be, simply superb. We must see each other soon."

than Salamis or Marathon. This pale Massachusetts sky, this sandy soil and raw wind, all shall nurture us. Unlike all the world before us, our own age and land shall be classic to ourselves."

We shall have to think *something else* of America than simply preferring it if we are to save it.

Love to you all,

Gerald

[Gerald enclosed copies of the wording on the posters as follows:] Our contest is not only whether we ourselves shall be free, but whether there shall be left to mankind an asylum on earth for civil and religious liberty.
SAMUEL ADAMS, 1776

If we desire to avoid insult, we must be able to repel it; if we desire to secure peace, it must be known that we are at all times ready for war.
GEORGE WASHINGTON, Dec. 3, 1793

They tell us, sir, that we are weak—unable to cope with so formidable an adversary. But when shall we be stronger? . . . Gentlemen may cry peace, peace—but there is no peace. The war is actually begun! The next gale that sweeps from the north will bring to our ears the clash of resounding arms! Our brethren are already in the field! Why stand we here idle? . . . Is life so dear, or peace so sweet, as to be purchased at the price of chains and slavery? Forbid it, Almighty God! I know not what course others may take; but as for me, give me liberty or give me death!
PATRICK HENRY, 1775

God grants liberty only to those who live it and are always ready to guard and defend it.
DANIEL WEBSTER, June 3, 1843

These are the times that try men's souls. The summer soldier and the sunshine patriot will, in this crisis, shrink from the service of their country; but he that stands it now, deserves the love and thanks of man and woman. Tyranny, like Hell, is not easily conquered; yet we have this consolation with us, that the harder the conflict, the more glorious the triumph.
THOMAS PAINE, 1776, at Valley Forge

They that can give up essential liberty to obtain a little temporary safety deserve neither liberty nor safety.
BENJAMIN FRANKLIN, 1755

LC

200. KATY DOS PASSOS TO SARA MURPHY
Fort Walton, Florida, 14 April 1942

Dearest Mrs. Puss,

We've found a beach here, you ought to be sitting on. Pure white sand, white as sugar, a delicious blue sea, pines, magnolia, flowers and solitude. We are staying in a nice inn, too, which is on the shore of an inlet. There are several young officers from the air-force, and I was struck by their appearance. They are all intensely blonde. They look quite sensational, with ash-blonde hair, dark blue suits—uniforms, rather, and gold-braid. The ash-blonde hair was so universal that I asked about it. Sara, they *all* dye their hair—with peroxide and vinegar. One hundred and fifty of them. I don't know why. It's a striking effect. Is it to scare the enemy, or just a navy whim? The landlady here told me (she has a son in camp at Pensacola) that her son has dyed his hair too. It's the fashion, he said. He'd look queer if he didn't. This is true. But *why*? It just goes to show this is not like the last war.

Dos and I had a fine time in Texas. Saw more funny people and handsome men and lovely girls than you could imagine in one state. Next time you and Pusser must come to Texas. We spent one whole day at the great air field, Randolph Field, and it was a thriller. We went up in the control tower to see the cadets practice night-flying. They were a splendid lot of young men, all tall, tough, polite, and grim. It's very fancy, white gloves, spit and polish, drill, elegance in a military fashion, and driving hard training for 16 hours a day. Texas is very exciting, and it makes you feel good about the country. We need to feel good about our future, the way things are going. It's going to be a hard job to Knock the Kimonos off those little yellow men.

Darling, we've been missing you. Please ask us to dinner—to a pusser meal, when we get back to New York. We have not had a *single* vegetable for six weeks. Just steak and fish and hush-puppies. Dos and I are quite fat and pasty, and I'm afraid that roll around my hips is permanent. We ate creole food in New Orleans, washed down with [?], till we were all out of shape, like a couple of stuffed dates. But had a wonderful time.

The plans are all drawn for the Virginia house. More than that I dassn't say. We're going to Tappahannock from here. Should be there in two days. Then New York—and Pussers again. Love to you and Gerald and Honoria—Eliza sends her respecks—Always your devoted

Katy

UVA

282

201. Pauline Hemingway to Gerald and Sara Murphy
Key West, 17 December 1942

Dearest Sara and Dow,

This is a combination bred-and butter (and *such* bread and butter!) and holiday-greetings letter—the fomer (Jewish spelling) a little late, and the latter a bit early.

Despite the global war, the Hemingways are managing to have a pretty fine Christmas holidays, as *all* the boys are here. Bumbi got here last week and Patrick arrives today, the three to stay until the day after Christmas when they go to Cuba to Ernest, if the passports come through and the plane reservations hold up. It's been marvellous getting birth certificates and photographs for young men in Hanover, New Milford and Key West. Have a technique now that certainly ought to be of value to the War Department if I could just think of some way of making it available to them.

Key West is now a boom town (and will be a ghost town after the war), with wages in the clouds and housing accomadations in the gutter. And three and four house robberies every night, with the police force consisting of three very baffled men leaping around to one place after another where the robber has just operated and disappeared. Sort of like the old Treasure Hunt of fascist days. Help is practically a thing of the past. I press my bed spread as I dress in the morning, keep my room neat as a pin, paint at parts of the wood work that have become too bad, rake in the garden, mend the hose, wash the curtains, drive the truck, steer the ship and generally burn myself in the home fires. Fortunately, I still have Ada, and she does all the *real work*. Then of course there is the War Work.

What are you two up to? I miss you both very much—as much as I miss a handy man, or the good old days. The unfortunate thing about the good old days is they are like the couplet—

The only really perfect wives
Have beds beneath the willows.

About the only only comforts left are Old Friends, and Very Best Wishes to two Old Friends and their lovely daughter

From,

a

VERY

OLD

Friend,

P. Hemingway

HMD

During the early months of 1943, Gerald Murphy tried to help one of his employees, Christian Meyeringh—"a Hollander by birth"—to enlist, even though his naturalization papers had not come through. He corresponded regularly with both MacLeish and MacLeish's secretary, Miss Bakey, hoping that Archie's influence in Washington might be of service, which it was. By April 1943 Archie had gotten through to the right people and Meyeringh was "well on his way . . . to being allowed to volunteer for pilot training." When Gerald wrote for Archie's advice, he was also remembering Alexander Woollcott, who had just died on 23 January 1943.

202. GERALD MURPHY to ARCHIBALD MACLEISH
New York, 8 February 1943

Archie:—

A great many thanks for the time you gave Meyeringh. He fears that he imposed on Miss Bakey's patience,—but his zeal *is* pardonable, I do believe. I've never seen a greater determination to serve.

I want to ask you something. Living as one does in a city which is (tragically I think) out of the stream of consciousness regarding the war, it is hard to establish one's own relation to it. Nevertheless it never has left my mind these last months,—in spite of the fact that I've foreseen the difficulties of a retrenchment of this monument to the non-essential, the Mark Cross Company. . . .

Now my question: toward what kind of service do you think it would be best for me to direct myself when the moment comes. Granted my age (55 this coming March) am I fitted for anything in which I would be of value? Physically I'm in pretty good condition, although Sara and I do notice that we have recently been pretty much slowed up due to the wallop that that bumpy period of Baoth's and Patrick's illnesses took out of us. My eyesight is not good without glasses. My waist still is 32 (not 30!)

Simply think it over for me, will you? For the moment I am essential, as I say, to the pulling-in-of-the-neck of this Company in the face of the *essential* civilian industry curtailments;—but I wish to direct my mind toward something. Possibly there is some training which is being organized.

Just bear me in mind. Don't attempt to answer this till you have an idea.

Just the same, one finds that Alec—behind all that nonsense—had something very human. He had become more tractable and was dining *alone* quietly with us each week. His gift was to make the people he loved feel valuable. Few have it.

284

Love to you both,

Affectionately,

Gerald.

LC

*On a visit with the MacLeishes in Washington, D.C., the Murphys met
Secretary of State Dean Acheson and Supreme Court Justice Felix
Frankfurter. After MacLeish received Murphy's letter, he forwarded it to
Frankfurter with a note attached: "Mr. Justice FF This should indeed
please you Pls return A." Frankfurter responded at the bottom of Mac-
Leish's attached note: "Archie My pleasure over that warm festation of a
charmingly civilized man exceeds its ministrations to my ego! Thank
you F."*

203. GERALD MURPHY to ARCHIBALD and ADA MACLEISH
New York, 14 April 1943

Ada: Archie:

Well! . . . As we wired Honoria—from the station on leaving—'. . . Have
had most inspiring time.' And so it was. What an addition is made to that long
litany of remarkable experiences we four have shared! (I felt almost as if we
were all behind the scenes at the rebirth of a nation.):

The pleasure at seeing you in what is the asylum you both *deserve*—that
gracious house and garden; the evening with high diplomacy in the Jamesian
atmosphere of the Achesons (do you recall 'the Europeans'?); my trip to the
moon up through the amazing carcass of the Library of Congress in quest of
the mystical vellum; the good dry sack and the sun on the neck in the garden;
the delicious country luncheon in the bright dining-room followed by the
tussle and buzz of the moving of box—with its attendant 'odour of immortal-
ity;' the hunching—in concert—for the success of the 'Patriots' and the excitement of *feeling* it succeed; the gay becoming dinner-party and the rarified
delight of listening to the play of such minds—and withal the privilege of
seeing revealed the *feelings* of Justice Frankfurter for Thomas Jefferson—after
five months of their distillation; at the monument in the open air and the
words spoken there; the precious gleanings from the seminar; the inspired,
challenging oration of that man with oracular insight on that last evening, all
of it, all of it . . . was life at one of the highest points I shall ever be able to
remember—out beyond its own limitations—.

And we have you to thank for wanting us to be among the ones to share it with you.

We *do* thank you—with all our hearts—and will be doing so for a long time to come,

devotedly,

Gerald.

p.s. Please tell those nice people—all of them—how we enjoyed ourselves,—and do thank them.

LC

204. Katy Dos Passos to Sara Murphy
Provincetown, 1 November 1943

Dearest Sara,

Ay wullah how lovely it was at your house dear Mrs. Puss, Protector of the poor. I did enjoy everything so much and Dos too—especially breakfast—you have the best breakfast in the world and the pleasantest company. I miss you all very much and had a letter from Dos the other day complaining that he missed you too, in Coon Rapids Iowa. Doesn't Coon Rapids sound like a nice place?

Have you heard that Mr. Edmund Wilson, the Marxist critic, or AntiChrist as I have nicknamed him, is taking over Clifton Fadiman's job at the New Yorker on January first. He is already sharpening his fangs. He demanded a free hand with the Catholic Church and also any life of Churchill that happened to come out during his incumbency—or else! His dog Rex, whom he refers to sappily as Angel Doggie, has been killing chickens and turkies in Wellfleet to such an extent that the enraged poultry raisers have demanded the dog's life, so Mr. Wilson, in an effort to save his life by breaking him of the habit has been taking him to the scene of the crime and there beating and scolding him. But this has been seen by several kindhearted ladies who were deeply shocked and have reported him to the Humane Society so they are after him too. So now he is known as Dogbeater Wilson.

Jack Hall's dog bit Polly Boyden twice in the knee last week. The knee is very much swollen and inflamed. It was the fault of Angel Doggie again because he followed her out to the Hall's farm and their dog attacked him and Polly sprang between them. The way I heard it first was that Angel Doggie had torn Polly Boyden to pieces but Mr. Wilson says it was the other dog and Polly does too. Angel Doggie was not injured and killed two chickens while at the Hall's farm.

This is not all because in Provincetown a very strange incident occurred that has never happened before in our whole history. We heard wild cries from the harbor at two thirty with the tide running in and on rushing out saw a small skiff with Abuchykoff, a poor little Russian refugee who lives by fishing, out in the bay about two hundred feet away shouting for help—he was being followed by a shark—in a few minutes we could see the shark as big as a Japanese submarine swimming round the boat, keeping between Abuchykoff and the shore and every now and then running at the boat and hitting it with his nose. By using the telescope we could also see him turn over showing his open mouth and greedy fangs. The Russian who is very small was standing up in the boat crying for help and hitting the shark feebly on the head with an oar—the shark's tail would slap the water as he rushed at the boat and the way he kept between it and the shore was simply satanic. People ran to the beach but nothing could be done and Abuchykoff was almost capsized by the fiendish fish when two men rowed down from Long Wharf and began shooting at the shark with rifles barely missing the boat—Abuchykoff kept yelling for help even more wildly then but they killed the shark and brought him and the boat in. The shark was fourteen feet long and his liver weighed twenty seven and a half pounds and Abuchykoff sold it at the Wharf for seventeen dollars. He said the shark had been following him for three hours. Nothing like this has ever been seen in Provincetown before. This incident, and the attack on Polly Boyden by the Hall's dog Shemus, have made people wonder if there is not some upheaval in the animal kingdom and we are looking now for lions to whelp in the streets. I have also to report shocking behavior on the part of Eliza Poodle who tore open and ate a package of dog food which was left with her in the car. She also has destroyed the half of an entire panelled wall in the living room because she was left alone for a short time while I went to tea with Marjorie Ball. We had brownies, which Robert Ball had made himself, the poor wretch, as Marjorie said. But when I came back Eliza had torn out the wall. I don't see how she could have got her teeth in it as it is a perfectly smooth surface but the wall was splintered from end to end. Not only that but she suddenly and secretly attacked our cat with whom she has been on good terms, when the poor animal was quietly sitting enjoying the air on the back step. I was just in time to save her from Eliza's jaws. She leaves the house at midnight and does not return till day, coming back wet and dirty with garbage on her face. She seems a hardened and impenitent sinner and I scarce know how to proceed with her. She gets into people's beds at night and then gets out of them and makes them up again. The Shay's have been having similar trouble with their dog Dancer, who suddenly and for no reason refuses insolently to sleep on her blanket and goes to bed with her mistress, biting and growling when reproved. I don't know what to make of this and would be grateful if you would report any similar incidents you hear of. There has been a sudden and unprecedented increase in fox and owl depredations on chickens. A large savage animal is tunneling under our Truro house and has torn off most of the shingles as high as six feet on the east side. Well that is all for this time. I send love to all Pussers.

As ever affectionately,

Katy

UVA

205. JOHN DOS PASSOS to GERALD and SARA MURPHY
San Francisco [4 December 1944]

Dear Gerald and Sara—

What a delightful going away party—we wished we could have stayed after we'd been seen off—in fact we wished we were all seeing somebody else off. When I finally got on the plane it was with the cosiest feeling of having been wined and dined. New York looked like millions of birthday cakes with all their candles blowing in the wind. The swoop into Salt Lake was one of the most amazing things I've ever seen—level after level of odd yellow and bronze reflections among [illegible] clouds and the blue lake steaming far below— then the climb over the Sierra Nevadas and the Cascades and the gentle glide over the fat plains of the Sacramento Valley had me with my nose glued to the cabin window—a lovely smooth easy trip. Today San Francisco is all robins egg blue and cream color—earliest spring kind of day.

Dont tell anybody but your guests last week—the ones in the parlor suite went away without paying their telephone bill—Hope this is an approximation of it. I'm already eating Saras vitamins—leaving here soon—

lots of love

Dos

HMD

206. JOHN DOS PASSOS to GERALD and SARA MURPHY
Philippines, 21 February 1945

Dear Gerald and Sara,

How are you all? I'd have written sooner but this little vacation I'm taking seems to keep me most amazingly busy. Particularly now that I'm cabling stuff instead of just noting it down for future reference. Today I'm taking a little rest in a ruined sugar plantation set among big trees draped with Bougainvillea and an immense growth of philodendron. There are immense wallowing carabao with big black buffalo horns and the tiny dusty underfed people drive little painted up twowheel carts a little like the tartanas in Valencia. The horses are amazingly tiny, hardly bigger than the widow poodle. The burning and pillaging and murdering of the retreating Nips has left the civilians in a heartbreaking plight. Popeyed correspondents keep sending off horrible atrocity stories. The surprizing thing about them is that they tend to be understated rather than exaggerated. This is the grimmest I've seen since South Russia way back in '21.

It's perfectly absurd but in spite of the constant aeroplane hopping, jeep and truck riding and the heat and the dust and the mud and the general carnage I seem to remain in raging health. I attribute it entirely to Sara's vitamins which I religiously crunch every morning. Lots of love

Dos

Isn't it time for Sara to go southish? I wish you were both here today. It's a delicious hot summer day out in the Press's country retreat.

Katy said Gerald had a bad throat. I do hope that's mended now. Dont you think you ought to take each other somewhere for a short bake in the sun.
HMD

207. GERALD MURPHY to ARCHIBALD MACLEISH
New York, 21 February 1945

Dear Archie:

When you were here we spoke of a cable from Vladimir. I enclose a copy. I suppose what he means is that he wants to get out of Monaco but that someone must send for him in order that he be allowed to travel to another part of France. He doubtless read of your appointment and thought of you as being the first person he knew who would one day be in Paris.

I don't know his experience of the last years except that he felt it essential to sell the Weatherbird as he was to be put in concentration camp by the Germans as being a Russian. He was later released and built himself a stone hut outside of Ramatuelle, a hill-town above St. Tropez overlooking the Ferme Blanche. He grew his own vegetables and lived without artificial light for two years.

The boat he sold to a Swiss resident of Paris and Geneva, named Capitaine Gerard de l'Oriol. The whereabouts and amount of the money we know nothing although he assures us it's safe. I instructed him to withdraw from it periodically wages for himself, Joseph, the gardener, and family. de l'Oriol, a count, is apparently a louche [shady] character, as I was several times interviewed concerning him by the F.B.I. last year. I know nothing of him nor has Vladimir ever spoken of him except as purchaser. He wrote me once asking me to have the American passport of the Weatherbird for foreign waters transferred to his name. I sent the application to Washington which I think precipitated the inquiry, as I had never reported the sale of the boat never having known exactly what amount or kind of currency was paid for it or its disposition.

I thought I'd give you the whole picture. I naturally have no idea what can be done about Vladimir, nor can I see how you could.

I'm writing him soon and will ask for more details if he can give them.

A bientôt,

Gerald.

P.S. The town is ringing about your speech. I've never known more unanimous comment.

LC

208. KATY DOS PASSOS to GERALD and SARA MURPHY
Provincetown, 21 March 1945

Dearest Pussers:

Are you back from the Hot? I missed myself not being there with you. My life here is both sordid and inspiring, as life is all over the world today. I am always shoveling and digging and toting and pulling like a seabee, during the day. At night I read and try to instruct Jean [Kaeselau] in the rudiments of English. I write to Mr. Dos Passos and worry about him. I worry subconsciously as I will not allow myself to worry in the open. But yesterday I had a cable from him saying he would be home soon. He has left the Phillipines and his last letter from a strange island seemed to indicate New Guinea. He has had a really hair raising time and several close shaves. While flying over the burning city of Manilla in a plane was shot down by a Jap shell which crashed through the right motor of the plane. If there had been any enemy planes in the sky, he wrote, they would have been a sitting duck. Then he was

290

clipped on the head by an aeroplane after that, sustaining damages which he says he has completely recovered from. I wrote and told him this sort of thing must stop.

If I were to come to New York in about a week could I stay with you for a night or two? It was nice of you dear Pusser to speak of Captain Shaw. It seems to be having a modest success. I am trying to be off hand and easy about the whole thing and never mention the book unless I happen to be talking to someone.[1]

How is Honoria? Do send me a line.

So much Love,

Katy

UVA

---

1. Katy and Edith Shay had co-authored *The Private Adventure of Captain Shaw*, published by Houghton Mifflin in 1944. The book had just been selected as the June 1945 Book of the Month offering.

209. KATY DOS PASSOS to SARA MURPHY
Provincetown, 8 April 1945

My Dearest Mrs. Puss:

Oh I am afraid I have been making myself a nuisance like a weather forecast that keeps people nervous but doesn't materialize—rain tomorrow and then you put on your rubbers and go out and then you have to carry them all day. I am so put about too, but have been unable to leave because of my dear Eliza— she is awfully low, my poor Eliza, and I was going to take her to Edie Shay's while I was gone but then Frank [Shay] got sick and had to go to the hospital so they could not have her and the vet could not take her till the first of the week—she may get better, they say, so I am determined to try everything. Well I was coming this Monday and then all of a sudden comes a cable from Dos and he said to stand by—he was coming home. The cable was from Pearl Harbor which is where he would take off from. He said he would telephone me from San Francisco—well Puss I was very stirred up as you may imagine. I've been awfully quiet and good but I must say his adventures have been wild enough to worry a sloth. Oh how I have missed you and Gerald—I have really *needed* to see you—well will be there next week and if you have other guests coming why think no more of it, I will come anyway. Thought would call you up in advance but can hole up with friends if my dear Pussers have rented their spare rooms. Oh Sara *what* a winter—but it is about over now—the spring peepers are out. I suppose maybe Dos *might* be home next week but I aint saying so. I have got to go down to Virginia soon. Oh dear.

This morning saw the most lovely sight. A great finback whale sporting and playing in the Bay. He was so big that I thought he was a patrol boat. He was going like a locomotive, spouting and rolling, and yet he was sort of idling too. They are very rare, you know. Have seen three seals.

You would laff if you could see me. I am sitting in the living room *under* a rubber tree. Not beside it. Under it. It has grown so that it is against the ceiling. I have cut off the top but it has just grown harder. Unless it behaves I have threatened to sell it to the Hood Rubber Company in New Bedford . . .

Tell Gerald I have so enjoyed his postal cards. Not enough of them though. I keep them all. Am very proud of my collection. In fact would like to have all his postal cards even those he has written to others—do you suppose people would be willing to sell them—I think they ought because I am going to be an Authority on Pusser's cards. Do you realize that he is the only man who has actually created a Post Card Style? I am planning a monograph on this with examples—it will be known as the Murphy Telescope Style or something of that kind—probably just known as "The Murphy Style."

Well now it is late and I must be off to bed—it is a queer Spring—awfully hot and then very cold again. I was going to mention the war but it is too late now thank goodness.

I wonder how is Honoria. I hope you are well darling. Hope Gerald is well. Oh I have so much to talk about. Love you so much.

Dos wrote that when he was flying over New Guinea a naked savage ran out of a house in a village deep in the hills and hurled a spear at the plane!

Jean and I were trying to clean up some of the hurricane damage—we have been at it all winter, and Jean said to me, "Katy, we don't know *where* to start. We don't know *what* to do. And we'll never get it done." Everything is like that, it seems. Well goodnight dearest Pussers.

Your devoted loving

Katy

UVA

210. ERNEST HEMINGWAY to SARA MURPHY
Finca Vigía, 5 May 1945

Dearest Sara:

Just got your lovely letter asking for news of Bumby. Three days ago heard he was liberated. Maybe you saw it in the paper. He had three wounds and was captured in the Voges on October 28. Now we ought to be seeing him pretty soon. I just missed him in Paris as they were sending him up to see me when I came down before the Hurtgen Forest fight. He was to come up two days after the day he had his bad luck. I got to know most of the guys in his outfit and they thought he was a fine soldier and very good kid. He took his trout fishing rod with him when he parachuted in.

Last week had a fairly bad scare when Pauline called up and told me Patrick had a spot on right lung etc. But it turned out to be a defective plate. I thought a lot about you and our other wonderful Patrick in the three days before found out things were o.k. They really are according to the Dr. Patrick has turned out to be a swell painter. Think maybe he will be very good.

Gigi is comeing out fine. Husky, funny, very good shot and athlete. Good company.

I never got to see Honoria because got smashed up almost as soon as got to London and then there was the invasion and the rest of the time I was flying and never had any time of my own. Then in July of last year went with an Infantry Division for the St. Lo breakthrough and stayed with them, or up ahead with French Maquis, in the fighting through Normandy, up to Argentan and then Chartres, Epernon, Rambouillet, Toussus le Noble, Buc, Porte Clamart, Bas Meudon, Porte de St. Cloud, Auteuil, Hotel Majestic, the Etoile and on down the Concorde and into the Vendome. We liberated the Travellers Club and the Ritz and I kept a room at the Ritz from then on to come back to from the front. Michel, George the Chasseur, all the barmen all fine.

We went on up north then to Compiegne, La Fere, St. Quentin, Wassigny, Landrecies, Le Cateau. Sometimes fighting sometimes chaseing. Then through the Ardennes, takeing St. Hubert, Houfallize, Bastogne and on into Germany in the Schnee Eifel country. We assaulted the Siegfried line on Sept. 14th. From then on it was a terribly tough fall and winter. Coldest and snowiest winter I ever saw in Europe—and terrible fighting, Sara, all winter long. I came back when I knew we had the German army broken. Was fairly badly beaten up with three concussions and hadn't seen the kids for a year and Drs. said ought to take three months complete rest and convalescence (chest was bad too) so thought would go to the showers instead of waiting for the pulling up of the goal posts.

Marty and I split up its hard to say exactly where. But I need a wife in bed and not just in even the most widely circulated magazines. Been in love with a girl named Mary Welsh since last June. She wants to quit work and have children and look after me and I need that plenty. Also she is a great believer in bed which I believe is probably my true Patria and we carved as good a life as anybody could make under the circumstances right out of the middle of the worst times you can imagine.

Also she is the only woman ever knew besides you who really loves a boat and the water: which is a break for me.

Paris is not place to go to yet. Neither food nor wine nor aperetifs. But plenty of good champagne tho. Must have drunk couple of thousand bottles as would always load up a trailer full of Perrier Jouet every time would go through where she comes from.

When I got to N.Y. never saw anybody, not you, nor Dawn [Powell], nor Waldo [Peirce] nor any old friends because expected to be there for ten days anyway and one night they called up and said Patrick and I had reservations for the next morning. So missed everybody. First days were there was over head in elapsed years business, Scribners, legal etc. people certainly rob the what do you call it out of you when you are away. I guess you know that.

It was terrible not to see Honoria. And so many years since we have been ship-mates. Please give my love to Ada and to Dawn and we will all go out together.

I saw Noel [Murphy] in Paris, looking as gaunt as one of my cats when we got back here.

About other people I can't remember who or what would be interesting but will tell you when see you. Was out a couple of times with Picasso. His stuff painted while the krauts were there is very good. Wonderful. I call Welsh my pocket Rubens and he was going to paint her but we didn't have time. Maybe next year.

Give my love to Gerald. Please write if you have time. I love to hear from you.

Have so many things to tell you.

Ernest Hemingway

What news of Archie? Give him my love when you see Ada.

HMD

211. KATY DOS PASSOS to SARA MURPHY
Hague, Virginia, 5 August 1945

Dearest Mrs. Puss:

We found ourselves refreshed by seeing you and Pusser and Honoria, who was looking so lovely and was lovely. It was like a drink from the well at the World's End. Indeed dear, Puss dear if those poor searchers after the Fountain of Youth were to come again I would tell them where to look. They would find it on the sixth floor of 131 East 66th Street, guarded only by two small dogs.

I am reading Scott's book the Crack Up as edited by Wilson—held by it in a trance of personal fascination and sadness, with a sense of Time and of the Past blowing through the book, like a night wind from the marsh, sweet and deathly. I wish he had lived to finish The Great Tycoon. I wonder what you will think of it. The strange thing about the book is that this Past which is so close and really ours, seems already as far distant as the Parthenon—not quite that far perhaps, but it seems very long ago.

We are going from here today to visit Dr. Gantt in Nelson County some two hundred miles from here. All the Cabells come from there. I reckon James Branch was the black sheep of the family. The rest are still there. They drive poor Dr. Gantt frantic telling him that the first Gantt came over as a tutor to the early young Cabells. They always mention this and then add "He was an educated man—quite the gentleman, I assure you." Horsley Gantt's labored breathing can be heard from one end of the piazza to the other but he swallows this in silence. I would try to think up a reply after all these years. I look forward to calling on the Cabells again—Horsley always calls once a year. They never do—and hearing the story told again. Fortunately they know nothing of Dos Passos and we are received as friends of Horsley—no more. Our reception while civil does not run to any form of entertainment and we are not asked into the house by Mr. Cabell, who always welcomes us, because Mrs. Cabell is lying down. This reminds me of a brief but fascinating item I read once about alpacas. Referring to the alpaca Von Tschudi states that he knows of no animal which is more stubborn. "When an alpaca has been separated from the herd and it is necessary to conduct it to some other place it simply lies down on the ground and it is practically impossible to persuade the animal to move. Neither persuasive tactics nor the threat of punishment, nothing in fact, will influence the animal. The alpaca prefers to die a painful death rather than abandon its position."

Now dearest Puss I will put this in the mail and start out on a ten mile stroll over our estate. Do not forget that you are my Ideal. Love to Pusser. Love to Honoria. We hope to see you in about ten days.

Always your affectionate

Katy

UVA

212. DOROTHY PARKER to GERALD and SARA MURPHY
Hollywood [29 October 1945]

I don't know. I just thought that you should realize that the moving picture which had been entitled "Thanks, God, I'll Take It from Here" has now had its name changed to "Miss Klotz Is No Beetle". The reason for the alteration is that it was considered that "Thanks, God, I'll Take It from Here" might be regarded as having to do with the war.

Come at once.

Dorothy

HMD

213. ARCHIBALD MACLEISH to GERALD MURPHY
Uphill Farm, 12 October 1946

Dear Dow;

It suddenly came over me today—I don't know why today more than any other day except that there is a warm rainy autumn wind like the presence of memory driving the leaves down and the summer visibly with them—it suddenly came over me that I haven't seen you since the summer was first full and the elms full and green as you said like bunches of young parsley and the maples green and full and round and the grass under it all like time's reflection of eternity—which is surely blue in itself but green in the earth's reflection because green is brief. But "came over me" is wrong for it was like a blow. I count on your being in the world and not only in *the* world but in mine. So I write you this letter to tell you and to say that I miss you. Quite simply and truly that.

yours

Archie

HMD

214. KATY DOS PASSOS to SARA MURPHY
Crystal River, Florida, 22 March 1947

Dear Sara

Report on Sarasota and Gulfview Inn:
Inn Crowded but Unsafe as Gulf has washed away most of the Beach and is trying to get into the Dining Room. We stayed one night but the Glamor had gone. The proprieter asked warmly after you. We *missed* you.

Midnight Pass:

Alas. All full of Trailers and Cottages. Everything in Florida now costs $10,000, even an overnight sub-standard cottage.

Sarasota Itself. Booming and Building. Coldest Winter since the Big Freeze.

Key West. Housing and Art Boom. We found it full of people from Provincetown who were starting Little Theaters and Fashion Shows. We stayed 2 days. Saw those Johnsons again. They entertained a vivid recollection of That Evening. Pauline is in Business. Decorating Business. She does Night Clubs and hopes to do over the Casa Marina. Has bought a House in the Town near Duval St for her Shoppe and seems very busy with Bandstands.

We can think of nothing but Birds. This is too long a story to write you now. But I may say we saw two Sand-Hill Cranes in their native habitat, also a Burrowing Owl eye to eye. Also the King Rail and a Limpkin.

Now on way to the North which met us here when we arrived. There has been no sun anywhere but Key West and Miami but we were only there 8 days in all. Rest of the time it Rained. We hope you are well—Please give love to Miss Puss and Gerald. We'll be in Virginia before long—then home.

Love from us both and Rufus sends his respecks—

Affectionately

Katy

UVA

215. KATY DOS PASSOS to GERALD and SARA MURPHY
London, 19 August 1947

Dearest Pussers,

Your [Mark Cross] factory is a most energetic, careful, hardworking, and attractive set-up in the distracted and I fear collapsing economy of this island. Mr. Beck was wonderful, and besides being a nice, clever young man, was a great help to Dos. Showed him a great many things. Through him we are coming home tomorrow on the Queen Mary, as he arranged it himself when Life expressed doubts. I *love* the factory. So do the people who work there. We'll tell all on arriving.

Oh what a trip! The weather is wonderful, so are the inhabitants, so is the scenery. The dark side is inside. Sara, there's nothing to eat but flour and tea. Don't think we're grumbling though. We *were* hungry for a few weeks but now we're not hungry any more—a little weak and apathetic perhaps, but so is everyone, and the weather is so hot.

297

Well darlings, it was wonderful to hear from you. We're almost on the boat now. I must stop as I have a big washing to do. You can't get any laundry done here short of 3 or 4 weeks. We'll call up on landing. Send a great deal of love. Very anxious to meet Mr. Young pug

As ever

Katy

Saw Cyril Connolly who sent his love to you. He said "Tell them I sent my love—Oh no, I musn't say that—yes, I will. Say I sent my love." He was awfully nice and very witty.

As ever again

Katy

Love from Dos.
UVA

216. SARA MURPHY to JOHN and KATY DOS PASSOS
New York, 3 September [1947]

Dearest Dos & Katy

I am so *glad* you are back! Only a thin telephone conversation between you & us & 2 atlantic crossings, & god knows what in England, & perhaps France? Maybe grim, & partly pleasant? One is always glad of travel—like a dip in salt water—*afterwards,*—if not at the time—It's been a rather queer summer—not bad, not too good—I *don't like* all those dead fish, washed up on Florida coast, & some on L. I.—it looks too much like radioactivity—& I think also radioactivity causes there being no cleaning women *at all*—So G. & I had to do *all* our own work for 2 or 3 weeks. Everybody had a holiday but us!—Of course Honoria, clever girl, stayed in N.Y. most—if not all—of the summer—(the café type). She hates country life—So Gerald & I made beds,—3 meals—& the care & feeding of 2 dogs, quite unassisted—I don't think *any* harm was done. My waist got thinner even if dishpan hands *did* set in, but I did get rather a horrid bunyan (is that the sp?) & I don't know who to blame, but would like someone.—Mr Alchermes chiropodist at the Plaza, is indignant & has nothing on me—Too many comfortable sandals always does it—Nothing like good high heels, I always say, for keeping *feet* in order—I do hope you are getting *rested*? Gerald, you know is setting out a wk from Sat. 13th to be gone a month—England,—& now Denmark & Italy have been added to his agenda. So he will be a busy boy. When Dos finishes his articles, I do hope you will be coming down to N.Y. again. I long to see you. Get a good lot of *sleep* too, & take care of yourselves—Welcome to these shores! & <u>very</u> *best* love from old ohia girl

Sara

You heard Alice Lee found G's paintings? Unesco thought it best to keep them—but were foiled.[1]

UVA

---

1. When Archibald MacLeish left to attend a United Nations conference in Paris in 1947, Gerald Murphy contacted Vladimir Orloff about his paintings, which had been left behind at Villa America. Murphy asked Orloff to ship the paintings to MacLeish in Paris, but due to some mix-up, MacLeish never received them. When Alice Lee Myers came to Paris later, she was able to retrieve the paintings from UNESCO. Four of Murphy's paintings have never been recovered: *Boatdeck; Portrait; Engine Room*; and *Roulement à Billes.*

The Murphys did not see the Dos Passoses again before the fatal car accident on 12 September. The next day, Gerald Murphy left for his Mark Cross buying trip in Europe. He felt Katy's loss and Dos Passos's tragedy throughout his travels, as Sara remained behind to help out Dos Passos in any way she could. She went to Boston for Katy's funeral, and she traveled to Virginia with Dos Passos and the Lloyd Lowndeses. At one point during his trip, Gerald would tell Sara: "Even now with yr. very vivid picture of Dos and the funeral I can not grasp it. I think it must be because I have no one to talk to about it. I feel that I heard that it happened and that it hasn't been confirmed. What is it that determines that people be swept out of life by a sudden meaningless violence? You must have been prostrated" (22 September 1947).

217. GERALD MURPHY to SARA MURPHY
in flight to London, 13 September 1947

Sal dear:—

We're all serene at 9 M feet above a floor of cotton wisps with the road leading to EH [East Hampton] quite visible off to the right . . . now there's Gardiners Island and I can distinguish the arc of Sammi's Beach. We're veering over Connecticut and Montauk goes out to sea with a line of fleecy torn clouds over it. Only 10 souls aboard. The air floor is very smooth and everything most comfortable . . . over Boston now and I think of dear Dos lying there below . . . and of the anguish in his mind when he wakes . . . the anguish that he cannot be spared. Write me how they say he is in mind. Where *can* he put this nightmare? Where can he go where Katy will not be? . . . I keep wondering what he'll do. Stand it, I guess. I think she *must* have lost all consciousness. I pray she did. But how awful for him not to have and to have known at once the horror of the reality . . .

* * * * *

I was saying to Daughter that possibly it isn't necessary to wait for me to get back before going out West. [. . . .] She's a lovely creature, more ravishing and original looking everyday (everyone says so). She deserves the best,—and she must *have* it, damn it. She's got a real interest in the theatre and she found it all herself. I think we should now meet her friends, and have them to the house. We've not managed to do that enough and I for one feel remiss about it. I think she needs and deserves our *support*. Tell all this to the dear girl for me, and that I admire and love her in spite of being a haranguing unskillful parent. She's poised to act now and I hate my absence delaying her.

Buy yourself all kinds of repair and cleaning and decorating help and lets give 131 E. the good old 1–2. It will be an economy compared to moving.

* * * * *

Just had tea: how comforting the English make it. I hope you are not too crushed after this day. We're over Nova Scotia now and I think of how enterprising Dos & Katy were about travelling and how cheerfully always they took wing . . .

Give my love to dear Daughter and thank her for the addresses and all her offers to help. I'm really hoping this merger and my work from now on will bring her something in the future. I feel sure it will. The dividends will be at least 4 or 5 M a year and I want her to begin to have them. As the Company expands they'll increase.

Sal dear, many thanks for all the work you did getting this nourishment & these remedies ready. (I thought I'd bring some stuff to Mme Helene & to mail to Vova from Paris. Are there any other French? Pl. send me Mme H's address.)

Don't let Edward impose on you. He's a tender little thing and will do anything if you insist—and stick it out. He begins to know now when he's done something he deserves punishment for. This a.m. he was the picture of guilt when he'd offended *for the 2nd time* at the entrance to the guest room. He needs a moment near his paper when he wakes up (with the cage removed). This a.m. I let him out of the room too soon.

We're nearing Gander. My dearest love to you both dear ones. I'm sorry we had such a tragic and sad day, but I know now how necessary it would be *to be with you* both when such a tragedy comes to our friends,

Devotedly,

daou.

HMD

218. GERALD MURPHY to SARA MURPHY
London, 14 September 1947

Sal: 10 a.m. here
   Smooth crossing. Slept considerably. Found myself praying for Dos. I wonder if it didn't reach him from that point over the Atlantic. Eire looks verdant through a fine drizzle checkerboard paysage with tight little stone farmsteads; people with pink and white skins and thick brogues. Miss you both. Glad Dawn [Powell] was with you. Dearest love to you 2.

d.

HMD

219. GERALD MURPHY to SARA MURPHY
London, 15 September 1947

Sal dear:—

   Had occasion to drive down into the old city to-day past St. Paul's, etc. and suddenly got the sense (for the first time) of what they'd been through. What shocks you is that suddenly—in some remote and now quiet and peaceful square—a house is missing. It has been violently obliterated while the others stand by dozing. You wonder where the people are who were living in it.
   (Honoria: I see so many girls that at a distance look like you,—especially silhouette, hair-do, general tenue. There's one difference: their skins. These have not improved,—and one can see why. The young men look more like the king than they did: blunt noses and more of a muzzle than before)
   Monday I went down to the Kleinwort's cavernous Bank and was back in the Dickens period in two minutes. We lunched in their banqueting room, they two men in their black morning coats, striped trousers. An aged retainer (called Lightfoot) served us. It was all tres International Banker. It's a *very*

different London and one should expect nothing else,—and gets it. The style (if they had it) has gone,—especially if one knew another.

As yet we've not accomplished much (they've slowed up so!) Going to Manchester by car to-morrow, via Walsall. Then back to London Fri. eve. and out to the Kleinwort's Sat. They all live in houses on the old estate. Next wk. Walsall and Ireland. Will advise by cable.

Saw N[oel] Coward's 'Peace in our Time' (alone; tried to get Ruby) to-night. Trash,—with background music out of Sibelius (recorded) and the US Marines saving London while an underdressed English audience sat lumpily through the Star Spangled Banner blared out of a radio in a pub as the final curtain. Two hours of chipper conversation, in an ideal setting, stained-glass clearstories and dark, dark corners. The 2 brothers are in their forties, prosperous versions of Franz Weininger of Vienna,—not at all English in nature,—only in manner and custom. Very volatile. Large estates in the country,—so that all my (your) little gifts shall go to the children and servants (EE Velyn and Lightfoot, aged 72) as they have farm produce of all kinds. The wives are extremely chic, soft-spoken Englishwomen, both like Kate Shepherd, refined but friendly, with restricted horizons. They're being very nice, and I *am* their guest. They spend 2 nights a week in town, so I'm alone in the house, when I'm there. Days are in the equivalent of Wall St. & with the manufacturers,—so that I see nothing of the districts one knew. But the shops are dowdy and uninviting, from what see from taxis.

The English need to be prosperous to be English. Same of us, I guess. The French no. Suddenly it's like Canada here,—with many, many more foreigners: 200,000 refuges in London alone.

Hope Edward hasn't wrecked things and that Wookie doesn't mind him as much.

* * * * *

Show was at 7 p.m. to-night so have finished this in the Buttery. Melon (thin slice), pinladeau, potatoes, peas, 1 bread, cheese, demi-tasse.

* * * * *

Tues. night and no word from you yet. Hope all is well with you dear Sal, Honoria, Wookie, Edw'd, Theresa, Molly,—and Dos.

daou.

HMD

302

220. GERALD MURPHY to SARA MURPHY
Paris, 26 September 1947

Sal, dear:—

The trip here was like a kind of inconsequential taxi-ride by air. No départ, no sense of leave-taking, no sense of arrival. Much too soon Normandy is gone (with now and then a shell hole in a forest where it doesn't interfere) and suddenly one is in a bus passing old names like Avenue des Ternes. We waited for a taxi—tout mité [very run-down]—which brought us to the Claridge 4 blocks away for 35 fr. (a newspaper costs 10 fr.). Claridge's is an ornate friendly caravanserai with corridors miles long, cavernous bathrooms, but with the wonderful flexible front the French always put on. There is no light in our arrondissement except from 7 p.m. to 11 p.m. daily & one shaves gropingly in dark bathrooms. Each arrondissement is deprived 3 days a week. They have really suffered but are still as eager, receptive, elastic, inventive, intelligent and gay. (The English admit they've lost something but are being sporting about it.) The French spirit is untouched, the English facade has been tarnished. Paris is strange tho. Touching, silent, pensive. Everyone scuttling about his business swiftly, deftly with none of the real free leisurely gayety of old. Values are so distorted that the purchase of an aperitif is no longer an idle gesture but takes on the mood of a major operation. You spend $30.00 in dollars (thousands of francs) and have no record of where or how or for what.

Yesterday was manufacturers all p.m. (we arrived at 1 p.m.) dinner near the hotel, to-day mfrs. from 9 a.m. to 6. They're all so inventive, original, searching, impatient—and with no materials. The French genius is rising again. We're all half-alive compared to them,—and they have *nothing* to work with.

Mr. Schloss and his brothers send you their very best wishes and to Honoria too. I have a strange sense of stealing into a town I know and not making my presence known to it. To be here with strangers on a business mission is like a dream. Opposite is Fouquet's where one sat, the Pont Alexandre Trois, Larve, Langer,—one goes by them without comment to strangers. It's all very strange. Fortunately it never occurs to you to have time to ponder. Being one's age and wondering if it will ever return to itself gets all mixed up. There is no temptation to flaner [lounge], time, space and food are too uncertain and scarce.

Mme Helene (or anyone) is out of the question. I regret. Not allowed to bring food into France, anyway. Will try to call Noel [Murphy]. Somehow I can't go into shops knowing that the French are not allowed to buy the stuff. All desire goes in the face of their real *need*. Their clothes, their thin bodies, and taut skins are moving beyond words.

To-morrow eve. at 8:50 we fly back. Sunday by motor to Walsall, mingham, Sheffield. Thursday, London again till Sun. then Dublin for 2 1/2 days.

Hope you're both keeping well and that E. & W. are a comfort. There are more dogs here than in Eng. I think they're really *fonder* of them. Lots of love to you both. I keep trying to think if you'd both enjoy Paris. In a way you somehow feel you shouldn't because they're all so worried. There's not much one can do to help. Yet the young are so much the same: loving couples, tête à têtes at tables in cafes, just as always. What a race! Love to you, my dears,—

daou.

HMD

221. GERALD MURPHY to SARA MURPHY
London, 1 October 1947

Sal, dear:—

We went Sunday p.m. to Birmingham (150m.) by motor. Grim town but I'm getting used to blackened classic revival buildings, with their wet sooty smell and the acrid pall of smoke over everything, with people in threadbare paper clothing with raw faces. Manchester was worse. We stayed at the Midland Hotel with long corridors in impossible perspective and spacious rooms with 20 foot ceilings. Such waste of space and effort. Walsall is 10 miles away. I addressed the factory personnel and told them of the new scheme, omitting the fact of the passing of control out of the family. I was advised by Mr Beck and others that it would be adverse. [Archie's letter to Amb. Lewis Douglas worked like a charm. He gave me two interviews. The second time I brought Ivo Forde (the man Kleinwort sent to America to make the negotiations with us). Douglas was so gracious, keen and understanding and gave the scheme his blessing in the form of telling the British Board of Trade what a chance it was to further a name identified for years with British imports.][1] After the settling of factory matters I went on with the reopening of sources of related lines (sil-

---

1. Prior to Gerald's trip, MacLeish had provided him with letters of introduction, including one to Ambassador Douglas. MacLeish believed that Gerald's idea to draw more heavily upon British imports for the Mark Cross Company would be of "very great concern" to Douglas. "He would want to know about it and to know about it from you," MacLeish told Murphy on 5 September. The brackets in this letter are Gerald's.

ver, crystal, etc.) developed by Father years ago. It meant visiting firms all over Walsall and Birmingham who were desperate to export but who have no materials. It was very touching. Next day we went to Sheffield and worked the cutlery sources. Everywhere the name is so wonderfully well received. It is most gratifying. To-day we came back to London through the country known as 'the Dukeries.' Our road led thro' Chatsworth (Devonshire's place). Monumental free standing trees in cropped pastures with scatterings of Southdown sheep, the river Trent winding smooth and wide through the 30 sq. mile estate and the elegant Georgian house with smiling coloured gardens surrounding it. You wonder for whom it was contrived. It seems so remote, removed, and heedless of the world one lives in. Only the difficulties of its maintenance occur to you who should admire. Then there was Welbeck Abbey, and Burghley Park. Domains so secret and apart that you think of them as if they were in some imagined realm like Graustark. Sad and mute, but so beautiful. We passed the entrance to Haddon Hall and I recalled Granby telling you that replacing the leaden gutters took almost his income. It was picture-book country and I am not convinced now I've seen it.

Got yr. cable in Walsall, Tuesday. I decided not to go on the Eliz. with Givner on the 11th as I don't think I could stand four days of sharing a cabin, meals, drinks, constant enforced companionship (I shall have had 3 wks and more of it) with him. It isn't incompatibility, etc. but when one hasn't got business as a reason, it becomes intolerable. I'll explain. Anyway I'd rather get back. The luxury of those boats suffocates me unless I'm with somebody. I feel fine. (It's yr. vitamins and yr. foods I brought, I think.) Not one bit tired, and it surprises me. Givner (45 yrs.) is the complainer! I'll know how to take the flying better this time. I had no technique before. Don't worry really. Much love to both you dears. A scrunch for W. and E.

daou.

p.s. Cabling you Flight #, hours arrival etc.   g.
HMD

When Gerald Murphy arrived back in New York from Europe, Sara and Honoria were still in the West. Sara had invited Dos Passos to go with them to help him get his mind off Katy, and Dos Passos left for the Midwest a few days before Sara returned home. Honoria remained in the West a while longer.

222. SARA MURPHY to JOHN DOS PASSOS
New York, 2 November [1947]

Dear Dos—

Thank you for your wire, rec'd this am—I *wondered* how you made out—We had a rather horrid time—& I reflected longingly on sitting in a train, & reading—in spite of weather.—They took us to Chicago & then said "flight was terminated"—which meant every man for himself after that.—Every man, unfortunately, seemed woman with child or children—all wanting to get to N.Y. immediately & most planes grounded, so pandemonium ensued—Screaming babies—all unfed & frantic people—By that time I had become intimate friends with a little girl who got on at Reno with me—She looked about 16—but has a husband & 2 babies at home in Reno—She is going to look up Honoria—She turned out to be a niece of Lefty Lewis & was going alone to visit her mother in Boston—So we joined forces & stormed the desk at Chicago airport. *Finally*—about 8 P.M. we climbed onto a D.C. 6—happy enough to dance—which we did—& I arrived at the apt—*very* bedraggled, about 11:30 at night, with one of the mothers & a baby—Gerald had about given me up—as he could get *nothing* out of the United Lines—& was so pleased—(if a little surprised)—at seeing our little group—Laguardia was 2 ft under water—So we had to be *towed*—Well, all is well that ends well, & I am nearly rested up, we stayed here instead of going to Easthampton—I was good & cross though—& made a scene at the desk, because we found one of the mothers giving her baby Coca Cola in a feeding bottle—They could at least have had some milk for children at those airports, where they waited so many hours—It was all infuriating & I think I'll travel by train hereafter. Best love, Dos—all is well here—You have a pile of mail—Wire if you want it forwarded—I've talked to Honoria on phone & she sounded fine—Take *good Care* of yourself—I thought we had quite a nice time—& Everyone wants to hear about our adventures—

à bientôt!—& love again

Sara

UVA

223. JOHN DOS PASSOS to SARA MURPHY
Coon Rapids, Iowa, 5 November [1947]

Dear Sara,

Thanks for such a nice letter. Certainly United Airlines isn't what it's

306

cracked up to be. I'm starting east Monday by train to Chicago and then taking a chance on a flight to Washington (not by United). I'll be turning up in New York after a rapid run to Virginia the fifteenth or sixteenth.

It's wonderful here. Nobody talks about anything but corn and hogs and oats and fertilizers and it's a liberal education in the art of farming. The weather has been miserable.

I'm so glad Honoria sounded cheerful. I think she'll get to love it. Hope she's started riding.

Please let my mail accumulate. I'll tackle it when I get back—

love to you and Gerald,
Yrs

Dos

HMD

224. JOHN DOS PASSOS TO SARA MURPHY
Havana, 8 September 1948

Dear Sara—

Got in just in time for the Despedida de Hemingway which is described inimitably in the enclosed—The old Monster was much better than the sour Mr. Juarez (who wasn't invited) implies, had his weight down and seemed in splendid fettle. The trouble with the party was not the champagne which was excellent but the fact that the steamer, which was Polish, kept forgetting to leave. First it was 10:30, then 12:00 noon and then when I had to tear myself away to go about my business 4 p.m. The good old Monster kept ordering up more giggle-water with the results that are described within. Love to Gerald: the briefcase travels marvellously.

Yrs ever

Dos

[Dos Passos included an article from a local English-language paper as follows:]
Ernest Hemingway, United States author and in an exceptionally large way, left Havana for Europe yesterday on the "Jagiello". Some said he is going to Italy. They all gave him a farewell however as though he quit Havana. Many have been here with him long. The inseparable ones, as Juan Dunabeita, skipper or chief officer for a ship. C. G. Echevarria, one more in that capacity and

307

career, he of the "Atlantico," and others would keep him company for ever if left to them. Bakques, and particularly such people as mentioned, team up with him because he is one American that can match them in their mother tongue and in their acts including bridge and the jai-alai. And he can almost outbid them in travels by sea, which is their game, by land and by air. When it comes to drinks, few can reach his level. Mr. Hemingway in the past war took risks for his country and for the Allies. He had an accident in London, nearly died, stayed in the hospital, and again *reincorporated to live in full swing* [Dos Passos's underlining]. He makes news wherever he goes, as he will now, and as he did in Africa, in Asia and all abouts. His books sell by the thousands, so it was "For Whom the Bell Tolls," which turned out the more in his profit for the picture. The only thing he gets out of them is money, and that serves to keep him going and well. His yacht here Pilar II is one of his precious relics, a relic in his absence, for the yacht moves much while he is on it, even as he is heavy, if only in the sense of size and weight. Friends were with him till the ship parted from the docks. They all wish him well and back him up to that extent. Julio Hidalgo, the pilot gave him his send-off aboard ship. It was his turn to put ship and him on trail out. They hugged each other till they next be together shortly again. Mr. Hemingway owns home and piece of property, or resort, at San Francisco de Paula near Havana.

HMD

225. JOHN DOS PASSOS TO SARA MURPHY
Buenos Aires, Argentina, 7 November [1948]
good lord how the time goes [written by date]

Dear Sara—

Now it is B.A.—a large synthetic city that looks very much like the Paris of the Parc Monceau region—Everybody looks well fed and well shod and rather stuffy. People on the street have a rather disagreeable expression on their faces like Chicago without the humor. The steaks are sensational but the rest of the cookery is done with linseed and cotton seed oil and pretty quelquonque [mediocre]. Huge German style restaurants full of people getting red in the face over gigantic slabs of prime beef—No matter how hot it is nobody is allowed to take off his jacket on the street. Even little children have to wear neck ties to get into the moving picture theatres. And all this dominated by the extraordinary figures of Mr. & Mrs Peron.

Sara it was sweet of you to send the flowers to Truro. I cant yet find words to write. After a year the void is as deep as ever. The only thing is to keep busy.

I cant wait to see the raised cottage in the course of transformation—
there's still a lot of work to be done before I can start home
Love to Gerald & Honoria—

Yrs ever

Dos

HMD

226. ARCHIBALD MACLEISH to GERALD MURPHY
Conway [c. November 1948]

Dear Dow:

I don't know. I only know that you & I feel it alike. A year ago now I wrote
in a piece in "1948"—
"October in New England was a parable. For more than three weeks the
days turned slowly in an enchanted stillness of blue overhead, gold underfoot.
The trees held their foliage or let it fall little by little from motionless branches
& the sun at noon was hot in the high silence. . . . It was perfect weather, or
weather as nearly perfect as living men have ever seen. And nevertheless there
was no quiet in it. Even before the brush fires started in the pines you felt a
sense of tragic imminence, of waiting. October is the time for change and the
change had not come——" "A kind of boding" you say. It is true. Or at least it
is true for you & me. But why, unless because the autumn is the time for
change & we await it, our hearts beating faster than the season, I do not know.
What a beautiful letter. Thank you for it. My love to you both

Archie

HMD

227. GERALD MURPHY to JOHN DOS PASSOS
New York, 20 November 1948

Dos:

To-day it was 66° at 7 a.m. but we are told of transcontinental buses lost in
the snows which descended on 75 mile winds on Kansas and the Dakotas.
This strange suspension of the seasons continues here. I wrote Archie and

309

tried to define my feelings about the very thing I wrote you about and cried out to him for help. He answered: [Gerald here copies Archie's letter which precedes this letter, word for word, save for its closing paragraph.]

How grateful I find myself to Archie for his ability to think and to write about the feelings one has in relation to nature—in the American scene. So few poets to-day are willing to or can do so. I've never felt so intensely as now about my memories of the natural peace and kind of assurance which one has felt at certain times on this continent on a hill once in Vermont on a ridge in Virginia—not an awe of Nature or the spreading panorama—but the almost intolerable satisfaction seated on the ground with your back against a tree. Where is it? I would go forth now on a pilgrimage in search of it, willing never to return.

The project at Sneden's creeps apace. We plough next week. The willow is in and looks lovely also the Paulownia stands on the rear terrace. It's so nice to think of its being a stray seedling given us by our neighbours, les Lowndes. My quest for two larches was answered. They went in yesterday and I already await their shrill Spring green. Next a smoke-bush. Then in the Spring a pair of hollys. But alas our contractor is apathetic. We have no estimate yet!!

We shall miss you mightily next Thursday. I'm contributing some Chateau Palmer '37 Bordeaux to the pheasant. We'll be drinking your health about 8 p.m. Lloyd [Lowndes] is godfather at noon to the Tomkins. The *entire* T. family—in a mass movement—are being baptized. I cannot help picturing them all in graduating sequence and in white shifts being dunked off a plank into the Hudson and crying Hallelujah! Sara and Honoria and I send you as much love as they'll allow across the border,

Gerald.

p.s. The temp. went to 73° yesterday. Cloudless sky. To-day continues with its ominous benediction.   g.

p.p.s. Such a nice Mr Bass called for yr. address. He said that yr. name ran *throughout* 'The Legacy of Sacko-Vanzetti.'

UVA

228. JOHN DOS PASSOS to SARA MURPHY
Palisades, N.Y., 15 January 1949

Dear Sara—

You cant imagine how empty New York feels getting back there and finding no Sara in it. Last night Gerald read excerpts from yours and Honoria's letters and it sounds as if Windsor Cottage [in Nassau] were just what its name implies, and working out. I cant get over your picture of Mrs M. If you haven't seen the Marquands yet do call them up and give them my best. I'll certainly try to get down some time in February but dont know just when I can work it yet

Last night turned out to my amazement to be my birthday. Gerald and Teresa even had a cake. The Lowndes came and we drank Gerald's best Martinis followed by clam broth, deliciously cooked squab with [illegible word], giggle water and the theatre. Gerald in some way managed to get seats to Kiss Me Kate and we all roared and clapped all evening. It's definitely one of Cole Porter's better products. The only thing we missed was the presence of Mrs. Puss.

Tonight I'm off to Virginia to visit the cattle for a few days. I wish I could stop dashing up and down the country. Maybe I shall very suddenly one day.

Love to Honoria—Yrs ever

Dos

HMD

John Dos Passos did get down to see Sara in Nassau as he had hoped. Gerald wrote Sara there on 22 February 1949: "So glad you've got Dos there. Diddy Lowndes says: 'He needs Sara as much as the sun.' He's such fun to do things with and loves doing the things one prefers to. Rare. Make him stay as long as you can." Archie MacLeish had just been with Gerald and was preparing to join Ada and Sara in Nassau in early March, following an extensive stint of lecturing.

229. JOHN DOS PASSOS to SARA MURPHY
Havana, 28 February 1949

Dear Sara—

I seem to be established at the old Ambos Mundos for a while. I'm afraid I was a horrid sickly guest. I bought you another bottle of Kaopectate but before I could get it to the post office I was drinking it and then the post office was closed and my plane left first thing in the morning so I couldn't even make the pretty gesture of mailing you a bottle of the precious fluid. Either that or old Dr. Cass's white powder or both brought me around so I'm now virtually on my feet again. Havana seems completely unchanged. The old monster unfortunately is still in Europe, in Austria so they say at the Ambos Mundos.

Nassau seemed lovely and it was a pleasure to see our Mrs Puss so sturdy—I'm writing Gerald that he must go down and take a look himself. I still think longingly of that little fat freshly painted boat I didn't get to go out in. Give my love to Ada and Archie and the Marquands. Let me have a card occasionally—

Yrs ever

Dos

[Ernest had apparently written Dos Passos asking him to give Sara the following message, enclosed in this letter on a separate scrap of paper.]

Tell Sara Mary and I lost baby in Casper Wyo. If you are going to lose anything Casper is the place. Sara wrote lovely letter about maybe we would have a daughter and never answered. Tell her am glad she has a daughter and will have to do for all of us. Tell her also that I love her very much.

H.

HMD

230. JOHN DOS PASSOS to GERALD MURPHY
Havana, 28 February 1949

Dear Gerald—

I had an all too short but very pleasant visit with our Sadie—she was looking very well and seemed in excellent spirits although perhaps a little missing her 'interieur' [home]. I'm sure Nassau is doing her good. The little town is so picturebook pretty and the air is so fresh and the bays and inlets are so clear I'm sure you would enjoy a glimpse of it. Arriving there is fantastically easy. I left Washington at one thirty a.m. one morning was in Miami at six and in Nassau at ten. The water is delicious at the beaches, and right in front of the house for that matter. I found Sara surrounded by Ada and the Kenny MacL's and with her Cincinnati Bishop coming to lunch.

I'm afraid I was a rather sickly guest as I was having just a touch of the rheumatics and felt a little done in by the trip and was injudicious enough to come down with the traveller's disease. Left after having been very much cared for and medicated to such a point that I was virtually cured by the time I arrived in Havana.

Havana is very much the same as it's always been. I wish we could all take a trip together again some time.

                    Yrs

                              Dos

Love to Honoria.
HMD

231. ARCHIBALD MACLEISH to GERALD MURPHY
Conway, 29 April [1949]

Dear Daou:

It isn't that I object to the efficiency of the self-addressed, return, perforated, hand-deckled, prepaid post-card. Its just that I've got more to say than will fit its little oblong.

The anthology is Huntington Cairn's *Limits of Art* published by Pantheon Books. Its excellent if you can take it for what it is, not for what it pretends. The blurbs by great minds at the ends of the several selections are irritating until you have read enough so that they cancel each other out. Then they are merely funny and can be neglected. Also there is far too much Dryden. Which is another way of saying that Cairns is far too much impressed with the local divinity of this age, Mr. T.S. E [Eliot]. But there are wonderful things.

The quotation is Measure for Measure, III–1. It *does* sound like Milton. Which is rare in both.

And now I must ask a favor. Somewhere, somehow, I have lost the note-book I was working on last summer. I am badly confused about it but my best memory is that I took it to your flat with some other papers (including a check-book which is also missing) when I repacked *on March 1* just before I left for Nassau. I'm not at all sure but that's my best guess. But the trouble with that theory is that none of these things were in my attaché case which was neatly tucked away just where I left it on the closet shelf in the little bed-room. If, therefore, I left the note-book there at all I must have put it in some other container. Which brings me, with a thousand apologies, to the favor. Would you ask Theresa to look around a bit to see if I could possibly have put the note-book and a few other papers somewhere else? If it doesn't come to light at once please don't let anyone worry about it. I'm apparently irresponsible. But if it did happen to lie there somewhere I should be much relieved. It had one poem in it which *might* turn out to *be* one.

Love to that Sal. I hope Cheer Hall looks as vernal as I am sure it must with the river before and the hill-side behind all facing the morning sun. The Boylston business is apparently going through in the next ten days.[1] I feel fine about it too. Not in the least trapped. Why?

affectionately as ever

Archie

And <u>WHEN</u> <u>ARE</u> <u>YOU</u> <u>COMING?</u>

HMD

---

1. MacLeish had accepted the position as the Boylston Professor of Rhetoric and Oratory at Harvard.

232. JOHN DOS PASSOS to SARA MURPHY
Wiscasset, Maine [25 July 1949]

Dear Sara,

It was sweet seeing old friends on the Cape but its still too painful there. I had to go to do some things. Tell Gerald I put those lines—"How to keep . . . from vanishing away" on the little tablet, on the back. Wiscasset seems deliciously remote after the crowded Cape. Lloyd and Diddy [Lowndes] and I spent a large part of suppertime last night wishing you and Gerald were here. I'll be through New York for a second next week on my way to Maryland—where Betty Holdridge and I are going to get married privately in a cornfield and then hurry down to Spence's Point to go to work on the farming and house organization there. I've gotten tangled up with an event in Venice in mid September similar to the one Gerald packed me off to years ago in England. We'll be back October 1 and eager to receive a brace of Murphies in those rural solitudes along the Potomac—Anyway I'm hoping to see you in New York or Snedens on my way through—

love

Dos

HMD

233. SARA MURPHY to JOHN and BETTY DOS PASSOS
Snedens Landing, 24 November [1949]

Mr dear Dos & Betty—

I thought I would, on Thanksgiving, write you both how *wonderful* we think the news is—brought back from Virginia by the Lowndeses! (In secret, of course.) I can't think of *anything* that would give us more rejoicing—It is just the best news in years & years!—Well, blessings on you both, and especially on the expected newcomer. I cannot help hoping (although I've no idea what *your* feelings are in the matter,)—that it's to be a daughter—Daughters are a very *good thing,*—and so pretty too! I can hardly wait! But I suppose we must,—till May,—isn't it? The Lowndeses say you are both perfectly fine, & the house lovely, & that you have *electricity!* & *perhaps* a telephone—How immeasurably easier that will make everything—We are all well, & going along in the usual country style—dogfights, head colds, deranged plumbing (we found they had thought it best not to give us a cess-pool! So our lawn is now all dug up—with 4 street lights you know, bomb-shaped,—at night,—rather like 42nd St.)—& cooks come & go—mostly go—however, we love it—our air & view remain,—& the house *is* cute & comfortable, even if we can't take baths—What are a few baths among friends? Dawnie [Powell] came, & spent a couple of nights in our sans-sol guestroom, & said she felt exactly like the Folle de Chaillot—It *is* rather red & underground. The Mac-Leishes are coming on the 2nd or 3rd Dec. I think we may be considered settled in, in spite of all the workmen & their travaux—I go to N.Y. about once a week, feeling quite hayseedy—Honoria *loves* her apt—& entertaining her friends—She has been here for thanksgiving, & it was a *beautiful* day—& we are all rather drowsy with turkey & pie—not to mention Gerald's drinks. I *hope* we shall see you sometime soon—perhaps you will both be obliged to run up to N.Y. on some pretext, & that you can spend a night or 2 with us?—Do, please—And in the meantime I must say again how we *treasure* your news! With *very* best love from us all—I am your obliged & devoted friend

Sara—

UVA

234. JOHN DOS PASSOS to SARA MURPHY
Baltimore, Maryland, 10 April [1950]

Dear Sara,

These Baltimore races are informal gentleman jockey affairs and lots of fun.

You have to get there early usually to find parking places and suitable points of vantage etc as there are no stands. The crowd just mills around along the edges of the track. If you could come up for the Grand National on Saturday the 22nd it would be splendid. If the day is anything near decent (today it feels like snow) we can ride out in the stationwaggon and take our lunch. I'm afraid it will be a little too strenuous for Betty but we can tell her about it at supper. We hope to take her to Milady's Manor this Saturday. Maybe you would rather come on the train Friday afternoon, or maybe a spring glimpse of Pennsylvania would be agreeable from Mr Murphy's gleaming locomotive. If Mrs B [Boynton] isnt occupying her room we can place you and Gerald in it. I'll probably be in New York for two days that week and could perhaps come back with you. If we have to get you a hotel room we'd better do it right away as Baltimore is packed to the gills in April. If the 29th which is the Maryland Hunt Cup turns out more convenient we could still manage it but it would be un peu juste [a little tight] as we have to move to 317 Thornhill Road the 28th. We are very much in the position of the cuckoo laying its eggs (for a price) in other people's nests. Let us know and meanwhile I think I'll try to make a reservation at the Belvedere or the Emerson just in case for Friday and Saturday nights (21st and 22nd). We do want to see you

Love to the McCloskeys—

Yrs ever

Dos

HMD

In May of 1950, Gerald Murphy arrived in Europe for another Mark Cross buying trip. This one would take him to England, France, Italy and Scandinavia, and it would include as well his firming up the arrangements for the sale of Villa America. The Murphys had begun to explore the possibility of selling the property as early as 1947, when Ellen and Philip Barry went over and checked out the condition of the villa. After placing the property with an agent and having Vladimir oversee the details of the sale, Gerald Murphy secured a buyer and made the sale in conjunction with his 1950 stay. During Murphy's stay in Europe, Ellen Barry was there also. Philip Barry had died of a massive heart attack on 3 December 1949, and Ellen's loss was quickened by the memories which the Riviera evoked. Besides selling Villa America, Vladimir had also arranged in 1945 for the sale of the Weatherbird *to Gerard de Loriol, a Swiss resident of Geneva and Paris.*

235. GERALD MURPHY to SARA MURPHY
Paris, 23 April [May] 1950

Sal dear:—

Vova left last night for St. Tropez. He had brought de l'Oriol for a drink before luncheon. He proves to be the *most charming* person. Apparently he was disapproved of by his very rich Father as being a playboy and decided he'd go to the Gold Coast where he made a fortune in ivory. He's tall, dark with an open plain face. Enormous vitality. Loves to laugh. Loves danger, adventure, travel, exploration. Is leaving on the Vagrant early in July pour aller aux Indes. (Sleeps on board when it's calm. Stays up on deck all night if its rough, stormy or dangerous.) Vraiement un grand esprit. He and E. Hemingway should know each other. Vlad. feels we should get the furniture—which is in cases according to kind—over to his boat's entrepot at Monte Carlo. It is empty now. We could sort the various things, sell what we don't want and send the choice things back to USA. All this whether sale goes thro' or not. M. Uhers (acheteur) sec'y came to see me yesterday. They're acting (mostly Platano, the vieux requin of an agent) peculiar and he's trying to get occupation before first payment which I won't allow. We told them so, yet trying not to lose sale. It all may come out all right. Hope so. I've decided to leave on Parisienne, July 6th in order to go down to Nice. I shall send you my list to-morrow and you mark what you *think* you'd like & I'll be guided by that. Wonder if you could join me for last two weeks here in France & go down to Nice. Would you be disposed to attempt it. The sale of furniture would pay for (ultimately) yr. expenses over here and return. Vova longs so to see you. It's touching. Of course travel, reservations, etc. is *awful*. (Ellen had to leave this hotel [Meurice] and go to another as they are so booked up & she had to stay over on account of her car, etc.) (She's fine and seems to be making her way pretty well. Every one *loves* her.) I do not care to go to the Villa, especially if it's sold. V. thinks best not. I guess it's right to preserve a memory if one can. Please advise. V. says the Americans spoiled the Cote d' Azur. St. Trop. has lost all its primitiveness & is now a seriously 'important' watering-place. I wish V. could come to see us. The Gdynia Polish line sails from Villefranche every two weeks for USA. He could come en touriste, I think. Paris is strange. All life goes off the streets at 8 p.m. It's dark and taxis run with dimmed parking lights. Cafes close early. You're reminded of the French provincial towns. Esther [Murphy], I see now, is not well. After all these years of neglect her teeth are in terrible condition, her appetite gone and she has insomnia. I don't think she 'drinks,' but she tries to get support from alcohol, and of course that doesn't work. Noel [Murphy] came last night. More so than ever, but I suppose she means well. She's worried about E. Esther is taking injections from Miss Barney's doctor & trying to get well. She's much underweight. Leave for Florence Fri. 8 p.m. Will keep in close touch with you by cable. The address in Rome will be Hotel Excelsior. Should you get confused ever about my movements and reaching me Miss Robbins will advise.

Am lunching Thu. with de' l'Oriol & am keeping eye on Ellen. Esther is lunching with her today. She's so dependent on Whiskers. I don't know what she'd do without him. Her nephew is coming up from Antibes to drive down with her. She's at the Hotel Lotti now.

Dearest love to you and Daughter am writing her to-morrow. Esther & Noel drank to you both last night,

daou

[written on back of envelope]: Did you feel that awful explosion?
HMD

236. GERALD MURPHY to SARA MURPHY
Florence, Italy, 28 May 1950

Sal dearest:—

Excuse pencil. The paper (like this hotel [Majestic]) is rather flimsy. We came by train overnight arriving last evening. The sight, smell and look of la Méditerranée at Genoa was for an instant almost intolerably nostalgic. All that it had meant to us everywhere with everyone rushed into my mind. I missed you and ours painfully and yet I knew that we had had something (with all its flaws) which one could not set about finding to-day. It was more grey than blue and glistened restlessly par un soleil voilé [through a veiled sun]. I felt that it had changed because of what it had seen those years of the war. All along the coast thro' Rapallo and down to Pisa there are cruel gaping ruins of innocent houses, gardens and villas along the RR and especially near the little bridges crossing the many streams. People living in half a house which [had] been cut like cake, but with pots of flowers on every sill. Pisa is a waste with its duomo and campanile and baptisteria looking like forgotten toys in the middle of it. As I came on Florence I recalled so clearly our first visit (with all the memories I had of yr. stays here). It is shocking the destruction. I found myself saying, right around this corner there's a . . . and it would not be there. Only two bridges remain. Our hotel (and many houses near it) is gone. Still gaping ruins with entrails hanging. And worse is what they're building in its place! Our new commissionaire Giorgini is a charming cultivated man. The great antiquaire of Florence. We dined with him at his palazzo near the Pitti with a huge botanical garden along the Arno all walled in. His wife and children (21 to 25) charming. They keep it up as best they can. The Germans occupied it & drove trucks and put gravel throughout the ancient parterres, used garden sculptures as targets, played 'darts' with bayonets on the boisserie [wooden] doors of the salon and ball-room, etc, etc. One tries not to notice, but it takes you so unawares. Giorgoni says it can not be restored, possibly. The sight of living desecration is hard to bear. The sky is the same, long lozenze-shaped Benozzo Gozzali clouds, soft dry cool air stirring and the bells——There are 1800 Unesco people (with families) here, the French Opera Company, and les touristes. This poor little provincial upland town groans in its sleep. On the walls one reads 'Vota cosi el partito communista' [Vote the communist party] To-day we looked at the shop windows which are open. It is odd to know what there is behind walls and in buildings and to do nothing about it. I *couldn't* even if I had the time. How one needs to *share* things. You *always* knew this.

I'm so glad of your reports that things are running smoothly. I hope that you do get *some* rest tho'. The garden *is* a boon. Two years ago and less it was a dream. I'll try to find you a little statue here if time allows. What a comfort Daughter is. Give her my love. Edward (I know) can manage. He has too much to do to mope, I'm glad to say. It was Wookies neck, back length (nape to tail) and girth I want. Also Edward's *actual* neck measurement. Sorry. They asked me for a verification and I gave it.

Is the hydrangea bush coming back? I do hope so & feel it will. Hope weather isn't continuing damp. You *should* have some sun. Is the knee troubling you still. Answer. I suppose it's too late for holly & too disturbing and costly. They should be good specimens or none.

Ellen [Barry] saw Hoytie [Wiborg] but ducked. Give my best to the entourage and dearest love to yrself & Daughter,

daou.

HMD

237. GERALD MURPHY to SARA MURPHY
en route Rome–Paris, 9 June 1950

Dearest Sal:——

We've come up from Rome along the coast. I've been looking inland with my map to towns with names to conjure with: Orvieto (the wine from there: dry but heady) Perugia, Siena, Orvieto, Pisa, Firenze, Pistoia (I finally tracked down the Lima-Pistoiese you loved so. It's almost extinct.) Elba is off to the left. (I recall your visit with Honoria in a red-striped dress, Fanny, & L. [Louise] Bowers) Now its Spezia with its superb port, and soon San Margharita & Portofino. Remember?! Ours was the great epoque at those places. Now all is so breathed upon, standardized & popularized. Soon it will be Genoa of old memory and then over Torino and Milano off to the East, Geneva ahead with Mont Blanc in the distance. In Rome this time my memory went back so clearly—for some reason—to your stories of yr. earliest visits, the people you knew, la Campagna, etc. It's a completely past era, possibly that's why it came back thro' the corridors of memory. Rome is beautiful, but unbecomingly crowded and breathed upon. (Clouds too heavy, we've avoided Mt. Blanc and gone S.W. toward Lyon.) Annezy is below looking peaceful in the sun. We'll be over Beaune soon. I miss you, seeing these things that we've always shared: Chalon, Verdun, Semur, Avallon . . . are all there in the sun below. I wish you were here beside me. We're over the region Archie and I bicycled thro'. How beautiful and *human* it is! Approach Paris!

All my love to you both.

daou.

p.s. Trib. says it was 90 in NYC yesterday. Hope you're not getting it bad.   d.
HMD

238. GERALD MURPHY to SARA MURPHY
Copenhagen, Denmark, 13 June 1950

Sal dear:—

We flew up over Belgium, the Netherlands, the British zone of Germany (with the Rhine glistening below) then out up this peninsula with its 600 islands (100 of which are inhabited) to Copenhagen. Got here at 7:00 so that I've no impression yet. Somewhat German in looks, naturally,—tho' there's was a resistance 'second to none' as Montgomery said. It's cool,—but I allowed for it and have warm clothes.

On the 10th I was leaving the hotel to go out with Esther at about 8:15 p.m. when I was called to the phone. It was Ellen. She was sitting on the terrace of the hotel du Cap and said she felt us so much there that she had to call me. I told her that I'd just had a letter from you saying you hoped to go with the Brennans to Wilton. She was so touched and said: 'It's going on now. How sweet of Sara and Honoria!' She appreciated yr. thought so. She said the Cap was calm, serene and so beautiful. I asked if she was enjoying it and she said: 'Yes, but it's difficult.' Adele [Lovett] is going to her the 29th. I'm going to try to stop there with Vladimir during my 3 days between Nice, Monte-Carlo, St. Tropez and Marseille. Vladimir when he saw her in Paris said: 'Qu'elle est devenue belle!' [What a beautiful woman she has become!] I had written him about Phil. He liked them so from the time we gave them the boat to cruise on.

My last days in Paris were so chopped up that I didn't have a moment to write you. Saw Esther one evening and met Noel in the street. The North and its people seem strange after the Latins. They're extremely nice and friendly tho' and *love* foreigners. The commissionaire whom I'd never seen in my life sent flowers with a card saying 'Welcome to Denmark.' He came to see me and when I thanked him he said: 'Those were a little thanks from a small man of Denmark for the great Marshall Plan.' Very sweet. The Germans did wicked damage here,—and took out reprisals on the most beloved buildings on account of the Resistance which was *openly* bitter. What a scourge they've been!

Reports of the heat in NY sound awful. I do hope you're not too uncomfortable. Find out the cool spots at the different times of day. Isn't Edwd a nuisance taking on so about the heat? I suppose he makes you feel it worse.

I'll write you to-morrow after I get an idea of what it's like here. Much, much love to you and to Daughter,

daou.

HMD

239. GERALD MURPHY TO SARA MURPHY
Paris, 26 June 1950

Sara dear:—

Am writing this at Pierre's (he recognized me and asked for you at once!) opposite Drouant, where in a salon particulier we dined with Clemenceau (le Tigre de France) and Hoytie (la Tigresse). The place has prospered but not grown too much of a moustache. The little triangular square looks more like a stage set than ever. I am sitting alone (for the 1st time in 5 weeks! My compagnonne has gone to the USA via London) among begonias and geraniums as of yore. The moon is just over the roof tops, a dog with Edward's meaningless bark has taken over,—and I wish you were here. I just ate green almonds and I'm bringing you some. A fine quiet Sunday yesterday, unpacking and repacking all my samples to send back by boat. In the afternoon I went to the Louvre (it was the day of the Grand Prix: 100,000 souls at Longchamps). What a stupendous collection it is in those long narrow salons of the Palace so beautifully lighted. It seemed strange to be in a crowd so young. Thirty years ago I saw it first. They were so orderly, leisurely and quietly appreciative. The Italian school can't be matched even in mia Italia. Afterwards I walked in the Tuileries and sat near the very pond where I recall sailing a tin boat with elastic band rigging. Mother who had come with her friend Mr Holmes had bought it for me. It was a dismal failure: wouldn't sail. I recall it as my first disappointment in life. Nearby was the old Punch and Judy show,—now 'Marionettes.' At a pavillion under the trees I had a glass of beer and watched the amazing French people all doing just what they wanted and knowing what that was. Walked up by the Pavillion 'Jeu de Paume' and sat looking out over the Place. What a sight, with its perspectives darting in all directions and overhead that great expanse of sky. To-day finished the shops on the boulevards. Went into Prevost (thinking surely it no longer existed) sat at the same table you brought me to on that winter day so long ago. Yes the girl had the same wooden stirrer she twirls: I had a brioche. The chocolat was all too much the same: of a heartiness. Later I went into Loche. He remembered me at once and asked for you and the children. Madame 'est decedée il ya douze ans, Monsieur.' [His wife has been dead for twelve years.] His son is proprietaire. He's 73;—and sent such affectionate messages.

My days will now be scheduled rendezvous with mfrs. at the commissionaires or out in the suburbs at the source.

Back of it all is that for which there is no substitute: Paris. I see you here— not in the past but in the future. You will come and find what was always here and will continue to be. Nothing changes. No sign of the Germans having been here. It was just a bad dream. *They* called it La Ville sans Regard. No French person ever looked at them.

Much love,

daou.

HMD

240. GERALD MURPHY to SARA MURPHY
Antibes, France, 30 June 1950

S. d.

Immediately one is caught up by the compelling beauty of it—that shining *transparent* sea, the high healthy palms, the mixed smell of watered parks with oleander dominating (laurier rose just at its height). The stillness and peace and the air stirred constantly by the sea. I had come with misgivings, prepared to be saddened, but no! The villa *is* untended in appearance, but the garden no! The palms, the large conifer, the linden, the eucalyptus (like a tower) have now eclipsed the view of the water, so that it's a secret garden, not the free outlook it had. Joseph [Revello] so sweet, unchanged, affectionate and Baptistine [Revello] as young as ever. Both sent 1000 warm messages with brimming eyes to you and Hoho. Lovely eve. with Vova. Cool empty hotel. Stopped to see Ellen. More later. Love, d.

HMD

241. ALAN CAMPBELL to SARA MURPHY
West Los Angeles, 14 January [1951]

Dear Sara,

Dotty and I were so pleased to get your warm, good letter. We think of you and Gerald so often—with resultant missing of you—so it was lovely to have direct news.

We tried desperately to call you on New Year's Eve, but didn't have a telephone number. I first tried information at Sneeden's Landing (how did that extra E pop in?) and got a number which, when I called it, said that Mr. Gerald Murphy had moved to Niagara Falls in 1920. Then I tried Monte Wooley here at the Bel-Air Hotel, but he was out, as was everybody else we tried, both here and on the East coast. We even tried Archie and Ada in Cambridge, but they, too, were helling around somewhere in Boston. We were frustrated and furious and—by the time we had finished trying, extremely full of champagne.

In any case, I shall now give you our message which is that we hope you will have a fine, happy, abundant New Year. We were both so pleased by Honoria's marriage and when we get North will instantly call her. Meantime, do give her our love when you write.[1]

Dotty looks—and is—wonderful. She has a new short haircut, a permanent wave, and a beautiful figure, and feels fine besides. She sends you both much love and so do I.

Yours

Alan

HMD

---

1. Honoria married William M. Donnelly in New York on 14 November 1950.

242. GERALD MURPHY to JOHN DOS PASSOS
in flight, New York to California, 31 October 1951

Dear Dos:—

As Sara said when yr. card came: 'I like it when people write about nothing in particular but just what they're feeling.' What a boon it was for me to
know that someone else was feeling as I was standing in the field by the river
ranging hay-cocks and full of a well-nigh unsupportable ecstase at the day
around me wide spacious high with sounds far off directionless but clear lim-
itless distance yet the feeling of haze   a strong sense of pause   pause in
time and space   a sense of brooding   boding   an imminence an imminence of Peace   a Peace we somehow know . . . above and through
it all the air (whose base is cool and full of that acrid incense of fallen
leaves) . . . I'd better stop this litany of my perceptions   I've never felt it
anywhere but here   I knew it first gathering hickory nuts in Ridgefield
Connecticut as a child   I wonder if it's linked to that almost obscured
sense we sometimes have of being a creature on a *continent* spreading wide
between two oceans   all somehow blessed   It certainly has to do with
being (and feeling) an American. As you know for years I've been pleading
with you and Archie *to do* something about it   I'm glad to see you're
haunted   Archie has written me now in answer to my question as to *what*
it is we feel: [Here Gerald once again quotes the letter he had quoted to Dos
Passos on 20 November 1948]

* * * * *

And so you have it. I'm so glad you had it. I felt it was *everywhere* through
the land. I can imagine it in Westmoreland! And our Miss Lucy [only child of
John and Betty Dos Passos]? I have two engaging photos of her I took during
her passage thro' Snedens. She's so obviously taking the strange photographer
gentleman *in*. We are winging this All Hallows Eve on broomsticks to see our
grandson, John Charles. He has thrived steadily and looks so really bonnie in
his pictures: 16 lbs. 10 oz. 4 mos. the 20th of October! Strawberry blond with
blue eyes which close at sudden smiles. I've never seen him. We're pretty excited. Returning the 15th. Much love from us to you all three

Gerald

Our warmest remembrances to the Griffiths!
UVA

243. GERALD MURPHY to ELLEN BARRY
Snedens Landing, 14 November 1952

Ellen, dear:—

Here it is with winter closing in and no word from me to you in thanks for the lovely and thoughtful 'tubereuses' (I shall always think of them as essentially French) which you sent me on my couch of pain. At night especially with the cool air from outside their parfum recalled Antibes and Cannes (oddly enough your father's funeral) and I got to thinking of what an Age of Innocence our pleasures on the Riviera seemed during those first few years before the great American Invasion when even the Hotel du Cap was taken over. (Hotel Universe reflects it.) Those were the days when Jonathan [Barry] would do his long-strided swinging Marathon way down the Garoupe beach.—all by himself,—be brought back and start out all over again. I can see him still. St. Paul du Var was an adventure; Monte Carlo was as described by your parents; the dinner-flowers-gala at the Ambassadeurs when Hopkins said of Raquel Meller: 'She goes in my book.' I asked 'What book?', and he said: 'The people who don't try.' By and large what we did had a kind of personal style. I don't see its like around anywhere to-day.

As soon as the house gets out of its present turmoil you must come out. Just now the 'guest' room is clogged with Antibes linen on top of my winter clothes on top of *all* the rugs from the cleaners.

Our dearest love to you. We cherish so much our memories of all the things we did with you and Phil,

Gerald.

*p.s. I took Sara (as a cadeau de naissance de jour de fête) [as her birthday gift and celebration] to see Bea Lillie. Either Miss Lillie or I or both have grown older along with that kind of humour. Yet I recall rolling in the aisle during 'March, March, April, May and June . . .'
HMD

The Murphys and MacLeishes had been vacationing together in Antigua in late 1953 when Sara took ill with bronchial flu and had to cancel their planned activities. As the MacLeishes returned home, they heard of Ernest Hemingway's supposed death. He had been involved in two small airplane crashes in January 1954 while in Africa, and some newspapers erred in reporting him dead.

244. ARCHIBALD MacLEISH to GERALD MURPHY
Cambridge, Massachusetts, 2 February [1954]

Dear Daow:

It was wonderfully reassuring to hear the Clerk at the Westbury say you had checked out Sunday afternoon. We knew our anxieties could be put away in moth balls for the winter. And then came Sadie's letter—so gay and so touching. She really was an angel through that whole long wait that must have been such a disappointment to her and such a trial in so many ways. I've never seen anyone more patient or sweeter in the face of adversity—and Sadie was never a girl to suffer fools or sickness lightly or gladly. Our whole trip back was devoted to the singing of praises.

We are happy for the landfall but of course it can't fall on us. Christmas presents can't flow back uphill. Gresham's law or something. Perhaps if you put it away in the toe of something—maybe even a stocking—it will grow and grow until you can come back to the Isle again. Where cheering thousands will stand waiting. And mostly us. There were so many things we wanted to show you and do with you.

The one thing to regret ever seems to me to be time lost. And in a way it was lost. Time *planned* was lost anyway. But then we have so much time to be grateful for—the four of us. Those days that become richer and more beautiful with every day that passes and has passed since. And Antigua isn't wholly lost we'll find. For all the anxiety there were moments that will lift themselves in our memories. They always have for us, haven't they?

Did Sadie hear of Ernest's death before she heard of his undeath? That worried us. Our phone was ringing as we walked in and it wasn't till the next day we knew it wasn't true. I must say I suspected it wasn't. He's immortal.

our very dear love to you both

Archie

HMD

MacLeish had been recuperating from surgery for removal of a benign tumor, and Murphy had probably sent him a get-well card. After two years of a strained relationship, MacLeish's comments about sickness take on double meaning—both in light of the Murphy family tragedies and Sara's taking ill in Antigua in late 1953. The Murphys had appar-

ently taken offense at what they saw as MacLeish's insensitivity to Sara's illness and had declined an invitation to share in the MacLeishes' fortieth wedding celebration in Conway.

245. ARCHIBALD MACLEISH to GERALD MURPHY
Uphill Farm, 3 June [1956]

Dear Daouw:

Your card. You are (as always) so right about those countries. One does not know how to figure them—whether as a kind of vast out-back of pain surrounding an island of not-pain as the darkness surrounds the not-dark, or, the other way around, as the intensely feeling center which, in the thoughtlessness of unpain, we circle and into which, from time to time, and always at the end, we fall. The one certainty is the one you name—that it is intensely personal—that there is only room within it for one's self alone—that no matter how one craves sympathy one resents too the intrusion of those who are not part of it— are only trespassers however generous. But it is in part for all these reasons that one feels at the end he would not for anything give up the journey through that place. Malraux says in that weak novel, La Voie Royale, that it is only in the presence of death one learns what one really loves. Pain, I suppose is that presence, and it does sort out the meanings. I am no wiser than I was and certainly no better but I have seen something which I can go back to and see again even though I can't bring it forward with me. And when I see it again, as I shall, I shall recognize it. Which, for one who has been as ignorant of pain as I have been all my life, is a gift. I think you have always known more about it because you sense more than I do. Also you have been there more often.

I am sad about the 21st of June. Not that these returning dates mean anything in themselves but because they make a kind of structure on which one can hang the continuances of one's life—of which our long love for S and G is one of the dearest. I know you feel that that continuance is broken—broken by me—and I am sure you have good reason to think so, but it is not true. I wish you had felt you could come. But your instinct in these things is, as I have long known, truer than mine. You have made an art of what I have only blundered at. Perhaps the time will come when you will find it possible again. But we shall be thinking most of you.

Yours as always

Archie

HMD

246. GERALD MURPHY to ARCHIBALD MACLEISH
Snedens Landing, 11 June 1956

Dear Archie:—

You may—from your letter—feel that I have been nursing some lingering resentment. Everyone, I guess, thinks of himself as one who never harbours a grudge. I must admit to flattering myself that I do not.

You are wrong, I think, in saying that my 'instinct' in that uncertain realm of human relationships is 'truer' than yours. Indeed, years ago I was for resigning from *all* of them in sheer desperation at my inadequacy. I even wrote you and Ada a mistaken and churlish letter on the subject [Letter 26]. Mercifully enough, I received a corrective one from you in return for which I have ever since been grateful.

I suppose that the even maintenance of a friendship calls for a complete emotional stability on the part of one of the friends,—preferably on the part of both. In all the years I've known her, I've remarked that Sara, once she has told herself that a person is her friend, never is even tempted to depart for an instant from her apparent acceptance and understanding of incidents which another person might consider unfriendly. Not out of blind loyalty this, but due rather to a kind of humane wisdom through which she seems to see more clearly and farther than anyone else.

I am not thus endowed. It is sad, when a difference arises between friends, to feel that nuisance—one's amour propre raising its head, and to hear the low whine of hurt feelings. Worse than the general feeling of lowered consequence, however, is the loss of confidence in one's ability to safeguard the precious friendship. This is pretty close to loss of confidence in oneself.

Doubtless, with the approach of la viellesse, one's feelings when hurt do not have the resilience they once had. One is tempted not to allow them again to take on more than they know how to handle. I am not so tempted.

Time, for some reason, does play a part in such things. Let me tell you here how much I have appreciated your generous letters from the beginning.

I have no heart of oak, but I cannot see life—either past or future—without in it an enduring affection for you and Ada.

On se reverra!

daou

LC

247. SARA MURPHY to ERNEST HEMINGWAY
Snedens Landing, 24 May 1961

Dear Ernest,—

We read—too often, in the papers—about your being in the Mayo

Clinic,—mentioning various ailments, and please write me a card, saying it *isn't so,*—or at least that you are all recovered—It isn't in character for you to be ill—I want to picture you—as always—as a burly bearded young man—with a gun or on a boat—Just a line, please—I always remember old times with the *greatest* pleasure—and that you were helpful to me at a time when I certainly *needed* it—We hope some time to meet Mary too.

affectionately,
your *very* old friend

Sara

JFK

The Murphys sold Cheer Hall, Snedens Landing, in April 1963, and in August Gerald underwent surgery for intestinal cancer. He recuperated at East Hampton, where the Murphys now lived.

248. SARA MURPHY TO GERALD MURPHY
East Hampton, 7 August 1963

Dearest Gerald—

Here I am "at home"—"without you,"—and it is no longer a home, just a place to live—You *must know* that without you—*nothing* makes any sense—I am only half a person,—and you are the other half—It is *so,* however I may try—and always will be—*Please please* get well soon—and come back to me—

With love—all I *have*—

Sara

HMD

249. JOHN DOS PASSOS TO GERALD MURPHY
Westmoreland, 7 September 1963

Dear Gerald,

We were all delighted to get your letter.

We returned to find a disastrous drouth. In spite of a two day northeaster not a drop of rain fell on us last week. This has been the driest summer in history with almost total loss of the corn crop and soy beans. Thank God we were away all of August. It is heartbreaking to see magnificent crops wither away in the fields without being able to do anything to help. Again our poor Northern Neck is labeled a disaster area.

The summer trip turned out a delight. I'll have many things to tell you about when I see you. We thought of you especially in the Indian pueblos and ruins we poked about in in New Mexico, and looking into George Eastman, the Kodak man's, house in Rochester. It has been turned into a remarkably good museum of photography. His strange character broods over the place. I find myself trying to write a little piece about him.

What do you remember of him? Didn't you and Sara take me to the Chateau des Enfants once? Wasn't there something tragic about how he met his end? I'd be obliged if you would jot down a few things to freshen my recollection—just a line or two.

Love to Sara—We're all very proud of you for bouncing up so marvelously—I still feel my stitches but otherwise splendid—

Yrs ever

Dos

HMD

250. GERALD MURPHY to JOHN DOS PASSOS
East Hampton, 12 September 1963

Dear Dos:—

We were distressed to hear about the drought in your area. Of course we were surrounded by it at Snedens and here, but finally a series of thunder showers and cloudbursts relieved it,—but just in time. What a heart-rending shock it must have been for you all—the sight of those fields on your return! You really wonder how farmers face the risk year after year,—so often they lose everything, including the hours of labour devoted to planting and tending a crop. As you say, you were all spared the spectacle of your investments' slow death. Poor comfort!

We are aiming to leave for Snedens the 16th to face our Nov. 1st deadline after having lost two months of time. Like all things that appear to be laughably impossible to accomplish I suppose we'll end by doing so. It's what Wm James called 'the wear and tear of discrimination' which gets you. What to do with something you've kept carefully in the attic for years because it had a very special future which in the meantime you have forgotten. We know someone who had to visit their attic. The first thing she found was a box neatly corded and marked: 'Pieces of string too small to use.'

Well, we'll see.

I now marvel that one can feel tolerably human, having gained only one pound in two weeks of 'convalescence.' Really how formidable the human carcass is!

We shall be bivouacing at what was once Cheer Hall until Nov. 1st, then here which for the nonce must be H. Q.

> Very much love to you all three from Sara
> and me,
>
> Gerald.

P.S. Yes we did all go to the Chateau des Enfants together. My memory of the visit is opaque (André Sella, proprietor of le Grand Hotel du Cap at Antibes would be a good source. Great friend of ours and a authority on the Cap's history.) Father was implored for years to go to Rochester with his friend Eastman to visit his factories, laboratories, etc. of which he was inordinately proud. Father finally said 'all right.' It was deep winter and bitterly cold. Father who never wore underwear or overcoats but summerweight suits all year, went hatless from steaming laboratories to frigid rooms for storage of films, often 1/4 of a mile apart. The tour took 7 hours in all. He took the midnight sleeper which was airless and suffocatingly hot, went to his office with a fever. Next day pneumonia et finis. We learned afterwards that many of E's friends had the same experience. He was apparently pitiless about subjecting people to his pride in the place, tho' technically it was incomprehensible to most people. People got to dreading they'd have to toil to Rochester in dead of winter and put over the hurdles. Of course this bit is of no use to you but I have such a clear memory of it all.

> G.

UVA

251. GERALD MURPHY to ARCHIBALD MACLEISH
East Hampton, 15 September 1963

Dear Archie:—

Your letters of July 19th and then August 20th I have kept and reread. One of them I acknowledged, I remember. Neither of them could be adequately answered,—so much have they meant to me.

One thing was borne in upon me during those days: that nothing, nothing brings as much comfort as *knowing* that you are in the thoughts of those you love. There must be the letter, the message, the inquiry, in order to *Know*. One tells over to oneself the names of those who 'communicated'—like beads of prayer. Sedation is as nothing.

I seem to have mended to the doctors' satisfaction. Sitting in the sun and gazing out over the Ocean to a featureless horizon has been my therapy. I can leave in a day or two to cope with our grim deadline of Nov. 1st. Our Mrs. Wessberg here is coming to help. Honoria too, later on.

It's what the attics hold which begins to alarm me. I feel sure I'll come across the two skeletons of our former selves. A young woman we know fell heir to all the possessions of an aged Aunt, known to be a magpie (as is Sara). Lawyers for the estate insisted she alone must pass on every article in the large house. Deciding to start at the attic, she mounted the ladder. Inside the hatchway, on the nearest of innumerable cartons neatly wrapped was one labelled in her Aunt's handwriting: 'Pieces of string too small to use.'

Ada: your calls and letters were such a comfort to Sara and warming for me to hear about from her.

Christ, let us sit upon the ground, all four of us, and relate, recount, describe our various coups d' age. *We* have some beauts!

Best love to you both from us two,

Aff'y—

Gerald.

p.s. I prize what you say about 'les oeuvres du maitre'. Yesterday I was sent an account of their being shown in Oakland, Cal. It's a little spooky to meet oneself in the dark 30 years later! *You had courage* when you *bought* one.[1] Blessings on you. G.

LC

---

1. Gerald had donated *Watch* and *Razor* to the permanent collection of the Dallas Museum of Art when they exhibited his works in 1960, and, thereafter, some of his paintings were independently exhibited throughout America. The MacLeishes had initially purchased *Watch* but then later exchanged it for the smaller *Wasp and Pear*. Close to the time of Gerald's death in 1964, MacLeish donated *Wasp and Pear* to the Museum of Modern Art in New York.

252. ARCHIBALD MACLEISH to GERALD MURPHY
Uphill Farm, 19 September [1963]

Dear Gerald:

I was still wondering whether a letter would be an intrusion when yours came. Featureless horizon—yes. That is precisely what one sees from the un-inhabited bare hills old men climb to, though only you would think of the just word. But the point is—or at least I think the point is—the horizon, not the featurelessness. When one expects to go on "forever" as one does in one's youth or even in middle age, horizons are merely limits, not yet ends. It is when one first sees the horizon as an end that one first begins to *see*. And it is then that the featurelessness, which one would not have noticed, or would have taken for granted, before, becomes the feature. Ends are the hardest things in the world to see—and precisely because they aren't *things*, they are the end of things. And yet they are wonderful. What would life be without them! Or art—imagine a work of art without ends: it would be worse than a novel by Thomas Wolfe. So that this featureless sky is as far as it is possible to be from negation. It is affirmation. It says the world is possible to man because to man there are horizons, there are beginnings and ends, there are things known and things unknown. Frost said (I don't believe he thought so) that the world was God's joke on him. Meaning, I suppose, that because we die, be-cause everything dies, vanishes, blows away, our lives are nonsense and our works worse. But it isn't true. Because if we didn't die there would be no works—not works of art certainly, the only ones that count. There would be no painter's line to include and exclude and so create. Death is the perspective of every great picture ever painted and the underbeat of every measurable poem and the enviable men are the ripe men who can sit as you do and look at a featureless sky above an endless sea that does, nevertheless, and at that point, *end*. I like to think of you there looking. Or at the rose, that other in-ward horizon of horizon on horizon. We have time to think of all this, you and I—much time—summers and winters. And time, I hope, trust and pray, to talk about it. Because *now* THERE IS SO MUCH TO talk about. No richer gift to any of us than a glimpse of death and then time after—even to one who has had to live with death as much as you—or one whose glimpse was brief as mine. Think of you? You would not believe how much or with what love. We will see each other soon. Meantime a great hug to that darling ever young Sadie.

yours

Archie

HMD

333

253. Gerald Murphy to Archibald MacLeish
East Hampton, 30 May 1964

Dear Archie:—

What a nice, warming letter, yours of April 18th, for one to get. Nourishment. Mother's milk.

We left Washington, April 25th, to come here—now our home. You must have had the same weather that we have since: beautiful blue days in a row. Certain of them poignant with clarity and beauty. You have, in 'Queen Elizabeth's Virginal,' 'Sweet day, so cool, so calm, so bright. The bridal of the earth and sky . . .' We all used to sing it. I've never felt May so keenly in my life. GMH [Gerard Manley Hopkins] called it 'peeléd May.' Whatever he meant, it seems somehow right. Sans doute Ada has been at her flowers and loving the feel of a soil different from Bahamian;—while you have presided over the vegetable Department,—scolding against the hoax that Bibb Lettuce is.

Has anyone, anywhere, written of the *nature* of la vieillesse? We have been told so little of how it comes,—in the night or when one is off one's guard. I wish I had known. It is strange to be aware of it in such a Spring as this has been. What is the poem with the words '—as if a Queen, once young, were dead—'?

I am at the grim task of reviewing all check book stubs, cancelled cheques, receipts, data, data, data covering the renovations and improvements of Cheer Hall, Snedens Landing from 1948–1963 Nov. It must be ready by June 15th. (I have a two month extension due to age and general goddam debility.)

Somehow, somewhere, when we least expect it we must convene this year. When the fall-out rises, we shall confer. It is a time to sit together and be wise, as wise as possible, in this disorderly world. I wish it were not that on se deplace difficilement [it is difficult now to move]. Every once in a while we pull out a drawer and go through our memories of the things we did together—we four. What an age of innocence it was, and how beautiful and free! Thank you, you two!

Gerald.

p.s. I am—contre coeur [reluctantly]—in Ernest's book [*A Moveable Feast*]. What a strange kind of bitterness—or rather accusitoriness. Aren't the rich (whoever they are) rather poor prey? What shocking ethics! How well written, of course. What an indictment. Poor Hadley!
p.s.s. I hope you didn't overdo, struggling to comply with that strange request of the Animal Rescue Mission.[1]

---

1. Gerald had asked Archie on 13 April if he could contribute to the Animal Rescue Mission by way of autographing a photo "of you (with Finn, for instance?) or write some apt remark on a photo . . . or picture or donate what is known here as a 'figurine,' etc.—anything to make it easier for you".

p.s.s.s. It was the Alexander sisters: Harriet (Adrich, Ambassadress to Britain); Janetta (Mrs Arnold Whitridge); and Mary (Mrs Sheldon Whitehouse), who said in unison, when their imagination was caught: "Recount! Relate! Descri-i-i-i-i-be! *You* found the genesis of it as said by one of those three comic characters that keep appearing in one of Shakespeare's not-so-often-read plays.

G.

LC

254. ARCHIBALD MACLEISH to GERALD MURPHY
Uphill Farm, 26 June [1964]

Dear Gerald:

I have a constant and urgent need to talk to you—hear you talk—which seems to have the least possible chance of realizing itself. The process of getting older throws one more & more, in one's deepest self, on the friends (& how few they are) with whom one has lived through this curious journey (to nowhere? somewhere? where?). Again & again as I feel the loss of myself I find myself thinking that you would understand this—perhaps only you—& whether you know the loss in yourself or not. Louise Lavelle says the words for it—"la solitude la plus tragique est celle qui m' simpeche le force les barrieres que safarect ce que je crois êtue le ce que je suis . . ."[1] I send you the context—with my love. And to S. Always.

Archie

HMD

—————————————————

1. MacLeish is quoting from the French philosopher Louis Lavelle, *Le mal et la Souffrance* (Plon: Paris, 1940). The passage in the letter translates as: "The most tragic solitude is that which does not permit me to break open the fence which separates what I hold to be from what I am." MacLeish enclosed two additional paragraphs from Lavelle.

255. ARCHIBALD MACLEISH to GERALD MURPHY
Uphill Farm, 4 July [1964]

Dear Gerald:

Your voice yesterday—I think you have gone farther than any of us. Camus says in an essay, "To a conscious man old age & what it portends is not a surprise." You have always been a conscious man: there is no higher praise.

love

Archie

P.S. Camus also says, a propos of your remark that we are not taught preparation for old age: "There was in Athens a temple dedicated to old age. Children were taken there."

A.

HMD

256. GERALD MURPHY to ARCHIBALD and ADA MACLEISH
East Hampton, 18 July 1964

Dear Archie, dear Ada:—

Your call from so far away brought me so much. Then your letters! What it means! How rare to know it! Archie: the Camus was just what I had hoped to hear.

We are so delighted that you will come down in August. We'll manage to make you comfortable. Bring your bathing-dresses. At present I am incapable of sustained conversation.

Apparently it is to be a matter of protracted (and only partial adjustment). So I am cultivating GMH [Gerard Manley Hopkins]'s—'patience exquisite, which plumes to peace thereafter—' and trying to envisage an existence (?) of amiable and regulated debility.

I had so wanted to know and greet old age.

We'll keep in touch. Let us know your preferred date.

Oh, the comfort you have brought me!

Gerald.

LC

257. GERALD MURPHY to ARCHIBALD MACLEISH
East Hampton, 29 August 1964

Dear Archie:—

You have sent me a book such as I have been yearning for these last weeks.[1]

336

When you spoke of it here, I knew from the words you used that it would be balm to the attenuated spirit which accompanies me these days.

What a joy to be with this man as his mind and his senses play over 'Carp,' 'The Pink Oleanders,' . . .

I am enthralled. I wander starry-eyed through his world.

What distinction, what elegance and innate taste!

You had said you would send it to me, and you did. Dear Archie, my heart to you.

For me it was a milestone: seeing you and Ada.

We send you both best love,

Gerald.

LC

---

1. MacLeish probably gave Gerald a book on Gerard Manley Hopkins, Gerald's favorite poet, some of whose poems Gerald could recite flawlessly from memory. MacLeish had introduced Gerald to Hopkins's work after they first met in France, and Gerald had many of Hopkins's poems on his mind prior to his death.

258. ARCHIBALD MACLEISH to GERALD MURPHY
Uphill Farm, 2 September [1964]

Dear Daouw:

I'm delighted it worked for you. I am reading it out loud to Ada and I felt as I went along that it belonged personally and privately to you—the same unerring sense of the *scene* which you and Sara have always had—not only the loveliness of the particular world but *why* it is lovely—the color of a kitchen bowl full of new, boiled potatoes—the richness of a linden tree. This is the great creative gift of *sight*—what Rodin meant when he told Rilke that he would teach him to *see*. And this, of course, is what you taught us all—the treasure you gave us so far as we had strength to take it. I know of only one comparable gift—what Frost called "freedom of the material"—freedom to make those unexpected "connections", as he calls them, which actually create meaning—Baudelaire's "analogie universelle". But God knows where that "freedom" comes from or how it can be taught—even by you. Dear love to you and to Sadie and "ancient love" to Honoria—thank her for that.

Archie

HMD

In his sermon "The Book of Job," of which a thousand copies were printed, MacLeish stresses that "no man can believe in the imitation of life in art who does not first believe in life itself, and no man can believe in life itself who does not believe that life can be justified," something difficult to do "in a world in which the innocent perish in vast meaningless massacres, and brutal and dishonest men foul all the lovely things." MacLeish concludes that "our labor always, like Job's labor, is to learn through suffering to love . . . to love even that which lets us suffer." MacLeish added a handwritten note on the cover of the copy he sent to Gerald: "Dear Dow: I don't think I sent you this when I did it seven or eight years ago. Rereading it today I thought at once of you because you have said it all so much better. At bottom it is still a question of the love of life isn't it? We will be down very soon   love Archie."

259. GERALD MURPHY to ARCHIBALD MACLEISH
East Hampton, 4 September 1964

Dear Archie:—

How clear and how sustained: your message about Job, about love! It has the clarion-quality of a trumpet-call, of something declarative, something that's been *said*.

The very conception of eternity, infinite space, birth, death, love . . . have always, I must admit, left me awestruck,—and possibly intimidated. My conception of God was hopelessly disfigured for me by a rigorous institutional Catholic training, beginning at a convent at 7 years. At 15 at Hotchkiss I rebelled and chose 'Chapel,' rather than go to the village Roman Catholic Church. Sara's and my 'Mixed Marriage' as it was called by the 'Church' was a nightmare of bigotry [. . . .] But to-day the sight of a priest or nun affects me. I doubt if one recovers.

Assez de ca!

So your Job was like drinking from a pure source. I wish it were not so late. I bless you for sending it. I heard every note of your clarion-call.

Your both coming, as you did, down this long unsightly Island to visit with us—goes into my Pantheon of memories. How like you both! My heart in thanks. It would be lovely if you were to come down in September. One feels less the impact of this now, alas, trivial community. It becomes as it was when Sara and I met here in the very early 1900's.

Honoria was exhilarated and moved by seeing you both. All her ancient love for you welled up, she said.

From us: our dearest love . . .

Gerald.

LC

260. ARCHIBALD MACLEISH to GERALD MURPHY
Uphill Farm, 16 September [1964]

Dear Gerald:

It occurred to me this morning that this age in which we have lived, you and I, is actually, if one looks through the trash, plastic containers, paper cups, half-used words and soiled hypocrisies which float on its surface like the steamer-leavings on the precipitous deep blue of Lake Como—is actually a heroic age and that that is its tragedy. The heroic ages in the myths—those only true rememberers—were the ages in which men, some men, perhaps only one, dared to believe that it might be possible—that it WAS possible— with nothing but human head and hands to slaughter the great beasts, to over-come the monsters, to go down into the dark, into death itself, and drag the dog up howling and so, as Herakles was assured by the oracle, to live there-after like gods.

I have known for a long time that that myth was our myth. That is why I have been struggling for five years with a play about Herakles [*Herakles: A Play in Verse*, 1967]. But not until this morning did I see what I must have known all along—that it is because our age like his life is heroic in that highest and most daring sense that we take our meaning from him. For our age is tragic as his life was and as all the heroic ages must be. The deeds are per-formed, the miracles accomplished, the wonders visited—and there is still the world as it was—the dog as it was . . . except that the dog is now tied up in the cook's slops in Eurystheus' kitchen. Le prince d' Acquitaine a la tour abolie. It is true tragedy—tragedy to wring the heart: all these tremendous intelligences daring to take space and time and matter apart and to dig deep down under into the eternal dark and returning in triumph to what? Night as usual. Dust as usual. Someone sprinkling water on the dust as usual—the old sad smell. But then one reminds one's self that in the myth Herakles DOES become a god at the end. So that the oracle comes true in the myth. So what should we think of ourselves—of our destiny? The myths are always right—but right in

339

other language. Are we also gods, we victims of ourselves—but in some sense we do not understand?

Certainly not in the sense of your beloved friend Hopkins to whom the just man

Acts in God's eye what in god's eye he is—
Christ—for Christ plays in ten thousand places,
lovely in limbs, and lovely in eyes not his
to the Father through the features of men's faces.

Not in that sense but in some other?

Let the last word be his too—Hopkins: "How to keep—is there any, is there none such, nowhere known some, bow or brooch or braid or brace, lace, latch, catch or key to keep

Back beauty, keep it, beauty, beauty, beauty . . . from vanishing away?
our dear and always love to you both

Archie

HMD

261. ARCHIBALD MACLEISH to GERALD MURPHY
Uphill Farm, 29 September [1964]

Dear Gerald:

When I got back from Chicago yesterday I found a letter from Alfred Barr, the Director of Acquisitions at the Museum of Modern Art, asking me to tell you that the Museum of Modern Art is proud to have a work by you in its permanent collection. He is referring to the Pear and the Wasp. When you told me a few weeks ago about the loss of the picture Vladimir had [*Portrait*], I wrote the Museum telling them that, if I could keep it in my house as long as I live, I should like to give the painting to the Museum. They accepted at once and with the greatest eagerness and Alfred now sends this word to you by me. I don't need to tell you how happy I am that the picture is to go where it belongs and where it will long represent your great work. Ada and I send our dear love to you and Sarah as always.

hurriedly

Archie

HMD

262. DAWN POWELL to JOHN DOS PASSOS
[New York] 26 October 1964

Dear Dos—

Counted on you at Gerald's funeral but heard you were reciting Gunga Din at the Odd Fellows Banquet or was it the Elks? Anyway I quailed at thought of long ride out there which shakes up my internes perilously but it turned out to be a suave Murphy-organized do with station wagon by the Vaills (Honoria's friends) & Chas Cornish & Billy MacLeish so we had a charming ride— charming party chez Murphy before & after church—all like a small perfect Murphy party—Maidstone [Club] bartender in charge & Mrs Westbrook [Wessberg] and four lovely local waitresses servicing delicacies to about 20 or 25—all carefully organized by Gerald I'm sure including the brief church service—poignant & perfect. Honoria's lovely children leant the Edwardian touch to the scene. Sara was marvellous—controlled & I believe relieved that Gerald did not have to go through any more of the unchic indignities and embarrassments of pain & dying. It was—as you might know—a lesson in courage disguised as *taste*.

MacLeishes & Brennans [Hank and Fanny Myers Brennan] & Ellen Barry (looking amazingly like Alice Myers)—and the young man [Calvin Tomkins] who wrote Gerald's biog in N. Yorker ["Living Well Is the Best Revenge," 1962] were on hand but no [Diddy and Lloyd] Lowndes—it was a parlous trip & the others had been on hand when he was alive. You were missed of course but probably not as much as the vast absentee list of Benchley, Woolley, Porter, Ernest, Fitzgeralds et al. I'm surprised we are still alive but sometimes I don't notice it—especially now that I have six days to turn in a story desired by Sat Ev. Post and all I do is fall asleep 20 hrs a day (I believe all my medication is studded with dope) but the Sat Ev Post may be gone before I get there anyway.

Rosalind [Wilson] & I keep a hot line between Boston & here as she is waiting for a yes to a story at Curtis. She is apparently in fine shape—certain her novel will be accepted & already quibbling over who shall get it—sure of herself and off to Yaddo & the tracks next week.

Best to Lucy & Betty & the Worlds Fair sends regrets

love

Dawn

UVA

263. ARCHIBALD MACLEISH to SARA MURPHY
Antigua, West Indies, 3 December [1964]

Darling Sadie:

What wonderful talking letters! I don't mean like talking dogs. I mean like talking *you*. I was reading the last one out loud to Ada & you were *there*. I mean, here. I wish we could *see* you talking.

I'm proud to be asked to think of something for Gerald's stone. I have thought. First I wanted something of Hopkins' because Gerald loved him so. But I can find nothing that will fit the space: Hopkins needs room to build up those marvellous rhythms. So I am going to propose three words from *King Lear*: RIPENESS IS ALL. Many readers of Shakespeare think the phrase is Shakespeare's greatest: certainly his most searching. But that isn't my reason. My reason is that it is so like Gerald who achieved the most complete maturity I have ever seen. Think about it. Perhaps you will like it. It goes wonderfully with the words he chose for you ["And she made all of light"]:[1] those two "all"s marry each other & mean more side by side. Dear love from us both.

Archie

HMD

------

1. Gerald had chosen the inscription for Sara's gravestone—a line from the Elizabethan poet Thomas Campion—shortly before his own death.

Notes

INTRODUCTION

1. References made to letters published in this book will not be footnoted but will be indicated by their dates. Murphy family letters not included in this book are in the Honoria Murphy Donnelly Collection.

2. William Rubin, *The Paintings of Gerald Murphy* (New York: Museum of Modern Art, 1974), p. 30.

3. During 1962, Douglas MacAgy was preparing a manuscript on Murphy's art which appeared as "Gerald Murphy: 'New Realist' of the Twenties," *Art in America* 51.2 (1963): 49–57. Murphy corresponded with MacAgy at this time, and MacAgy's questions to Murphy regarding his art and life in France during the 1920s generated two particularly rich hand-written responses from Murphy, both of which are in the "Gerald Murphy File," Douglas MacAgy Papers, The Archives of American Art, Smithsonian Institution, Washington, D.C. Citations from these two pieces are identified according to Murphy's own numbering systems, which employ both Arabic numbers and Roman numerals. These quotes here are from Files III and VI, respectively.

4. Archibald MacLeish, *Riders on the Earth: Essays and Recollections* (Boston: Houghton Mifflin, 1978), p. 78; and Murphy, MacAgy Papers, File 12.

5. Calvin Tomkins, *Living Well Is the Best Revenge* (1962; rpt. New York: Viking, 1972), p. 29.

6. MacAgy Papers, Files 3 and 4.

7. Rudi Blesh, *Modern Art USA: Men, Rebellion, Conquest 1900–1956* (New York: Alfred A. Knopf, 1956), pp. 93–96.

8. MacLeish, *Riders*, pp. 79, 126.

9. John Dos Passos, *The Best Times: An Informal Memoir* (New York: New American Library, 1966), p. 146.

10. Carlos Baker, *Ernest Hemingway: A Life Story* (New York: Scribners, 1969),

p. 259; also Hemingway to Fitzgerald, 28 May 1934, in *Ernest Hemingway Selected Letters, 1917–1962*, ed. Carlos Baker (New York: Scribners, 1981), p. 407.

11. *Tender Is the Night* (1934; rpt. New York: Scribners, 1962), p. 27.

12. *The Notebooks of F. Scott Fitzgerald*, ed. Matthew J. Bruccoli (New York: Harcourt Brace Jovanovich/Bruccoli Clark, 1972), pp. 225, 149, 229, and 146.

13. Andrew Turnbull, *Scott Fitzgerald* (1962; rpt. New York: Ballantine Books, 1971), pp. 163, 166.

14. *Tender*, pp. 151, 35–36, 152.

15. Dos Passos, *Best Times*, p. 146.

16. Lillian Hellman, *An Unfinished Woman: A Memoir* (1969; rpt. New York: Bantam Books, 1970), p. 65.

17. Murphy to John and Betty Dos Passos, 27 August 1957, Dos Passos Papers, University of Virginia.

18. Hemingway to MacLeish, 15 October 1958, in *Hemingway Letters*, p. 885.

19. *Riders*, p. 79; and MacLeish to author, 17 October 1979.

20. This poem was first published in *Streets in the Moon* (1926) and then reprinted in various collected works. See Archibald MacLeish, *New and Collected Poems 1917–1976* (Boston: Houghton Mifflin, 1976), pp. 107–109.

21. *Tender*, pp. 24, 33, 34, 21, 17, 42, 34.

22. Dos Passos, *Best Times*, p. 146.

23. Turnbull, *Fitzgerald*, p. 160; and Hadley Hemingway, quoted in Nancy Milford, *Zelda: A Biography* (New York: Harper & Row, 1970), p. 132.

24. *Tender*, pp. 26, 29.

25. Edmund Wilson to Arthur Mizener, 4 April 1950, in *Edmund Wilson: Letters on Literature and Politics 1912–1972*, ed. Elena Wilson (New York: Farrar, Straus & Giroux, 1977), p. 479.

26. Fitzgerald, "The Jazz Age," in *The Crack-Up: F. Scott Fitzgerald*, ed. Edmund Wilson (1945; rpt. New York: New Directions Paperbook, 1956), p. 22.

27. *Crack-Up*, p. 19.

28. Tomkins, *Living Well*, p. 42.

29. Fitzgerald to Maxwell Perkins, 20 February 1926, in *Dear Scott/Dear Max: The Fitzgerald-Perkins Correspondence*, eds. John Kuehl and Jackson R. Bryer (New York: Scribners, 1971), p. 134.

30. MacLeish to Bishop [c. April 1933] in *Letters of Archibald MacLeish 1907–1982*, ed. R. H. Winnick (Boston: Houghton Mifflin, 1983), p. 257.

31. Murphy to Calvin Tomkins, 31 January 1962, copy in Murphy Papers, Donnelly Collection.

32. Tomkins, *Living Well*, pp. 15–16.

33. Murphy to Tomkins, 31 January 1964, copy in Murphy Papers, Donnelly Collection.

34. MacLeish, *Riders*, p. 79.

35. Dos Passos, *Best Times*, pp. 140, 147.

36. MacLeish to author, letter of 13 February 1978; and *Riders*, p. 79.

37. MacLeish to Hemingway, [14 October 1936], in *MacLeish Letters*, p. 285.

38. MacLeish to Bishop, 8 August 1925, ibid., p. 169.
39. Murphy to Calvin Tomkins, 27 November 1963, copy in Murphy Papers, Donnelly Collection.
40. Ellen Barry to author, interview of 4 June 1982, Washington, D.C.
41. Patricia Frazer Lamb, "Women's Letters: Touchstones of Friendship," *The CEA Forum*, 15:4 (1985): 10.

PART ONE: *1925–1932*

1. Dos Passos, *Best Times*, pp. 147–148.
2. MacLeish, *Riders*, p. 76.
3. Dos Passos, *Best Times*, p. 148.
4. Edmund Wilson, *The Twenties: From Notebooks and Diaries of the Period*, ed. Leon Edel (New York: Farrar, Straus & Giroux, 1975), p. 94.
5. Dos Passos, *Best Times*, p. 140.
6. Fitzgerald to Seldes, [June or July 1925], in *The Letters of F. Scott Fitzgerald*, ed. Andrew Turnbull (1963; rpt. New York: Bantam Books, 1971), p. 491.
7. Tomkins, *Living Well*, p. 31; and Hemingway to Fitzgerald, 15 December 1925, in *Hemingway Letters*, p. 176.
8. Dos Passos, *Best Times*, pp. 158–159; and Hemingway, *A Moveable Feast* (New York: Scribners, 1964), pp. 196–205.
9. *Tender*, pp. 28–29.
10. Dos Passos, *Best Times*, pp. 149–150.
11. *Moveable Feast*, pp. 185–186.
12. Ibid., pp. 209–211.
13. Alice Hunt Sokoloff, *Hadley: The First Mrs. Hemingway* (New York: Dodd, Mead & Co., 1973), p. 89.
14. Milford, *Zelda*, p. 134; and Baker, *Hemingway*, p. 170.
15. James R. Gaines, *Wit's End: Days and Nights of the Algonquin Round Table* (New York: Harcourt Brace, 1977), p. 160; and Malcolm Cowley, *Exile's Return: A Literary Odyssey of the 1920s* (1934; rpt. New York: Viking, 1956), p. 241.
16. Murphy to Tomkins, 9 September 1960, copy in Murphy Papers, Donnelly Collection. When Tomkins was beginning his work on the Murphys and life in France during the 1920s, Murphy and Tomkins corresponded, and Tomkins also conducted several taped interviews. Transcriptions from these interviews as well as copies of the Murphy-Tomkins correspondence are in the Murphy Papers. Notes on Hemingway drawn from these transcriptions are hereinafter referred to as Hemingway Notes, Tomkins Interviews.
17. Dos Passos, *Best Times*, p. 159.
18. MacAgy Papers, File 4.
19. Fitzgerald to Hemingway, [Fall 1926], in Turnbull, *Fitzgerald Letters*, p. 301.
20. Turnbull, *Fitzgerald*, p. 175.
21. Zelda Fitzgerald to Perkins, September 1926, as quoted in Turnbull, *Fitzgerald*, p. 173.

22. Fitzgerald to Hemingway, [Fall 1926], in *Fitzgerald Letters*, p. 301.
23. Rubin, *Paintings of Gerald Murphy*, pp. 17–18.
24. MacLeish to Hemingway, 19 June [1927], in *MacLeish Letters*, p. 202.
25. MacLeish to Hemingway, 13 August [1927], ibid., p. 206.
26. Hemingway Notes, Tomkins Interviews, Donnelly Collection.
27. As quoted in Milford, *Zelda*, p. 153.
28. Ibid., p. 141.
29. Fitzgerald to Hemingway, [probably July 1928], in Matthew Bruccoli, *Scott and Ernest: The Authority of Failure and the Authority of Success* (New York: Random House, 1978), p. 67.
30. MacLeish to Hemingway, 5 June 1935, Hemingway Papers, JFK Library, Boston.
31. Author's interview with King Vidor, Beverly Hills, California, 29 June 1982.
32. Bruccoli, *Scott and Ernest*, p. 73.
33. Milford, *Zelda*, pp. 153–155.
34. Fitzgerald to Hemingway, 9 September 1929, in *Fitzgerald Letters*, p. 310.
35. Fitzgerald to Hemingway, 23 August 1929, ibid., p. 309.
36. Fitzgerald to Hemingway, 9 September 1929, ibid., p. 310.
37. Marion Meade, *Dorothy Parker: What Fresh Hell Is This?* (New York: Penguin Books, 1989), pp. 203–204.
38. Dos Passos, *Best Times*, p. 202.
39. Ibid., pp. 202–203.
40. Tomkins, *Living Well*, p. 137.
41. MacLeish to Fitzgerald, 15 September [1930], in *MacLeish Letters*, p. 236.
42. Turnbull, *Fitzgerald*, p. 201.
43. Milford, *Zelda*, pp. 200–203.
44. Honoria Murphy Donnelly with Richard N. Billings, *Sara & Gerald: Villa America and After* (New York: Time Books, 1982), pp. 63–64.
45. *The Collected Essays of John Peale Bishop*, ed. Edmund Wilson (New York: Scribners, 1948), pp. 129–130.
46. MacLeish, *Riders*, p. 92.

PART TWO: *1933–1940*

1. MacLeish to Hemingway, 31 May 1933, in *MacLeish Letters*, p. 259.
2. Hemingway to Wilder, May 1929, as paraphrased in Richard H. Goldstone, *Thorton Wilder: An Intimate Portrait* (New York: Saturday Review Press, 1975), p. 73.
3. Donnelly, *Sara and Gerald*, pp. 77–78.
4. Dos Passos to Hemingway, [July 23 (?), 1935], in *The Fourteenth Chronicle: Letters and Diaries of John Dos Passos*, ed. Townsend Ludington (Boston: Gambit, 1973), p. 479.
5. MacLeish to John and Katy Dos Passos, [20 March 1935], in *MacLeish Letters*, p. 275.
6. James Vermillion to Archibald MacLeish, letter of 29 October 1971, Box 48, MacLeish Papers, Library of Congress.

7. MacLeish to John and Katy Dos Passos, [20 March 1935], in *MacLeish Letters*, p. 275.

8. Sheilah Graham in her *The Real F. Scott Fitzgerald Thirty-five Years Later* (New York: Warner Books, 1976), p. 101, points out that scholars have assumed that Fitzgerald was referring to himself in this poem, but they have overlooked the caption to it which clearly states "For BAOTH 2nd stanza poem."

9. "Words to Be Spoken" was later published in Archibald MacLeish, *Public Speech* (1936) and then reprinted in various collections. See *New and Collected Poems*, p. 315.

10. MacLeish to Brendan Gill, 8 October 1971, MacLeish Papers, Library of Congress.

11. Donnelly, *Sara and Gerald*, p. 94.

12. Ibid., pp. 85–86.

13. Dos Passos to Hemingway, [July 23(?), 1935], in *Fourteenth Chronicle*, p. 479.

14. Dos Passos to Hemingway, 9 January 1937, ibid., p. 504.

15. Donnelly, *Sara and Gerald*, pp. 114–115.

16. Bruccoli, *Scott and Ernest*, p. 130.

17. Turnbull, *Fitzgerald*, p. 244.

18. Dos Passos, *Best Times*, pp. 209–210.

19. Ibid., p. 128.

20. Donald Ogden Stewart, *By a Stroke of Luck! An Autobiography* (New York: Paddington Press Ltd., 1975), pp. 86–87.

21. MacLeish, *Riders*, pp. 79–80.

22. Dos Passos to Hemingway, 27 July 1934, in *Fourteenth Chronicle*, p. 437.

23. Donnelly, *Sara and Gerald*, p. 91.

24. MacLeish, *Riders*, p. 125.

25. Turnbull, *Fitzgerald*, pp. 331–332.

26. Fitzgerald to Perkins, 20 May 1940, in *Dear Scott/Dear Max*, p. 261.

27. *The Dialogues of Archibald MacLeish and Mark Van Doren*, ed. Warren V. Bush (New York: E. P. Dutton & Company, Inc., 1964), pp. 86–87; and Baker, *Hemingway*, pp. 261–262.

28. *Fourteenth Chronicle*, pp. 495–496; and Dos Passos, *Best Times*, p. 219.

29. Zelda to Scott, Fall 1938, as quoted in Milford, *Zelda*, p. 339.

PART THREE: *1941–1964*

1. Murphy to Katy Dos Passos, 1 April 1942, Dos Passos Papers, University of Virginia.

2. *The Van Wyck Brooks Lewis Mumford Letters: The Record of a Literary Friendship, 1921–1963*, ed. Rober E. Spiller (New York: E. P. Dutton & Company, Inc., 1970), p. 202.

3. John Peale Bishop, "The Social Muse Once More," in *The Collected Essays*, pp. 278–279.

4. Edmund Wilson, *Classics and Commercials: A Literary Chronicle of the Forties* (New York: Farrar, Straus, 1950), p. 7.

5. MacLeish, "The Isolation of the American Artist," *The Atlantic* 201 (January 1958), p. 58.

6. *MacLeish Letters*, pp. 343–344.

7. Gertrude Stein's *Paris France* (London: Batsford, 1940) reemphasizes the idea that while Stein lived in France, she still felt herself to be an American.

8. MacLeish to Hemingway, [30 September 1958], *MacLeish Letters*, pp. 411–412.

9. Ibid.

10. Hemingway, *Moveable Feast*, pp. 207–209.

11. Baker, *Hemingway*, pp. 298–299, 495.

12. *Moveable Feast*, unpublished manuscript, Hemingway Papers, JFK Library.

13. Dos Passos to Hemingway, 28 April 1961, as quoted in Baker, *Hemingway*, p. 561.

14. Dos Passos to Hemingway, 23 October 1951, *Fourteenth Chronicle*, p. 597.

15. Dos Passos to Sara Murphy, [August 1961], ibid., p. 623.

16. Murphy to Tomkins, [c. Summer 1961], copy in Donnelly Collection.

17. Sara Murphy to John and Betty Dos Passos, 19 April 1963, Dos Passos Papers, University of Virginia.

18. Sara Murphy to John and Betty Dos Passos, 14 September 1962, 19 April 1963, Dos Passos Papers.

19. Murphy to Archibald and Ada MacLeish, 10 July 1963, MacLeish Papers, Library of Congress.

20. *New York Times*, 18 October 1964, p. 89, col. 1.

21. MacLeish, *Riders*, pp. 125–126; and MacLeish to author, letter of 13 February 1978.

22. Murphy, as quoted in Blesh, *Modern Art USA*, pp. 93–96.

23. MacLeish, *Riders*, p. 124.

24. Tomkins, *Living Well*, p. 13.

25. *Tender*, pp. 18, 38, 43–44.

26. MacLeish, *Riders*, p. 124.

27. Foreword to *in their time/1920–1940: An Exhibition at The University of Virginia Library December 1977–March 1978* (Bloomfield Hills, Mich.: Bruccoli Clark, 1977).

28. Wilson to Dos Passos, in *Wilson Letters*, pp. 638–639.

29. *Fourteenth Chronicle*, p. 574.

30. *MacLeish-Van Doren Dialogues*, pp. 147–148.

31. Hemingway to Ada MacLeish, [1941], MacLeish Papers, Box 48, Library of Congress.

32. Hemingway to MacLeish, 4 April, early May, 30 June, and 10 August 1943, as quoted in Baker, *Hemingway*, p. 383; and Hemingway to Ada MacLeish, [1941], MacLeish Papers.

33. Dos Passos to Ada MacLeish, 24 December 1964, MacLeish Papers.

34. As told to author by Miranda Barry, quoting her grandmother Ellen Barry, phone conversation, c. March 1989.

35. Meade, *Parker*, p. 406.

36. Dos Passos Papers.

Index